A NORTON CRITICAL

William Shakespeare
THE MERCHANT OF VENICE

AUTHORITATIVE TEXT
SOURCES AND CONTEXTS
CRITICISM
REWRITINGS AND APPROPRIATIONS

Edited by

LEAH S. MARCUS
VANDERBILT UNIVERSITY

W. W. NORTON & COMPANY
New York • London

W. W. Norton & Company has been independent since its founding in 1923, when William Warder Norton and Mary D. Herter Norton first published lectures delivered at the People's Institute, the adult education division of New York City's Cooper Union. The Nortons soon expanded their program beyond the Institute, publishing books by celebrated academics from America and abroad. By mid-century, the two major pillars of Norton's publishing program—trade books and college texts—were firmly established. In the 1950s, the Norton family transferred control of the company to its employees, and today—with a staff of four hundred and a comparable number of trade, college, and professional titles published each year—W. W. Norton & Company stands as the largest and oldest publishing house owned wholly by its employees.

This title is printed on permanent paper containing 30 percent post-consumer waste recycled fiber.

Copyright © 2006 by W. W. Norton & Company, Inc.

All rights reserved.
Printed in the United States of America.
First Edition.

Every effort has been made to contact the copyright holders of each of the selections in this volume. Rights holders of any selections not credited should contact W. W. Norton & Company, Inc., 500 Fifth Avenue, New York, NY 10110, for a correction to be made in the next printing of our work.

The text of this book is composed in Fairfield Medium
with the display set in Bernhard Modern.
Composition by PennSet, Inc.
Manufacturing by the Courier Companies—Westford Division.
Production manager: Benjamin Reynolds.

Library of Congress Cataloging-in-Publication Data
Shakespeare, William, 1564–1616.
    The merchant of Venice: authoritative text, sources and contexts, criticism, rewritings and appropriations / William Shakespeare; edited by Leah S. Marcus.
        p. cm. — (A Norton critical edition)
    Includes bibliographical references (p.   ).

ISBN 0-393-92529-3 (pbk.)

1. Moneylenders—Drama. 2. Jews—Italy—Drama. 3. Venice (Italy)—Drama. 4. Shylock (Fictitious character)—Drama.
5. Shakespeare, William, 1564–1616. Merchant of Venice.
I. Marcus, Leah S. (Leah Sinanoglou) II. Title. III. Series.

PR2825.A2M36 2005
822.3'3—dc22

2005053425

W. W. Norton & Company, Inc., 500 Fifth Avenue, New York, NY 10110-0017
www.wwnorton.com

W. W. Norton & Company Ltd., Castle House,
75/76 Wells Street, London W1T 3QT

6   7   8   9   0

Contents

Rewritings and Appropriations

Illustrations

Preface

The Merchant of Venice is one of Shakespeare's most beautiful plays; it is arguably also one of his ugliest. Modern audiences have difficulty placing its ravishing, idealistic praise of heavenly and musical harmonies within the same conceptual frame as its materialism and its racism. Of course, to apply the term "racism" to a work of the late sixteenth century is in one sense anachronistic: defenders of the play have pointed out that neither Moors nor Jews were sufficiently visible in England of the 1590s, when the play was written and first performed, to constitute a distinct cultural category and to receive the systematic institutional discrimination that we now associate with the twentieth-century term "racism."

But even if that rather optimistic view of Elizabethan culture is generally accepted, and several of the readings in this Norton Critical Edition will suggest that it is not, we are still left with the question of shifting audience response to the characters and attitudes in the play. Where do audiences stand on the issue of the color line? When and under what circumstances is Portia's eager suitor—the "tawny" Prince of Morocco—as disagreeable to audiences on account of his "complexion" as Portia states that he is for her? And how do we respond to Portia if our own perceptions are completely at odds with hers? Is Shylock the Jew a comical figure, as the first published version of the play suggests in its running titles: "The comical history of the Merchant of Venice"? When the play was published in the collected folio edition of Shakespeare's plays in 1623, it was placed firmly among the comedies. Or is Shylock a tragic character, deprived of family, religion, and identity by his forced conversion to an alien faith at the end of the play? Because of these problems in interpretation, during the twentieth century *The Merchant of Venice* came to be categorized not as a comedy but as a "problem play" in which the impediments to comedy were sufficiently pressing to disrupt its generic labeling. We have tended to assume that responses were simpler in Shakespeare's own day; that *Merchant* was performed and received as untroubled comedy with a Jew, and to a lesser degree Moors, Moroccans, and various others, as its butts; and that it became problematic only in the twentieth century, as a result of shifting attitudes toward Jews, blacks, and racial stereotyping in general. But there is evidence that the play was problematic from the start, at least in terms of its portrayal of the Jew. In the trial scene, Portia asks, "Which is the merchant here, and which the Jew," suggesting that there is not much perceptible difference between them. When it was first registered with the Stationers' Company for publication in 1598, the play that we call *The Merchant of Venice* was registered under the title of *The Jew of Venice*, which suggests that the story of Shylock loomed larger in sixteenth-century perceptions than we used to assume it did. As early as 1709, we find Nicholas Rowe, one of the first Shakespearean editors, protesting in print that the play, though staged as a comedy in his day, was "designed tragically by the author" (see below, p. 135).

The readings in this Norton Critical Edition have been selected to highlight the diversity of frames within which the play can be interpreted, both in Shakespeare's time and more recently. On the one hand we have the philosemitism of the judaizing Christians of the 1590s and beyond (see Heylyn, p. 124, and Nicholas, p. 129). On the other hand we have examples of rank antisemitism, as in the Lopez affair and the continuation of age-old blood libels against the Jews (see Camden, p. 121, and Calvert, p. 123). Indeed, it is noteworthy that editors have traditionally dated the play with reference to the Lopez affair of 1594, in which Queen Elizabeth I's personal physician Dr. Rodrigo Lopez, who was Jewish by birth but at least ostensibly converted to Christianity, was hanged for alleged treason against the queen—a charge of which he was almost certainly innocent. The assumption among Shakespearean editors has been that Shakespeare wrote *The Merchant of Venice* to capitalize on the sensationalism that surrounded Lopez's trial and execution, much as Christopher Marlowe's earlier *The Jew of Malta* was revived to tap into the same popular interest. We have, in fact, no direct evidence that Shakespeare knew of the Lopez affair when he wrote the play, unless we count a possible pun on "wolf" and "Lopez" in Act 4, scene 1 (line 136). What does it mean that the play's very origin is assumed to be bound up in antisemitism?

Of course the heavily freighted question of antisemitism is not the only issue that has divided audiences and readers of *The Merchant of Venice*. In the "Criticism" section, explanations of the Christian and Neoplatonic roots of the play are counterpoised with feminist, queer, and postcolonial critiques of those very roots. This Norton Critical Edition offers readings that on the one hand, strongly critique usury and on the other hand, offer strong evidence that Shakespeare and his father were themselves usurers (see D'Ewes, p. 127, Coryat, p. 114, and Edelman, p. 243). Readers are invited not only to assess what is at stake in different interpretive positions, but also to consider how *The Merchant of Venice* may be seen as a particularly striking bellwether of critical and ideological differences across a wide spectrum of issues involving religion, race, nation, economics, gender, art, music, and even the drama itself.

That bellwether effect has by no means been limited to the play in its Shakespearean form. The section of this Norton Critical Edition titled "Rewritings and Appropriations" offers ample testimony to *The Merchant of Venice*'s rich afterlife in drama, poetry, fiction, film, and television. Space limitations precluded me from including any full texts of the rewritings or imagined sequels of the play, sorely tempting though it would have been to do so. However, through the miniaturized lens of the selection of poems about Shylock that I was able to include (pp. 335–40), readers will get a glimpse of the strength and diversity of the play's imaginative afterlife. The selected bibliography represents this afterlife in a different form, pointing readers toward additional critical studies that extend our understanding of the range and complexity of the play across four hundred years of interpretation.

While it is outside the scope of Norton Critical Editions to offer full-dress editions of Shakespearean texts, that does not mean that we cannot provide readers with texts that are fresh and innovative. In editing *Merchant* here, I have followed some editorial traditions, but departed decisively from others in ways that reflect recent changes in our evaluation of early printed editions of Shakespeare. Traditionally, editors have strived to reproduce Shakespearean texts in the form that Shakespeare would ideally have wanted, insofar as that form can be determined. But the editions that have resulted from that process have often taken it as axiomatic that Shakespeare anticipated modern syntax, grammar (especially subject-verb agreement!), and sentence structure, not to mention more minor matters such as "correct" line divisions. To the extent that early printed texts of the plays failed to reflect these modern forms, they were assumed to be deficient. But Shakespeare's English, his grammar and syntax, were not ours; quite demonstrably, he was less than punctilious about subject-verb agreement! What if we thought of the early texts of the plays not as deficient but instead—even in what look to modern eyes like mistakes or confusion—as relatively faithful reproductions of the play as written by Shakespeare or as presented in early theatrical performances? Recent editorial practice has become more tolerant of what earlier editors might have considered "defects" on grounds that they may offer important evidence about the composition, performance, or reception of the play.

Textual editing always involves negotiating between modern expectations and historical fidelity (insofar as we can determine it), between our sense of what constitutes quality and the quite different standards of the period in which the play was written and performed. Here, I have tried to strike a balance that is more tilted toward the latter than toward the former of each of the above alternatives. All modern editions use the first quarto edition of *The Merchant of Venice* (printed in 1600) as their base text, but I have followed it with greater fidelity—some might say servility!—than most past editors have. I have modernized spelling and punctuation in accordance with Norton practice; I have also used the standardized act and scene divisions (which the quarto does not supply), and accepted some standard normalizations of names and speech prefixes that are extremely confusing in the first quarto version. But I have preserved "anomalies" in the 1600 text where they appeared to offer fruitful material for twenty-first-century cultural interpretation. In particular, I have kept the speech prefix "Jew" which occurs instead of the expected "Shylock" at key points in the text (see "A Note on the Text," p. 76). I have also offered a few suggestions for reading quarto lines that have traditionally been emended. For example, in the quarto scene that corresponds with our modern 5.1, Launcelot the Clown, who is forever uttering hilarious malapropisms, addresses Lorenzo without recognizing him in the darkness, "did you see M. *Lorenzo*, & M. *Lorenzo*," which modern editors tend to emend, dropping the "&," as "Did you see Master Lorenzo? Master Lorenzo!" That interpretation is plausible, but I offer another that is arguably more faithful to Launcelot's capacity for confusion, as also to the 1600 printed text. "M." in Elizabethan usage could be an abbreviation for either "Master" or "Mistress." So the best reading of the line may well be "did you see Master Lorenzo and Mistress Lorenzo," in which case Launcelot is asking about Lorenzo and his wife, Jessica, but comically mistaking Lorenzo's given name for his surname. In this case and a few others, I have explained my suggested wordings in the notes. The play will read slightly differently than it has in other modern versions, but its departures will, I hope, be interesting and useful to those who study the play.

In preparing this Norton Critical Edition, I have received much help, for which I offer warm thanks. My trusty research assistant Jennifer Clement proofread and corrected nearly everything and found many of the items listed in "Rewritings and Appropriations." Douglas Lanier generously supplied materials on revisions and appropriations from his own ongoing research. Georgianna Ziegler of the Folger Shakepeare Library and Sue Erickson of the Central Library at Vanderbilt University provided timely assistance with research. The Interlibrary Loan Office at Vanderbilt endured and supplied many obscure requests. I owe special thanks to Carol Be-mis, my Norton editor; Brian Baker, Assistant Editor; Benjamin Reynolds, Production Manager; Marian Johnson, Managing Editor, College; Kurt Wildermuth, Project Editor; and Katrina Washington, who cleared permissions. Of course, in the nature of things, errors will remain, and I invite readers to call them to our attention so they can be corrected in future printings. My thanks also to the College of Arts and Science at Vanderbilt, which provided research money for travel, photos, and permissions. My daughter, Lauren Marcus, offered the valuable perspective of a sixteen-year-old by vetting the text and notes to let me know what I had failed to make clear. My husband, David, provided his usual blend of support and healthy skepticism. Last of all, I thank Bakula Trivedi, to whom this project is dedicated, and who has taught me more about friendship than Antonio ever knew.

The Text of
THE MERCHANT OF
VENICE

The moſt excellent

Hiſtorie of the *Merchant* of *Venice*.

VVith the extreame crueltie of *Shylocke* the Iewe
towards the ſayd Merchant, in cutting a iuſt pound
of his fleſh: and the obtayning of *Portia*
by the choyſe of three
cheſts.

*As it hath beene diuers times acted by the Lord
Chamberlaine his Seruants.*

Written by William Shakeſpeare.

AT LONDON,

Printed by *I. R.* for Thomas Heyes,
and are to be ſold in Paules Church-yard, at the
ſigne of the Greene Dragon.
1600.

The Comical History of the Merchant of Venice

Act 1 Scene 1

[*Venice*] *Enter* ANTONIO, SALERIO, *and* SOLANIO.

ANTONIO   In sooth I know not why I am so sad.
   It wearies me, you say it wearies you,
   But how I caught it, found it, or came by it,
   What stuff 'tis made of, whereof it is born,
   I am to learn;   5

3

And such a want-wit sadness makes of me
That I have much ado to know myself.
SALERIO   Your mind is tossing on the ocean,
There where your argosies with portly sail
Like signiors and rich burghers on the flood,   10
Or as it were the pageants of the sea,
Do over-peer the petty traffickers
That curtsey to them, do them reverence,
As they fly by them with their woven wings.
SOLANIO   Believe me, sir, had I such venture forth,   15
The better part of my affections would
Be with my hopes abroad. I should be still
Plucking the grass to know where sits the wind,
Peering in maps for ports and piers and roads;
And every object that might make me fear   20
Misfortune to my ventures, out of doubt
Would make me sad.
SALERIO   My wind cooling my broth
Would blow me to an ague when I thought
What harm a wind too great might do at sea.
I should not see the sandy hourglass run   25
But I should think of shallows and of flats,
And see my wealthy Andrew docks in sand,
Vailing her high top lower than her ribs,
To kiss her burial. Should I go to church   30
And see the holy edifice of stone
And not bethink me straight of dangerous rocks,
Which touching but my gentle vessel's side
Would scatter all her spices on the stream,
Enrobe the roaring waters with my silks—   35
And in a word, but even now worth this,
And now worth nothing? Shall I have the thought
To think on this, and shall I lack the thought
That such a thing bechanced would make me sad?
But tell not me; I know Antonio   40
Is sad to think upon his merchandise.

9. **argosies:** large merchant ships.
10. **signiors:** gentlemen.
11. **pageants:** floats in a parade.
12. **over-peer . . . traffickers:** look down on the small boats.
17. **still:** always.
19. **roads:** safe waters for anchorage.
23. **wind:** breath.
24. **ague:** fit of shivering.
28. **see . . . sand:** see my ship (*The Andrew*) run aground.
29. **Vailing:** lowering.
39. **bechanced:** come to pass.

ANTONIO   Believe me, no. I thank my fortune for it.
  My ventures are not in one bottom trusted,
  Nor to one place, nor is my whole estate
  Upon the fortune of this present year;   45
  Therefore my merchandise makes me not sad.
SOLANIO   Why then you are in love.
ANTONIO   Fie, fie!
SOLANIO   Not in love neither? Then let us say you are sad
  Because you are not merry; and 'twere as easy   50
  For you to laugh and leap and say you are merry
  Because you are not sad. Now, by two-headed Janus,
  Nature hath framed strange fellows in her time:
  Some that will evermore peep through their eyes
  And laugh like parrots at a bagpiper,   55
  And other of such vinegar aspect
  That they'll not show their teeth in way of smile
  Though Nestor swear the jest be laughable.

      Enter BASSANIO, LORENZO, *and* GRATIANO.

  Here comes Bassanio, your most noble kinsman,
  Gratiano, and Lorenzo. Fare ye well!   60
  We leave you now with better company.
SALERIO   I would have stayed till I had made you merry
  If worthier friends had not prevented me.
ANTONIO   Your worth is very dear in my regard.
  I take it your own business calls on you,   65
  And you embrace th'occasion to depart.
SALERIO   Good morrow, my good lords.
BASSANIO   Good signiors both, when shall we laugh? Say, when?
  You grow exceeding strange! Must it be so?
SALERIO   We'll make our leisures to attend on yours.   70

      Exeunt SALERIO *and* SOLANIO.

LORENZO   My Lord Bassanio, since you have found Antonio,
  We two will leave you; but at dinner time
  I pray you have in mind where we must meet.
BASSANIO   I will not fail you.
GRATIANO   You look not well, Signior Antonio.   75
  You have too much respect upon the world.
  They lose it that do buy it with much care.

---

52. **Janus:** Roman god of the threshold with two faces that could look simultaneously happy and sad.
56. **vinegar aspect:** sour expressions.
58. **Nestor:** wise and sober leader from *The Iliad*.
76. **respect upon:** concern about.

Believe me, you are marvelously changed.
ANTONIO   I hold the world but as the world, Gratiano—
   A stage where every man must play a part,   80
   And mine a sad one.
GRATIANO   Let me play the fool—
   With mirth and laughter let old wrinkles come,
   And let my liver rather heat with wine
   Than my heart cool with mortifying groans.   85
   Why should a man whose blood is warm within
   Sit like his grandsire, cut in alabaster;
   Sleep when he wakes, and creep into the jaundice
   By being peevish? I tell thee what, Antonio,
   I love thee, and 'tis my love that speaks: 90
   There are a sort of men whose visages
   Do cream and mantle like a standing pond,
   And do a willful stillness entertain
   With purpose to be dressed in an opinion
   Of wisdom, gravity, profound conceit—   95
   As who should say, "I am Sir Oracle,
   And when I ope my lips let no dog bark."
   O my Antonio, I do know of these
   That therefore only are reputed wise—
   For saying nothing; when I am very sure   100
   If they should speak, would almost damn those ears
   Which hearing them would call their brothers fools.
   I'll tell thee more of this another time.
   But fish not with this melancholy bait
   For this fool gudgeon, this opinion.   105
   Come, good Lorenzo, fare ye well awhile.
   I'll end my exhortation after dinner.
LORENZO   Well, we will leave you then till dinner time.
   I must be one of these same dumb wise men,
   For Gratiano never lets me speak.   110
GRATIANO   Well, keep me company but two years moe—
   Thou shalt not know the sound of thine own tongue!
ANTONIO   Fare you well! I'll grow a talker for this gear.
GRATIANO   Thanks i'faith, for silence is only commendable
   In a neat's tongue dried and a maid not vendable.   115

---

87. like . . . alabaster: like his grandfather's statue carved in fine white stone (as on a tomb).
88. jaundice: condition associated in the Renaissance with depression and bitterness.
91–92. visages . . . mantle: whose faces become clouded as a pond with scum.
105. gudgeon: type of fish.
111. moe: more.
113. for this gear: because of all this.
115. neat's tongue: ox tongue.
115. vendable: marketable (as in marriage).

Exeunt [LORENZO *and* GRATIANO].

ANTONIO   It is that—anything now.

BASSANIO   Gratiano speaks an infinite deal of nothing, more
than any man in all Venice. His reasons are as two grains of
wheat hid in two bushels of chaff: you shall seek all day ere
you find them, and when you have them they are not worth   120
the search.

ANTONIO   Well, tell me now—what lady is the same
   To whom you swore a secret pilgrimage
   That you today promised to tell me of?

BASSANIO   'Tis not unknown to you, Antonio,   125
   How much I have disabled mine estate
   By something showing a more swelling port
   Than my faint means would grant continuance.
   Nor do I now make moan to be abridged
   From such a noble rate; but my chief care   130
   Is to come fairly off from the great debts
   Wherein my time something too prodigal
   Hath left me gaged. To you, Antonio,
   I owe the most in money and in love,
   And from your love I have a warranty   135
   To unburden all my plots and purposes
   How to get clear of all the debts I owe.

ANTONIO   I pray you, good Bassanio, let me know it,
   And if it stand, as you your self still do,
   Within the eye of honor, be assured   140
   My purse, my person, my extremest means
   Lie all unlocked to your occasions.

BASSANIO   In my school days, when I had lost one shaft,
   I shot his fellow of the selfsame flight
   The selfsame way, with more advised watch,   145
   To find the other forth; and by adventuring both,
   I oft found both. I urge this childhood proof
   Because what follows is pure innocence.
   I owe you much, and like a willful youth
   That which I owe is lost; but if you please   150
   To shoot another arrow that self way
   Which you did shoot the first, I do not doubt,

---

116. **It is . . . now:** Cryptic comment that may mean, "It's true—anything goes now."
127. **something:** somewhat.
127. **swelling port:** lavish lifestyle.
129–30. **abridged from . . . noble rate:** to be obliged to be more economical.
133. **gaged:** indebted.
143. **shaft:** arrow.
144. **selfsame flight:** another arrow that had the same characteristics in flight.

As I will watch the aim, or to find both,
Or bring your latter hazard back again,
And thankfully rest debtor for the first.   155
ANTONIO   You know me well, and herein spend but time
To wind about my love with circumstance;
And out of doubt you do me now more wrong
In making question of my uttermost
Than if you had made waste of all I have.   160
Then do but say to me what I should do
That in your knowledge may by me be done,
And I am pressed unto it—therefore speak.
BASSANIO   In Belmont is a lady richly left,
And she is fair, and fairer than that word,   165
Of wondrous virtues. Sometimes from her eyes
I did receive fair speechless messages.
Her name is Portia, nothing undervalued
To Cato's daughter, Brutus' Portia.
Nor is the wide world ignorant of her worth,   170
For the four winds blow in from every coast
Renowned suitors; and her sunny locks
Hang on her temples like a golden fleece,
Which makes her seat of Belmont Colchos' strond;
And many Jasons come in quest of her.   175
O my Antonio, had I but the means
To hold a rival place with one of them,
I have a mind presages me such thrift
That I should questionless be fortunate.
ANTONIO   Thou knowst that all my fortunes are at sea: 180
Neither have I money nor commodity
To raise a present sum. Therefore go forth—
Try what my credit can in Venice do;
That shall be racked even to the uttermost
To furnish thee to Belmont to fair Portia.   185
Go presently inquire, and so will I,
Where money is; and I no question make
To have it of my trust, or for my sake.

                                                   Exeunt

---

153. **or:** either.
157. **circumstance:** conditions.
159. **making . . . uttermost:** doubting whether I will do my utmost.
169. **Portia:** Roman woman noted for heroism and independence, daughter of Cato the Younger and wife of the Marcus Brutus who helped assassinate Julius Caesar.
174–75. **Colchos' strond . . . in quest of her:** The mythic Jason sailed to Colchis coast to win the Golden Fleece.
188. **of my trust . . . my sake:** because of my strong credit or out of friendship for me.

Act 1 Scene 2

[Belmont] Enter PORTIA *with her waiting woman,* NERISSA.

PORTIA   By my troth, Nerissa, my little body is a-weary of this
great world.

NERISSA   You would be, sweet madam, if your miseries were in
the same abundance as your good fortunes are. And yet for
aught I see, they are as sick that surfeit with too much as   5
they that starve with nothing. It is no mean happiness,
therefore, to be seated in the mean: superfluity comes
sooner by white hairs, but competency lives longer.

PORTIA   Good sentences, and well pronounced.

NERISSA   They would be better if well followed.   10

PORTIA   If to do were as easy as to know what were good to do,
chapels had been churches and poor men's cottages, princes'
palaces. It is a good divine that follows his own instructions.
I can easier teach twenty what were good to be done than to
be one of the twenty to follow mine own teaching. The brain   15
may devise laws for the blood, but a hot temper leaps o'er a
cold decree: such a hare is madness, the youth, to skip o'er
the meshes of good counsel, the cripple. But this reasoning
is not in the fashion to choose me a husband. O me! The
word "choose"! I may neither choose who I would nor refuse   20
who I dislike; so is the will of a living daughter curbed by the
will of a dead father. Is it not hard, Nerissa, that I cannot
choose one, nor refuse none?

NERISSA   Your father was ever virtuous, and holy men at their
death have good inspirations; therefore the lottery that he   25
hath devised in these three chests of gold, silver, and lead,
whereof who chooses his meaning chooses you, will no
doubt never be chosen by any rightly but one who you shall
rightly love. But what warmth is there in your affection towards any of these princely suitors that are already come?   30

PORTIA   I pray thee, over-name them, and as thou namest
them I will describe them, and according to my description
level at my affection.

NERISSA   First there is the Neapolitan prince.

PORTIA   Aye, that's a colt indeed! For he doth nothing but talk   35

6. **mean:** slight.
7. **seated in the mean:** located in the middle.
8. **competency lives longer:** moderation lives longer than excess.
13. **divine:** preacher.
18. **meshes:** nets to catch hares.
19. **in the fashion:** of the right sort.
23. **none:** any.
31. **over-name them:** go over their names.

of his horse, and he makes it a great appropriation to his
own good parts that he can shoe him himself. I am much
afeared my lady his mother played false with a smith.

NERISSA   Then is there the County Palatine.

PORTIA   He doth nothing but frown—as who should say, "And   40
you will not have me, choose." He hears merry tales and
smiles not. I fear he will prove the weeping philosopher
when he grows old, being so full of unmannerly sadness in
his youth. I had rather be married to a death's head with a
bone in his mouth than to either of these. God defend me   45
from these two!

NERISSA   How say you by the French lord, Monsieur Le Bon?

PORTIA   God made him; and therefore let him pass for a man.
In truth I know it is a sin to be a mocker, but he—why he
hath a horse better than the Neapolitan's, a better bad habit   50
of frowning than the Count Palatine: he is every man in no
man. If a throstle sing he falls straight a capering; he will
fence with his own shadow. If I should marry him I should
marry twenty husbands. If he would despise me, I would forgive him; for if he love me to madness, I shall never requite   55
him.

NERISSA   What say you then to Falconbridge, the young baron
of England?

PORTIA   You know I say nothing to him, for he understands
not me, nor I him: he hath neither Latin, French, nor Ital-   60
ian; and you will come into the court and swear that I have a
poor pennyworth in the English. He is a proper man's picture, but alas! Who can converse with a dumb show? How
oddly he is suited! I think he bought his doublet in Italy, his
round hose in France, his bonnet in Germany, and his be-   65
havior everywhere.

NERISSA   What think you of the Scottish lord, his neighbor?

PORTIA   That he hath a neighborly charity in him, for he borrowed a box of the ear of the Englishman and swore he
would pay him again when he was able. I think the French-   70
man became his surety and sealed under for another.

36–37. **appropriation . . . parts:** addition to his accomplishments.
39. **County:** Count.
40–41. **"And you . . . choose":** "If you don't want me, choose whom you wish!"
42. **weeping philosopher:** Heraclitus, Greek philosopher known for melancholy.
52. **throstle:** thrush.
61–62. **I have . . . English:** I speak little English.
63. **dumb show:** pantomine.
64. **doublet:** coat.
65. **round hose:** breeches.
69–71. **Englishman . . . another:** A series of political references: England had defeated
Scotland at Flodden Field in 1513; in later Scottish wars, the French became "surety" for
and "underwrote" the Scots by serving as their allies against England.

NERISSA How like you the young German, the Duke of Sax-
ony's nephew?

PORTIA Very vilely in the morning when he is sober, and most
vilely in the afternoon when he is drunk. When he is best, he   75
is a little worse than a man, and when he is worst, he is little
better than a beast. And the worst fall that ever fell, I hope I
shall make shift to go without him.

NERISSA If he should offer to choose, and choose the right
casket, you should refuse to perform your father's will if you   80
should refuse to accept him.

PORTIA Therefore, for fear of the worst, I pray thee set a deep
glass of Rhenish wine on the contrary casket; for if the devil
be within and that temptation without, I know he will
choose it. I will do anything, Nerissa, ere I will be married to   85
a sponge!

NERISSA You need not fear, lady, the having any of these lords.
They have acquainted me with their determinations, which
is indeed to return to their home and to trouble you with no
more suit, unless you may be won by some other sort than   90
your father's imposition, depending on the caskets.

PORTIA If I live to be as old as Sibylla, I will die as chaste as
Diana unless I be obtained by the manner of my father's will.
I am glad this parcel of wooers are so reasonable, for there is
not one among them but I dote on his very absence, and I   95
pray God grant them a fair departure.

NERISSA Do you not remember, lady, in your father's time, a
Venetian—a scholar and a soldier that came hither in company of the Marquess of Montferrat?

PORTIA Yes, yes—it was Bassanio; as I think, so was he called.   100

NERISSA True, madam. He of all the men that ever my foolish
eyes looked upon was the best deserving a fair lady.

PORTIA I remember him well, and I remember him worthy of
thy praise.

Enter a serving man.

How now? What news?   105

SERVING MAN The four strangers seek for you, madam, to take
their leave; and there is a forerunner come from a fifth, the

---

77. **worst . . . fell:** if worst comes to worst (and the German prince wins her hand).
78. **make shift:** manage.
83. **Rhenish:** Rhine.
83. **contrary casket:** wrong casket.
90. **sort:** method.
92. **Sibylla:** classical prophetess to whom Apollo promised as many years of life as she held grains of sand.
93. **Diana:** perpetually unmarried Roman goddess of the hunt.

Prince of Morocco, who brings word the prince his master
will be here tonight.

PORTIA   If I could bid the fifth welcome with so good heart as   110
I can bid the other four farewell, I should be glad of his approach. If he have the condition of a saint and the complexion of a devil, I had rather he should shrive me than wive
me. Come, Nerissa; sirrah, go before. Whiles we shut the
gate upon one wooer, another knocks at the door.   *Exeunt*   115

Act 1 Scene 3

[Venice] Enter BASSANIO *with* SHYLOCK *the Jew.*

SHYLOCK   Three thousand ducats—well.

BASSANIO   Aye, sir—for three months.

SHYLOCK   For three months—well.

BASSANIO   For the which, as I told you, Antonio shall be
bound.   5

SHYLOCK   Antonio shall become bound—well.

BASSANIO   May you stead me? Will you pleasure me?
Shall I know your answer?

SHYLOCK   Three thousand ducats for three months, and Anto-
nio bound.   10

BASSANIO   Your answer to that?

SHYLOCK   Antonio is a good man.

BASSANIO   Have you heard any imputation to the contrary?

SHYLOCK   Ho, no, no, no, no: my meaning in saying he is a
good man is to have you understand me that he is sufficient.   15
Yet his means are in supposition: he hath an argosy bound to
Tripolis, another to the Indies. I understand, moreover, upon
the Rialto, he hath a third at Mexico, a fourth for England,
and other ventures he hath squand'red abroad. But ships are
but boards, sailors but men; there be land rats and water   20
rats, water thieves and land thieves—I mean pirates. And
then there is the peril of waters, winds, and rocks. The man
is, notwithstanding, sufficient. Three thousand ducats: I
think I may take his bond.

BASSANIO   Be assured you may.   25

112–13. **complexion . . . devil:** Devils were frequently imagined as black.
113. **shrive me:** hear my confession.
114. **sirrah:** addressed to the serving man.
1. **ducats:** units of Venetian currency. This sum would equal approximately £270,000 or
$500,000, depending on the exchange rate.
7. **stead:** accommodate.
16. **supposition:** doubt.
18. **Rialto:** merchants' exchange along the Grand Canal in Venice.

JEW   I will be assured I may; and that I may be assured, I will
   bethink me. May I speak with Antonio?

BASSANIO   If it please you to dine with us.

JEW   Yes—to smell pork, to eat of the habitation which your
   prophet the Nazarite conjured the devil into? I will buy with   30
   you, sell with you, talk with you, walk with you, and so following. But I will not eat with you, drink with you, nor pray
   with you. What news on the Rialto? Who is he comes here?

     Enter ANTONIO.

BASSANIO   This is Signior Antonio.

JEW   How like a fawning publican he looks!   35
   I hate him for he is a Christian,
   But more for that in low simplicity
   He lends out money gratis and brings down
   The rate of usance here with us in Venice.
   If I can catch him once upon the hip,   40
   I will feed fat the ancient grudge I bear him.
   He hates our sacred nation and he rails,
   Even there where merchants most do congregate,
   On me, my bargains, and my well-won thrift,
   Which he calls interest. Cursed be my tribe   45
   If I forgive him.

BASSANIO   Shylock, do you hear?

SHYLOCK   I am debating of my present store,
   And by the near guess of my memory,
   I cannot instantly raise up the gross   50
   Of full three thousand ducats. What of that?
   Tubal, a wealthy Hebrew of my tribe,
   Will furnish me. But soft—how many months
   Do you desire? Rest you fair, good signior,
   Your worship was the last man in our mouths.   55

ANTONIO   Shylock, albeit I neither lend nor borrow
   By taking nor by giving of excess,
   Yet to supply the ripe wants of my friend
   I'll break a custom. Is he yet possessed
   How much ye would?   60

---

26. JEW: This edition reproduces a significant pattern in the first quarto, where the
speech prefixes sometimes refer to Shylock by name, and sometimes as "Jew."
30. Nazarite: Jesus, who cast devils into a herd of swine (Luke 8.26–33).
35. publican: Either an innkeeper or a tax collector, as in Luke 18.10–14, where a
publican humbles himself and asks for mercy. Shylock interprets the publican as trying to ingratiate himself with Jesus because he wants a favor.
39. usance: interest rate charged on loans.
40. If I . . . the hip: If I can just get him under my control (from wrestling).
50. gross: full sum.
58. ripe: urgent.

SHYLOCK   Aye, aye—three thousand ducats.

ANTONIO   And for three months.

SHYLOCK   I had forgot: three months. You told me so.
  Well then, your bond. And let me see, but hear you—
  Methoughts you said you neither lend nor borrow   65
  Upon advantage.

ANTONIO   I do never use it.

SHYLOCK   When Jacob grazed his Uncle Laban's sheep,
  This Jacob from our holy Abram was
  (As his wise mother wrought in his behalf)   70
  The third possessor; aye, he was the third.

ANTONIO   And what of him? Did he take interest?

SHYLOCK   No, not take interest—not, as you would say,
  Directly interest. Mark what Jacob did:
  When Laban and himself were compromised   75
  That all the eanlings which were streaked and pied
  Should fall as Jacob's hire, the ewes, being rank,
  In end of autumn turned to the rams;
  And when the work of generation was
  Between these wooly breeders in the act,   80
  The skillful shepherd peeled me certain wands,
  And in the doing of the deed of kind
  He stuck them up before the fulsome ewes,
  Who then conceiving, did in eaning time
  Fall particolored lambs; and those were Jacob's.   85
  This was a way to thrive, and he was blessed;
  And thrift is blessing, if men steal it not.

ANTONIO   This was a venture, sir, that Jacob served for—
  A thing not in his power to bring to pass,
  But swayed and fashioned by the hand of heaven.   90
  Was this inserted to make interest good?
  Or is your gold and silver ewes and rams?

SHYLOCK   I cannot tell; I make it breed as fast.
  But note me, signior—

ANTONIO   Mark you this, Bassanio—   95

---

68. Jacob: Biblical son of Abraham (Abram) and Rebecca and son-in-law of Laban, who promised Jacob the spotted and black sheep from his flocks as wages, then removed them before Jacob could collect them (Genesis 30.25–36).

75. compromised: agreed.

76. eanlings . . . pied: lambs that were striped or spotted.

77. rank: in heat.

81. peeled me: peeled (colloquial usage).

81–85. The skillful . . . particolored lambs: In front of the pregnant ewes, Jacob placed sticks that looked striped because they had been partially peeled. Since it was popularly believed that the nature of the offspring was influenced by what the mothers saw during their pregnancy, the ewes then gave birth to striped and spotted offspring that, by previous agreement with Laban, became Jacob's (Genesis 30.37–43).

91. Was this . . . interest good: was this story brought up to defend the taking of interest?

The devil can cite scripture for his purpose.
An evil soul producing holy witness
Is like a villain with a smiling cheek,
A goodly apple rotten at the heart.
O what a goodly outside falsehood hath!　　　　100
SHYLOCK　　Three thousand ducats—'tis a good round sum.
　　Three months from twelve—then let me see the rate.
ANTONIO　　Well, Shylock, shall we be beholding to you?
SHYLOCK　　Signior Antonio, many a time and oft
　　In the Rialto you have rated me　　　　105
　　About my moneys and my usances.
　　Still have I borne it with a patient shrug,
　　For sufferance is the badge of all our tribe.
　　You call me misbeliever, cut-throat dog,
　　And spit upon my Jewish gaberdine,　　　　110
　　And all for use of that which is mine own.
　　Well then, it now appears you need my help.
　　Go to, then—you come to me and you say,
　　"Shylock, we would have moneys," you say so—
　　You that did void your rheum upon my beard　　　　115
　　And foot me as you spurn a stranger cur
　　Over your threshold. Moneys is your suit.
　　What should I say to you? Should I not say
　　"Hath a dog money? Is it possible
　　A cur can lend three thousand ducats?" Or　　　　120
　　Shall I bend low and in a bondman's key,
　　With bated breath and whispering humbleness,
　　Say this: "Fair sir, you spit on me on Wednesday last;
　　You spurned me such a day; another time
　　You called me dog, and for these courtesies　　　　125
　　I'll lend you thus much moneys"?
ANTONIO　　I am as like to call thee so again—
　　To spit on thee again, to spurn thee too.
　　If thou wilt lend this money, lend it not
　　As to thy friends, for when did friendship take　　　　130
　　A breed for barren metal of his friend?
　　But lend it rather to thine enemy
　　Who, if he break, thou mayst with better face
　　Exact the penalty.

105. **rated:** scolded harshly.
108. **sufferance . . . badge:** suffering is the mark.
110. **gaberdine:** long coat.
115. **void your rheum:** spit your mucus.
116. **foot . . . cur:** kick me as you turn back a strange dog.
131. **breed:** offspring (interest, the "child" of money).
133. **break:** fail to pay.

SHYLOCK   Why look you, how you storm!   135
   I would be friends with you and have your love,
   Forget the shames that you have stained me with,
   Supply your present wants and take no doit
   Of usance for my moneys—and you'll not hear me.
   This is kind I offer.   140
BASSANIO   This were kindness.
SHYLOCK   This kindness will I show:
   Go with me to a notary; seal me there
   Your single bond, and in a merry sport,
   If you repay me not on such a day   145
   In such a place, such sum or sums as are
   Expressed in the condition, let the forfeit
   Be nominated for an equal pound
   Of your fair flesh, to be cut off and taken
   In what part of your body pleaseth me.   150
ANTONIO   Content, in faith: I'll seal to such a bond,
   And say there is much kindness in the Jew.
BASSANIO   You shall not seal to such a bond for me;
   I'll rather dwell in my necessity.
ANTONIO   Why fear not, man—I will not forfeit it.   155
   Within these two months—that's a month before
   This bond expires—I do expect return
   Of thrice three times the value of this bond.
SHYLOCK   O father Abram, what these Christians are,
   Whose own hard dealings teaches them suspect   160
   The thoughts of others! Pray you, tell me this:
   If he should break his day, what should I gain
   By the exaction of the forfeiture?
   A pound of man's flesh taken from a man
   Is not so estimable, profitable neither,   165
   As flesh of muttons, beefs, or goats. I say
   To buy his favor, I extend this friendship.
   If he will take it, so; if not, adieu,
   And for my love I pray you wrong me not.
ANTONIO   Yes, Shylock, I will seal unto this bond.   170
SHYLOCK   Then meet me forthwith at the notary's.
   Give him direction for this merry bond,
   And I will go and purse the ducats straight,
   See to my house, left in the fearful guard
   Of an unthrifty knave; and presently   175
   I'll be with you.   *Exit.*

138. **doit:** small coin.

ANTONIO   Hie thee, gentle Jew!
   The Hebrew will turn Christian—he grows kind.
BASSANIO   I like not fair terms and a villain's mind.
ANTONIO   Come on—in this there can be no dismay;   180
   My ships come home a month before the day.   *Exeunt.*

Act 2 Scene 1

[BELMONT] *Enter* [*the Prince of*] MOROCCO, *a tawny*
moor all in white, and three or four followers accordingly,
with PORTIA, NERISSA, *and their train.*

MOROCCO   Mislike me not for my complexion,
   The shadowed livery of the burnished sun,
   To whom I am a neighbor and near bred.
   Bring me the fairest creature northward born,
   Where Phoebus' fire scarce thaws the icicles,   5
   And let us make incision, for your love,
   To prove whose blood is reddest—his or mine.
   I tell thee, lady, this aspect of mine
   Hath feared the valiant; by my love I swear
   The best regarded virgins of our clime   10
   Have loved it too. I would not change this hue
   Except to steal your thoughts, my gentle queen.
PORTIA   In terms of choice I am not solely led
   By nice direction of a maiden's eyes.
   Besides, the lottery of my destiny   15
   Bars me the right of voluntary choosing.
   But if my father had not scanted me
   And hedged me by his wit to yield myself
   His wife who wins me by that means I told you,
   Yourself, renowned prince, then stood as fair   20
   As any comer I have looked on yet
   For my affection.
MOROCCO   Even for that I thank you.
   Therefore I pray you lead me to the caskets

---

177. Hie thee: hurry.
STAGE DIRECTION *accordingly:* of similar complexion and dress.
2. The shadowed . . . sun: Morocco describes his tawny skin as a dark "uniform" he
wears to indicate his allegiance to the sun.
3. near bred: a close relative.
5. Phoebus': the sun god's.
9. feared: brought fear to.
14. nice: fastidious, picky.
17. scanted: limited.

To try my fortune. By this scimitar   25
That slew the Sophy and a Persian Prince,
That won three fields of Sultan Suleiman,
I would o'er-stare the sternest eyes that look,
Out-brave the heart most daring on the earth,
Pluck the young sucking cubs from the she-bear;   30
Yea, mock the lion when 'a roars for prey,
To win the lady. But, alas the while,
If Hercules and Lychas play at dice
Which is the better man, the greater throw
May turn by fortune from the weaker hand—   35
So is Alcides beaten by his rage.
And so may I, blind Fortune leading me,
Miss that which one unworthier may attain,
And die with grieving.

PORTIA   You must take your chance   40
And either not attempt to choose at all,
Or swear before you choose, if you choose wrong
Never to speak to lady afterward
In way of marriage. Therefore be advised.

MOROCCO   Nor will not. Come, bring me unto my chance.   45

PORTIA   First forward to the temple; after dinner
Your hazard shall be made.

MOROCCO   Good fortune, then,
To make me blest or cursed'st among men.   *Exeunt.*

Act 2 Scene 2

[Venice] Enter [LAUNCELOT GOBBO,] *the clown, alone.*

LAUNCELOT   Certainly, my conscience will serve me to run
from this Jew, my master. The fiend is at mine elbow and
tempts me, saying to me, "Gobbo, Launcelot Gobbo, good
Launcelot" or "good Gobbo" or "good Launcelot Gobbo, use
your legs, take the start, run away." My conscience says,   5
"No, take heed, honest Launcelot; take heed honest Gobbo,"
or, as aforesaid, "honest Launcelot Gobbo, do not run, scorn
running with thy heels." Well, the most courageous fiend
bids me pack: "Fia!" says the fiend; "away!" says the fiend,

25–26. **By this scimitar . . . the Sophy:** by my sword that slew the Shah of Persia.
27. **Sultan Suleiman:** Ottoman Turkish ruler known for great military prowess.
31. **'a:** he (colloquialism).
33. **Lychas:** servant of Hercules.
36. **Alcides . . . rage:** Alcides (Hercules) is beaten not only by the servant but by his own rage at the injustice of the defeat.
9. **Fia:** away! (From Italian *via*).

"for the heavens rouse up a brave mind," says the fiend, "and   10
run!" Well, my conscience, hanging about the neck of my
heart, says very wisely to me, "My honest friend Launcelot,
being an honest man's son," or rather, "an honest woman's
son"—for indeed my father did something smack, something
grow to; he had a kind of taste. Well, my conscience says,   15
"Launcelot, budge not." "Budge," says the fiend. "Budge
not," says my conscience. "Conscience," say I, "you counsel
well." "Fiend," say I, "you counsel well." To be ruled by my
conscience I should stay with the Jew my master, who (God
bless the mark) is a kind of devil. And to run away from the   20
Jew, I should be ruled by the fiend, who (saving your reverence) is the devil himself. Certainly the Jew is the very devil
incarnation. And in my conscience, my conscience is but a
kind of hard conscience to offer to counsel me to stay with
the Jew. The fiend gives the more friendly counsel: I will run.   25
Fiend, my heels are at your commandment; I will run!

Enter old GOBBO *with a basket.*

GOBBO   Master young man—you, I pray you—which is the
way to Master Jew's?
LAUNCELOT   O heavens! This is my true-begotten father, who,
being more than sand blind—high gravel blind—knows me   30
not. I will try confusions with him.
GOBBO   Master young gentleman, I pray you, which is the way
to Master Jew's?
LAUNCELOT   Turn up on your right hand at the next turning,
but at the next turning of all on your left. Marry, at the very   35
next turning turn of no hand, but turn down indirectly to the
Jew's house.
GOBBO   By God's sonties, 'twill be a hard way to hit! Can you
tell me whether one Launcelot that dwells with him dwell
with him or no?   40
LAUNCELOT   Talk you of young Master Launcelot? Mark me
now—now will I raise the waters. Talk you of young Master
Launcelot?
GOBBO   No "Master," sir, but a poor man's son. His father,
though I say't, is an honest exceeding poor man, and, God be   45
thanked, well to live.

15. **he had . . . taste:** he was a womanizer.
19–20. **God . . . mark:** Lord help us.
21–22. **saving your reverence:** apologies in advance.
23. **incarnation:** incarnate, in the flesh.
30. **more than . . . gravel blind:** more than half blind—almost stone blind.
38. **sonties:** saints.
42. **raise the waters:** bring on the tears.
46. **well to live:** living comfortably.

LAUNCELOT Well, let his father be what 'a will, we talk of
young Master Launcelot.

GOBBO Your worship's friend and Launcelot, sir.

LAUNCELOT But, I pray you, ergo, old man, ergo, I beseech   50
you, talk you of young Master Launcelot?

GOBBO Of Launcelot an't please your mastership.

LAUNCELOT Ergo, Master Launcelot! Talk not of Master
Launcelot, father, for the young gentleman, according to
fates and destinies and such odd sayings, the sisters three   55
and such branches of learning, is indeed deceased, or as you
would say in plain terms, gone to heaven.

GOBBO Marry God forbid! The boy was the very staff of my
age, my very prop!

LAUNCELOT Do I look like a cudgel or a hovel post, a staff or   60
a prop? Do you know me, father?

GOBBO Alack the day! I know you not, young gentleman; but
I pray you tell me: is my boy, God rest his soul, alive or dead?

LAUNCELOT Do you not know me, father?

GOBBO Alack, sir, I am sand blind. I know you not.   65

LAUNCELOT Nay, indeed, if you had your eyes you might fail
of the knowing me: it is a wise father that knows his own
child. Well, old man, I will tell you news of your son.
[Kneels.] Give me your blessing. Truth will come to light;
murder cannot be hid long; a man's son may, but in the end   70
truth will out.

GOBBO Pray you sir, stand up. I am sure you are not
Launcelot, my boy.

LAUNCELOT Pray you, let's have no more fooling about it, but
give me your blessing. I am Launcelot—your boy that was,   75
your son that is, your child that shall be.

GOBBO I cannot think you are my son.

LAUNCELOT I know not what I shall think of that, but I am
Launcelot, the Jew's man; and I am sure Margery, your wife,
is my mother.   80

GOBBO Her name is Margery indeed. I'll be sworn if thou be
Launcelot, thou art mine own flesh and blood. Lord, wor-
shiped might He be, what a beard hast thou got! Thou hast
got more hair on thy chin than Dobbin my fill-horse has on
his tail.   85

50. **ergo:** therefore (Latin).
52. **an't:** if it.
55. **sisters three:** the three fates who controlled human destiny.
60. **hovel post:** post propping up a shed.
67–68. **it is . . . own child:** Reverses the proverb "It's a wise child that knows his own father."
83. **what a . . . thou got:** He mistakes Launcelot's hair for a beard.
84. **fill-horse:** cart horse.

LAUNCELOT   It should seem then that Dobbin's tail grows
backward. I am sure he had more hair of his tail than I have
of my face when I last saw him. [*Stands.*]

GOBBO   Lord, how art thou changed! How dost thou and thy
master agree? I have brought him a present; how 'gree you   90
now?

LAUNCELOT   Well, well. But for mine own part, as I have set
up my rest to run away, so I will not rest till I have run some
ground. My master's a very Jew: give him a present—give
him a halter. I am famished in his service. You may tell every   95
finger I have with my ribs. Father, I am glad you are come.
Give me your present to one Master Bassanio, who indeed
gives rare new liveries. If I serve not him, I will run as far as
God has any ground. O rare fortune! Here comes the man:
to him, father, for I am a Jew if I serve the Jew any longer.   100

Enter BASSANIO *with* [LEONARDO *and*] *a follower or two.*

BASSANIO   You may do so, but let it be so hasted that supper
be ready at the farthest by five of the clock. See these letters
delivered, put the liveries to making, and desire Gratiano to
come anon to my lodging.

LAUNCELOT   To him, father!   105

GOBBO   God bless your worship.

BASSANIO   Gramercy. Would'st thou aught with me?

GOBBO   Here's my son, sir, a poor boy.

LAUNCELOT   Not a poor boy, sir, but the rich Jew's man that
would, sir, as my father shall specify.   110

GOBBO   He hath a great infection, sir, as one would say, to serve.

LAUNCELOT   Indeed the short and the long is, I serve the Jew
and have a desire as my father shall specify.

GOBBO   His master and he, saving your worship's reverence,
are scarce cater-cousins.   115

LAUNCELOT   To be brief, the very truth is that the Jew, having
done me wrong, doth cause me, as my father, being I hope
an old man, shall fructify unto you—

92–93. **set up my rest**: determined.
94. **ground**: distance.
95. **halter**: hangman's noose.
95–96. **You may . . . my ribs**: As usual he gets things backwards: "You may count all
my ribs with my finger."
97. **Give me**: give (colloquialism).
101. **hasted**: speeded up.
102. **farthest**: latest.
103. **put . . . to making**: put the servants' uniforms out to be tailored.
104. **anon**: at once.
107. **Gramercy**: many thanks.
111. **infection**: blunder for "affection."
115. **cater-cousins**: close friends.

GOBBO   I have here a dish of doves that I would bestow upon
  your worship, and my suit is—   120
LAUNCELOT   In very brief, the suit is impertinent to myself, as
  your worship shall know by this honest old man and, though
  I say it, though old man, yet poor man, my father—
BASSANIO   One speak for both: what would you?
LAUNCELOT   Serve you, sir.   125
GOBBO   That is the very defect of the matter, sir.
BASSANIO   I know thee well; thou hast obtained thy suit.
  Shylock thy master spoke with me this day,
  And hath preferred thee—if it be preferment
  To leave a rich Jew's service to become   130
  The follower of so poor a gentleman.
LAUNCELOT   The old proverb is very well parted between my
  Master Shylock and you, sir: you have the grace of God, sir,
  and he hath enough.
BASSANIO   Thou speak'st it well. Go, father, with thy son;   135
  Take leave of thy old master and inquire
  My lodging out. Give him a livery
  More guarded than his fellows'—see it done.
LAUNCELOT   Father, in. I cannot get a service—no! I have
  ne'er a tongue in my head. Well, if any man in Italy have a   140
  fairer table which doth offer to swear upon a book—I shall
  have good fortune. Go to—here's a simple line of life; here's
  a small trifle of wives. Alas, fifteen wives is nothing! Eleven
  widows and nine maids is a simple coming in for one man,
  and then to 'scape drowning thrice, and to be in peril of my   145
  life with the edge of a featherbed. Here are simple scapes!
  Well, if Fortune be a woman, she's a good wench for this
  gear. Father, come. I'll take my leave of the Jew in the twin-
  kling.

          Exit [LAUNCELOT *the*] *clown* [*with old* GOBBO].

BASSANIO   I pray thee, good Leonardo, think on this.   150
  These things being bought and orderly bestowed,
  Return in haste, for I do feast tonight
  My best esteemed acquaintance. Hie thee, go!
LEONARDO   My best endeavors shall be done herein.

133–34. **you have . . . hath enough:** Quip on the proverb "He who has the grace of God
has enough."
138. **guarded:** decorated.
141. **table:** palm, which he reads like a "table" or notebook.
141. **swear . . . book:** take an oath by swearing with one's palm upon a Bible.
144. **coming in:** income (with sexual connotations).
145–46. **peril . . . featherbed:** allusion to a fantasized future sexual adventure.
147. **scapes:** escapades.

Enter GRATIANO.

GRATIANO   Where's your master?   155
LEONARDO   Yonder, sir, he walks.   [*Exit*]
GRATIANO   Signior Bassanio!
BASSANIO   Gratiano!
GRATIANO   I have suit to you.
BASSANIO   You have obtained it.   160
GRATIANO   You must not deny me. I must go with you to
     Belmont.
BASSANIO   Why then you must; but hear thee, Gratiano:
     Thou art too wild, too rude and bold of voice—
     Parts that become thee happily enough
     And in such eyes as ours appear not faults.   165
     But where thou art not known, why there they show
     Something too liberal. Pray thee, take pain
     To allay with some cold drops of modesty
     Thy skipping spirit, lest through thy wild behavior
     I be misconstered in the place I go to,   170
     And lose my hopes.
GRATIANO   Signior Bassanio, hear me.
     If I do not put on a sober habit,
     Talk with respect, and swear but now and then,
     Wear prayer books in my pocket, look demurely,   175
     Nay more—while grace is saying, hood mine eyes
     Thus with my hat and sigh and say "Amen";
     Use all the observance of civility
     Like one well studied in a sad ostent
     To please his grandam—never trust me more.   180
BASSANIO   Well, we shall see your bearing.
GRATIANO   Nay, but I bar tonight—you shall not gauge me
     By what we do tonight.
BASSANIO   No, that were pity!
     I would entreat you rather to put on   185
     Your boldest suit of mirth, for we have friends
     That purpose merriment. But fare you well;
     I have some business.
GRATIANO   And I must to Lorenzo and the rest;
     But we will visit you at supper time.   *Exeunt.*   190

---

167. **Something . . . liberal:** somewhat too unrestrained.
170. **misconstered:** misconstrued, misunderstood.
179–80. **sad ostent . . . grandam:** a sober appearance to please his grandmother.
182. **bar:** make exception of.

Act 2 Scene 3

Enter JESSICA *and* [LAUNCELOT] *the Clown.*

JESSICA   I am sorry thou wilt leave my father so;
　　Our house is hell and thou, a merry devil,
　　Didst rob it of some taste of tediousness.
　　But fare thee well; there is a ducat for thee.
　　And, Launcelot, soon at supper shalt thou see   5
　　Lorenzo, who is thy new master's guest.
　　Give him this letter; do it secretly,
　　And so farewell. I would not have my father
　　See me in talk with thee.
LAUNCELOT   Adieu! Tears exhibit my tongue, most beautiful   10
　　pagan, most sweet Jew. If a Christian do not play the knave
　　and get thee, I am much deceived. But adieu! These foolish
　　drops do something drown my manly spirit. Adieu!   *Exit.*
JESSICA   Farewell, good Launcelot.
　　Alack, what heinous sin is it in me   15
　　To be ashamed to be my father's child!
　　But though I am a daughter to his blood
　　I am not to his manners. O Lorenzo,
　　If thou keep promise, I shall end this strife—
　　Become a Christian and thy loving wife.   *Exit.*   20

Act 2 Scene 4

Enter GRATIANO, LORENZO, SALERIO, *and* SOLANIO.

LORENZO   Nay, we will slink away in supper time,
　　Disguise us at my lodging, and return
　　All in an hour.
GRATIANO   We have not made good preparation.
SALERIO   We have not spoke us yet of torch-bearers.   5
SOLANIO   'Tis vile unless it may be quaintly ordered,
　　And better in my mind not undertook.
LORENZO   'Tis now but four of clock; we have two hours
　　To furnish us.

Enter LAUNCELOT [*with a letter*].

　　Friend Launcelot, what's the news?   10

10. **exhibit:** blunder for "inhibit."
11. **do not:** did not.
12. **get:** beget.
6. **quaintly ordered:** nicely arranged.

LAUNCELOT   And it shall please you to break up this, it shall
   seem to signify.
LORENZO   I know the hand: in faith 'tis a fair hand,
   And whiter than the paper it writ on
   Is the fair hand that writ.   15
GRATIANO   Love news in faith.
LAUNCELOT   By your leave, sir—
LORENZO   Whither goest thou?
LAUNCELOT   Marry, sir, to bid my old master the Jew to sup
   tonight with my new master the Christian.   20
LORENZO   Hold—here, take this. Tell gentle Jessica
   I will not fail her; speak it privately.

                                    Exit [LAUNCELOT, *the*] *clown.*

   Go, gentlemen.
   Will you prepare you for this masque tonight?
   I am provided of a torch-bearer.   25
SALERIO   Aye, marry, I'll be gone about it straight.
SOLANIO   And so will I.
LORENZO   Meet me and Gratiano
   At Gratiano's lodging some hour hence.
SALERIO   'Tis good we do so.   30

                                    Exit [*with* SOLANIO].

GRATIANO   Was not that letter from fair Jessica?
LORENZO   I must needs tell thee all: she hath directed
   How I shall take her from her father's house,
   What gold and jewels she is furnished with,
   What page's suit she hath in readiness.   35
   If e'er the Jew her father come to heaven,
   It will be for his gentle daughter's sake;
   And never dare misfortune cross her foot
   Unless she do it under this excuse:
   That she is issue to a faithless Jew.   40
   Come—go with me, peruse this as thou goest.
   Fair Jessica shall be my torch-bearer.

                                    Exit [*with* GRATIANO].

11. **break up**: unseal.
13. **hand**: handwriting.

Act 2 Scene 5

[*Venice*] *Enter* [SHYLOCK *the*] *Jew and his man*
[LAUNCELOT] *that was the clown.*

JEW   Well, thou shalt see—thy eyes shall be thy judge—
The difference of old Shylock and Bassanio.
[*Calling.*] What, Jessica? Thou shalt not gourmandize
As thou hast done with me. [*Calling.*] What Jessica?
And sleep, and snore, and rend apparel out.   5
[*Calling.*] Why, Jessica, I say!
LAUNCELOT   Why, Jessica!
SHYLOCK   Who bids thee call? I do not bid thee call.
LAUNCELOT   Your worship was wont to tell me I could do noth-
ing without bidding.   10

        Enter JESSICA.

JESSICA   Call you? What is your will?
SHYLOCK   I am bid forth to supper, Jessica.
There are my keys; but wherefore should I go?
I am not bid for love—they flatter me—
But yet I'll go in hate to feed upon   15
The prodigal Christian. Jessica, my girl,
Look to my house. I am right loath to go;
There is some ill a-brewing towards my rest
For I did dream of money bags tonight.
LAUNCELOT   I beseech you, sir, go. My young master doth ex-   20
pect your reproach.
SHYLOCK   So do I his.
LAUNCELOT   And they have conspired together. I will not say
you shall see a masque, but if you do, then it was not for
nothing that my nose fell a-bleeding on Black Monday last,   25
at six o-clock i'th' morning, falling out that year on Ash
Wednesday was four year in th'afternoon.
SHYLOCK   What, are there masques? Hear you me, Jessica:
Lock up my doors and when you hear the drum
And the vile squealing of the wry-necked fife,   30
Clamber not you up to the casements then,
Nor thrust your head into the public street
To gaze on Christian fools with varnished faces;

---

21. **reproach:** blunder for "approach."
25. **Black Monday last:** Easter Monday of last year.
26–27. **Ash Wednesday was four year:** Ash Wednesday four years ago (Launcelot's calen-
dar is markedly confused).
30. **wry-necked fife:** fife played with the head twisted sideways.
33. **varnished:** painted or masked.

But stop my house's ears—I mean my casements.
Let not the sound of shallow foppery enter   35
My sober house. By Jacob's staff I swear
I have no mind of feasting forth tonight;
But I will go. Go you before me, sirrah.
Say I will come.

LAUNCELOT   I will go before, sir.   40
Mistress, look out at window for all this—
There will come a Christian by
Will be worth a Jewess' eye.   [*Exit.*]

SHYLOCK   What says that fool of Hagar's offspring? Ha?

JESSICA   His words were "Farewell mistress," nothing else.   45

SHYLOCK   The patch is kind enough, but a huge feeder,
Snail-slow in profit, and he sleeps by day
More than the wildcat. Drones hive not with me;
Therefore I part with him, and part with him
To one that I would have him help to waste   50
His borrowed purse. Well, Jessica, go in.
Perhaps I will return immediately.
Do as I bid you: shut doors after you.
Fast bind, fast find:
A proverb never stale in thrifty mind.   *Exit.*   55

JESSICA   Farewell, and if my fortune be not crossed,
I have a father, you a daughter, lost.   *Exit.*

Act 2 Scene 6

Enter the masquers, GRATIANO *and* SALERIO.

GRATIANO   This is the penthouse under which Lorenzo
Desired us to make stand.

SALERIO   His hour is almost past.

GRATIANO   And it is marvel he outdwells his hour,
For lovers ever run before the clock.   5

SALERIO   O ten times faster Venus' pigeons fly
To seal love's bonds new made than they are wont
To keep obliged faith unforfeited.

GRATIANO   That ever holds: who riseth from a feast
With that keen appetite that he sits down?   10
Where is the horse that doth untread again

---

44. fool of Hagar's offspring: The biblical Hagar was a gentile slave who bore Abraham a son, Ishmael; both were sent into exile after Abraham's legitimate son Isaac was born (Genesis 21. 9–14).
46. patch: fool.
1. penthouse: overhanging upper story.
8. To keep . . . unforfeited: to keep promised faithfulness unbroken.
11. untread: retrace.

His tedious measures with the unbated fire
That he did pace them first? All things that are
Are with more spirit chased than enjoyed.
How like a younker or a prodigal   15
The scarfed bark puts from her native bay,
Hugged and embraced by the strumpet wind;
How like the prodigal doth she return
With over-weathered ribs and ragged sails,
Lean, rent, and beggared by the strumpet wind!   20

    Enter LORENZO.

SALERIO   Here comes Lorenzo; more of this hereafter.
LORENZO   Sweet friends, your patience for my long abode;
  Not I but my affairs have made you wait.
  When you shall please to play the thieves for wives,
  I'll watch as long for you then. Approach—   25
  Here dwells my father Jew. How? Who's within?

    [Enter] JESSICA *above [dressed like a boy.]*

JESSICA   Who are you? Tell me for more certainty,
  Albeit I'll swear that I do know your tongue.
LORENZO   Lorenzo, and thy love.
JESSICA   Lorenzo, certain, and my love indeed;   30
  For who love I so much? And now who knows
  But you, Lorenzo, whether I am yours?
LORENZO   Heaven and thy thoughts are witness that thou art.
JESSICA   Here—catch this casket. It is worth the pains.
  I am glad 'tis night—you do not look on me—   35
  For I am much ashamed of my exchange.
  But love is blind, and lovers cannot see
  The pretty follies that themselves commit.
  For if they could, Cupid himself would blush
  To see me thus transformed to a boy.   40
LORENZO   Descend, for you must be my torchbearer.
JESSICA   What? Must I hold a candle to my shames?
  They in themselves, good sooth, are too, too light.
  Why, 'tis an office of discovery, love,
  And I should be obscured.   45
LORENZO   So are you, sweet,
  Even in the lovely garnish of a boy.

15. **younker:** youth.
16. **scarfed bark:** ship decked with streamers.
19. **over-weathered ribs:** weather-beaten hull.
36. **exchange:** change of dress.
44. **office of discovery:** means to make something visible.
47. **garnish:** dress.

But come at once,
For the close night doth play the runaway,
And we are stayed for at Bassanio's feast.   50
JESSICA   I will make fast the doors, and gild myself
  With some moe ducats, and be with you straight.
                                        [*Exit above.*]
GRATIANO   Now by my hood, a gentle and no Jew.
LORENZO   Beshrow me but I love her heartily;
  For she is wise, if I can judge of her;   55
  And fair she is, if that mine eyes be true;
  And true she is, as she hath proved herself.
  And therefore like herself—wise, fair, and true—
  Shall she be placed in my constant soul.

        Enter JESSICA [*below*].

What, art thou come? On, gentleman, away.   60
Our masquing mates by this time for us stay.

        Exit [LORENZO *with* JESSICA *and* SALERIO].

        Enter ANTONIO.

ANTONIO   Who's there?
GRATIANO   Signior Antonio?
ANTONIO   Fie, fie, Gratiano—where are all the rest?
  'Tis nine o'clock; our friends all stay for you.   65
  No masque tonight; the wind is come about.
  Bassanio presently will go aboard.
  I have sent twenty out to seek for you.
GRATIANO   I am glad on't. I desire no more delight
  Than to be under sail and gone tonight.   *Exeunt.*   70

Act 2 Scene 7

[BELMONT] *Enter* PORTIA *with* [*the Prince of*] MOROCCO
and both their trains.

PORTIA   Go, draw aside the curtains and discover
  The several caskets to this noble prince.
  Now make your choice.
MOROCCO   This first of gold, who this inscription bears:
  "Who chooseth me shall gain what many men desire."   5
  The second silver, which this promise carries:

49. **the close night . . . runaway:** the secret night is slipping away fast.
53. **gentle:** with pun on "gentile."
54. **Beshrow me but:** evil befall me unless.

"Who chooseth me shall get as much as he deserves."
This third, dull lead, with warning all as blunt:
"Who chooseth me must give and hazard all he hath."
How shall I know if I do choose the right?   10
PORTIA   The one of them contains my picture, prince;
    If you choose that, then I am yours withal.
MOROCCO   Some God direct my judgment. Let me see.
    I will survey th'inscriptions back again.
    What says this leaden casket?   15
    "Who chooseth me must give and hazard all he hath."
    Must give for what? For lead—hazard for lead?
    This casket threatens; men that hazard all
    Do it in hope of fair advantages.
    A golden mind stoops not to shows of dross;   20
    I'll then nor give nor hazard aught for lead.
    What says the silver with her virgin hue?
    "Who chooseth me shall get as much as he deserves."
    As much as he deserves—pause there, Morocco,
    And weigh thy value with an even hand.   25
    If thou be'st rated by thy estimation
    Thou dost deserve enough, and yet enough
    May not extend so far as to the lady.
    And yet to be afeared of my deserving
    Were but a weak disabling of myself.   30
    As much as I deserve: why that's the lady!
    I do in birth deserve her and in fortunes,
    In graces, and in qualities of breeding;
    But more than these, in love I do deserve.
    What if I strayed no farther but chose here?   35
    Let's see once more this saying graved in gold:
    "Who chooseth me shall gain what many men desire."
    Why that's the lady! All the world desires her;
    From the four corners of the earth they come
    To kiss this shrine, this mortal breathing saint.   40
    The Hyrcanian deserts and the vasty wilds
    Of wide Arabia are as thoroughfares now
    For princes to come view fair Portia.
    The watery kingdom, whose ambitious head
    Spits in the face of heaven, is no bar   45
    To stop the foreign spirits, but they come

12. **withal:** with it.
29. **afeared:** doubtful.
36. **graved:** engraved.
41. **Hyrcanian deserts:** thinly populated area southwest of the Caspian Sea (in modern-day Iran).
41. **vasty:** immense, vast.

As o'er a brook to see fair Portia.
One of these three contains her heavenly picture.
Is't like that lead contains her? 'Twere damnation
To think so base a thought. It were too gross   50
To rib her cerecloth in the obscure grave.
Or shall I think in silver she's immured,
Being ten times undervalued to tried gold?
O sinful thought! Never so rich a gem
Was set in worse than gold. They have in England   55
A coin that bears the figure of an angel
Stamped in gold, but that's insculpt upon.
But here an angel in a golden bed
Lies all within. Deliver me the key!
Here do I choose, and thrive I as I may.   60
PORTIA   There—take it, prince, and if my form lie there
Then I am yours.

   [*He opens the golden casket.*]

MOROCCO   O hell! What have we here?
A carrion death within whose empty eye
There is a written scroll. I'll read the writing: 65

   All that glisters is not gold.
   Often have you heard that told.
   Many a man his life hath sold
   But my outside to behold.
   Gilded timber do worms enfold: 70
   Had you been as wise as bold,
   Young in limbs, in judgment old,
   Your answer had not been inscrolled.
   Fare you well; your suit is cold.

Cold indeed and labor lost.   75
Then farewell heat, and welcome frost.
Portia adieu; I have too grieved a heart
To take a tedious leave. Thus losers part.   *Exit.*
PORTIA   A gentle riddance! Draw the curtains; go.
Let all of his complexion choose me so.   *Exeunt.*   80

---

49. **like:** likely.
51. **rib her cerecloth:** enclose her shroud (since coffins were lined in lead).
53. **tried:** tested.
57. **insculpt upon:** engraved on its surface.
64. **carrion death:** decayed skull.

Act 2 Scene 8

[*Venice*] *Enter* SALERIO *and* SOLANIO.

SALERIO   Why, man, I saw Bassanio under sail.
  With him is Gratiano gone along,
  And in their ship I am sure Lorenzo is not.
SOLANIO   The villain Jew with outcries raised the duke,
  Who went with him to search Bassanio's ship.   5
SALERIO   He came too late; the ship was under sail.
  But there the duke was given to understand
  That in a gondola were seen together
  Lorenzo and his amorous Jessica.
  Besides, Antonio certified the duke   10
  They were not with Bassanio in his ship.
SOLANIO   I never heard a passion so confused,
  So strange, outrageous, and so variable
  As the dog Jew did utter in the streets:
  "My daughter, O my ducats, O my daughter!   15
  Fled with a Christian, O my Christian ducats!
  Justice, the law, my ducats, and my daughter!
  A sealed bag—two sealed bags of ducats,
  Of double ducats, stolen from me by my daughter;
  And jewels—two stones, two rich and precious stones   20
  Stolen by my daughter! Justice! Find the girl.
  She hath the stones upon her, and the ducats."
SALERIO   Why all the boys in Venice follow him
  Crying his stones, his daughter, and his ducats.
SOLANIO   Let good Antonio look he keep his day   25
  Or he shall pay for this.
SALERIO   Marry, well rememb'red.
  I reasoned with a Frenchman yesterday
  Who told me in the narrow seas that part
  The French and English there miscarried   30
  A vessel of our country richly fraught.
  I thought upon Antonio when he told me,
  And wished in silence that it were not his.
SOLANIO   You were best to tell Antonio what you hear.
  Yet do not suddenly, for it may grieve him.   35
SALERIO   A kinder gentleman treads not the earth.
  I saw Bassanio and Antonio part.

25. **his day:** the day on which he agreed to pay his debt.
28. **reasoned:** talked.
30. **miscarried:** was lost.
31. **richly fraught:** loaded with expensive wares.

Bassanio told him he would make some speed
Of his return; he answered, "Do not so;
Slubber not business for my sake, Bassanio;   40
But stay the very riping of the time.
And for the Jew's bond which he hath of me,
Let it not enter in your mind of love.
Be merry and employ your chiefest thoughts
To courtship and such fair ostents of love   45
As shall conveniently become you there."
And even there, his eye being big with tears,
Turning his face, he put his hand behind him
And with affection wondrous sensible
He wrung Bassanio's hand; and so they parted.   50
SOLANIO   I think he only loves the world for him.
I pray thee, let us go and find him out
And quicken his embraced heaviness
With some delight or other.
SALERIO   Do we so.   *Exeunt.*   55

Act 2 Scene 9

[*Belmont*] *Enter* NERISSA *and a servitor.*

NERISSA   Quick, quick, I pray thee, draw the curtain straight;
The Prince of Aragon hath ta'en his oath
And comes to his election presently.

Enter [*the Prince of*] ARAGON, *his train, and* PORTIA.

PORTIA   Behold, there stand the caskets, noble prince.
If you choose that wherein I am contained   5
Straight shall our nuptial rites be solemnized;
But if you fail, without more speech, my lord,
You must be gone from hence immediately.
ARAGON   I am enjoined by oath to observe three things:
First, never to unfold to anyone   10
Which casket 'twas I chose; next, if I fail
Of the right casket, never in my life
To woo a maid in way of marriage; lastly,
If I do fail in fortune of my choice,
Immediately to leave you and be gone.   15

40. **slubber:** perform carelessly.
41. **stay the . . . of the time:** wait until the time is right.
45. **ostents:** shows.
53. **quicken . . . heaviness:** lighten up the sadness he has embraced.
1. **straight:** immediately.

PORTIA   To these injunctions everyone doth swear
That comes to hazard for my worthless self.
ARAGON   And so have I addressed me. Fortune now
To my heart's hope! Gold, silver, and base lead.
"Who chooseth me must give and hazard all he hath."   20
You shall look fairer ere I give or hazard.
What says the golden chest? Ha, let me see:
"Who chooseth me shall gain what many men desire."
What many men desire—that "many" may be meant
By the fool multitude that choose by show,   25
Not learning more than the fond eye doth teach,
Which pries not to th'interior, but like the martlet
Builds in the weather on the outward wall,
Even in the force and road of casualty.
I will not choose what many men desire   30
Because I will not jump with common spirits,
And rank me with the barbarous multitudes.
Why then, to thee, thou silver treasure house.
Tell me once more what title thou dost bear:
"Who chooseth me shall get as much as he deserves."   35
And well said too, for who shall go about
To cozen fortune, and be honorable
Without the stamp of merit? Let none presume
To wear an undeserved dignity.
O that estates, degrees, and offices   40
Were not derived corruptly, and that clear honor
Were purchased by the merit of the wearer!
How many then should cover that stand bare;
How many be commanded that command;
How much low peasantry would then be gleaned   45
From the true seed of honor; and how much honor
Picked from the chaff and ruin of the times
To be new varnished? Well—but to my choice:
"Who chooseth me shall get as much as he deserves."
I will assume desert: give me a key for this,   50
And instantly unlock my fortunes here.

[*He opens the silver casket.*]

PORTIA   Too long a pause for that which you find there.
ARAGON   What's here—the portrait of a blinking idiot

27. **martlet:** purple martin.
29. **casualty:** mishaps.
37. **cozen:** trick.
43. **cover that stand bare:** wear hats who now stand bare (as a sign of respect to their "superiors").
48. **varnished:** refurbished.

Presenting me a schedule? I will read it.
How much unlike art thou to Portia!   55
How much unlike my hopes and my deservings!
"Who chooseth me shall have as much as he deserves"?
Did I deserve no more than a fool's head?
Is that my prize; are my deserts no better?
PORTIA   To offend and judge are distinct offices,   60
    And of opposed natures.
ARAGON   What is here?

    The fire seven times tried this;
    Seven times tried that judgment is
    That did never choose amiss.
    Some there be that shadows kiss;   65
    Such have but a shadow's bliss.
    There be fools alive, iwis,
    Silvered o'er, and so was this.
    Take what wife you will to bed,   70
    I will ever be your head.
    So be gone; you are sped.

Still more fool I shall appear
By the time I linger here.
With one fool's head I came to woo,   75
But I go away with two.
Sweet, adieu; I'll keep my oath
Patiently to bear my wroth.

        [Exit the Prince of Aragon with his train.]

PORTIA   Thus hath the candle singed the moth.
    O these deliberate fools—when they do choose   80
    They have the wisdom by their wit to lose!
NERISSA   The ancient saying is no heresy:
    Hanging and wiving goes by destiny.
PORTIA   Come draw the curtain, Nerissa.

    Enter MESSENGER.

MESSENGER   Where is my lady?
                                                                   85
PORTIA   Here—what would my lord?
MESSENGER   Madam, there is alighted at your gate
    A young Venetian, one that comes before
    To signify th'approaching of his lord,
    From whom he bringeth sensible regreets: 90

60. **To offend . . . distinct offices:** i.e., the offender can't be his own judge.
68. **iwis:** certainly.
72. **sped:** finished off.
78. **wroth:** resentment.
90. **sensible regreets:** tangible greetings.

To wit, besides commends and courteous breath,
Gifts of rich value. Yet I have not seen
So likely an ambassador of love.
A day in April never came so sweet
To show how costly summer was at hand,   95
As this fore-spurrer comes before his lord.
PORTIA   No more, I pray thee. I am half afeared
Thou wilt say anon he is some kin to thee,
Thou spend'st such high-day wit in praising him.
Come, come, Nerissa, for I long to see   100
Quick Cupid's post that comes so mannerly.
NERISSA   Bassanio, Lord Love, if thy will it be.   *Exeunt.*

Act 3 Scene 1

[*Venice. Enter*] SOLANIO *and* SALERIO.

SOLANIO   Now, what news on the Rialto?
SALERIO   Why yet it lives there unchecked that Antonio hath a
ship of rich lading wracked on the narrow seas—the Goodwins I think they call the place, a very dangerous flat, and fa-
tal, where the carcasses of many a tall ship lie buried, as   5
they say, if my gossip Report be an honest woman of her
word.
SOLANIO   I would she were as lying a gossip in that as ever
knapped ginger or made her neighbors believe she wept for
the death of a third husband. But it is true, without any slips   10
of prolixity or crossing the plain highway of talk, that the
good Antonio, the honest Antonio—O that I had a title good
enough to keep his name company—
SALERIO   Come, the full stop.
SOLANIO   Ha, what sayest thou? Why the end is, he hath lost a   15
ship.
SALERIO   I would it might prove the end of his losses.
SOLANIO   Let me say amen betimes lest the devil cross my
prayer, for here he comes in the likeness of a Jew.

96. **fore-spurrer:** forerunner, messenger.
99. **high-day:** holiday (and therefore especially fine).
101. **post:** messenger.
102. **Lord Love:** Cupid.
3–4. **the Goodwins:** Goodwin Sands, off the coast of England.
6. **my gossip Report:** Dame Rumor.
9. **knapped:** nibbled.
10–11. **slips of prolixity:** slipping into wordiness.
11. **crossing the . . . of talk:** going beyond normal speech.
14. **full stop:** end of the sentence.
18. **betimes:** quickly (he imagines that the appearance of the "devil" Shylock will nullify
his prayers for Antonio).

Enter SHYLOCK.

How now, Shylock, what news among the merchants?   20

SHYLOCK   You knew, none so well, none so well as you, of my
daughter's flight.

SALERIO   That's certain. I, for my part, knew the tailor that
made the wings she flew withal.

SOLANIO   And Shylock, for his own part, knew the bird was fledge,   25
and then it is the complexion of them all to leave the dam.

SHYLOCK   She is damned for it.

SALERIO   That's certain, if the devil may be her judge.

SHYLOCK   My own flesh and blood to rebel!

SOLANIO   Out upon it, old carrion! Rebels it at these years?   30

SHYLOCK   I say my daughter is my flesh and my blood.

SALERIO   There is more difference between thy flesh and hers
than between jet and ivory; more between your bloods than
there is between red wine and Rhenish. But tell us: do you
hear whether Antonio have had any loss at sea, or no?   35

SHYLOCK   There I have another bad match: a bankrout, a
prodigal who dare scarce show his head on the Rialto, a beg-
gar that was used to come so smug upon the mart! Let him
look to his bond. He was wont to call me usurer; let him look
to his bond. He was wont to lend money for a Christian curt-   40
sey; let him look to his bond.

SALERIO   Why I am sure if he forfeit thou wilt not take his
flesh. What's that good for?

SHYLOCK   To bait fish withal. If it will feed nothing else, it will
feed my revenge. He hath disgraced me and hind'red me half   45
a million, laughed at my losses, mocked at my gains, scorned
my nation, thwarted my bargains, cooled my friends, heated
mine enemies, and what's his reason? I am a Jew. Hath not a
Jew eyes? Hath not a Jew hands, organs, dimensions, senses,
affections, passions—fed with the same food, hurt with the   50
same weapons, subject to the same diseases, healed by the
same means, warmed and cooled by the same winter and
summer as a Christian is? If you prick us do we not bleed? If
you tickle us do we not laugh? If you poison us do we not
die, and if you wrong us shall we not revenge? If we are like   55
you in the rest, we will resemble you in that. If a Jew wrong
a Christian, what is his humility? Revenge! If a Christian
wrong a Jew, what should his sufferance be by Christian ex-

25. **fledge:** fledgling, ready for flight.
26. **dam:** mother (here, in reference to Shylock).
30. **Rebels . . . these years:** Solanio pretends to misunderstand Shylock as referring to his
own sexual appetites.
36. **bankrout:** bankrupt.
58. **sufferance:** forbearance.

ample? Why revenge! The villainy you teach me I will execute, and it shall go hard but I will better the instruction.   60

    Enter a man from ANTONIO.

MAN   Gentlemen, my master Antonio is at his house and desires to speak with you both.
SALERIO   We have been up and down to seek him.

    Enter TUBAL.

SOLANIO   Here comes another of the tribe; a third cannot be
matched unless the devil himself turn Jew.   65

    Exeunt Gentlemen [SALERIO, SOLANIO, *and man*].

SHYLOCK   How now, Tubal! What news from Genoa? Hast
thou found my daughter?
TUBAL   I often came where I did hear of her, but cannot find
her.
SHYLOCK   Why there, there, there, there—a diamond gone   70
cost me two thousand ducats in Frankfort! The curse never
fell upon our nation till now. I never felt it till now: two
thousand ducats in that and other precious, precious jewels!
I would my daughter were dead at my foot and the jewels in
her ear! Would she were hearsed at my foot and the ducats   75
in her coffin! No news of them? Why so? And I know not
what's spent in the search. Why thou loss upon loss, the
thief gone with so much, and so much to find the thief, and
no satisfaction, no revenge, nor no ill luck stirring but what
lights a' my shoulders, no sighs but a' my breathing, no tears   80
but a' my shedding.
TUBAL   Yes, other men have ill luck too. Antonio, as I heard in
Genoa—
SHYLOCK   What, what, what? Ill luck, ill luck?
TUBAL   —hath an argosy cast away coming from Tripolis.   85
SHYLOCK   I thank God! I thank God! Is it true, is it true?
TUBAL   I spoke with some of the sailors that escaped the
wrack.
SHYLOCK   I thank thee, good Tubal. Good news, good news.
Ha, ha, heard in Genoa!   90
TUBAL   Your daughter spent in Genoa, as I heard, one night
fourscore ducats.
SHYLOCK   Thou stick'st a dagger in me; I shall never see

60. but I will: if I do not.
71. The curse: the curse Jews suffered (according to Christian belief) because they
had killed Christ.
75. hearsed: in a hearse.
80. a': of or on (colloquialism).

my gold again: fourscore ducats at a sitting, fourscore
ducats!   95

TUBAL   There came divers of Antonio's creditors in my company to Venice that swear he cannot choose but break.

SHYLOCK   I am very glad of it. I'll plague him; I'll torture him.
I am glad of it.

TUBAL   One of them showed me a ring that he had of your   100
daughter for a monkey.

SHYLOCK   Out upon her; thou torturest me, Tubal! It was my
turquoise; I had it of Leah when I was a bachelor. I would
not have given it for a wilderness of monkeys.

TUBAL   But Antonio is certainly undone.   105

SHYLOCK   Nay, that's true, that's very true. Go, Tubal, fee me
an officer; bespeak him a fortnight before. I will have the
heart of him if he forfeit, for were he out of Venice I can
make what merchandise I will. Go, Tubal, and meet me at
our synagogue. Go, good Tubal; at our synagogue, Tubal.   110

Exeunt.

Act 3 Scene 2

[*Belmont*] *Enter* BASSANIO, PORTIA, [NERISSA,] GRATIANO,
and all their trains.

PORTIA   I pray you, tarry, pause a day or two
Before you hazard, for in choosing wrong
I lose your company. Therefore forbear awhile.
There's something tells me (but it is not love)
I would not lose you; and you know yourself   5
Hate counsels not in such a quality.
But lest you should not understand me well—
And yet a maiden hath no tongue but thought—
I would detain you here some month or two
Before you venture for me. I could teach you   10
How to choose right, but then I am forsworn;
So will I never be. So may you miss me,
But if you do, you'll make me wish a sin—
That I had been forsworn. Beshrew your eyes!
They have o'erlooked me and divided me.   15
One half of me is yours, the other half yours—
Mine own I would say—but if mine then yours,

106–07. **fee me . . . bespeak him:** hire an officer's services (so Antonio can be arrested).
109. **make what . . . I will:** make whatever bargains I wish.
6. **quality:** manner.
14. **Beshrew:** may evil befall.

And so all yours. O these naughty times
Puts bars between the owners and their rights.
And so, though yours, not yours. Prove it so,   20
Let fortune go to hell for it, not I.
I speak too long, but 'tis to peise the time,
To eke it and to draw it out in length
To stay you from election.
BASSANIO   Let me choose.   25
For as I am I live upon the rack.
PORTIA   Upon the rack, Bassanio? Then confess
What treason there is mingled with your love.
BASSANIO   None but that ugly treason of mistrust,
Which makes me fear th'enjoying of my love.   30
There may as well be amity and life
'Tween snow and fire, as treason and my love.
PORTIA   Aye, but I fear you speak upon the rack
Where men enforced do speak anything.
BASSANIO   Promise me life, and I'll confess the truth.   35
PORTIA   Well then, confess and live.
BASSANIO   Confess and love
Had been the very sum of my confession.
O happy torment when my torturer
Doth teach me answers for deliverance!   40
But let me to my fortune and the caskets.
PORTIA   Away, then. I am locked in one of them;
If you do love me, you will find me out.
Nerissa and the rest, stand all aloof.
Let music sound while he doth make his choice.   45
Then if he lose, he makes a swanlike end,
Fading in music. That the comparison
May stand more proper, my eye shall be the stream
And watery death bed for him. He may win,
And what is music then? Then music is   50
Even as the flourish when true subjects bow
To a new-crowned monarch. Such it is
As are those dulcet sounds in break of day
That creep into the dreaming bridegroom's ear
And summon him to marriage. Now he goes,   55

20. **Prove it so:** if it prove so.
22. **peise:** suspend.
23. **eke:** increase.
26. **the rack:** instrument of torture used to extract confessions of treason against the state.
46–47. **swanlike . . . in music:** Swans were said to sing just before they died.
51. **flourish:** fanfare.
53–55. **Those dulcet sounds . . . to marriage:** By custom, music was played under the respective windows of the bride and groom on the morning of their wedding.

With no less presence but with much more love,
Than young Alcides when he did redeem
The virgin tribute paid by howling Troy
To the sea monster. I stand for sacrifice;
The rest aloof are the Dardanian wives   60
With bleared visages come forth to view
The issue of th'exploit. Go Hercules!
Live thou, I live! With much, much more dismay
I view the fight than thou that mak'st the fray.

> A *song, the whilst* BASSANIO *comments on the caskets to himself.*

Tell me where is fancy bred: 65
Or in the heart or in the head;
How begot, how nourished?
     Reply, reply!
It is engend'red in the eye,
With gazing fed; and fancy dies   70
In the cradle where it lies.
Let us all ring fancy's knell.
I'll begin it: Ding dong, bell.
ALL   *Ding, dong, bell.*

BASSANIO   So may the outward shows be least themselves.   75
The world is still deceived with ornament.
In law, what plea so tainted and corrupt
But being seasoned with a gracious voice,
Obscures the show of evil? In religion,
What damned error but some sober brow   80
Will bless it and approve it with a text,
Hiding the grossness with fair ornament?
There is no voice so simple but assumes
Some mark of virtue on his outward parts.
How many cowards whose hearts are all as false   85
As stairs of sand, wear yet upon their chins
The beards of Hercules and frowning Mars,
Who, inward searched, have livers white as milk;
And these assume but valor's excrement
To render them redoubted. Look on beauty,   90
And you shall see 'tis purchased by the weight,

57–59. Alcides . . . sea monster: Alcides (Hercules) rescued the daughter of the Trojan king from sacrifice to a sea monster.
60. Dardanian: Trojan.
61. bleared: swollen from weeping.
87. Hercules . . . Mars: gods particularly associated with valor.
88. livers white as milk: white (bloodless) livers were considered signs of cowardice.
89. excrement: outward sign.

Which therein works a miracle in nature,
Making them lightest that wear most of it.
So are those crisped, snaky golden locks,
Which maketh such wanton gambols with the wind   95
Upon supposed fairness, often known
To be the dowry of a second head—
The skull that bred them in the sepulcher.
Thus ornament is but the guiled shore
To a most dangerous sea, the beauteous scarf   100
Veiling an Indian beauty—in a word,
The seeming truth which cunning times put on
To entrap the wisest. Therefore, then, thou gaudy gold,
Hard food for Midas, I will none of thee.
Nor none of thee, thou pale and common drudge   105
'Tween man and man. But thou! Thou meager lead
Which rather threaten'st than dost promise aught,
Thy paleness moves me more than eloquence,
And here choose I—joy be the consequence!

PORTIA   How all the other passions fleet to air—   110
As doubtful thoughts and rash-embraced despair
And shudd'ring fear and green-eyed jealousy!
O love, be moderate, allay thy ecstasy,
In measure rein thy joy, scant this excess.
I feel too much thy blessing; make it less   115
For fear I surfeit!

[BASSANIO *opens the leaden casket.*]

BASSANIO   What find I here?
Fair Portia's counterfeit! What demigod
Hath come so near creation? Move these eyes,
Or whether riding on the balls of mine,   120
Seem they in motion? Here are severed lips
Parted with sugar breath; so sweet a bar
Should sunder such sweet friends. Here in her hairs
The painter plays the spider and hath woven
A golden mesh t'entrap the hearts of men   125
Faster than gnats in cobwebs. But her eyes—
How could he see to do them? Having made one,

94. **crisped:** curled.
98. **skull . . . sepulcher:** Golden locks are often a wig that came from the skull of a dead person.
99. **guiled:** beguiling.
104. **Midas:** King Midas could not eat because his touch turned everything to gold.
105–06. **thou pale . . . and man:** silver, "common" because used for coins.
120. **Or . . . balls of mine:** or, only moving along with my eyeballs.
121. **severed:** separated.
123. **sunder . . . friends:** i.e., separate her two lips.

Methinks it should have power to steal both his
And leave itself unfurnished. Yet look—how far
The substance of my praise doth wrong this shadow   130
In underprizing it, so far this shadow
Doth limp behind the substance. Here's the scroll,
The continent and summary of my fortune:

> You that choose not by the view
> Chance as fair and choose as true.   135
> Since this fortune falls to you,
> Be content and seek no new.
> If you be well pleased with this,
> And hold your fortune for your bliss,
> Turn you where your lady is   140
> And claim her with a loving kiss.

A gentle scroll! Fair lady, by your leave—

[*Kisses her.*]

I come by note to give and to receive.
Like one of two contending in a prize
That thinks he hath done well in people's eyes—   145
Hearing applause and universal shout,
Giddy in spirit, still gazing in a doubt
Whether those peals of praise be his or no—
So, thrice-fair lady, stand I even so,
As doubtful whether what I see be true   150
Until confirmed, signed, ratified by you.
PORTIA   You see me, Lord Bassanio, where I stand,
Such as I am. Though for myself alone
I would not be ambitious in my wish
To wish myself much better, yet for you   155
I would be trebled twenty times myself—
A thousand times more fair, ten thousand times
More rich; that only to stand high in your account
I might in virtues, beauties, livings, friends
Exceed account. But the full sum of me   160
Is sum of something, which to term in gross
Is an unlessoned girl, unschooled, unpracticed;
Happy in this, she is not yet so old
But she may learn; happier than this,
She is not bred so dull but she can learn;   165
Happiest of all, is that her gentle spirit
Commits itself to yours to be directed

---

129. **unfurnished:** without its other eye.
161. **term in gross:** state in full.

As from her lord, her governor, her king.
Myself and what is mine to you and yours
Is now converted. But now, I was the lord   170
Of this fair mansion, master of my servants,
Queen o'er myself; and even now, but now,
This house, these servants, and this same myself
Are yours, my lord's. I give them with this ring,
Which when you part from, lose, or give away,   175
Let it presage the ruin of your love
And be my vantage to exclaim on you.
BASSANIO   Madam, you have bereft me of all words.
Only my blood speaks to you in my veins;
And there is such confusion in my powers   180
As after some oration fairly spoke
By a beloved prince, there doth appear
Among the buzzing, pleased multitude—
Where every something, being blent together,
Turns to a wild of nothing save of joy   185
Expressed and not expressed. But when this ring
Parts from this finger, then parts life from hence.
O then be bold to say Bassanio's dead.
NERISSA   My lord and lady, it is now our time
That have stood by and seen our wishes prosper   190
To cry good joy, good joy, my lord and lady!
GRATIANO   My Lord Bassanio and my gentle lady,
I wish you all the joy that you can wish,
For I am sure you can wish none from me.
And when your honors mean to solemnize   195
The bargain of your faith, I do beseech you
Even at that time I may be married too.
BASSANIO   With all my heart, so thou canst get a wife.
GRATIANO   I thank your lordship, you have got me one.
My eyes, my lord, can look as swift as yours.   200
You saw the mistress; I beheld the maid.
You loved, I loved; for intermission
No more pertains to me, my lord, than you.
Your fortune stood upon the caskets there,
And so did mine too as the matter falls.   205
For wooing here until I sweat again,
And swearing till my very roof was dry
With oaths of love, at last, if promise last,

169–70. **what is mine . . . converted:** By English law (but not Venetian), the wife's
goods became the possession of the husband.
177. **vantage . . . you:** opportunity to reproach you.
202. **intermission:** inactivity.
207. **roof:** roof of the mouth.

I got a promise of this fair one here
To have her love, provided that your fortune   210
Achieved her mistress.
PORTIA   Is this true, Nerissa?
NERISSA   Madam it is, so you stand pleased withal.
BASSANIO   And do you, Gratiano, mean good faith?
GRATIANO   Yes, faith, my lord.   215
BASSANIO   Our feast shall be much honored in your marriage.
GRATIANO   We'll play with them the first boy for a thousand
   ducats.
NERISSA   What, and stake down?
GRATIANO   No, we shall ne'er win at that sport and stake   220
   down!
   But who comes here? Lorenzo and his infidel?
   What, and my old Venetian friend Salerio?

   Enter LORENZO, JESSICA, *and* SALERIO [*as*] *a messenger
   from Venice.*

BASSANIO   Lorenzo and Salerio, welcome hither
   If that the youth of my new interest here   225
   Have power to bid you welcome. By your leave,
   I bid my very friends and countrymen,
   Sweet Portia, welcome.
PORTIA   So do I, my lord; they are entirely welcome.
LORENZO   I thank your honor. For my part, my lord,   230
   My purpose was not to have seen you here,
   But meeting with Salerio by the way
   He did entreat me past all saying nay
   To come with him along.
SALERIO   I did, my lord,   235
   And I have reason for it. Signior Antonio
   Commends him to you.

   [*Gives* BASSANIO *a letter.*]

BASSANIO   Ere I ope his letter
   I pray you tell me how my good friend doth.
SALERIO   Not sick, my lord, unless it be in mind;   240
   Nor well, unless in mind: his letter there
   Will show you his estate.

   [BASSANIO *opens*] *the letter.*

---

217. **play:** wager.
219. **stake down:** money for the bet put down now.
220. **and stake down:** with stake down (i.e., without an erection).

GRATIANO   Nerissa, cheer yond stranger; bid her welcome.
    Your hand, Salerio; what's the news from Venice?
    How doth that royal merchant, good Antonio?   245
    I know he will be glad of our success.
    We are the Jasons; we have won the fleece.
SALERIO   I would you had won the fleece that he hath lost.
PORTIA   There are some shrewd contents in yond same paper
    That steals the color from Bassanio's cheek—   250
    Some dear friend dead, else nothing in the world
    Could turn so much the constitution
    Of any constant man. What, worse and worse?
    With leave, Bassanio—I am half yourself,
    And I must freely have the half of anything   255
    That this same paper brings you.
BASSANIO   O sweet Portia,
    Here are a few of the unpleasant'st words
    That ever blotted paper. Gentle lady,
    When I did first impart my love to you,   260
    I freely told you all the wealth I had
    Ran in my veins—I was a gentleman—
    And then I told you true. And yet, dear lady,
    Rating myself at nothing, you shall see
    How much I was a braggart. When I told you   265
    My state was nothing I should then have told you
    That I was worse than nothing; for indeed
    I have engaged myself to a dear friend,
    Engaged my friend to his mere enemy
    To feed my means. Here is a letter, lady,   270
    The paper as the body of my friend,
    And every word in it a gaping wound
    Issuing lifeblood. But is it true, Salerio?
    Hath all his ventures failed? What, not one hit,
    From Tripolis, from Mexico and England,   275
    From Lisbon, Barbary, and India,
    And not one vessel scape the dreadful touch
    Of merchant-marring rocks?
SALERIO   Not one, my lord.
    Besides, it should appear that if he had   280
    The present money to discharge the Jew,
    He would not take it. Never did I know
    A creature that did bear the shape of man
    So keen and greedy to confound a man.

247. fleece: the mythological Golden Fleece (see note to 1.1.173–75).
249. shrewd: evil.
252. turn: change.

He plies the duke at morning and at night,   285
And doth impeach the freedom of the state
If they deny him justice. Twenty merchants,
The duke himself, and the magnificos
Of greatest port have all persuaded with him,
But none can drive him from the envious plea   290
Of forfeiture, of justice, and his bond.
JESSICA   When I was with him I have heard him swear
To Tubal and to Chus, his countrymen,
That he would rather have Antonio's flesh
Than twenty times the value of the sum   295
That he did owe him; and I know, my lord,
If law, authority, and power deny not,
It will go hard with poor Antonio.
PORTIA   Is it your dear friend that is thus in trouble?
BASSANIO   The dearest friend to me, the kindest man,   300
The best conditioned and unwearied spirit
In doing courtesies; and one in whom
The ancient Roman honor more appears
Than any that draws breath in Italy.
PORTIA   What sum owes he the Jew?   305
BASSANIO   For me, three thousand ducats.
PORTIA   What, no more?
Pay him six thousand and deface the bond;
Double six thousand and then treble that,
Before a friend of this description   310
Shall lose a hair through Bassanio's fault.
First go with me to church and call me wife,
And then away to Venice to your friend.
For never shall you lie by Portia's side
With an unquiet soul. You shall have gold   315
To pay the petty debt twenty times over.
When it is paid, bring your true friend along.
My maid Nerissa and myself meantime
Will live as maids and widows. Come away,
For you shall hence upon your wedding day.   320
Bid your friends welcome; show a merry cheer;
Since you are dear bought, I will love you dear.
But let me hear the letter of your friend:
[BASSANIO *reads*.] Sweet Bassanio, my ships have all mis-
carried; my creditors grow cruel; my estate is very low; my   325
bond to the Jew is forfeit; and since in paying it, it is impos-
sible I should live, all debts are cleared between you and I if

---

286. impeach . . . state: accuse the state of hindering free trade.
288. magnificos: Venetian magnates.

I might but see you at my death. Notwithstanding, use your
pleasure; if your love do not persuade you to come, let not
my letter.   330
PORTIA   O love, dispatch all business and be gone!
BASSANIO   Since I have your good leave to go away,
   I will make haste; but till I come again
   No bed shall e'er be guilty of my stay,
   Nor rest be interposer 'twixt us twain.   *Exeunt.* 335

Act 3 Scene 3

[Venice] Enter the JEW *and* [SOLANIO] *and* ANTONIO *and
the Jailor.*

JEW   Jailor, look to him; tell not me of mercy.
   This is the fool that lent out money gratis.
   Jailor, look to him.
ANTONIO   Hear me yet, good Shylock—
JEW   I'll have my bond; speak not against my bond.   5
   I have sworn an oath that I will have my bond.
   Thou call'dst me dog before thou hadst a cause;
   But since I am a dog, beware my fangs.
   The duke shall grant me justice. I do wonder,
   Thou naughty jailor, that thou art so fond   10
   To come abroad with him at his request.
ANTONIO   I pray thee, hear me speak.
JEW   I'll have my bond; I will not hear thee speak.
   I'll have my bond, and therefore speak no more.
   I'll not be made a soft and dull-eyed fool,   15
   To shake the head, relent and sigh, and yield
   To Christian intercessors. Follow not.
   I'll have no speaking; I will have my bond.

                                               Exit JEW.

SOLANIO   It is the most impenetrable cur
   That ever kept with men.   20
ANTONIO   Let him alone.
   I'll follow him no more with bootless prayers.
   He seeks my life; his reason well I know:
   I oft delivered from his forfeitures
   Many that have at times made moan to me;   25

---

335. **be interposer . . . twain:** come between the two of us.
11. **come . . . him:** bring him out of jail.
22. **bootless:** useless.

Therefore he hates me.
SOLANIO   I am sure the duke
Will never grant this forfeiture to hold.
ANTONIO   The duke cannot deny the course of law,
For the commodity that strangers have   30
With us in Venice, if it be denied,
Will much impeach the justice of the state,
Since that the trade and profit of the city
Consisteth of all nations. Therefore go.
These griefs and losses have so bated me   35
That I shall hardly spare a pound of flesh
Tomorrow to my bloody creditor.
Well, jailor, on! Pray God Bassanio come
To see me pay his debt, and then I care not.   *Exeunt.*

Act 3 Scene 4

[Belmont] Enter PORTIA, NERISSA, LORENZO, JESSICA, *and*
[BALTHAZAR,] *a man of Portia's.*

LORENZO   Madam, although I speak it in your presence,
You have a noble and a true conceit
Of godlike amity, which appears most strongly
In bearing thus the absence of your lord.
But if you knew to whom you show this honor,   5
How true a gentleman you send relief,
How dear a lover of my lord your husband,
I know you would be prouder of the work
Than customary bounty can enforce you.
PORTIA   I never did repent for doing good,   10
Nor shall not now; for in companions
That do converse and waste the time together,
Whose souls do bear an equal yoke of love,
There must be needs a like proportion
Of lineaments, of manners, and of spirit;   15
Which makes me think that this Antonio,
Being the bosom lover of my lord,
Must needs be like my lord. If it be so,
How little is the cost I have bestowed
In purchasing the semblance of my soul   20
From out the state of hellish cruelty!

---

30. **commodity:** trading privileges.
35. **bated:** reduced.
20. **purchasing . . . soul:** redeeming Antonio, who is the likeness of my soul, Bassanio.

This comes too near the praising of myself;
Therefore no more of it. Hear other things:
Lorenzo, I commit into your hands
The husbandry and manage of my house   25
Until my lord's return. For mine own part
I have toward heaven breathed a secret vow
To live in prayer and contemplation,
Only attended by Nerissa here,
Until her husband and my lord's return.   30
There is a monastery two miles off,
And there we will abide. I do desire you
Not to deny this imposition,
The which my love and some necessity
Now lays upon you.   35
LORENZO   Madam, with all my heart
I shall obey you in all fair commands.
PORTIA   My people do already know my mind,
And will acknowledge you and Jessica
In place of Lord Bassanio and myself.   40
So fare you well till we shall meet again.
LORENZO   Fair thoughts and happy hours attend on you!
JESSICA   I wish your ladyship all heart's content.
PORTIA   I thank you for your wish, and am well pleased
To wish it back on you. Fare you well, Jessica!   45

                    Exeunt [LORENZO *and* JESSICA.]

Now, Balthazar,
As I have ever found thee honest true,
So let me find thee still: take this same letter
And use thou all th'endeavor of a man
In speed to Mantua; see thou render this   50
Into my cousin's hands, Doctor Belario,
And look what notes and garments he doth give thee.
Bring them, I pray thee, with imagined speed
Unto the tranect, to the common ferry
Which trades to Venice. Waste no time in words   55
But get thee gone; I shall be there before thee.
BALTHAZAR   Madam, I go with all convenient speed.   [*Exit*]
PORTIA   Come on, Nerissa—I have work in hand
That you yet know not of. We'll see our husbands
Before they think of us!   60
NERISSA   Shall they see us?
PORTIA   They shall, Nerissa, but in such a habit

---

54. tranect: ferry (from Italian *traghetto*).

That they shall think we are accomplished
With that we lack. I'll hold thee any wager
When we are both accoutered like young men,   65
I'll prove the prettier fellow of the two,
And wear my dagger with the braver grace,
And speak between the change of man and boy
With a reed voice, and turn two mincing steps
Into a manly stride, and speak of frays   70
Like a fine bragging youth, and tell quaint lies
How honorable ladies sought my love,
Which I denying, they fell sick and died—
I could not do withal! Then I'll repent
And wish, for all that, that I had not killed them;   75
And twenty of these puny lies I'll tell,
That men shall swear I have discontinued school
Above a twelve-month. I have within my mind
A thousand raw tricks of these bragging Jacks,
Which I will practice.   80
NERISSA   Why, shall we turn to men?
PORTIA   Fie, what a question's that,
If thou wert near a lewd interpreter!
But come, I'll tell thee all my whole device
When I am in my coach, which stays for us   85
At the park gate; and therefore haste away,
For we must measure twenty miles today.   *Exeunt.*

Act 3 Scene 5

Enter [LAUNCELOT *the*] *Clown and* JESSICA.

LAUNCELOT   Yes truly, for look you, the sins of the father are to
be laid upon the children; therefore I promise you, I fear you.
I was always plain with you and so now I speak my agitation
of the matter. Therefore be a' good cheer for truly I think you
are damned. There is but one hope in it that can do you any   5
good, and that is but a kind of bastard hope neither.
JESSICA   And what hope is that, I pray thee?
LAUNCELOT   Marry, you may partly hope that your father got
you not, that you are not the Jew's daughter.

63. **accomplished:** equipped.
65. **accoutered:** dressed.
69. **reed:** piping.
74. **I . . . withal:** I couldn't help it!
78. **Above a twelve-month:** at least a year.
81. **turn to men:** turn into men or (a bawdy second meaning) start sleeping with men.
3. **agitation:** blunder for "cogitation."
6. **neither:** too.

JESSICA   That were a kind of bastard hope indeed—so the sins   10
of my mother should be visited upon me!

LAUNCELOT   Truly then, I fear you are damned both by father
and mother; thus when I shun Scylla, your father, I fall into
Charybdis, your mother. Well, you are gone both ways.

JESSICA   I shall be saved by my husband. He hath made me a   15
Christian.

LAUNCELOT   Truly the more to blame he! We were Christians
enow before, in as many as could well live one by another.
This making of Christians will raise the price of hogs; if we
grow all to be pork eaters, we shall not shortly have a rasher   20
on the coals for money.

    Enter LORENZO.

JESSICA   I'll tell my husband, Launcelot, what you say—here
he comes!

LORENZO   I shall grow jealous of you shortly, Launcelot, if you
thus get my wife into corners.   25

JESSICA   Nay, you need not fear us, Lorenzo. Launcelot and I
are out. He tells me flatly there's no mercy for me in heaven
because I am a Jew's daughter; and he says you are no good
member of the commonwealth, for in converting Jews to
Christians you raise the price of pork.   30

LORENZO   I shall answer that better to the commonwealth
than you can the getting up of the negro's belly: the Moor is
with child by you, Launcelot!

LAUNCELOT   It is much that the Moor should be more than
reason, but if she be less than an honest woman she is in-   35
deed more than I took her for.

LORENZO   How every fool can play upon the word! I think the
best grace of wit will shortly turn into silence, and discourse
grow commendable in none only but parrots. Go in, sirrah;
bid them prepare for dinner.   40

LAUNCELOT   That is done, sir; they have all stomachs.

LORENZO   Goodly Lord! what a wit snapper are you! Then bid
them prepare dinner!

13–14. Scylla . . . Charybdis: Joking variant of the proverbial phrase "Between Scylla and
Charybdis"—a sea monster and whirlpool between which mariners in Homer's *Odyssey* had
to steer in order to pass the Straits of Messina.
17–18. We were . . . before: There were enough of us Christians already.
20. rasher: slab of bacon (which is pork and therefore forbidden to observant Jews).
27. are out: have quarreled.
34–35. It is much . . . than reason: It makes sense that the Moor is unreasonably large
(with pun on "more") since she is pregnant.
35–36. she is . . . her for: i.e., I thought she was a prostitute. There may be a joking topical reference here to a well-known black woman, Lucy Negro, who was a London prostitute in the 1590s.
41. They . . . stomachs: They are all hungry (and therefore do not need to be prepared).

LAUNCELOT   That is done too, sir, only "cover" is the word.
LORENZO   Will you cover then, sir?   45
LAUNCELOT   Not so, sir, neither; I know my duty.
LORENZO   Yet more quarreling with occasion! Wilt thou show
the whole wealth of thy wit in an instant? I pray thee understand a plain man in his plain meaning: go to thy fellows, bid
them cover the table, serve in the meat, and we will come in   50
to dinner.
LAUNCELOT   For the table, sir, it shall be served in; for the
meat, sir, it shall be covered; for your coming in to dinner,
sir, why let it be as humors and conceits shall govern.

Exit [LAUNCELOT *the*] *clown.*

LORENZO   O dear discretion, how his words are suited!   55
The fool hath planted in his memory
An army of good words, and I do know
A many fools that stand in better place,
Garnished like him, that for a tricksy word
Defy the matter. How cheer'st thou, Jessica?   60
And now, good sweet, say thy opinion—
How dost thou like the Lord Bassanio's wife?
JESSICA   Past all expressing! It is very meet
The Lord Bassanio live an upright life,
For having such a blessing in his lady   65
He finds the joys of heaven here on earth.
And if on earth he do not mean it, it
Is reason he should never come to heaven.
Why if two gods should play some heavenly match
And on the wager lay two earthly women,   70
And Portia one, there must be something else
Pawned with the other, for the poor rude world
Hath not her fellow.
LORENZO   Even such a husband
Hast thou of me as she is for wife.   75
JESSICA   Nay, but ask my opinion too of that!
LORENZO   I will anon; first let us go to dinner.
JESSICA   Nay, let me praise you while I have a stomach.
LORENZO   No, pray thee, let it serve for table talk—

---

44. cover: set the table.
46. Not so . . . duty: Launcelot pretends to take "cover" to mean "appear in a hat," which
would be inappropriate with a superior.
58–59. In better place . . . Garnished like him: many fools having higher social rank, resembling him.
59–60. for a . . . Defy the matter: defeat meaning for the sake of a play on words.
72. Pawned: wagered.
78. have a stomach: am still hungry.

Then howsome'er thou speak'st, 'mong other things   80
I shall digest it.
JESSICA   Well, I'll set you forth.   *Exit [with* LORENZO.]

Act 4 Scene 1

[*Venice*] *Enter the* DUKE, *the magnificos,* ANTONIO, BAS-
SANIO, [SALERIO,] *and* GRATIANO.

DUKE   What, is Antonio here?
ANTONIO   Ready, so please Your Grace.
DUKE   I am sorry for thee. Thou art come to answer
A stony adversary, an inhuman wretch,
Uncapable of pity, void and empty   5
From any dram of mercy.
ANTONIO   I have heard
Your Grace hath ta'en great pains to qualify
His rigorous course; but since he stands obdurate,
And that no lawful means can carry me   10
Out of his envy's reach, I do oppose
My patience to his fury, and am armed
To suffer with a quietness of spirit
The very tyranny and rage of his.
DUKE   Go one, and call the Jew into the court.   15
SALERIO   He is ready at the door; he comes, my lord.

[*Enter* SHYLOCK.]

DUKE   Make room and let him stand before our face.
Shylock, the world thinks, and I think so too,
That thou but leadest this fashion of thy malice
To the last hour of act; and then, 'tis thought,   20
Thou'lt show thy mercy and remorse more strange
Than is thy strange apparent cruelty.
And where thou now exacts the penalty,
Which is a pound of this poor merchant's flesh,
Thou wilt not only loose the forfeiture,   25
But, touched with human gentleness and love,
Forgive a moiety of the principal,
Glancing an eye of pity on his losses
That have of late so huddled on his back—
Enow to press a royal merchant down   30

80. **howsome'er:** howsoever.
82. **set you forth:** serve you up (like food); praise you highly.
19–20. **leadest . . . act:** carry your show of malice to the last possible minute.
27. **moiety:** share, half.
30. **enow:** enough.

And pluck commiseration of this state's,
From brassy bosoms and rough hearts of flints,
From stubborn Turks and Tartars never trained
To offices of tender courtesy.
We all expect a gentle answer, Jew.   35
JEW   I have possessed Your Grace of what I purpose,
And by our holy Sabaoth have I sworn
To have the due and forfeit of my bond.
If you deny it, let the danger light
Upon your charter and your city's freedom!   40
You'll ask me why I rather choose to have
A weight of carrion flesh than to receive
Three thousand ducats. I'll not answer that,
But say it is my humor. Is it answered?
What if my house be troubled with a rat   45
And I be pleased to give ten thousand ducats
To have it baned? What—are you answered yet?
Some men there are love not a gaping pig;
Some that are mad if they behold a cat;
And others, when the bagpipe sings i'th'nose,   50
Cannot contain their urine; for affection
Masters of passion—sways it to the mood
Of what it likes or loathes. Now for your answer:
As there is no firm reason to be rend'red
Why he cannot abide a gaping pig,   55
Why he a harmless necessary cat,
Why he a woolen bagpipe, but of force
Must yield to such inevitable shame
As to offend, himself being offended;
So can I give no reason, nor I will not,   60
More than a lodged hate and a certain loathing
I bear Antonio, that I follow thus
A losing suit against him. Are you answered?
BASSANIO   This is no answer, thou unfeeling man,
To excuse the current of thy cruelty!   65
JEW   I am not bound to please thee with my answers.
BASSANIO   Do all men kill the things they do not love?
JEW   Hates any man the thing he would not kill?
BASSANIO   Every offense is not a hate at first.
JEW   What—wouldst thou have a serpent sting thee twice?   70
ANTONIO   I pray you, think you question with the Jew?
You may as well go stand upon the beach

47. baned: poisoned.
51–52. affection . . . passion: inclination (likes and dislikes) controls passion.
55. gaping pig: a roast pig served with its mouth propped open.

And bid the main flood bate his usual height;
You may as well use question with the wolf
Why he hath made the ewe bleak for the lamb;   75
You may as well forbid the mountain of pines
To wag their high tops and to make no noise
When they are fretten with the gusts of heaven;
You may as well do anything most hard
As seek to soften that than which what's harder—   80
His Jewish heart. Therefore, I do beseech you,
Make no moe offers, use no farther means,
But with all brief and plain conveniency
Let me have judgment and the Jew his will.
BASSANIO   For thy three thousand ducats here is six.   85
JEW   If every ducat in six thousand ducats
Were in six parts, and every part a ducat,
I would not draw them. I would have my bond.
DUKE   How shalt thou hope for mercy, rend'ring none?
JEW   What judgment shall I dread, doing no wrong?   90
You have among you many a purchased slave,
Which like your asses and your dogs and mules,
You use in abject and in slavish parts
Because you bought them. Shall I say to you,
"Let them be free; marry them to your heirs!   95
Why sweat they under burdens? Let their beds
Be made as soft as yours, and let their palates
Be seasoned with such viands"? You will answer,
"The slaves are ours." So do I answer you.
The pound of flesh which I demand of him   100
Is dearly bought, as mine, and I will have it.
If you deny me, fie upon your law!
There is no force in the decrees of Venice.
I stand for judgment. Answer! Shall I have it?
DUKE   Upon my power I may dismiss this court   105
Unless Bellario, a learned doctor
Whom I have sent for to determine this,
Come here today.
SALERIO   My lord, here stays without
A messenger with letters from the doctor,   110
New come from Padua.
DUKE   Bring us the letters. Call the messenger.
BASSANIO   Good cheer, Antonio! What, man—courage yet!

73. **flood bate his:** flood tide reduce its.
75. **bleak:** bleat.
78. **fretten:** fretted, agitated.
91. **purchased slave:** Venice was an important slave market during this period.
98. **viands:** food.

This Jew shall have my flesh, blood, bones and all,
Ere thou shalt lose for me one drop of blood!   115
ANTONIO   I am a tainted wether of the flock,
Meetest for death. The weakest kind of fruit
Drops earliest to the ground, and so let me.
You cannot better be employed, Bassanio,
Than to live still and write mine epitaph.   120

        Enter NERISSA *[disguised as* BELLARIO'S *assistant].*

DUKE   Come you from Padua, from Bellario?
NERISSA   From both, my lord. Bellario greets Your Grace.

        [Presents a letter.]

BASSANIO   Why dost thou whet thy knife so earnestly?
JEW   To cut the forfeiture from that bankrout there.
GRATIANO   Not on thy sole, but on thy soul, harsh Jew,   125
Thou mak'st thy knife keen. But no metal can—
No, not the hangman's axe—bear half the keenness
Of thy sharp envy. Can no prayers pierce thee?
JEW   No, none that thou hast wit enough to make.
GRATIANO   O be thou damned, inexecrable dog,   130
And for thy life let justice be accused.
Thou almost mak'st me waver in my faith—
To hold opinion with Pythagoras
That souls of animals infuse themselves
Into the trunks of men! Thy currish spirit   135
Governed a wolf who hanged for human slaughter;
Even from the gallows did his fell soul fleet,
And whilst thou layest in thy unhallowed dam,
Infused itself in thee; for thy desires
Are wolvish, bloody, starved, and ravenous.   140
JEW   Till thou canst rail the seal from off my bond
Thou but offend'st thy lungs to speak so loud.
Repair thy wit, good youth, or it will fall
To cureless ruin. I stand here for law.
DUKE   This letter from Bellario doth commend   145
A young and learned doctor to our court.
Where is he?

116. **wether:** castrated ram.
125–26. **thy sole . . . keen:** The pun on sole/soul suggests that Shylock is sharpening the
knife on the sole of his shoe.
133. **Pythagoras:** Greek philosopher who believed in the transmigration of souls.
136. **wolf . . . slaughter:** In Elizabethan times, animals could be hanged for crimes against
humans. Since the Latin for "wolf" is *lupus*, there may also be an allusion to Doctor Lopez
(= *lupus*), a Jew who was executed for treason in 1594 (see pp. 121–22).
137. **fell soul fleet:** cruel soul hasten.
138. **layest . . . dam:** lay in the womb of your unholy mother.

NERISSA   He attendeth here hard by
　To know your answer whether you'll admit him.
DUKE   With all my heart. Some three or four of you   150
　Go give him courteous conduct to this place;
　Meantime the court shall hear Bellario's letter:

> [*Reads.*] Your Grace shall understand that at the receipt of
> your letter I am very sick, but in the instant that your mes-
> senger came, in loving visitation was with me a young doc-   155
> tor of Rome; his name is Balthazar. I acquainted him with
> the cause in controversy between the Jew and Antonio the
> merchant. We turned o'er many books together. He is fur-
> nished with my opinion which, bettered with his own
> learning—the greatness whereof I cannot enough com-   160
> mend—comes with him at my importunity to fill up Your
> Grace's request in my stead. I beseech you, let his lack of
> years be no impediment to let him lack a reverend estima-
> tion; for I never knew so young a body with so old a head.
> I leave him to your gracious acceptance, whose trial shall   165
> better publish his commendation.

　　　Enter PORTIA [*disguised as*] BALTHAZAR.

You hear the learn'd Bellario, what he writes;
And here, I take it, is the doctor come.
Give me your hand; come you from old Bellario?
PORTIA   I did, my lord.   170
DUKE   You are welcome; take your place.
　Are you acquainted with the difference
　That holds this present question in the court?
PORTIA   I am informed thoroughly of the cause.
　Which is the merchant here and which the Jew?   175
DUKE   Antonio and old Shylock, both stand forth.
PORTIA   Is your name Shylock?
JEW   Shylock is my name.
PORTIA   Of a strange nature is the suit you follow,
　Yet in such rule that the Venetian law   180
　Cannot impugn you as you do proceed.
　You stand within his danger, do you not?
ANTONIO   Aye, so he says.
PORTIA   Do you confess the bond?
ANTONIO   I do.   185
PORTIA   Then must the Jew be merciful.
SHYLOCK   On what compulsion must I? Tell me that.
PORTIA   The quality of mercy is not strained;

148. **hard by**: close by.
182. **danger**: power.

It droppeth as the gentle rain from heaven
Upon the place beneath. It is twice blest: 190
It blesseth him that gives and him that takes.
'Tis mightiest in the mightiest; it becomes
The throned monarch better than his crown.
His scepter shows the force of temporal power,
The attribute to awe and majesty   195
Wherein doth sit the dread and fear of kings.
But mercy is above this sceptered sway;
It is enthroned in the hearts of kings;
It is an attribute to God himself,
And earthly power doth then show likest God's   200
When mercy seasons justice. Therefore, Jew,
Though justice be thy plea, consider this—
That in the course of justice none of us
Should see salvation. We do pray for mercy,
And that same prayer doth teach us all to render   205
The deeds of mercy. I have spoke thus much
To mitigate the justice of thy plea,
Which if thou follow, this strict court of Venice
Must needs give sentence 'gainst the merchant there.
SHYLOCK   My deeds upon my head! I crave the law,   210
The penalty and forfeit of my bond.
PORTIA   Is he not able to discharge the money?
BASSANIO   Yes, here I tender it for him in the court—
Yea, twice the sum; if that will not suffice,
I will be bound to pay it ten times o'er   215
On forfeit of my hands, my head, my heart.
If this will not suffice, it must appear
That malice bears down truth. And I beseech you—
Wrest once the law to your authority;
To do a great right do a little wrong,   220
And curb this cruel devil of his will.
PORTIA   It must not be. There is no power in Venice
Can alter a decree established.
'Twill be recorded for a precedent,
And many an error by the same example   225
Will rush into the state. It cannot be.
SHYLOCK   A Daniel come to judgment! Yea, a Daniel!
O wise young judge, how I do honor thee!
PORTIA   I pray you, let me look upon the bond.
SHYLOCK   Here 'tis, most reverend doctor, here it is.   230
PORTIA   Shylock, there's thrice thy money off'red thee.

---

227. **Daniel:** In the Apocrypha, young Daniel judges Susanna innocent of charges of unchastity and instead condemns the elders who had falsely accused her.

SHYLOCK   An oath, an oath, I have an oath in heaven.
Shall I lay perjury upon my soul?
Not, not for Venice!
PORTIA   Why, this bond is forfeit,   235
And lawfully by this the Jew may claim
A pound of flesh to be by him cut off
Nearest the merchant's heart. Be merciful—
Take thrice thy money; bid me tear the bond!
SHYLOCK   When it is paid according to the tenure.   240
It doth appear you are a worthy judge;
You know the law; your exposition
Hath been most sound. I charge you by the law
Whereof you are a well-deserving pillar,
Proceed to judgment. By my soul I swear   245
There is no power in the tongue of man
To alter me! I stay here on my bond.
ANTONIO   Most heartily I do beseech the court
To give the judgment.
PORTIA   Why then, thus it is: 250
You must prepare your bosom for his knife.
SHYLOCK   O noble judge, O excellent young man!
PORTIA   For the intent and purpose of the law
Hath full relation to the penalty,
Which here appeareth due upon the bond.   255
JEW   'Tis very true. O wise and upright judge,
How much more elder art thou than thy looks!
PORTIA   Therefore lay bare your bosom.
JEW   Aye—his breast.
So says the bond, doth it not, noble judge?   260
"Nearest his heart"; those are the very words.
PORTIA   It is so. Are there balance here to weigh
The flesh?
JEW   I have them ready.
PORTIA   Have by some surgeon, Shylock, on your charge,   265
To stop his wounds lest he do bleed to death.
JEW   Is it so nominated in the bond?
PORTIA   It is not so expressed, but what of that?
'Twere good you do so much for charity.
JEW   I cannot find it; 'tis not in the bond.   270
PORTIA   You, merchant, have you anything to say?
ANTONIO   But little. I am armed and well prepared.
Give me your hand, Bassanio, fare you well;
Grieve not that I am fall'n to this for you,

240. tenure: authority (of the bond).
262. balance: scales.

For herein Fortune shows herself more kind   275
Than is her custom: it is still her use
To let the wretched man outlive his wealth,
To view with hollow eye and wrinkled brow
An age of poverty; from which ling'ring penance
Of such misery doth she cut me off.   280
Commend me to your honorable wife:
Tell her the process of Antonio's end;
Say how I loved you; speak me fair in death.
And when the tale is told, bid her be judge
Whether Bassanio had not once a love.   285
Repent but you that you shall lose your friend
And he repents not that he pays your debt;
For if the Jew do cut but deep enough,
I'll pay it instantly with all my heart.
BASSANIO   Antonio, I am married to a wife   290
Which is as dear to me as life itself;
But life itself, my wife, and all the world
Are not with me esteemed above thy life.
I would lose all—aye, sacrifice them all
Here to this devil—to deliver you.   295
PORTIA   Your wife would give you little thanks for that
If she were by to hear you make the offer.
GRATIANO   I have a wife who I protest I love—
I would she were in heaven so she could
Entreat some power to change this currish Jew.   300
NERISSA   'Tis well you offer it behind her back;
The wish would make else an unquiet house.
JEW   These be the Christian husbands! I have a daughter—
Would any of the stock of Barrabas
Had been her husband rather than a Christian!   305
We trifle time; I pray thee pursue sentence.
PORTIA   A pound of that same merchant's flesh is thine:
The court awards it and the law doth give it.
JEW   Most rightful judge!
PORTIA   And you must cut this flesh from off his breast: 310
The law allows it and the court awards it.
JEW   Most learned judge, a sentence! Come, prepare!
PORTIA   Tarry a little. There is something else:
This bond doth give thee here no jot of blood.
The words expressly are "A pound of flesh."   315
Take then thy bond, take thou thy pound of flesh;

304. **stock of Barrabas**: Thieves like Barrabas in the Bible, whom the Jews wanted released instead of Christ (Mark 15.6–15); also a possible reference to Barrabas, the unscrupulous title character from Christopher Marlowe's popular play, *The Jew of Malta*.

But in the cutting it, if thou dost shed
One drop of Christian blood, thy lands and goods
Are by the laws of Venice confiscate
Unto the state of Venice.   320
GRATIANO   O upright judge! Mark Jew, O learned judge!
SHYLOCK   Is that the law?
PORTIA   Thyself shall see the act;
   For as thou urgest justice, be assured
   Thou shalt have justice more than thou desir'st.   325
GRATIANO   O learned judge! Mark, Jew, a learned judge!
JEW   I take this offer then; pay the bond thrice
   And let the Christian go.
BASSANIO   Here is the money.
PORTIA   Soft—   330
   The Jew shall have all justice! Soft, no haste—
   He shall have nothing but the penalty.
GRATIANO   O Jew, an upright judge, a learned judge!
PORTIA   Therefore prepare thee to cut off the flesh.
   Shed thou no blood, nor cut thou less nor more   335
   But just a pound of flesh. If thou tak'st more
   Or less than a just pound, be it but so much
   As makes it light or heavy in the substance
   Or the division of the twentieth part
   Of one poor scruple—nay if the scale do turn   340
   But in the estimation of a hair—
   Thou diest and all thy goods are confiscate.
GRATIANO   A second Daniel, a Daniel, Jew!
   Now, infidel, I have you on the hip!
PORTIA   Why doth the Jew pause? Take thy forfeiture!   345
SHYLOCK   Give me my principal and let me go.
BASSANIO   I have it ready for thee; here it is.
PORTIA   He hath refused it in the open court.
   He shall have merely justice and his bond.
GRATIANO   A Daniel, still say I; a second Daniel!   350
   I thank thee, Jew, for teaching me that word.
SHYLOCK   Shall I not have barely my principal?
PORTIA   Thou shalt have nothing but the forfeiture
   To be so taken at thy peril, Jew.
SHYLOCK   Why then, the devil give him good of it!   355
   I'll stay no longer question.
PORTIA   Tarry, Jew—
   The law hath yet another hold on you.
   It is enacted in the laws of Venice

---

340. scruple: a very small weight.

If it be proved against an alien   360
That by direct or indirect attempts
He seek the life of any citizen,
The party 'gainst the which he doth contrive
Shall seize one half his goods; the other half
Comes to the privy coffer of the state;   365
And the offender's life lies in the mercy
Of the duke only, 'gainst all other voice.
In which predicament I say thou stand'st:
For it appears by manifest proceeding
That indirectly, and directly too,   370
Thou hast contrived against the very life
Of the defendant; and thou hast incurred
The danger formerly by me rehearsed.
Down, therefore, and beg mercy of the duke.

GRATIANO   Beg that thou mayst have leave to hang thyself!   375
And yet, thy wealth being forfeit to the state,
Thou hast not left the value of a cord;
Therefore thou must be hanged at the state's charge.

DUKE   That thou shalt see the difference of our spirit,
I pardon thee thy life before thou ask it.   380
For half thy wealth, it is Antonio's;
The other half comes to the general state,
Which humbleness may drive unto a fine.

PORTIA   Aye, for the state, not for Antonio.

SHYLOCK   Nay, take my life and all, pardon not that.   385
You take my house when you do take the prop
That doth sustain my house; you take my life
When you do take the means whereby I live.

PORTIA   What mercy can you render him, Antonio?

GRATIANO   A halter gratis—nothing else, for God's sake!   390

ANTONIO   So please my lord the duke, and all the court,
To quit the fine for one half of his goods
I am content, so he will let me have
The other half in use, to render it
Upon his death unto the gentleman   395
That lately stole his daughter.
Two things provided more: that for this favor
He presently become a Christian;
The other, that he do record a gift
Here in the court of all he dies possessed   400
Unto his son Lorenzo and his daughter.

365. privy coffer: private treasury.
390. A halter gratis: a free hangman's noose.
401. son: son-in-law.

DUKE   He shall do this or else I do recant
  The pardon that I late pronounced here.
PORTIA   Art thou contented, Jew? What dost thou say?
SHYLOCK   I am content.   405
PORTIA   Clerk, draw a deed of gift.
SHYLOCK   I pray you, give me leave to go from hence;
  I am not well. Send the deed after me
  And I will sign it.
DUKE   Get thee gone, but do it.   410
GRATIANO   In christ'ning shalt thou have two godfathers.
  Had I been judge, thou should'st have had ten more
  To bring thee to the gallows, not to the font.

                                          Exit [SHYLOCK.]

DUKE   Sir, I entreat you home with me to dinner.
PORTIA   I humbly do desire Your Grace of pardon—   415
  I must away this night toward Padua,
  And it is meet I presently set forth.
DUKE   I am sorry that your leisure serves you not.
  Antonio, gratify this gentleman,
  For in my mind, you are much bound to him.   420

                                  Exit DUKE *and his train.*

BASSANIO   Most worthy gentleman, I and my friend
  Have by your wisdom been this day acquitted
  Of grievous penalties, in lieu whereof
  Three thousand ducats due unto the Jew
  We freely cope your courteous pains withal.   425
ANTONIO   And stand indebted over and above
  In love and service to you evermore.
PORTIA   He is well paid that is well satisfied;
  And I, delivering you, am satisfied,
  And therein do account myself well paid.   430
  My mind was never yet more mercenary.
  I pray you, know me when we meet again.
  I wish you well, and so I take my leave.
BASSANIO   Dear sir, of force I must attempt you further.
  Take some remembrance of us as a tribute,   435
  Not as fee. Grant me two things, I pray you:
  Not to deny me, and to pardon me.
PORTIA   You press me far, and therefore I will yield.
  Give me your gloves; I'll wear them for your sake.
  And for your love I'll take this ring from you.   440

412–13. ten more . . . gallows: a jury of twelve to condemn you to hanging.
425. cope: repay.

Do not draw back your hand; I'll take no more,
And you, in love, shall not deny me this!
BASSANIO   This ring, good sir, alas—it is a trifle;
    I will not shame myself to give you this!
PORTIA   I will have nothing else but only this,   445
    And now methinks I have a mind to it!
BASSANIO   There's more depends on this than on the value.
    The dearest ring in Venice will I give you,
    And find it out by proclamation.
    Only for this, I pray you, pardon me.   450
PORTIA   I see, sir, you are liberal in offers.
    You taught me first to beg, and now, methinks,
    You teach me how a beggar should be answered.
BASSANIO   Good sir, this ring was given me by my wife,
    And when she put it on she made me vow   455
    That I should neither sell nor give nor lose it.
PORTIA   That 'scuse serves many men to save their gifts;
    And if your wife be not a madwoman,
    And know how well I have deserved this ring,
    She would not hold out enemy forever   460
    For giving it to me. Well, peace be with you.

                              Exeunt [PORTIA *and* NERISSA].

ANTONIO   My Lord Bassanio, let him have the ring.
    Let his deservings and my love withal
    Be valued 'gainst your wife's commandment.
BASSANIO   Go, Gratiano, run and overtake him.   465
    Give him the ring and bring him, if thou canst,
    Unto Antonio's house. Away, make haste!

                                        Exit GRATIANO.

Come, you and I will thither presently,
And in the morning early will we both
Fly toward Belmont. Come, Antonio.   *Exeunt.*   470

Act 4 Scene 2

Enter [PORTIA *and*] NERISSA [*still in disguise*].

PORTIA   Inquire the Jew's house out; give him this deed,
    And let him sign it. We'll away tonight
    And be a day before our husbands home.
    This deed will be well welcome to Lorenzo!

    Enter GRATIANO.

GRATIANO   Fair sir, you are well o'erta'en: 5
   My Lord Bassanio, upon more advice,
   Hath sent you here this ring, and doth entreat
   Your company at dinner.
PORTIA   That cannot be.
   His ring I do accept most thankfully,   10
   And so I pray you tell him. Furthermore,
   I pray you show my youth old Shylock's house.
GRATIANO   That will I do.
NERISSA   Sir, I would speak with you.
   [To PORTIA.] I'll see if I can get my husband's ring,   15
   Which I did make him swear to keep forever.
PORTIA   Thou mayst, I warrant. We shall have old swearing
   That they did give the rings away to men;
   But we'll outface them and outswear them too.
   Away, make haste! Thou know'st where I will tarry.   20
NERISSA   Come, good sir, will you show me to this house?
                                                          [Exeunt.]

Act 5 Scene 1

[Belmont] Enter LORENZO and JESSICA.

LORENZO   The moon shines bright. In such a night as this,
   When the sweet wind did gently kiss the trees
   And they did make no noise, in such a night
   Troilus methinks mounted the Trojan walls
   And sighed his soul toward the Grecian tents   5
   Where Cressid lay that night.
JESSICA   In such a night
   Did Thisbe fearfully o'ertrip the dew,
   And saw the lion's shadow ere himself,
   And ran dismayed away.   10
LORENZO   In such a night
   Stood Dido with a willow in her hand
   Upon the wild sea banks, and waft her love
   To come again to Carthage.
JESSICA   In such a night   15

17. old swearing: plenty of oaths.
4. Troilus: Trojan son of Priam from the *Iliad* who loved and lost Cressida.
6. Cressid: Troilus' beloved, who was forced to leave Troy for the Greek camp and subsequently abandoned **Troilus** for a Greek lover.
8. Thisbe: Lover of Pyramus who fled from their meeting place because she was frightened by a lion; thinking she had perished, Pyramus killed himself.
12. Dido . . . hand: Queen of Carthage forsaken by Aeneas in the *Aeneid*; she carries willow as a symbol of forsaken love.

Medea gathered the enchanted herbs
That did renew old Aeson.
LORENZO   In such a night
Did Jessica steal from the wealthy Jew,
And with an unthrift love did run from Venice   20
As far as Belmont.
JESSICA   In such a night
Did young Lorenzo swear he loved her well,
Stealing her soul with many vows of faith,
And ne'er a true one.   25
LORENZO   In such a night
Did pretty Jessica, like a little shrew,
Slander her love; and he forgave it her.
JESSICA   I would out-night you did nobody come,
But hark—I hear the footing of a man.   30

            Enter [STEPHANO,] *a messenger.*

LORENZO   Who comes so fast in silence of the night?
MESSENGER   A friend.
LORENZO   A friend? What friend? Your name I pray you, friend.
MESSENGER   Stephano is my name, and I bring word
My mistress will before the break of day   35
Be here at Belmont. She doth stray about
By holy crosses where she kneels and prays
For happy wedlock hours.
LORENZO   Who comes with her?
MESSENGER   None but a holy hermit and her maid.   40
I pray you, is my master yet returned?
LORENZO   He is not; nor we have not heard from him.
But go we in, I pray thee Jessica,
And ceremoniously let us prepare
Some welcome for the mistress of the house.   45

            Enter [LAUNCELOT *the*] *Clown.*

LAUNCELOT   Sola sola! Wo ha, ho sola, sola!
LORENZO   Who calls?
LAUNCELOT   Sola! Did you see Master Lorenzo and Mistress
Lorenzo? Sola, sola!
LORENZO   Leave holloaing, man! Here!   50
LAUNCELOT   Sola, where, where?

16. **Medea:** Sorceress from the story of Jason and the Golden Fleece. She is best known
for murdering her children after being abandoned by Jason.
17. **Aeson:** Jason's father, made young again by Medea's magic.
20. **unthrift:** reckless, spendthrift.
48–49. **Master . . . Lorenzo:** That is, Lorenzo and Jessica. Launcelot has mistaken
Lorenzo's first name for his surname.

LORENZO   Here!

LAUNCELOT   Tell him there's a post come from my master,
with his horn full of good news. My master will be here ere
morning, sweet soul.   [*Exit.*]   55

LORENZO   Let's in and there expect their coming.
And yet, no matter. Why should we go in?
My friend Stephano, signify, I pray you,
Within the house your mistress is at hand;
And bring your music forth into the air.   60

[*Exit* STEPHANO.]

How sweet the moonlight sleeps upon this bank.
Here will we sit and let the sounds of music
Creep in our ears. Soft stillness and the night
Become the touches of sweet harmony.
Sit, Jessica—look how the floor of heaven   65
Is thick inlaid with pattens of bright gold;
There's not the smallest orb which thou behold'st
But in his motion like an angel sings,
Still quiring to the young-eyed cherubins.
Such harmony is in immortal souls,   70
But whilst this muddy vesture of decay
Doth grossly close it in, we cannot hear it.
Come, ho! And wake Diana with a hymn.

[*Enter the house musicians.*]

With sweetest touches pierce your mistress' ear
And draw her home with music.   75

[*The house musicians*] *play music.*

JESSICA   I am never merry when I hear sweet music.

LORENZO   The reason is, your spirits are attentive;
For do but note a wild and wanton herd
Or race of youthful and unhandled colts
Fetching mad bounds, bellowing, and neighing loud,   80
Which is the hot condition of their blood:
If they but hear perchance a trumpet sound,
Or any air of music touch their ears,
You shall perceive them make a mutual stand,
Their savage eyes turned to a modest gaze   85

64. **Become:** are fitting for.
66. **inlaid . . . gold:** studded with stars like gold tiles on a floor.
69. **quiring . . . cherubins:** Reference to the music of the planetary spheres, imagined as singing like an angelic choir as they turned in the heavens.
71. **muddy . . . decay:** the body, imagined as only muddy clothing for the soul.
79–80. **unhandled . . . bounds:** untrained colts making wild leaps.

By the sweet power of music. Therefore the poet
Did feign that Orpheus drew trees, stones, and floods,
Since naught so stockish, hard, and full of rage
But music for the time doth change his nature.
The man that hath no music in himself,   90
Nor is not moved with concord of sweet sounds,
Is fit for treasons, stratagems, and spoils;
The motions of his spirit are dull as night,
And his affections dark as Erebus.
Let no such man be trusted! Mark the music.   95

    Enter PORTIA *and* NERISSA.

PORTIA   That light we see is burning in my hall;
How far that little candle throws his beams!
So shines a good deed in a naughty world.
NERISSA   When the moon shone we did not see the candle.
PORTIA   So doth the greater glory dim the less.   100
A substitute shines brightly as a king
Until a king be by, and then his state
Empties itself as doth an inland brook
Into the main of waters. Music, hark!
NERISSA   It is your music, madam, of the house.   105
PORTIA   Nothing is good, I see, without respect;
Methinks it sounds much sweeter than by day.
NERISSA   Silence bestows that virtue on it, madam.
PORTIA   The crow doth sing as sweetly as the lark
When neither is attended; and I think   110
The nightingale, if she should sing by day
When every goose is cackling, would be thought
No better a musician than the wren.
How many things by season seasoned are
To their right praise and true perfection!   115
Peace! How the moon sleeps with Endymion,
And would not be awaked.
LORENZO   That is the voice,
Or I am much deceived, of Portia.
PORTIA   He knows me as the blind man knows the cuckoo—   120
By the bad voice!

---

87. **Orpheus:** legendary classical figure whose music could charm even inanimate objects.
88. **stockish:** dull.
94. **Erebus:** area of hell in classical mythology.
102. **state:** the substitute's majesty.
106. **without respect:** except in relation to things around it.
114. **season:** coming at the right time.
116. **Endymion:** shepherd loved by Diana, goddess of the moon.

LORENZO   Dear lady, welcome home!

PORTIA   We have been praying for our husbands' welfare,
Which speed, we hope, the better for our words.
Are they returned?   125

LORENZO   Madam, they are not yet,
But there is come a messenger before
To signify their coming.

PORTIA   Go in, Nerissa.
Give order to my servants that they take   130
No note at all of our being absent hence—
Nor you, Lorenzo—Jessica, nor you.

    [*Trumpet sounds.*]

LORENZO   Your husband is at hand. I hear his trumpet.
We are no telltales, madam; fear you not.

PORTIA   This night methinks is but the daylight sick;   135
It looks a little paler. 'Tis a day
Such as the day is when the sun is hid.

    Enter BASSANIO, ANTONIO, GRATIANO, *and their followers.*

BASSANIO   We should hold day with the Antipodes,
If you would walk in absence of the sun.

PORTIA   Let me give light, but let me not be light;   140
For a light wife doth make a heavy husband,
And never be Bassanio so for me,
But God sort all. You are welcome home, my lord.

BASSANIO   I thank you, madam. Give welcome to my friend.
This is the man; this is Antonio   145
To whom I am so infinitely bound.

PORTIA   You should in all sense be much bound to him,
For, as I hear, he was much bound for you.

ANTONIO   No more than I am well acquitted of.

PORTIA   Sir, you are very welcome to our house.   150
It must appear in other ways than words;
Therefore I scant this breathing courtesy.

GRATIANO   By yonder moon I swear you do me wrong.
In faith, I gave it to the judge's clerk.
Would he were gelt that had it, for my part,   155
Since you do take it, love, so much at heart!

PORTIA   A quarrel, ho! Already? What's the matter?

138. **Antipodes:** area on the opposite side of the earth (where it is dusk instead of dawn).
140. **light:** unfaithful.
141. **heavy:** sad.
143. **sort all:** sort everything out.
152. **scant . . . courtesy:** cut short this courtesy of words.
155. **gelt:** castrated.

GRATIANO　About a hoop of gold, a paltry ring
　　That she did give me, whose posy was
　　For all the world like cutler's poetry　　　　　160
　　Upon a knife: "Love me and leave me not."
NERISSA　What talk you of the posy or the value?
　　You swore to me when I did give [it] you,
　　That you would wear it till your hour of death,
　　And that it should lie with you in your grave.　　165
　　Though not for me, yet for your vehement oaths,
　　You should have been respective and have kept it.
　　Gave it a judge's clerk! No, God's my judge,
　　The clerk will ne'er wear hair on's face that had it!
GRATIANO　He will and if he live to be a man.　　170
NERISSA　Aye, if a woman live to be a man!
GRATIANO　Now, by this hand, I gave it to a youth—
　　A kind of boy, a little scrubbed boy,
　　No higher than thyself—the judge's clerk,
　　A prating boy that begged it as a fee.　　175
　　I could not for my heart deny it him.
PORTIA　You were to blame, I must be plain with you,
　　To part so slightly with your wife's first gift,
　　A thing stuck on with oaths upon your finger,
　　And so riveted with faith unto your flesh.　　180
　　I gave my love a ring and made him swear
　　Never to part with it; and here he stands.
　　I dare be sworn for him he would not leave it,
　　Nor pluck it from his finger, for the wealth
　　That the world masters. Now, in faith, Gratiano,　　185
　　You give your wife too unkind a cause of grief;
　　And 'twere to me I should be mad at it.
BASSANIO　Why, I were best to cut my left hand off,
　　And swear I lost the ring defending it!
GRATIANO　My Lord Bassanio gave his ring away　　190
　　Unto the judge that begged it, and indeed
　　Deserved it too. And then the boy, his clerk,
　　That took some pains in writing, he begged mine;
　　And neither man nor master would take aught
　　But the two rings.　　195
PORTIA　What ring gave you, my lord?
　　Not that, I hope, which you received of me!
BASSANIO　If I could add a lie unto a fault,
　　I would deny it; but you see my finger

159. **posy:** inscription.
167. **respective:** careful.
173. **scrubbed:** short, scruffy.

Hath not the ring upon it. It is gone.   200
PORTIA   Even so void is your false heart of truth.
   By heaven, I will ne'er come in your bed
   Until I see the ring!
NERISSA   Nor I in yours till I again see mine!
BASSANIO   Sweet Portia,   205
   If you did know to whom I gave the ring,
   If you did know for whom I gave the ring,
   And would conceive for what I gave the ring;
   And how unwillingly I left the ring
   When naught would be accepted but the ring,   210
   You would abate the strength of your displeasure.
PORTIA   If you had known the virtue of the ring,
   Or half her worthiness that gave the ring,
   Or your own honor to contain the ring,
   You would not then have parted with the ring.   215
   What man is there so much unreasonable,
   If you had pleased to have defended it
   With any terms of zeal, wanted the modesty
   To urge the thing held as a ceremony?
   Nerissa teaches me what to believe: 220
   I'll die for't, but some woman had the ring!
BASSANIO   No, by my honor madam. By my soul,
   No woman had it, but a civil doctor,
   Which did refuse three thousand ducats of me
   And begged the ring, the which I did deny him,   225
   And suffered him to go displeased away—
   Even he that had held up the very life
   Of my dear friend. What should I say, sweet lady?
   I was enforced to send it after him.
   I was beset with shame and courtesy;   230
   My honor would not let ingratitude
   So much besmear it. Pardon me, good lady,
   For by these blessed candles of the night,
   Had you been there, I think you would have begged
   The ring of me to give the worthy doctor!   235
PORTIA   Let not that doctor e'er come near my house.
   Since he hath got the jewel that I loved,
   And that which you did swear to keep for me.
   I will become as liberal as you.
   I'll not deny him anything I have—   240

218. **wanted the modesty:** was so lacking in modesty.
219. **ceremony:** symbol (of their union).
223. **civil doctor:** doctor of civil law.
227. **held up:** sustained.

No, not my body nor my husband's bed!
Know him I shall; I am well sure of it.
Lie not a night from home; watch me like Argus.
If you do not, if I be left alone,
Now by mine honor, which is yet mine own,   245
I'll have that doctor for mine bedfellow.
NERISSA   And I his clerk. Therefore, be well advised
How you do leave me to mine own protection!
GRATIANO   Well, do you so. Let not me take him then;
For if I do, I'll mar the young clerk's pen.   250
ANTONIO   I am th'unhappy subject of these quarrels.
PORTIA   Sir, grieve not you; you are welcome notwithstanding.
BASSANIO   Portia, forgive me this enforced wrong,
And in the hearing of these many friends
I swear to thee—even by thine own fair eyes   255
Wherein I see myself—
PORTIA   Mark you but that?
In both my eyes he doubly sees himself—
In each eye one. Swear by your double self,
And there's an oath of credit!   260
BASSANIO   Nay, but hear me.
Pardon this fault, and by my soul I swear
I never more will break an oath with thee.
ANTONIO   I once did lend my body for his wealth,
Which but for him that had your husband's ring   265
Had quite miscarried. I dare be bound again,
My soul upon the forfeit, that your lord
Will never more break faith advisedly.
PORTIA   Then you shall be his surety: give him this
And bid him keep it better than the other.   270
ANTONIO   Here, Lord Bassanio, swear to keep this ring.
BASSANIO   By heaven, it is the same I gave the doctor!
PORTIA   I had it of him. Pardon me Bassanio,
For by this ring the doctor lay with me.
NERISSA   And pardon me, my gentle Gratiano,   275
For that same scrubbed boy, the doctor's clerk,
In lieu of this last night did lie with me.
GRATIANO   Why this is like the mending of highways
In summer, where the ways are fair enough!
What, are we cuckolds ere we have deserved it?   280

243. **Argus:** mythological guardian with a hundred eyes.
250. **pen:** i.e., his penis.
266. **miscarried:** been destroyed.
268. **advisedly:** intentionally.
277. **in lieu of:** in exchange for.
280. **cuckolds:** deceived husbands.

PORTIA　Speak not so grossly. You are all amazed.
　Here is a letter; read it at your leisure.
　It comes from Padua from Bellario.
　There you shall find that Portia was the doctor,
　Nerissa there her clerk. Lorenzo here　　　　　　　　　285
　Shall witness I set forth as soon as you
　And even but now returned. I have not yet
　Entered my house. Antonio, you are welcome,
　And I have better news in store for you
　Than you expect. Unseal this letter soon.　　　　　　290
　There you shall find three of your argosies
　Are richly come to harbor suddenly.
　You shall not know by what strange accident
　I chanced on this letter.
ANTONIO　I am dumb!　　　　　　　　　　　　　　　　295
BASSANIO　Were you the doctor and I knew you not?
GRATIANO　Were you the clerk that is to make me cuckold?
NERISSA　Aye, but the clerk that never means to do it,
　Unless he live until he be a man.
BASSANIO　Sweet doctor, you shall be my bedfellow.　　300
　When I am absent then lie with my wife.
ANTONIO　Sweet lady, you have given me life and living,
　For here I read for certain that my ships
　Are safely come to road.
PORTIA　How now, Lorenzo!　　　　　　　　　　　　305
　My clerk hath some good comforts too for you.
NERISSA　Aye, and I'll give them him without a fee.
　There do I give to you and Jessica
　From the rich Jew a special deed of gift
　After his death of all he dies possessed of.　　　　　310
LORENZO　Fair ladies, you drop manna in the way
　Of starved people.
PORTIA　It is almost morning,
　And yet I am sure you are not satisfied
　Of these events at full. Let us go in,　　　　　　　　315
　And charge us there upon interrogatories,
　And we will answer all things faithfully.
GRATIANO　Let it be so. The first interrogatory
　That my Nerissa shall be sworn on is
　Whether till the next night she had rather stay,　　320
　Or go to bed now, being two hours to day.

---

304. road: anchorage.
311. manna: bread from heaven (see Exodus 16).
316. charge . . . interrogatories: confront us with questions under oath (legal language).
320. stay: wait.

But were the day come, I should wish it dark
Till I were couching with the doctor's clerk.
Well, while I live I'll fear no other thing
So sore as keeping safe Nerissa's ring.   *Exeunt.*   325

FINIS

A Note on the Text

Since we do not have any of Shakespeare's manuscripts for his plays, we are dependent for our texts upon early printed editions, some of which were more carefully prepared than others. Many of Shakespeare's plays were published in small "comic book-style" quartos that appeared within a few years after the performance of the play on stage. There may well have been a quarto edition of *The Merchant of Venice* before the first version that has survived, which is dated 1600. But fortunately for us, the first extant quarto of the play is of relatively high quality, and is used as the base text in most modern editions of the play.

This Norton Critical Edition follows the first quarto more closely than most. With few exceptions, I have preserved its line divisions, which means that I have given a separate line to each speech rather than dividing verse lines among speakers, as is the practice in some modern editions. In several cases I have preserved quarto readings that previous editors have tended to alter. Because it will be of interest to many readers, I have also preserved the first quarto's variability when it comes to Shylock's name in speech prefixes. Sometimes he is "Shylock" and sometimes "Jew." At one point in Act 4, Portia addresses him, "Is your name Shylock?" and he answers "Shylock is my name" but the speech prefix before this answer calls him "Jew." What would the effect of this generic labeling, which becomes increasingly consistent in the Trial Scene, have been on early readers of the play? What might it suggest about attitudes toward Shylock on stage in Shakespeare's time and beyond? We cannot be certain of the answers to these questions, but having the evidence of the quarto edition before us will allow us to begin to ask them in a way that takes textual evidence into account.

There are other cases as well in which the first quarto of the play is inconsistent with names and speech prefixes. In all modern editions, the clown Launcelot Gobbo is called "Launcelot" or "Lancelot." But in the quarto his name is usually spelled "Launcelet," or little lance— a name that can resonate in interesting ways with Shylock's knife.[1]

---

1. See John F. Andrews, "Textual Deviancy in *The Merchant of Venice*," in *The Merchant of Venice: New Critical Essays*, ed. John W. Mahon and Ellen MacLeod Mahon (New York and London: Routledge, 2002), pp. 165–77.

Similarly, Launcelot (or Launcelet) in the quarto sometimes has a last name spelled "Iobbe," which could be interpreted as "Job" rather than "Gobbo." When Launcelot is not on stage with his father, he is usually called simply "Clown" in the speech prefixes—Shylock is therefore not the only character who can fall into generic labeling. But the variations in Launcelot's name did not seem to me to be significant enough in terms of their possible resonance with the rest of the play, or in terms of their cultural implications for the greater world outside it, to justify a departure from the regularized names and speech prefixes by which the clown has traditionally been identified.

Other characters in *The Merchant of Venice* are even more challenged in terms of nomenclature. G. Wilson Knight's reading of the music in the play, reproduced later in this volume, cites a speech by "Salarino," a character that occurs nowhere in this Norton Critical Edition's text of the play. How many S-named friends do Bassanio and Antonio have, and what are their names? Salerio, Salanio, Solanio, Salarino, Salaryno, Salario, Sal., Sol., Sola., Sala.—all of these forms occur in the first quarto version, and they are by no means used consistently. At some points, one of these seemingly interchangeable characters is indicated in the stage directions as entering, but the actual speech prefixes that follow name another. Tweedledum or Tweedledee? A case can be made for three characters rather than two—Salerio, Solanio, and Salarino—but even then, they are not differentiated in the quarto with anything approaching consistency. Obviously someone was imaginative, mischievous, neglectful and/or oblivious during the writing or publishing of the play—either Shakespeare himself, altering in the course of composition the names he had given these minor speakers; or a copyist later on, misreading, mis-remembering or revising as he wrote; or perhaps the compositors in the printing house. But this confusion, however interesting, is of a different order than that between "Jew" and "Shylock," and this Norton Critical Edition follows other modern texts of the play in regularizing the minor S-named characters as simply "Salerio" and "Solanio."

In this Norton Critical Edition, with the exception of "Shylock" and "Jew," characters' names are silently regularized throughout, as are spelling and punctuation. I have, however, preserved archaic forms from the quarto wherever their pronunciation would differ perceptibly from the modern equivalents. Readers will encounter "moe" instead of "more" if "moe" is the quarto reading, and "squand'red" rather than "squandered" if the quarto reading is "squandred," which suggests a variant pronunciation "squan-dred." I have resisted the temptation to include the customary editorially supplied accents to mark words that regular meter requires to be pronounced as disyllabics, as in the final word of line three from the song for Bassanio (3.2), which could have read "nourishèd" instead of "nourished," the reading in this Norton Critical Edition. I have similarly resisted the temptation to supply elisions to smooth out the roughness in Shakespeare's verse, or to supply indentation for speeches to indicate their completion of iambic pentameter lines commenced by an earlier speaker, as is common in modern editions. These are matters that can easily be adjusted as desired by readers in the process of reading and actors in the process of studying their roles. It is salutary for all of us to realize that Shakespeare may frequently have departed from strict metrical regularity—quite possibly for greater effectiveness in the theater, where absolute fidelity to iambic pentameter can be soporific rather than invigorating.

As is always the case with modern editing of Shakespeare, the demands of clarity and consistency need to be balanced against our desire to preserve idiosyncratic features of the early text. My editorial additions to the quarto text—in the list of "Persons of the Play" and very frequently in stage directions—are given in square brackets. At several points, I have silently emended the quarto's language if I could not figure out how to make sense of it. Following is a list of those emendations. But no amount of modern editorial apologetics will compensate readers for the experience of delving into the quarto text for themselves, either online or in a modern facsimile edition such as *Shakespeare's Plays in Quarto*, ed. Michael J. B. Allen and Kenneth Muir (Berkeley and London: University of California Press, 1981), pp. 449–86. In the following list, the reading adopted in this Norton Critical Edition is listed to the left of the square bracket, and the quarto reading is given in original spelling to the right. Alterations to stage directions and speech headings, as discussed above, are not included on this list. Several of my emendations are drawn from later texts of the play—particularly from the first folio (1623)—but providing a full list of variant readings in later texts is outside the scope of this edition.

1.2:
p. 10, line 39 Palatine] Palentine.
p. 10, line 57 Falconbridge] Fauconbridge.
p. 11, lines 74, 75 vilely] vildlie, vildly (word occurs twice).
p. 11, line 106 fifth] fift.
p. 12, line 110 fifth] fift.
1.3:
p. 12, line 18 Rialto] Ryalta.
p. 20, line 70 murder] muder.
p. 21, line 88 last] lost.
2.6:
p. 28, line 15 younker] younger.
2.8:
p. 32, line 8 gondola] Gondylo.
p. 33, line 40 slubber] slumber.
3.1:
p. 38, line 90 heard] heere.

3.3:
p. 48, Stage direction at beginning of 3.3
     Solanio] Salerio.
3.4:
p. 49, line 13 equal] egall.
p. 50, line 51 cousin's] cosin.
3.5:
p. 52, line 23 comes] come.
p. 53, line 68 Is] in.
4.1:
p. 63, line 390 for God's sake] for Godsake.
p. 64, line 411 Speech prefix
     Gratiano] Shylock.
5.1:
p. 68, line 58 Stephano] Stephen.
p. 69, line 94 Erebus] Terebus.

SOURCES AND CONTEXTS

RICHARD ROBINSON

[The Tale of the Three Caskets from the *Gesta Romanorum*]†

[In this story, the King of Naples's virgin daughter is promised to the son of the Emperor of Rome as surety for her father's tribute to Rome and peace between the two kingdoms. En route to Rome for the wedding, her ship wrecks in a storm and she is swallowed by a whale. She stabs the whale, it comes ashore to die, and she calls out for rescue. An earl opens the whale and takes her out, whereupon she tells him that she is to be married to the son of the Emperor of Rome, but has lost all of her treasure in the sea. The earl sends the damsel to the Emperor of Rome.]

* * * Then was the emperor right glad of her safety and coming, and had great compassion on her, saying, "Ah, good maid, for the love of my son thou hast suffered much woe. Nevertheless, if thou be worthy to be his wife, soon shall I prove." And when he had thus said, he let bring[1] forth three vessels. The first was made of pure gold well beset[2] with precious stones without, and within, full of dead men's bones, and thereupon was engraven this posey:[3] "Whoso chooseth me shall find that he deserveth." The second vessel was made of fine silver, filled with earth and worms, and the superscription was thus: "Whoso chooseth me shall find that his nature desireth." The third vessel was made of lead, full within of precious stones, and thereupon was insculpt this posey: "Whoso chooseth me shall find that God hath disposed for him."

These three vessels the emperor showed to the maiden and said, "Lo here, daughter—these be noble vessels. If thou choose one of these wherein is profit to thee and to other then shalt thou have my son. And if thou choose that wherein is no profit to thee nor to none other, soothly thou shalt not wed him."

When the maiden saw this she lift up her hands to God and said, "Thou Lord which knowest all things, grant me grace this hour so to choose that I may receive the emperor's son." And with that she beheld the first vessel of gold, which was graven royally, and read this superscription: "Who so chooseth me, etc.," saying thus: "Though this vessel be full precious and made of pure gold, nevertheless know not I what is within; therefore, my dear lord, this ves-

---

† From *A Record of Ancient Histories Entitled in Latin Gesta Romanorum*, trans. Richard Robinson (1571; rpt. London, 1595), "The 32nd History," sigs. O2r–O5r.
1. Had brought.
2. Set.
3. Saying.

sel will I not choose." And then beheld she the second vessel that was of pure silver, and read the superscription, "Whoso chooseth me shall find that his nature desireth," thinking thus within herself: if I choose this vessel, what is within I know not, but well I wot[4] there shall I find that nature desireth, and my nature desireth the lust of the flesh, and therefore this vessel will I not choose.

When she had seen those two vessels and given an answer as touching two of them, she beheld the third vessel of lead and read the superscription: "Whoso chooseth me shall find that God hath disposed," thinking within herself, this vessel is not passing rich, ne[5] thoroughly precious; nevertheless the superscription saith, "Whoso chooseth me shall find that God hath disposed," and without doubt God never disposed any harm. Therefore as now I will choose this vessel, by the leave of God.

When the emperor saw this he said, "O good maiden, open thy vessel, for it is full of precious stones, and see if thou hast well chosen or no." And when this young lady had opened it, she found it full of fine gold and precious stones, like as the emperor had foretold her before. And then said the emperor, "O my dear daughter, because thou hast wisely chosen, therefore shalt thou wed my son." And when he had so said, he ordained a marriage and wedded them together with great solemnity and much honor, and so continued to their lives' end.

SER GIOVANNI FIORENTINO

[The Merchant of Venice]†

*　*　*

There was once in Florence, in the house of the Scali, a certain merchant called Bindo, who had sailed many times to Tana, near to Alexandria, and had likewise adventured in those other long voyages which are made for the sake of traffic. This Bindo, who was very rich, had three stalwart sons, and when he lay on his deathbed he bade come to him the eldest and the second born, and in their presence he made his will and left them heirs of all he possessed in the world. But to the youngest he left nothing. When the will was completed, the youngest son, who was called Giannetto, heard tell of the same, and went to his father's bedside and said, "Father, I am greatly astounded at what you have done, in taking no thought of

4. Know.
5. Nor.
† From *Il Pecorone* (1558), trans. W. G. Waters in *The Italian Novelists*, 7 vols. (London: Society of Bibliophiles, 1901), pp. 111–56.

me in your testament." The father answered, "My Giannetto, there is no one living I hold dearer than you, therefore I am not minded that you should tarry here after my death, but rather that you should betake yourself to Venice to your godfather, who is named Messer Ansaldo. He has no son of his own, and has written to me more than once to send you to him; moreover, I must tell you that he is the richest of all the Christian merchants. Wherefore I desire that you go to him after my death and give him this letter. If you manage your affairs with prudence, you will become a rich man." The young man answered, "My father, I am ready to do what you command." Whereupon the sick man gave him his blessing, and in a few days' time breathed his last. All the sons lamented sorely, and buried their father with due honours.

When a few days had passed the two brothers called Giannetto, and said to him, "Brother, it is true indeed that our father has made a will leaving us his heirs, and making no mention of you. Nevertheless, you are our brother, and from this time you shall have share in whatever may be left, equally with ourselves." Giannetto answered, "I thank you, my brothers, for what you offer, but I have made up my mind to seek my fortune in some other place. On this I am fully determined; wherefore you can take the heritage sanctified and assigned to you." The brothers, when they saw what his will was, gave him a horse and money for his charges. Giannetto took leave of them, and having journeyed to Venice and gone to the warehouse of Messer Ansaldo, he delivered the letter which his father had handed to him on his deathbed; and Messer Ansaldo, when he had read the same, learned that the young man before him was the son of his dear friend Bindo. As soon as he had read it he straightway embraced Giannetto, saying, "Welcome, dear godson, whom I have so greatly desired to see." Then he asked news of Bindo, and Giannetto replied that he was dead; whereupon Ansaldo embraced and kissed him, weeping the while, and said, "I am sorely grieved over Bindo's death, inasmuch as it was by his aid that I won the greater part of my wealth; but the joy I feel at your presence here is so great that it takes away the sting of my sorrow." Then he led Giannetto to his house, and gave orders to his workpeople, and those about his person, as well as to his grooms and servants, that they should do service to Giannetto even more zealously than to himself. The first thing he did was to hand over to Giannetto the key of all his ready money, saying, "My son, spend what you will; buy raiment and shoes to suit your taste; bid the townsfolk to dine with you, and make yourself known; for I leave you free to do what you will, and the better you are liked by our citizens the better I shall love you." So Giannetto began to keep company with the gentlefolk of Venice, to entertain, to give banquets and presents, to keep servants in livery, and to buy fine horses; moreover, he would joust and tilt, because he was very expert, and magnanimous and courteous in everything he did. He never failed to give honour and respect where they might be due, and he reverenced Messer Ansaldo as if he had been a hundred times his father. So prudent was his carriage with men of all conditions that he won the good-will of all the people of Venice, who regarded him as a youth of the greatest intelligence and most delightful manners, and courteous beyond measure; so that all the ladies, and the men as well, seemed in love with him. Messer Ansaldo had no eyes for any but him, so charmed was he with Giannetto's bearing and manners. Nor was any feast ever given to which he was not bidden.

It happened one day that two good friends of his determined to sail for Alexandria with some wares laden in two ships, as was their annual custom. They said to Giannetto, "You ought to give yourself the pleasure of a voyage with us, in order to see the world, especially Damascus and the parts thereabout." Giannetto answered, "In faith I would go willingly, if only Messer Ansaldo would give me leave." They replied, "We will see that he does this, be sure of that." They went forthwith to Messer Ansaldo and said to him, "We beg you to let Giannetto go with us this spring to Alexandria, and to give him a bark or vessel so that he may see something of the world." Messer Ansaldo replied that he was willing to let Giannetto do as he liked, and the others assured him that the young man would be well pleased to go. Then Messer Ansaldo let prepare[1] a very fine ship, which he loaded with much merchandise, and supplied with banners and arms and all that was necessary. And when all was in readiness Messer Ansaldo gave orders to the captain and the crew of the ship that they should do whatever Giannetto might direct, and he committed him to their care. "For," said he, "I am not sending him out for the sake of gain, but so that he may see the world as it best pleases him." When Giannetto went to embark, all Venice came to see him, for it was long time since any ship so fine or so well furnished had left the port; and when he had taken leave of Messer Ansaldo and of his companions he put out to sea and hoisted sail, and steered the course for Alexandria in the name of God and of good fortune.

After these three friends in their three ships had sailed on several days it chanced that early one morning Giannetto caught sight of a certain gulf in which was a very fair port, whereupon he asked the captain what might be the name of the place. The captain replied that it belonged to a certain lady, a widow, who had brought many to ruin. Giannetto inquired how they had been undone, and the

1. Had prepared.

captain replied, "Messere, this lady is very beautiful, and she has made it a law that, if any stranger lands there, he must needs share her bed, and, if he should have his will of her, that he should have her to wife and be the lord of the town and of all the country round. But if he should fail in his venture, he must lose all he has." Giannetto meditated for a moment, and then bade the captain land him at the port by some means or other, but the captain cried to him, "Messere, take care what you do, for many gentlemen have landed there, and every one has been ruined." But Giannetto said, "Trouble not yourself about others; do what I tell you." His command was obeyed; they put the ship about at once and made sail for the port, and those on board the other ships perceived not what was done.

In the harbour the next morning, when the news was spread that a fine ship had come into port, all the people flocked to see her, and it was told likewise to the lady, who forthwith sent for Giannetto. He went to her with all haste and made respectful obeisance; whereupon she took him by the hand and asked who he was, and whence he had come, and whether he knew the custom of the land. Giannetto answered that he did, and that he had come there by reason of this custom alone. The lady said, "You are welcome a hundred-fold," and all that day she treated him with the greatest honour, and bid come divers counts and barons and knights who were under her rule to keep Giannetto company. All these were mightily pleased with Giannetto's manners and his polished and pleasant and affable presence. Almost everyone felt kindly towards him, and all that day they danced and sang and made merry at the court for the sake of Giannetto, and everyone would have been well content to own him as over-lord.

When evening was come the lady took him by the hand and led him into the bedchamber, and said, "Meseems[2] it is time for us to go to bed." Whereto Giannetto made answer, "Madonna, I am at your commands." Then two damsels came, one bearing wine and the other sweetmeats, and the lady said, "Surely you must be thirsty; drink of this wine." Giannetto took some sweetmeats and drank of the wine, which was drugged to make him sleep, and he unwitting drank half a glass thereof, as it had the taste of good wine. Then he undressed and lay down on the bed, and fell asleep at once. The lady lay down beside him, but he woke not till it was past nine o'clock the next morning. As soon as it was day the lady arose, and made them begin unload the ship, which was filled with rich and fine merchandise. When nine o'clock had struck the waiting-maid went to the bed where Giannetto lay, and bade him rise

2. It seems to me.

and go his way with God's help, forasmuch as he had forfeited his
ship and all that was therein. He was greatly ashamed, and conscious that he had fared very ill in his adventure. The lady bade
them give him a horse and money for the way; and he, after a sad
and doleful journey, arrived at Venice, but he dared not for shame
go home. He called by night at the house of one of his friends, who
marvelled greatly at the sight of him, and said, "Alas! Giannetto,
what means this?" and Giannetto made answer, "My ship struck
one night upon a rock, and became a wreck, and everything was
broken up. One was cast here and another there, and I caught hold
of a piece of wood, on which I reached the shore. I returned hither
by land, and here I am."

Giannetto tarried some time in the house of his friend, who went
one day to see Messer Ansaldo, and found him in very melancholy
mood. Ansaldo said, "I am so sorely afeared lest this son of mine
should be dead, or that he have met some ill fortune at sea, that I
can find nor peace nor happiness, so great is my love for him." The
young man answered, "I can tell you news of him; he has been
shipwrecked and has lost everything, but he has escaped with his
life." "God be praised for this," said Messer Ansaldo; "so long as he
has saved himself I am contented, and care naught for what he has
lost. But where is he?" The young man replied that Giannetto was
in his house; whereupon Messer Ansaldo arose forthwith and was
fain to go thither, and when he saw Giannetto he ran towards him
and embraced him, saying, "My son, you need feel no shame for
what has befallen you, inasmuch as it is no rare thing for a ship to
be wrecked at sea. Be not cast down, for, since no hurt has come to
you, I can rejoice." Then he took Giannetto home and cheered him
the best he could, and the news spread through Venice, everyone
being grieved for the loss which had befallen him.

Before long Giannetto's companions returned from Alexandria,
having won great profit from their venture, and as soon as they
landed they asked for news of him. When they heard his story they
went straightway to greet him, saying, "How did you leave our company, and where did you go? When we lost sight of you, we turned
back on our course for a whole day, but we could neither see aught
of your ship nor learn where you had gone. Thus we fell into such
grief that, for the whole of our voyage, we knew not what merriment was, deeming[3] you to be dead." Giannetto answered, "An ad-
verse wind arose in a certain inlet of the sea, which drove my ship
on a rock near the shore, and caused her to sink. I barely escaped
with my life, and everything I had was lost." This was the excuse
made by Giannetto to conceal his failure, and all his friends made

3. Believing.

merry with him, thanking God that his life had been spared, and saying, "Next spring, with God's help, we will earn as much as you have lost this voyage; so let us now enjoy ourselves without giving way to sadness," and they took their pleasure according to their wont.[4] But Giannetto could not banish the thought of how he might return to that lady, pondering with himself and saying, "Certes,[5] I must make her my wife or die," and he could not shake off his sadness. Wherefore Messer Ansaldo besought him often that he should not grieve; for that, with the great wealth he possessed, they could live very well, but Giannetto answered that he could know no rest until he should have once more made that voyage over seas.

When Messer Ansaldo saw what his longing was, he let furnish for him in due time another ship, laden with yet richer cargo than the first, spending in this venture the main portion of his possessions; and the crew, as soon as they had stored the vessel with all that was needful, put out to sea with Giannetto on board, and set sail on the voyage. Giannetto kept constant watch to espy the port where the lady dwelt, which was known as the port of the lady of Belmonte, and, having sailed one night up to the entrance thereof, which was in an arm of the sea, he suddenly recognized it, and bade them turn the sails and steer into it in such fashion that his friends on board the other ships might know naught of what he did. The lady, when she arose in the morning, looked towards the port, where she saw flying the flag of Giannetto's ship, and, having recognized it at once, she called one of her chambermaids and said to her, "Know you what flag that is?" and the maid replied that it was the ship of the young man who had come there just a year ago, and who had left with them all his possessions to their great satisfaction. Then said the lady, "It is true what you say, and certes he must be hugely enamoured of me, seeing that I have never known one of these to come back a second time." The maid said, "I indeed never saw a more courteous and gracious gentleman than he;" whereupon the lady sent out to Giannetto a troop of grooms and pages, who went joyfully on board the ship. He received them in like spirit, and then went up to the castle and presented himself to the lady.

She, when she met him, embraced him with joy and delight, and he returned her greeting with reverent devotion. All that day they made merry, for the lady had bid come to her court divers ladies and gentlemen, and these entertained Giannetto joyfully for the love they bore him. The men grieved over the fate which was in store for him, for they would gladly have hailed him as their lord on

4. Custom.
5. Certainly.

account of his charm and courtesy, while the women were almost all in love with him when they saw with what dexterity he led the dance, and how he always wore a merry face as if he had been the son of some great lord. When it seemed to her time to retire, the lady took Giannetto by the hand and said, "Let us go to bed," and when they had gone into the chamber, and had disposed themselves to rest, two damsels came with wine and sweetmeats, whereof they ate and drank, and then went to bed. Giannetto fell asleep as soon as he lay down; whereupon the lady undressed and placed herself beside him, but he did not awake from sleep all night. As soon as it was day the lady arose and bade them quickly unload the vessel, and when it was nine o'clock Giannetto awoke, but on seeking for the lady he could not find her. Then he lifted up his head and perceived that it was broad day; so he got up, covered with disgrace, and once more they gave him a horse and money for the journey, and said "Go your way," and he departed full of shame and sorrow. He journeyed for many days without halt till he came to Venice, and there he went by night to the house of his friend, who, when he saw him, was hugely amazed and said, "Alas! and what can this mean?" Giannetto replied," I am in evil case. Accursed be the fortune which led me into that land!" His friend replied, "Certes, you may well miscall your fortune, since you have ruined Messer Ansaldo, the greatest and the richest of our Christian merchants; but still your shame is worse than his loss."

Giannetto lay hid some days in his friend's house, knowing not what to say or do, and almost minded to return to Florence without speaking a word to Messer Ansaldo; but at last he determined to seek him, and when Ansaldo beheld him he arose and ran to him and embraced him, saying, "Welcome to you, my son," and Giannetto embraced him, weeping the while. Then, when he had learnt all, Messer Ansaldo said, "Listen to me, Giannetto, and give over grieving; for, as long as I have you back again, I am contented. We still have enough to allow us to live in modest fashion. The sea is always wont to give to one and to take from another." It was soon noised abroad in Venice what had happened, and all men were much grieved over the loss which Messer Ansaldo had suffered, for he was obliged to sell many of his chattels[6] in order to pay the creditors who had supplied him with goods. It happened that the adventurers who had set sail with Giannetto returned from Alexandria with great profit, and as soon as they landed they heard how Giannetto had come back broken in fortune; wherefore they were greatly amazed and said, "This is the strangest matter that ever was." Then they went with great laughter and merriment to Messer

6. Personal property.

Ansaldo and Giannetto and said, "Messere, be not cast down, for we have settled to go next year to trade on your account, seeing that we have been in a way the cause of your loss, in that we persuaded Giannetto to go with us. Fear nothing, for as long as we have anything you may treat it as your own." On this account Messer Ansaldo thanked them, and said that he had as yet enough left to give him sustenance.

But it came to pass that Giannetto, pondering these matters day and night, could not shake off his sorrow; wherefore Messer Ansaldo demanded to know what ailed him, and Giannetto answered, "I shall never know content till I have regained you what I have lost." Messer Ansaldo answered, "My son, I would not that you should leave me again, for it will be better for us to live modestly on what is left to us than for you to put aught else to hazard." Giannetto said, "I am determined to do all I can, forasmuch as I should hold myself to be in most shameful case were I to bide here in this fashion." Then Messer Ansaldo, seeing that his mind was set thereon, made provision to sell all that he had left in the world, and to equip for him another vessel; and, after he had sold everything, so that he had naught left, he loaded a fine vessel with merchandise, and, because he wanted yet ten thousand ducats to complete his venture, he went to a certain Jew of Mestri,[7] with whom he made an agreement that, if he should not repay the debt by Saint John's day in the June following, the Jew should have the right to take a pound of his flesh, and to cut the same from what place so ever he listed. Messer Ansaldo having duly agreed, and the Jew having drawn up a binding document with witnesses, using all the precautions and formalities which the occasion demanded, the ten thousand gold ducats were handed over, and with the same Messer Ansaldo supplied all that was wanting in the ship's cargo. In sooth, if the other two vessels had been fine and fair, this third was much richer and better furnished. In like manner Giannetto's friends fitted out their vessels, with the intention of giving to him whatever they might gain by traffic.

When the day of departure had come and they were about to sail, Messer Ansaldo said to Giannetto, "My son, you are going away, and you see with what bond I am bound. One favour I beg of you, which is, that if perchance you should again miscarry, you will return hither, so that I may see you again before I die; then I shall be content to depart;" and Giannetto answered that he would do all things which to him seemed agreeable to Messer Ansaldo's wishes. Then Ansaldo gave him his blessing, and, having taken leave, they set sail on their voyage. The two friends who sailed with Giannetto kept

7. Mestre, Italy, mainland town just across from the islands of Venice.

good watch over his ship, while he thought of nothing else than how he might again drop into the harbour of Belmonte. Indeed, he gained over to his interests one of the steersmen so completely that he caused the vessel to be brought one night into the port of the lady's city. When in the morning the light grew clear, his two friends in the other two ships conferred and deliberated, and, since they saw nothing of Giannetto's ship, they said one to the other, "In sooth, this is an evil turn for him," and then they kept on their course, wondering greatly the while. When the vessel entered the port all the people of the city ran to see her, and when they learned that it was Giannetto come once again they marvelled amain,[8] saying, "Certes, he must be the son of some great prince, seeing that he comes hither every year with such a fine ship and such great store of merchandise. Would to God that he were our ruler!" Then all the chief men and the barons and cavaliers of the land went to visit Giannetto, and word was carried to the lady how he was once more in the port. Whereupon she went to the window of the palace, and, as soon as she espied the fine vessel and the banner thereof, she made the sign of the holy cross and said, "Of a surety this is a great day for me, for it is the same gentleman who has already brought such wealth into the land." And she forthwith sent for Giannetto.

He repaired to her presence, and they embraced one another and exchanged greetings and reverence, and then the people set themselves to make merry all that day, and, for the love they had for Giannetto, they held a stately jousting, many barons and cavaliers running a course. Giannetto also was minded to show his skill, and indeed he wrought such marvellous deeds, and showed such great prowess both with his arms and his horse, and won so completely the favour of the barons, that they all desired to have him to rule over them. And when evening had come, and it was time to retire, the lady took Giannetto by the hand and said, "Let us go to bed." When they came to the chamber door one of the lady's waiting-women, who had pity for Giannetto, put her lips close to his ear and said in a whisper, "Make a show of drinking the wine, but taste it not." Giannetto caught the meaning of her words, and entered the room with the lady, who said, "I am sure you must be athirst; wherefore I will that you take a draught before you lie down to sleep." Straightway came two damsels, who were as fair as angels, bearing wine and sweetmeats according to their wont, and making ready the draught. Then said Giannetto, "Who could refuse to drink with cupbearers so lovely as these?" The lady laughed, and Giannetto took the cup and feigned to drink therefrom, but he poured the wine down into his breast. The lady however believed that he had indeed drunk of the same, and said to herself, "Thou

8. Greatly.

wilt sail here again with another ship, for thou hast lost the one in the port."

Giannetto got into bed and found himself with his wits clear and full of desire, and the time that sped before the lady came to his side seemed a thousand years. He said to himself, "Certes, I have caught her this time, and she shall no longer have reason to think of me as a glutton and a toper."[9] And, in order to let her come the quicker to bed, he began to snore and to feign to be sleeping. When the lady saw this she said, "All is well," and quickly undressed herself and lay down beside Giannetto, who lost no time, but, as soon as the lady was under the sheets, he turned and embraced her, saying, "Now I have that which I have so long desired," and with these words he gave her the greeting of holy matrimony, and all that night she lay in his arms; wherefore she was well content. The next morning she arose before dawn, and let summon all the barons and cavaliers and many of the citizens, and said to them, "Giannetto is your lord; so let us make merry," and at these words there went a shout through all the land, "Long live our lord, Giannetto!" The bells and the musical instruments gave notice of the feast, and word was sent to divers barons and counts who dwelt far from the city bidding them come and see their ruler. There were merrymakings and feastings many and sumptuous, and when Giannetto came forth from the chamber they made him a cavalier and set him upon the throne, giving him a wand to hold in his hand, and proclaiming him lord with much state and rejoicing.

When all the barons and ladies of the land were come to court, Giannetto took to wife the lady with rejoicings and delights so great that they can neither be described nor imagined. For at this time all the barons and nobles of the country came to the feast, and there was no lack of merry jesting, and jousting, and sword-play, and dancing, and singing, and music, and all the other sports appertaining to jollity and rejoicing. Messer Giannetto, like a high-spirited gentleman, made presents of silken stuffs and of other rich wares which he had brought with him. He was a strong ruler, and made himself respected by the equal justice he maintained towards men of all classes. Thus he lived his life in joy and gladness, and gave no thought to Messer Ansaldo, who, luckless wight as he was, remained a living pledge for the ten thousand ducats which he had borrowed from the Jew.

One day Messer Giannetto, standing with his wife at the window of the palace, saw, passing through the piazza, a band of men bearing lighted torches in their hands, as if they were going to make some offering. Giannetto inquired of her what this might mean;

9. Drunkard.

whereupon she replied that it was a company of craftsmen going to pay their vows at the church of San Giovanni on the festival of the saint. Messer Giannetto then remembered Messer Ansaldo, and, having gone away from the window, he sighed deeply and became grave of countenance, and walked up and down the hall thinking over what he had just seen. The lady asked what ailed him, and he replied that nothing was amiss; but she began to question him, saying, "Certes, you are troubled with something you are loth to tell me," and she spake so much on the matter that at last Messer Giannetto told her how Messer Ansaldo was held in pledge for ten thousand ducats, and that the time for repayment expired this very day. "Wherefore," he said, "I am smitten with great sorrow that my father should have to die for me; for unless his debt shall be repaid today, he is bound to have cut from his body a pound of flesh." The lady said, "Messere, mount your horse quickly, and travel thither by land, for you can travel more speedily thus than by sea. Take what following you wish, and a hundred thousand ducats to boot, and halt not till you shall be come to Venice. Then, if your father be still living, bring him back here with you." Whereupon Giannetto let the trumpets sound forthwith; and, having mounted with twenty companions and taken money enough, he set out for Venice.

When the time set forth in the bond had expired, the Jew caused Messer Ansaldo to be seized, and then he declared he meant to cut away from his debtor the pound of flesh. But Messer Ansaldo begged him to let him live a few days longer, so that, in case Giannetto should return, he might at least see his son once more. The Jew replied that he was willing to grant this favour, so far as the respite was concerned, but that he was determined to have his pound of flesh according to his agreement, though a hundred Giannettos should come; and Messer Ansaldo declared that he was content. All the people of Venice were talking of this matter, everyone being grieved thereanent,[1] and divers traders made a partnership together to pay the money, but the Jew would not take it, being minded rather to do this bloody deed, so that he might boast that he had slain the chief of the Christian merchants. Now it happened that, after Messer Giannetto set forth eagerly for Venice, his wife followed immediately behind him clad in legal garb and taking two servants with her.

When Messer Giannetto had come to Venice he went to the Jew's house, and, having joyfully embraced Messer Ansaldo, he next turned to the Jew, and said he was ready to pay the money that was due, and as much more as he cared to demand. But the Jew made answer that he wanted not the money, since it had not been paid in

1. About it.

due time, but that he desired to cut his pound of flesh from Ansaldo. Over this matter there arose great debate, and everyone condemned the Jew; but, seeing that equitable law ruled in Venice, and that the Jew's contract was fully set forth and in customary legal form, no one could deny him his rights; all they could do was to entreat his mercy.

On this account all the Venetian merchants came there to entreat the Jew, but he grew harder than before, and then Messer Giannetto offered to give him twenty thousand, but he would not take them; then he advanced his offer to thirty, then to forty, then to fifty, and finally to a hundred thousand ducats. Then the Jew said, "See how this thing stands! If you were to offer me more ducats than the whole city of Venice is worth, I would not take them. I would rather have what this bond says is my due." And while this dispute was going on there arrived in Venice the lady of Belmonte, clad as a doctor of laws. She took lodging at an inn, the host of which inquired of one of her servants who this gentleman might be. The servant, who had been instructed by the lady as to what reply he should make to a question of this sort, replied that his master was a doctor of laws who was returning home after a course of study at Bologna. The host when he heard this did them great reverence, and while the doctor of laws sat at table he inquired of the host in what fashion the city of Venice was governed; whereupon the host replied, "Messere, we make too much of justice here." When the doctor inquired how this could be, the host went on to say, "I will tell you how, Messere. Once there came hither from Florence a youth whose name was Giannetto. He came to reside with his godfather, who was called Messer Ansaldo, and so gracious and courteous did he show himself to everyone, that all the ladies of Venice, and the gentlemen as well, held him very dear. Never before had there come to our city so seemly a youth. Now this godfather of his fitted out for him, on three different occasions, three ships, all of great value, and every time disaster befell his venture. But for the equipment of the last ship Messer Ansaldo had not money enough, so he had perforce to borrow ten thousand ducats of a certain Jew upon these terms, to wit, that if by the day of San Giovanni in the following June he should not have repaid the debt, the Jew aforesaid should be free to cut away, from whatever part of his body he would, a pound of flesh. Now this much-desired youth has returned from his last voyage, and, in lieu of the ten thousand ducats, has offered to give a hundred thousand, but this villainous Jew will not accept them; so all our excellent citizens are come hither to entreat him, but all their prayers profit nothing." The doctor said, "This is an easy question to settle." Then cried the host, "If you will only take the trouble to bring it to an end, without letting this good man die, you will win the love and gratitude of the most worthy young man that ever was born, and besides this the goodwill of every citizen of our state."

After hearing these words of the host the doctor let publish a notice through all the state of Venice, setting forth how all those with any question of law to settle should repair to him. The report having come to the ears of Messer Giannetto that there was come from Bologna a doctor of laws who was ready to settle the rights and wrongs of every dispute, he went to the Jew and suggested that they should go before the doctor aforesaid, and the Jew agreed, saying at the same time that, come what might, he would demand the right to do all that his bond allowed him. When they came before the doctor of laws, and gave him due salutation, he recognized Messer Giannetto, who meantime knew not the doctor to be his wife, because her face was stained with a certain herb. Messer Giannetto and the Jew spake their several pleas, and set the question fully in order before the doctor, who took up the bond and read it, and then said to the Jew, "I desire that you now take these hundred thousand ducats, and let go free this good man, who will ever be bound to you by gratitude." The Jew replied, "I will do naught of this." Whereupon the doctor persuaded him again thereto, saying it would be the better course for him, but the Jew would not consent. Then they agreed to go to the proper court for such affairs, and the doctor, speaking on behalf of Messer Ansaldo, said, "Let the merchant be brought here," and they fetched him forthwith, and the doctor said, "Now take your pound of flesh where you will, and do your work."

Then the Jew made Messer Ansaldo strip himself, and took in his hand a razor which he had brought for the purpose; whereupon Messer Giannetto turned to the doctor and said, "Messere, this is not the thing I begged you to do." But the doctor bade him take heart, for the Jew had not yet cut off his pound of flesh. As the Jew approached, the doctor said, "Take care what you do; for, if you cut away more or less than a pound of flesh, you shall lose your own head; and I tell you, moreover, that if you let flow a single drop of blood, you shall die, for the reason that your bond says naught as to the shedding of blood. It simply gives you the right to take a pound of flesh, and says neither less nor more. Now, if you are a wise man, you will consider well which may be the best way to compass this task." Then the doctor bade them summon the executioner, and fetch likewise the axe and the block; and he said to the Jew, "As soon as I see the first drop of blood flow, I will have your head stricken off." Hereupon the Jew began to be afeared, and Messer Giannetto to take heart; and, after much fresh argument, the Jew said, "Messer doctor, you have greater wit in these affairs than I have; so now give me those hundred thousand ducats, and I will be satisfied." But the doctor replied that he might take his pound of flesh, as his bond said, for he should not be allowed a single piece of money now; he should have taken it when it was offered to him. Then the Jew came to ninety, and then to eighty thousand, but the doctor stood firmer than ever to his word. Messer Giannetto spake to the doctor, saying, "Give him what he asks, so that he lets Messer Ansaldo go free." But the doctor replied that the settlement of the question had better be left to himself. The Jew now cried out that he would take fifty thousand; but the doctor answered, "I would not give you the meanest coin you ever had in your pouch." The Jew went on, "Give me at least the ten thousand ducats that are my own, and cursed be heaven and earth!" Then said the doctor, "Do you not understand that you will get nothing at all? If you are minded to take what is yours, take it; if not, I will protest, and cause your bond to be annulled."

At these words all those who were assembled rejoiced exceedingly, and began to put flouts and jests upon the Jew, saying, "This fellow thought to play a trick, and see he is tricked himself." Then the Jew, seeing that he could not have his will, took his bonds and cut them in pieces in his rage; whereupon Messer Ansaldo was at once set free and led with the greatest rejoicing to Messer Giannetto's house. Next Giannetto took the hundred thousand ducats and went to the doctor, whom he found in his chamber making ready to depart, and said, "Messere, you have done me the greatest service I have ever known, and for this reason I would that you take with you this money, which, certes, you have well earned." The doctor replied, "Messer Giannetto, I thank you heartily; but as I have no need of the money, keep it yourself, so that your wife may not charge you with wasting your substance." Messer Giannetto answered, "By my faith, she is so generous and kindly and good, that, even were I to lavish four times the money I have here, she would not complain; in sooth, she was fain that I should take with me a much greater sum than this." The doctor inquired whether Giannetto were contented with this wife of his, and Giannetto replied, "There is no one God ever made who is so dear to me as she is; she is so prudent and so fair that nature could not possibly excel her. Now, if you will do me the favour to come and visit me, and see her, I trow you will be amazed at the honourable reception she will give you, and you can see for yourself whether or not she is all that I now tell you." The doctor of laws replied, "I cannot visit you as you desire, seeing that I have other business in hand; but, since you tell me that your wife is so virtuous a lady, salute her on my behalf when you see her." Messer Giannetto declared that he would not fail to do this, but he still urged the doctor to accept the money as a gift.

While they were thus debating the doctor espied upon Messer Giannetto's hand a ring, and said, "I would fain have that ring of yours, but money of any sort I will not take." Messer Giannetto answered, "It shall be as you wish, but I give you this ring somewhat unwillingly, for my wife gave me the same, saying that I must always keep it out of love for her. Now, were she to see me without the ring, she would deem that I had given it to some other woman, and would be wroth with me, and believe I had fallen in love otherwhere,[2] but in sooth I love her better than I love myself." The doctor replied, "Certes, if she love you as much as you say, she will believe you when you tell her that you gave it to me. But perchance you want to give it to some old sweetheart of yours here in Venice." Messer Giannetto answered, "So great are the love and the trust I have for her, that there is not a lady in the world for whom I would exchange her, so consummately fair is she in every sense," and with these words he drew from his finger the ring, which he gave to the doctor, and they embraced each other, saluting with due respect. The doctor asked Messer Giannetto if he would grant him a favour, and being answered in the affirmative, he went on to say, "I would that you tarry not here, but go straightway home to your wife." Messer Giannetto declared that the time yet to elapse before meeting her would be as long to him as a thousand years, and in this wise they took leave of one another.

The doctor embarked and went his way, while Messer Giannetto let celebrate divers banquets, and gave horses and money to his companions, and the merrymaking went on for several days. He kept open house, and at last he bade farewell to the Venetians, and took Messer Ansaldo with him, many of his old friends accompanying them on their voyage. Well nigh all the gentlemen and the ladies shed tears over his departure, so gracious had been his carriage with everyone what time he had abode in Venice, and thus he departed and returned to Belmonte. It happened that his wife had come there some days before, having given out that she had been away at the baths, and had once more put on woman's garb. Now she prepared great feastings, and hung all the streets with silk, and bade divers companies of men-at-arms array themselves; so when Messer Giannetto and Messer Ansaldo arrived all the barons and the courtiers met them, crying out, "Long live our lord!" When they had landed the lady ran to embrace Messer Ansaldo, but with Messer Giannetto she seemed somewhat angered, albeit she held him dearer than her own self. And they made high festival with jousting, and sword-play, and dancing, and singing, in which all the barons and ladies present at the court took part.

2. Somewhere else.

When Messer Giannetto perceived that his wife did not welcome him with that good humour which was her wont, he went into the chamber, and, having called her, asked her what was amiss, and offered to embrace her; but she said, "I want no caresses of yours, for I am well assured that you have met some old sweetheart of yours at Venice." Messer Giannetto began to protest; whereupon the lady cried, "Where is the ring I gave you?" Messer Giannetto answered, "That which I thought would happen has indeed come to pass, for I said you must needs think evil of what I did; but I swear to you, by the faith I have in God and in yourself, that I gave the ring to that doctor of laws who helped me win the suit against the Jew." The lady said, "And I swear to you, by the faith I have in God and in you, that you gave it to a woman. I am sure of this, and you are not ashamed to swear as you have sworn." Messer Giannetto went on, "I pray that God may strike me dead if I do not speak the truth; moreover, I spake as I told you to the doctor when he begged the ring of me." The lady replied, "You had better abide henceforth in Venice, and leave Messer Ansaldo here, while you take your pleasure with your wantons; in sooth, I hear they all wept when you left them." Messer Giannetto burst into tears, and, greatly troubled, cried out, "You swear to what is not and cannot be true;" whereupon the lady, perceiving from his tears that she had struck a knife into his heart, quickly ran to him and embraced him, laughing heartily the while. She showed him the ring, and told him everything: what he had said to the doctor of laws; how she herself was that same doctor, and in what wise he had given her the ring. Thereupon Messer Giannetto was mightily astonished; and, when he saw that it was all true, he made merry thereanent. When he went forth from the chamber he told the story to all the barons and to his friends about the court, and from this adventure the love between this pair became greater than ever. And afterwards Messer Giannetto let summon that same waiting-woman who had counselled him not to drink the wine, and gave her in marriage to Messer Ansaldo, and they all lived together in joy and feasting as long as their lives lasted.

ANONYMOUS

[Ballad of a Cruel Jew]†

[To be sung] to the tune of "Black and Yellow."

THE FIRST PART.

In Venice town not long ago
    A cruel Jew did dwell,
Which lived all on usury
    As Italian writers tell.

Gernutus called was the Jew,
    Which never thought to die,
Nor never yet did any good
    To them in streets that lie.

His life was like a barrow hog,
    That liveth many a day,
Yet never once doth any good,
    Until men will him slay.

Or like a filthy heap of dung,
    That lyeth in a hoard,
Which never can do any good
    Till it be spread abroad.

So fares it with the usurer.
    He cannot sleep in rest
For fear the thief will him pursue
    To pluck him from his nest.

His heart doth think on many a wile
    How to deceive the poor.
His mouth is almost full of muck,
    Yet still he gapes for more.

His wife must lend a shilling,
    For every week a penny;
Yet bring a pledge that's double worth
    If that you will have any.

---

† Reproduced in modernized spelling from *A New Variorum Edition of Shakespeare*, vol. 7: *The Merchant of Venice*, ed. Horace Howard Furness (Philadelphia and London: J. B. Lippincott, 1895), pp. 288–92. This ballad is probably from the sixteenth or seventeenth century, but since we cannot be precise about its date we cannot know certainly whether it preceded or followed Shakespeare's *Merchant of Venice*.

And see, likewise, you keep your day
   Or else you lose it all.
This was the living of the wife:
   Her "cow" she did it call.

Within that city dwelt that time
   A merchant of great fame,
Which being distressed in his need,
   Unto Gernutus came,

Desiring him to stand his friend
   For twelve month and a day,
To lend to him an hundred crowns,
   And he for it would pay

Whatsoever he would demand of him,
   And pledges he should have.
"No," quoth the Jew with fleering looks,[1]
   "Sir, ask what you will have.

"No penny for the loan of it
   For one year you shall pay.
You may do me as good a turn
   Before my dying day.

"But we will have a merry jest
   For to be talked long;
You shall make me a bond," quoth he,
   "That shall be large and strong.

"And this shall be the forfeiture:
   Of your own flesh a pound.
If you agree, make you the bond,
   And here is a hundred crowns."

"With right good will!" the merchant says,
   And so the bond was made.
When twelve month and a day drew on
   That back it should be paid,

The merchant's ships were all at sea,
   And money came not in.
Which way to take or what to do
   To think he doth begin.

---

1. Smiling obsequiously.

And to Gernutus straight he comes
   With cap and bended knee,
And said to him, "Of courtesy,
   I pray you bear with me.

"My day is come and I have not
   The money for to pay;
And little good the forfeiture
   Will do you, I dare say."

"With all my heart," Gernutus said,
   "Command it to your mind.
In things of bigger weight than this
   You shall me ready find."

He goes his way. The day once past,
   Gernutus doth not slack
To get a sergeant presently
   And clapped him on the back.

And laid him into prison strong,
   And sued his bond withal;
And when the judgment day was come,
   For judgment he did call.

The merchant's friends came thither fast,
   With many a weeping eye;
For other means they could not find,
   But he that day must die.

THE SECOND PART.

Some offered for his hundred crowns
   Five hundred for to pay;
And some a thousand, two or three,
   Yet still he did denay.[2]

And at the last ten thousand crowns
   They offered him to save.
Gernutus said, "I will no gold:
   My forfeit I will have.

"A pound of flesh is my demand,
   And that shall be my hire."
Then said the judge, "Yet, my good friend,
   Let me of you desire

2. Say no.

"To take the flesh from such a place
    As yet you let him live.
Do so, and lo! An hundred crowns
    To thee here will I give."

"No, no," quoth he, "No, judgment here!
    For this it shall be tried.
For I will have my pound of flesh
    From under his right side."

It grieved all the company
    His cruelty to see;
For neither friend nor foe could help,
    But he must spoiled[3] be.

The bloody Jew now ready is
    With whetted blade in hand
To spoil the blood of innocent
    By forfeit of his bond.

And as he was about to strike
    In him the deadly blow,
"Stay," quoth the judge, "thy cruelty—
    I charge thee to do so.

"Sith[4] needs thou wilt thy forfeit have,
    Which is of flesh a pound,
See that you shed no drop of blood,
    Nor yet the man confound.

"For if thou do, like murderer
    Thou here shalt hanged be.
Likewise of flesh see that thou cut
    No more than 'longs to thee.

"For if thou take either more or less
    To the value of a mite,
Thou shalt be hanged presently
    As is both law and right."

Gernutus now waxed frantic mad,
    And wotes[5] not what to say.
Quoth he at last, "Ten thousand crowns
    I will that he shall pay—

3. Pillaged, ravaged.
4. Since.
5. Knows.

"And so I grant to set him free."
    The judge doth answer make,
"You shall not have a penny given;
    Your forfeiture now take."

At the last he doth demand
    But for to have his own.
"No," quoth the judge, "do as you list,
    Thy judgment shall be shown.

"Either take your pound of flesh," quoth he,
    "Or cancel me your bond."
"O cruel judge," then quoth the Jew,
    "That doth against me stand!"

And so with griping, grieved mind
    He biddeth them farewell.
Then all the people praised the Lord
    That ever this heard tell.

Good people that do hear this song
    For truth, I dare well say
That many a wretch as ill as he
    Doth live now at this day.

That seeketh nothing but the spoil
    Of many a wealthy man,
And for to trap the innocent,
    Deviseth what they can.

From whom the Lord deliver me,
    And every Christian too;
And send to them like sentence eke[6]
    That meaneth so to do.

SIR THOMAS ELYOT

[The True Meaning of Friendship]†

Now let us ensearch[1] what friendship or amity is. Aristotle saith
friendship is a virtue or joineth with virtue. Which is affirmed by

6. Also.
† From *The Book Named the Governor* (1531; rpt. London, 1580), sigs. P6v–Q1v.
1. Search out.

Tully, saying friendship can not be without virtue, neither[2] but in good men only. Who be good men he after declareth to be those persons which so do bear themselves and in such wise do live that their faith, surety, equality, and liberality be sufficiently proved. Neither that there is in them any covetousness, wilfulness, or foolhardiness, and that in them is great stability or constance. Them suppose I (as they be taken) to be called good men which do follow, as much as men may, nature—the chief captain or guide of man's life. Moreover, the same Tully defineth friendship in this manner, saying it is none other thing but a perfect consent of all things appertaining as well to God as to man, with benevolence and charity; and that he knoweth nothing given of God, except sapience, to man more commodious. Which definition is excellent and very true. For in God and all thing that cometh of God, nothing is of more greater estimation than love, called in Latin *amor*, whereof *amicitia* cometh, named in English *friendship* or *amity*, the which taken away from the life of man, no house shall abide standing, no field shall be in culture.[3] And that is lightly[4] perceived if a man do remember what cometh of dissention and discord. Finally, he seemeth to take the sun from the world that taketh friendship from man's life.

Since friendship can not be but in good men, nor may not be without virtue, we may be assured that thereof none evil may proceed, or therewith any evil thing may participate. Wherefore in as much as it may be but in a few persons (good men being in a small number), and also it is rare and seldom (as all virtues be commonly), I will declare after the opinion of philosophers, and partly by common experience, who among good men be of nature most apt to friendship.

Between all men that be good cannot always be amity; but it also requireth that they be of semblable or much like manners or study, and specially of manners. For gravity and affability be every[5] of them laudable qualities; so be severity and placability; also magnificence and liberality be noble virtues. And yet frugality, which is a soberness or moderation in living, is—and that for good cause—of all wise men extolled. Yet where these virtues and qualities be separately in sundry persons assembled may well be perfect concord, but friendship is there seldom or never, for that which one for a virtue embraceth the other contemneth or at the least neglecteth. Wherefore it seemeth that wherein the one delighteth is repugnant to the other's nature. And where is any repugnancy may be none amity, since friendship is an entire consent of wills and desires.

2. Nor. "Tully": Roman orator Marcus Tullius Cicero.
3. Cultivation.
4. Easily.
5. Each.

Therefore it is seldom seen that friendship is between these persons: a man sturdy, of opinion inflexible, and of sour countenance and speech, with him that is tractable and with reason persuaded, and of sweet countenance and entertainment. Also between him which is elevate in authority and another of a very base estate or degree. Yea, and if they be both in an equal dignity, if they be desirous to climb, as they do ascend so friendship for the more part decayeth. For as Tully saith in his first book of *Offices*, what thing soever it be, in the which many cannot excel or have therein superiority, therein often times is such a contention that it is a thing of all other most difficile[6] to keep among them good or virtuous company—that is as much to say as to retain among them friendship and amity. And it is often times seen that divers, which before they came in authority were of good and virtuous conditions, being in their prosperity were utterly changed and, despising their old friends, set all their study and pleasure on their new acquaintance. Wherein men shall perceive to be a wonderful blindness, or, as I might say, a madness, if they note diligently all that I shall hereafter write of friendship.

But now to resort to speak of them in whom friendship is most frequent, and they also thereto be most aptly disposed, undoubtedly it is specially they which be wise and of nature inclined to beneficence, liberality, and constancy. For by wisdom is marked and substantially discerned the words, acts, and demeanor of all men between whom happeneth to be any intercourse or familiarity, whereby is engendered a favor or disposition of love. Beneficence, that is to say, mutually putting to their study and help in necessary affairs, induceth love. They that be liberal do withhold or hide nothing from them whom they love, whereby love increaseth. And in them that be constant is never mistrust or suspicion, or any surmise or evil report can withdraw them from their affection. And hereby friendship is made perpetual and stable. But if similitude of study or learning be joined unto the said virtues, friendship much rather happeneth, and the mutual interview and conversation is much more pleasant, specially if the studies have in them any delectable affection or motion. For where they be too serious or full of contention, friendship is oftentimes assaulted, whereby it is often in peril. Where the study is elegant and the matter illecebrous, that is to say, sweet to the reader, the course whereof is rather gentle persuasion and quick reasonings than over-subtle argument or litigious controversies, there also it happeneth that the students do delight one in another and be without envy or malicious contention.

6. Difficult.

Now let us try out what is that friendship that we suppose to be in good men. Verily it is a blessed and stable connection of sundry wills, making of two persons one in having and suffering. And therefore a friend is properly named of philosophers "the other I." For that in them is but one mind and one possession; and that which more is, a man more rejoiceth in his friend's good fortune than at his own.

Orestes and Pylades, being wonderful like in all features, were taken together and presented unto a tyrant who deadly hated Orestes. But when he beheld them both and would have slain Orestes only, he could not discern the one from the other. And also Pylades, to deliver his friend, affirmed that he was Orestes; on the other part, Orestes, to save Pylades, denied and said that he was Orestes, as the truth was. Thus a long time they together contending the one to die for the other, at the last so relented the fierce and cruel heart of the tyrant that, wondering at their marvelous friendship, he suffered them freely to depart without doing to them any damage.

Pithias and Damon, two Pythagorians, that is to say, students of Pythagoras'[7] learning, being joined together in a perfect friendship, for that one of them was accused to have conspired against Dionysus, king of Sicily, they were both taken and brought to the king, who immediately gave sentence that he that was accused should be put to death. But he desired the king that ere he died he might return home to set his household in order and to distribute his goods. Whereat the king laughing demanded of him scornfully what pledge he would leave him to come again. At the which words his companion stepped forth and said that he would remain there as a pledge for his friend, that in case he came not again at the day appointed, that he willingly would lose his head, which condition the tyrant received. The young man that should have died was suffered to depart home to his house, where he did set all thing in order and disposed his goods wisely. The day appointed for his return was come, the time much passed, wherefore the king called for him that was pledge, who came forth merrily without semblance of dread, offering to abide the sentence of the tyrant, and without grudging to die for the saving the life of his friend. But as the officer of justice had closed his eyen with a kerchief[8] and had drawn his sword to have stricken off his head, his fellow came running and crying that the day of his appointment was not yet past. Wherefore he desired the minister of justice to loose his fellow and to prepare to do execution on him that had given the occasion. Whereat the tyrant, being all abashed, commanded both to be

7. Ancient Greek philosopher and mathematician.
8. Covered his eyes with a blindfold.

brought to his presence, and when he had enough wondered at their noble hearts and their constancy in very[9] friendship, he, offering to them great rewards, desired them to receive him into their company, and so, doing them much honor, did set them at liberty.

Undoubtedly that friendship which doth depend either on profit or else on pleasure, if the ability of the person which might be profitable do fail or diminish, or the disposition of the person which should be pleasant do change or appare,[1] the ferventness of love ceaseth, and then is there no friendship.

EDWIN SANDYS

[Duties of Husband and Wife]†

How honorably a man should use his wife, St. Paul teacheth plainly in many places, but especially in his Epistle to the Ephesians: "Men love your wives as Christ hath loved His Church" (Ephesians 5.25). In which place he instructeth not only by precept, but also by setting a pattern before our eyes to follow—and that is Christ, the true spouse to His Church, the congregation of the faithful. The husband ought to love his wife even as Christ did His Church. But Christ suffered death to redeem His Church. Even so truly the husband, if necessity so required to save his wife, should jeopard[1] his own life. His life is well spent in saving of her, and by losing of her ill spared. Christ purged and made His Church beautiful, void of spot or wrinkle, that it might resemble himself, as near as might be in purity. Even so the husband should labor to reform his wife: to instruct and frame her to discretion, sobriety, all matron-like virtues, and all godliness. A wise wife maketh a happy husband and in her goodness he shall find gladness. The husband is called the head of his wife as Christ is of the congregation. Whenas the head espieth faults in the members of the body, it doth not study how to cut them off and make separation, but doth muse upon a remedy and labor to procure a medicine to apply unto the hurt parts, to recover the body and to cover the fault if he cannot cure it. A good husband is a good head; his endeavor will be to cure his diseased wife and not to cut her off from him, especially to win her unto Christ if she wander out of the right way. Her faults will make him

---

9. True.
1. Weaken.
† From Sermon Sixteen on marriage in *Sermons* (London, 1585), pp. 281–84. The most important of Sandys's marginal notations of biblical passages are incorporated into the text.
1. Endanger.

sorrowful, not furious, and to pity her infirmities without hating of her person. Wisdom is required in the head to rule and govern well the body which is placed under it. He that braggeth and boasteth that he is the head and yet wanteth[2] the prudence which the head should have is unworthy to be named that which indeed he is not.

*   *   *

Touching the duties of honor which the wife doth owe to the husband, we find in the beginning of the Book of Genesis that because of her transgression (for Eve seduced Adam, not Adam, Eve), God gave her a law of subjection to her husband, that she might ever after be better directed by him than he had been at that time by her. * * * Wives, be subject to your own husbands as to the Lord, because the man is the head of the wife as Christ is the head of the Church. And therefore, as the Church is in subjection to Christ, so ought wives to be in subjection to their husbands. What, should we seek more reasons? This one is sufficient: God hath set the husband over the wife in authority, and therefore she ought willingly and dutifully to obey him, else she disobeyeth that God who created woman for man's sake, and hath appointed man to be woman's governor. Peter also setteth forth this obedience, and bringeth Sarah for an example: "Wives, be obedient to your husbands even as Sarah obeyed Abraham, calling him sir, whose daughters ye are made in well doing" (I Peter 3.6). Yea, we are taught that wives should be of so good behavior and of such modest conversation that by their chaste and mild life and the sweetness of their godly manners, they might win their evil husbands unto God and of atheists make Christians. St. Paul in his Epistle to Titus also teacheth a wife her duty: that is, that she go appareled as becometh holiness, that she be no quarreler or false accuser but study to be sober, to love her husband, to love her children, to be discreet, chaste, abiding at home, good and obedient to her husband. * * * An honest and a modest woman is an honor to her husband, but the dissolute wife and indiscreet, is a death. She may not be a gadder abroad, a tattler, or a busybody, but sober, quiet, and demure, not an open teacher, but ready to learn of her husband at home, obedient in all lawful things, taking example of Sarah and giving example to the younger women of well demeaning themselves. Thus the man and wife joining themselves together in true love, endeavoring to live in the fear of God, and dutifully behaving themselves the one towards the other, either of them bearing wisely the other's infirmities, doubtless they shall reap joy and comfort by their marriage. They shall find this their estate, which is honorable in all, happy and profitable unto them.

2. Lacks.

DANIEL PRICE

The Merchant: A Sermon Preached at Paul's Cross†

Matthew 13.45–46: The kingdom of heaven is like to a merchant man that seeketh good pearls who, having found a pearl of great price, went and sold all that he had and bought it.

* * *

Our Savior in this chapter by seven parables setteth forth the state of the kingdom of heaven by the seed (verse 3), of the tares (verse 24), of the mustard seed (verse 31), of the leaven (verse 33), of the treasure (verse 44), of a net (verse 47), and here of a merchant in this [verse] 45, herein showing the ministers of the gospel their liberty left to them in performance of their calling—not only nakedly to lay open the truth but also to use helps of wit, invention, and art, the good gifts of God, which may be used in similitudes, allusions, applications, comparisons, proverbs, and parables which tend to edification and illustrating of the word, that so the weak may be comforted, the rude may be informed, the drowsy may be awakened, the hard-hearted may be suppled, the perverse overwhelmed, and so by all means God himself may be glorified and the hearers bettered. St. Paul, the doctor of the gentiles, professeth of himself that he became all unto all men that he might by all means win some of all (1 Corinthians 9.1). More truly may it be spoken of Christ, who was the schoolmaster of this master of the gentiles: He became all unto all men.

* * *

"The kingdom of heaven is like to a merchant man." If that complaint were true which Erasmus took up in his time against merchants, it is a marvel why I should compare the kingdom of heaven to a merchant, when so few merchants are like to the kingdom of heaven. His words are these: * * * "The trade of merchants account nothing good or holy, but only the only lucre of money, for the attaining of which they have dedicated and consecrated themselves as unto God. By this they measure piety, amity, honesty, credit, and fame, and all human and divine things." I am sure he spake by the figure of some in the name of all, for the stories and customs of Jews and gentiles, Grecians and barbarians, infidels and Christians, do acknowledge the necessity, dignity, and excellency of merchants; and they have approved the merchant of all men to be

† From *The Merchant: A Sermon Preached at Paul's Cross on Sunday the 24 of August, being the Day before Bartholomew Fair, 1607* (Oxford, 1608), sigs. Alr–Elv. Paul's Cross in London was the site of an outdoor pulpit where illustrious preachers often offered controversial and politically charged sermons that attracted crowds of auditors. Some of Price's marginal scriptural citations are incorporated into this text.

the most diligent for his life, the most assiduous in his labor, the most adventurous on the sea, the most beneficial to the land, the glory of his country, and the best pillar of his commonwealth.

* * *

There be two things to be observed in the merchant: the profit and the danger of the trade. Of the profit we shall find what great commodity came of Solomon by the triennial coming of the navy of Tharshish that brought unto him gold and silver, ivory and apes and peacocks, even all things for profit and for pleasure (1 Kings 10.22), where the Holy Ghost doth show that this trade was the occasion of the enriching of Solomon. And surely it doth mutually enrich all kingdoms, making the proper commodities of one country common to another. Witness our gold from India, our spices from Arabia, our silks from Spain, our wines from France, and so many other commodities from other countries, whereby the merchant is the key of the land, the treasurer of the kingdom, the venter of his soil's surplusage,[1] the combiner of nations, and the adamantine chain of countries. Of the danger David speaketh in the Psalm: "They that go down to the sea in ships and merchandise in great waters, these men see the works of the Lord and His wonders in the deep, for at His word the stormy winds arise, which lift up the waves thereof. They are carried up to heaven and down again to the deep, their soul melteth within them, and all their cunning is gone" (Psalm 107.22 etc.) Which peril and danger of them was the cause that Pittacus[2] held that sea adventurers were neither among the living nor the dead, but did hang between both. * * * They, their riches, and mariners and pilots and caulkers and merchants and men of war may be overthrown, perish, sunk, dispersed, and come to a fearful ruin. So that of all men I may say with David, these men "see the works of the Lord and His wonders in the deep." And surely so it is with the state of the godly: in this life in most danger, subject to the greatest affliction, they are in the waves of the world, yet they above all others see the works of the Lord and His wonders in the deepest of their misery.

* * *

The use then of this doctrine is to take heed of persuading ourselves that ease and quietness is the best trade. Lepidus the heathen was taxed for a sluggish and idle fellow that, sitting lazy in the sunshine, cried out *Utinam hoc esse laborare!*.[3] And so surely they that think Christianity an idle kind of life, God shall laugh them to scorn. We all have a goal for which we must run; we all have proposed to us a garland for which we must wrestle; we are all to have

1. Excess crops.
2. Statesman from Mytilene considered one of the seven sages of ancient Greece.
3. "Would that this were considered work!"

a crown for which we must strive. We are all mariners, and we must sail in danger before we come to the haven of happiness. * * * We are all merchants. We cannot find the pearl of great price until we have fought for many good pearls. O then run, wrestle, strive, sail, toil, labor, fight the good fight, finish the course, seek to be like to the good merchant. "The kingdom of heaven is like to a merchant man."

* * *

O remember, beloved, that if ye so much care and labor and travel for earthly things, how much more ought ye to care for spiritual things? I know not what reason many learned men have to condemn merchants and merchandise—so much that Tully[4] in his book *De republica* should affirm of the Phoenicians that, being merchants, they by their merchandise brought in covetousness, pride, luxury, and all kind of wickedness into Graecia.[5] That St. Jerome on the third of Jeremy calleth the Arabians, who much traded in merchandise, the thieves of the world. That the Carthaginians would not suffer them to be common with their citizens. That the Grecians would not let them enter their city, but caused them to keep their markets without the suburbs, as Cornelius Agrippa[6] observeth. That Plato admitted them not into his Commonwealth.[7] That Aristotle detested them and their life; that the ancient laws did not admit any merchant to bear any office or to be admitted into the council or senate; that Cicero affirmeth their getting of money to be most odious, giving this reason: * * * "That they get their living by lying." I hope the merchants of our time deserve not to be so thought of. Many of these merchants were Jews, gentiles, heathens, infidels, pirates, robbers; I hope none such are to be found among you, for you are Christians.

* * *

Lastly, my exhortation in a word is to this city in general. O London, thou that sittest like a queen, all thy citizens being as so many merchants, thy merchants as so many princes, nay, as so many polished corners of the temple, remember[8] them, that for all their port and state and dignity and riches, they are unworthy to enjoy the least of these blessings unless they be like to that good merchant here that seeketh good pearls. Their carelessness, haughtiness, oppression, wickedness, are but the worms and moths of their greatness, and these worms and moths will corrupt them and their greatness. Neither they, nor thou, shalt sin with impunity. The

---

4. Roman orator Marcus Tullius Cicero.
5. Latin name for Greece.
6. Early-sixteenth-century German writer who specialized in mysticism and the occult. "Without": outside.
7. Plato's imagined *Republic*, which banned many professions as corrupt.
8. Remind (addressing London).

A street procession from St. Mark's, Venice. From Giacomo Franco, *Habiti d'huomini et donne Venetiane* (1609). Courtesy of the New York Public Library.

mightiness of thy state, singularity of thy government, climbing of
thy walls, aspiring of thy towers, multitude of thy people, cannot
make thee secure against the wrath of the Lord. * * * In all the stories either rude or polite, profane or divine, I find no city more honored for merchants and merchandise than Tyrus in the prophecy of
Ezekiel (Ezekiel 27). * * * And they did bring fair horses and mules
and unicorns' horns and peacocks and emeralds, purple and broidered work and fine linen and pearl and coral and wheat and wine
and honey and oil and balm and cassia and calamus,[9] the chief of
all spices, of all precious stones and gold and raiments of blue silk
and broidered works and rich apparel. So that by her merchandise
she was replenished and made glorious in the midst of the sea. And
yet for all this, in the end of the chapter, the Lord threateneth this
fearful desolation to Tyrus for her abominable sins: "Thy riches and
thy fairs, thy merchandise, thy mariners, thy pilots, thy caulkers,
and all the occupiers of thy merchandise and all the men of war
that are in thee, and all the multitude which is in the midst of thee
shall fall in the midst of the sea, in the day of thy ruin."

*   *   *

O my beloved in the bowels of Christ Jesus, at the length remember that the fear of the Lord is your safest refuge, righteousness
your strongest bulwark, sobriety and sanctimony of life your walls
of brass, piety your best pearl, Christ Jesus your best jewel. O then
seek, search, labor, endeavor, find, buy this pearl, this peace—merchandise in this till He come that will come to judge the quick and
the dead! The Lord make you rich in His wisdom, and make you all
wise in Christ Jesus. Amen.

THOMAS CORYAT

[Description of Venice]†

The city is divided in the middest by a goodly fair channel, which
they call *Canal il grande*.[1] The same is crooked, and made in the
form of a Roman S. It is in length a thousand and three hundred
paces, and in breadth at the least forty, in some places more. The
six parts of the city whereof Venice consisteth are situate on both
sides of this *Canal il grande*. * * * Also both the sides of this channel are adorned with many sumptuous and magnificent palaces
that stand very near to the water and make a very glorious and

9. Chinese cinnamon and a root used to make medicinal oil.
† From *Coryat's Crudities* (London, 1611), sigs. O1r–Y3r.
1. The Grand Canal. "Middest": middle.

beautiful show. For many of them are of a great height—three or four stories high—most being built with brick and some with fair freestone.[2] Besides they are adorned with a great multitude of stately pillars made partly of white stone and partly of Istrian[3] marble.

*   *   *

There is only one bridge to go over the great channel, which is the same that leadeth from St. Mark's to the Rialto, and joineth together both the banks of the channel. This bridge is commonly called *Ponte de Rialto*,[4] and is the fairest bridge by many degrees for one arch that ever I saw, read, or heard of. For it is reported that it cost about fourscore thousand crowns, which do make four and twenty thousand pound sterling. Truly the exact view hereof ministered unto me no small matter of admiration to see a bridge of that length (for it is two hundred foot long, the channel being at the least forty paces broad, as I have before written) so curiously compacted together with one only arch.

*   *   *

There are in Venice thirteen ferries or passages, which they commonly call *traghetti*, where passengers may be transported in a gondola to what place of the city they will. Of which thirteen, one is under this Rialto Bridge. But the boatmen that attend at this ferry are the most vicious and licentious varlets about all the city. For if a stranger entereth into one of their gondolas and doth not presently tell them whither he will go, they will incontinently carry him of their own accord to a religious house, forsooth, where his plumes shall be well pulled before he cometh forth again.[5]

*   *   *

The Rialto, which is at the farther side of the bridge as you come from St. Mark's, is a most stately building, being the Exchange of Venice, where the Venetian gentlemen and the merchants do meet twice a day, betwixt eleven and twelve of the clock in the morning and betwixt five and six of the clock in the afternoon. This Rialto is of a goodly height, built all with brick as the palaces are, adorned with many fair walks or open galleries that I have before mentioned, and hath a pretty quadrangular court adjoining to it. But it is inferior to our Exchange in London, though indeed there is far greater quantity of building in this than in ours. In one of the higher rooms, which belongeth only to the state, there is kept wondrous abundance of treasure.

2. Fine-grained limestone or sandstone that can be easily cut.
3. Coastal area near Venice in modern-day Croatia.
4. The Rialto Bridge.
5. The "religious house," like the "nunnery" in *Hamlet*, is evidently a brothel. "Incontinently": quickly.

* * *

The fairest place of all the city (which is indeed of that admirable and incomparable beauty that I think no place whatsoever, either in Christendom or paganism may compare with it) is the Piazza, that is, the marketplace of St. Mark, or (as our English merchants commorant[6] in Venice do call it), the Place of St. Mark. * * * Here is the greatest magnificence of architecture to be seen that any place under the sun doth yield. Here you may both see all manner of fashions of attire, and hear all the languages of Christendom, besides those that are spoken by the barbarous ethnics, the frequency of people being so great twice a day, betwixt six of the clock in the morning and eleven and again betwixt five in the afternoon and eight, that (as an elegant writer saith of it) a man may very properly call it rather *orbis* than *urbis forum*—that is, a marketplace of the world, not of the city.

* * *

I was at the place where the whole fraternity of the Jews dwelleth together, which is called the ghetto, being an island, for it is inclosed round about with water. It is thought there are of them in all betwixt five and six thousand. They are distinguished and discerned from the Christians by their habits on their heads, for some of them do wear hats and those red, only those Jews that are born in the western parts of the world, as in Italy, etc.; but the eastern Jews, being otherwise called the Levantine Jews, which are born in Jerusalem, Alexandria, Constantinople, etc., wear turbans upon their heads as the Turks do. But the difference is this: the Turks wear white, the Jews yellow. By that word *turban* I understand a towel of fine linen wrapped together upon their heads, which serveth them instead of hats, whereof many have been often worn by the Turks in London. They have divers synagogues in their ghetto, at the least seven, where all of them, both men, women, and children, do meet together upon their Sabbath, which is Saturday. * * * The Levite that readeth the law to them hath before him at the time of divine service an exceeding long piece of parchment rolled up upon two wooden handles in which is written the whole sum and contents of Moses' law in Hebrew. That doth he (being discerned from the lay people only by wearing of a red cap, whereas the others do wear red hats) pronounce before the congregation not by a sober, distinct, and orderly reading, but by an exceeding loud yelling, indecent roaring, and as it were a beastly bellowing of it forth. And that after such a confused and headlong manner, that I think the hearers can very hardly understand him. Sometimes he cries out alone and sometimes again some others serving as it were

6. Resident.

his clerks hard without his seat and within, do roar with him; but for that his voice (which he straineth so high as if he sung for a wager) drowneth all the rest.

*   *   *

I observed some few of these Jews, especially some of the Levantines, to be such goodly and proper men that then I said to myself our English proverb "To look like a Jew"—whereby is meant sometimes a weather-beaten, warp-faced fellow, sometimes a frenetic and lunatic person, sometimes one discontented—is not true. For indeed I noted some of them to be most elegant and sweet-featured persons, which gave me occasion the more to lament their religion. For if they were Christians, then could I better apply unto them that excellent verse of the poet than I can now: *Gratior est pulchro veniens e corpore virtus.*[7]

In the room wherein they celebrate their divine service, no women sit, but have a loft or gallery proper to themselves only, where I saw many Jewish women, whereof some were as beautiful as ever I saw, and so gorgeous in their apparel, jewels, chains of gold, and rings adorned with precious stones, that some of our English countesses do scarce exceed them, having marvelous long trains like princesses that are borne up by waiting women serving for the same purpose. An argument to prove that many of the Jews are very rich. One thing they observe in their service which is utterly condemned by our Savior Christ, *Battologia*, that is, a very tedious babbling and an often repetition of one thing, which cloyed mine ears so much that I could not endure them any longer, having heard them at the least an hour, for their service is almost three hours long. They are very religious in two things only and no more: in that they worship no images, and that they keep their Sabbath so strictly that upon that day they will neither buy nor sell nor do any secular, profane, or irreligious exercise (I would to God our Christians would imitate the Jews herein!), no not so much as dress their victuals, which is always done the day before, but dedicate and consecrate themselves wholly to the strict worship of God. Their circumcision they observe as duly as they did any time betwixt Abraham (in whose time it was first instituted) and the Incarnation of Christ. For they use to circumcise every male child when he is eight days old with a stony knife. But I had not the opportunity to see it. Likewise they keep many of those ancient feasts that were instituted by Moses. Amongst the rest the Feast of Tabernacles is very ceremoniously observed by them. From swine's flesh they abstain as their ancient forefathers were wont to do, in which the

7. "Virtue is fairer when it appears in a beautiful person," slight misquotation of Virgil's *Aeneid* 5.344.

Turks do imitate them at this day. Truly, it is a most lamentable case
for a Christian to consider the damnable estate of these miserable
Jews, in that they reject the true Messias [sic] and Savior of their
souls, hoping to be saved rather by the observation of those Mosaical ceremonies the date whereof was fully expired at Christ's Incarnation, than by the merits of the Savior of the world, without
whom all mankind shall perish.

And as pitiful it is to see that few of them living in Italy are converted to the Christian religion. For this I understand is the main
impediment to their conversion: all their goods are confiscated as
soon as they embrace Christianity, and this I heard is the reason—
because whereas many of them do raise their fortunes by usury, insomuch as they do sometimes not only shear but also flay many a
poor Christian's estate by their gripping extortion, it is therefore de-
creed by the pope and other free princes in whose territories they
live that they shall make a restitution of all their ill-gotten goods,
and so disclog[8] their souls and consciences when they are admitted
by holy baptism into the bosom of Christ's church. Seeing, then,
when their goods are taken from them at their conversion they are
left even naked and destitute of their means of maintenance, there
are fewer Jews converted to Christianity in Italy than in any other
country of Christendom.

*   *   *

I was at one of [the Venetian] playhouses, where I saw a comedy
acted. The house is very beggarly and base in comparison of our
stately playhouses in England; neither can their actors compare
with us for apparel, shows, and music. Here I observed certain
things that I never saw before. For I saw women act, a thing that I
never saw before,[9] though I have heard that it hath been sometimes
used in London, and they performed it with as good a grace, action,
gesture, and whatsoever convenient for a player as ever I saw any
masculine actor. Also their noble and famous courtesans came to
this comedy, but so disguised that a man cannot perceive them.

*   *   *

[The music for a solemn festival in Venice] was so good, so delectable, so rare, so admirable, so super-excellent that it did even ravish and stupify all those strangers that never heard the like. But
how others were affected with it I know not; for mine own part I
can say this, that I was for the time even rapt up with St. Paul into
the third heaven.[1] Sometimes there sung sixteen or twenty men together, having their master or moderator to keep them in order, and

8. Unburden.
9. A reminder that in Shakespeare's theater, women's parts were played by men and boys.
1. According to the Gnostic "Apocalypse of Paul," the Holy Ghost raised the Apostle Paul
   up into the Third Heaven and beyond to enlighten his spirit.

when they sung, the instrumental musicians played also. * * * Of the singers there were three or four so excellent that I think few or none in Christendom do excel them, especially one who had such a peerless and (as I may in a manner say) such a supernatural voice for sweetness, that I think there was never a better singer in all the world, insomuch that he did not only give the most pleasant contentment that could be imagined to all the hearers, but also did as it were astonish and seize them.

*   *   *

Amongst many other things that moved great admiration in me in Venice, this was not the least—to consider the marvelous affluence and exuberancy of all things tending to the sustentation[2] of man's life. For albeit they have neither meadows nor pastures nor arable grounds near their city (which is a matter impossible because it is seated in the sea and distinguished with such a multitude of channels) to yield them corn and victuals, yet they have as great abundance (a thing very strange to be considered) of victuals, corn, and fruits of all sorts whatsoever, as any city, I think, of all Italy. Their victuals and all other provision being very plenteously ministered unto them from Padua, Vicenza, and other bordering towns and places of Lombardy, which are in their own dominion.

*   *   *

I observed one thing in Venice that I utterly condemned: that if two men should fight together at sharp[3] openly in the streets, whereas a great company will suddenly flock together about them, all of them will give them leave to fight till their hearts ache, or till they welter in their own blood, but not one of them hath the honesty to part them, and keep them asunder from spilling each other's blood. Also, if one of the two should be slain, they will not offer to apprehend him that slew the other, except the person slain be a gentleman of the city, but suffer him to go at random whither he list, without inflicting any punishment upon him. A very barbarous and unchristian thing to wink at such effusion of Christian blood, in which they differ (in my opinion) from all Christians. The like I understand is to be observed in Milan and other cities of Italy.

There happened a thing when I was in Venice that moved great commiseration and sympathy in me. I saw a certain Englishman, one Thomas Taylor, born in Leicestershire, endure great slavery in one of the Venetian galleys, for whose enlargement I did my uttermost endeavor, but all would not serve. I would to God he had not committed that fault which deserved that condemnation to the galleys, for indeed he took pay beforehand of the Venetians for service in their wars, and afterward fled away. But being again appre-

2. Sustaining.
3. With unsheathed weapons.

hended, they have made him with many trickling tears repent his flying from them.

* * *

There have been some authors that have distinguished the orders or ranks of the Venetians into three degrees, as the patricians, the merchants, and the plebeians. But for the most part they are divided into two: the patricians, which are otherwise called the *clarissimos* or the gentlemen; and the plebeians. By the patricians are meant those that have the absolute sway and government of the state or Signiory, both by sea and land, and administer justice at home and abroad. By the plebeians, those of the vulgar sort that use mechanical and manuary[4] trades and are excluded from all manner of authority in the commonweal.

* * *

Howbeit these gentlemen do not maintain and support the title of their gentility with a quarter of that noble state and magnificence as our English noblemen and gentlemen of the better sort do, for they keep no honorable hospitality nor gallant retinue of servants about them, but a very frugal table, though they inhabit most beautiful palaces and are enriched with as ample means to keep a brave port as some of our greatest English earls. For I have heard that the worst of five hundred of the principal Venetian gentlemen is worth a million of ducats, which is almost two hundred and fifty thousand pound sterling, having in many places of Lombardy goodly revenues yearly paid them, besides the possession of many stately palaces. But I understand that the reason why they so confine themselves within the bounds of frugality and avoid the superfluity of expenses in housekeeping that we Englishmen do use is because they are restrained by a certain kind of edict made by the Senate, that they shall not keep a retinue beyond their limitation.

* * *

So at length I finish the treatise of this incomparable city, this most beautiful queen, this untainted virgin, this paradise, this Tempe,[5] this rich diadem and most flourishing garland of Christendom, of which the inhabitants may as proudly vaunt as I have read the Persians have done of their Ormus, who say that if the world were a ring then should Ormus be the gem thereof. The same I say may the Venetians speak of their city, and much more truly. The sight whereof hath yielded unto me such infinite and unspeakable contentment, I must needs confess, that even as Albertus, Marquess of Guasto, as I have before spoken, were he to put to his choice to be lord of four of the fairest cities of Italy or the Arsenal[6] of Venice he

4. Performed by hand.
5. Beautiful Greek valley sacred to Apollo.
6. Venice's famed shipyard, described at length by Coryat in a passage not reproduced here.

would prefer the Arsenal; in like manner I say that had there been an offer made unto me before I took my journey to Venice either that four of the richest manors of Somersetshire (wherein I was born) should be gratis bestowed upon me if I never saw Venice, or neither of them if I should see it, although certainly those manors would do me much more good in respect of a state of livelihood to live in the world than the sight of Venice, yet notwithstanding I will ever say while I live that the sight of Venice and her resplendent beauty, antiquities, and monuments hath by many degrees more contented my mind and satisfied my desires than those four lordships could possibly have done.

WILLIAM CAMDEN

[The Case of Doctor Lopez]†

[In 1594 as some] learned English fugitives studied to advance by writing the Infanta of Spain to the scepter of England, so others of their number secretly attempted the same by the sword, sending privily[1] certain murderers to kill Queen Elizabeth, and some Spaniards [to kill her] by poison. The Spaniards, suspecting the fidelity of the English in a matter of so great weight, used the help of Rodrigo Lopez of the Jewish sect, the queen's physician for her household, and of Stephen Ferreira Gama and Emanuel Luis, Portugals[2] (for many Portugals in those days crept into England as retainers to the exiled Don Antonio[3]), who by means of letters intercepted, being apprehended, were about the end of February arraigned in Guildhall at London and charged by their own confessions to have conspired to make away the queen by poison.

Lopez, having been for a long time a man of noted fidelity, was not once suspected save that outlandish[4] physicians may by bribe and corruption be easily made poisoners and traitors. He confessed that he was drawn by Andrada, a Portugal, to employ his best and secret service for the King of Spain; that he had received from his

---

† From *The History of the Life and Reign of the Most Renowned and Victorious Princess Elizabeth* (London, 1630), year 1594, pp. 58–59. For an account much more favorable to Dr. Lopez, see Godfrey Goodman, *The Court of King James I*, ed. John Brewer (London: Richard Bentley, 1839), Book 1, pp. 149–56. According to Bishop Goodman, Lopez had been acting as a double agent to ferret out plots against Elizabeth and report them to the queen; he was framed by Elizabeth's favorite the earl of Essex, who was jealous of Lopez's influence; and he was executed, despite Elizabeth's promised protection, because his enemies managed to get him transferred from the Tower of London to a city prison from which he could be put to death without the express warrant of the queen.

1. Secretly.
2. Portuguese.
3. Elected king of Portugal who was expelled by the Spaniards and took refuge in England.
4. Foreign.

most inward councillor, Christophoro Moro, a rich jewel; that he had divers times advertised the Spaniards of such things as he could learn; that at length upon a contract for 50,000 ducats he had promised to poison the queen; and that this he signified to Count de Fuentez and Ibara, the king's secretary in the Netherlands.[5]

Stephanus Ferreira confessed that Count de Fuentez and Ibara had signified unto him both by letters and word of mouth that there was a plot laid to take away the queen's life by poison; that he wrote letters by Lopez his dictating wherein he promised the same, conditionally[6] that 50,000 ducats should be paid unto him; also that Emanuel Luis was secretly sent unto him by Fuentez and Ibara to excite Lopez to dispatch the matter speedily.

Emanuel confessed that Count Fuentez and Ibara, when he had given them his faith to keep close their counsels, showed him a letter which Andrada had written to Lopez his name[7] about making away the queen; and that he himself was likewise sent by Fuentez to deal with Ferreira and Lopez for hastening the queen's death, and to promise to Lopez himself money and honors to his children.

At the bar, Lopez spake not much, but cried out that Ferreira and Emanuel were wholly composed of fraud and lying; that he intended no hurt against the queen but hated the gifts of a tyrant; that he had given that jewel to the queen which was sent him from the Spaniard; and that he had no other meaning but to deceive the Spaniard and wipe him of his money. The rest spake nothing for themselves, many times accusing Lopez. They were all of them condemned, and after three months put to death at Tyburn, Lopez affirming that he had loved the queen as he loved Jesus Christ—which from a man of the Jewish profession was heard not without laughter.

---

5. During this period the king of Spain ruled much of the Netherlands.
6. On the condition that. "Dictating": dictated by Lopez.
7. Addressed to Lopez.

THOMAS CALVERT

[Causes of the Miseries of the Jews]†

First, there is the judgment of God upon them. They prayed
Christ's blood might be upon them and upon their children. It is so;
it follows and haunts them wherever they go. Few states and kingdoms entertain them, and where they are entertained they are kept
under and made to endure very hard things, the state serving their
own ends by them. In most places they use (if Christians) to distinguish them from others by place of dwelling by themselves and
some distinctive habit, as their own chronologer tells us, that at
Venice such a year the Jews were commanded to wear a yellow hat
that they might be known from Christians. Our Samuel[1] tells
enough of this wrath of God that dogs them at the heels all over.
Now besides this great sin of murdering Christ once, they have
other notorious vices that will make any Christian commonwealth
first or last vomit them out unless they leave their Jewish pranks.
Under Constantine[2] they used to set upon those Jews with stones
that had left them and turned Christians, till the emperor by edict
caused divers of them to be burnt, and withal appointed that if any
Christians turned Jews they should be burnt likewise. Many of
them rebelling, he caused their ears to be cut off. They used by
craft and by coin to buy and get of the consecrated bread which
was left at a Christmas Sacrament of the Lord's Supper, and prick
it, burn it, and very basely and scornfully abuse it, because they
heard Christians call it the body of Christ.

* * *

Sometimes they were accused for poisoning of wells and springs
to make an end of Christians, sometimes for beggaring Christians
by excessive usury and extortion, sometimes for clipping of coin, for
magic, for cozenage, etc. But their cursing of Christ and Christians, their cursing of Jews that turn Christians, their imprisoning
of their dearest friends, and laying some foul, false accusations
against them if they smell that they intend to turn Christians,
makes them oftentimes intolerable, some of their Rabbis reading
such lectures as these, "A Jew may murder or slay a baptized Jew
without sin." So much are they bent to shed the blood of Christians
that they say a Jew needs no repentance for murdering a Christian,

† From Preface to Rabbi Samuel of Morocco, *The Blessed Jew of Morocco, or, a Blackmoor
Made White* (London, 1648), pp. 16–20. This tract, while stating as its purpose the soft-
ening of Christian hearts against the Jews, offers a particularly concise compendium of
age-old accusations against them.
1. Author of the book Calvert is prefacing.
2. Emperor of Byzantium who lived from 718 to 775.

and they add to that sin to make it sweet and delectable that he who doth it, it is as if he had offered a corban[3] to the Lord, hereby making the abominable sin an acceptable sacrifice.

But beyond all these, they have a bloody thirst after the blood of Christians. In France and many kingdoms they have used yearly to steal a Christian's boy and to crucify him, fastening him to a cross, giving him gall and vinegar, and running him in the end through with a spear, to rub their memories afresh into sweet thoughts of their crucifying Christ, the more to harden themselves against Christ and to show their cursed hatred to all Christians. Thus they incensed Philip of France for such a fact, so as their goods were confiscate being Jews, whether guilty or innocent, and some imprisoned, others cast out of the kingdom. At Weissenburg in Germany they crucified a boy; at Verona they did it, and at Venice also, at Inmestar, a place near Antiochia.[4] Our diligent Foxe hath given us notice that when England gave Jews harbor, they got our English children and sometimes crucified them in divers places, as you may find in Acts and Monuments, and he publishes it withal in his Latin sermon at the baptism of a Jew.[5]

There is an excellent relation, if it can be proved to bear weight with truth, to show the original of child crucifying among the Jews. Cantipratanus saith he once heard a very learned Jew that in his time was converted to the faith say that a certain prophet of theirs, when he was at point of death, did prophecy of the Jews thus: "Know ye," saith he, "this for a most certain truth: that you can never be healed of this shameful punishment wherewith you are so vexed, but only by Christian blood." This punishment so shameful, they say, is that Jews, men as well as females, are punished *cursu menstruo sanguinis*,[6] with a very frequent blood flux. "These words" saith the converted Jew, "the Jews did take with a mistake, for hereupon to heal themselves they every year get the blood of some Christian child, whom they murder; whereas if they had understood aright, this *sanguine Christiano*[7] was Christ's blood that they should get, which in the Sacrament we receive, to the healing and saving of sinners. So many of us as are turned to Christ, we are presently healed of our Fathers' curse."

3. Ritual offering.
4. Antioch in Syria.
5. The works by John Foxe referred to are his very popular *Acts and Monuments* (London, 1596), pp. 213, 296; and his lesser-known *Sermon Preached at the Christening of a Certain Jew* (London, 1578).
6. Flow of menstrual blood (Latin).
7. Christian blood (Latin).

PETER HEYLYN

[Judaizing Christians in the 1590s]†

In the year 1595, some of that faction which before had labored with small profit to overthrow the hierarchy and government of this Church of England now set themselves on work to ruinate all the orders of it—to beat down at one blow all days and times which by the wisdom and authority of the Church had been appointed for God's service, and in the stead thereof to erect a Sabbath of their own devising. * * * Of these, the principal was one Doctor Bound, who published first his *Sabbath Doctrines anno*[1] 1595, and after with additions to it and enlargements of it, *anno* 1606. Wherein he hath affirmed in general over all the book that the commandment of sanctifying every seventh day, as in the Mosaical decalogue,[2] is natural, moral, and perpetual; that where all other things in the Jewish Church were so changed that they were clean taken away (as the priesthood, the sacrifices, and the sacraments), this day, the Sabbath, was so changed that it still remaineth (91). That there is great reason why we Christians should take ourselves as straitly bound to rest upon the Lord's Day as the Jews were upon their Sabbath, for being one of the moral commandments it bindeth us as well as them, being all of equal authority (247). And for the rest upon this day, that it must be a notable and singular rest, a most careful, exact, and precise rest, after another manner than men were accustomed (124).

Then for particulars: no buying of victuals, flesh, or fish, bread or drink (158). No carrier to travel on that day (160), nor packmen nor drovers (162). Scholars not to study the liberal arts, nor lawyers to consult the case and peruse men's evidences (163). Sergeants, apparitors, and summoners[3] to be restrained from executing their offices (164). Justices not to examine causes for preservation of the peace (166). No men to travail on that day (192). That ringing of more bells than one that day is not to be justified (202). No solemn feasts to be made on it (206), nor wedding dinners (209), with a permission notwithstanding to lords, knights, and gentlemen (he hoped to find good welcome for this dispensation! 211). All lawful pleasures and honest recreations, as shooting, fencing, bowling * * * which are permitted on other days were on this day to be for-

---

† From *The History of the Sabbath* (London, 1636), Part 2, pp. 250–56.
1. In the year (Latin). "Doctor Bound": Nicholas Bound, *The True Doctrine of the Sabbath* (1595; rpt. London, 1606); the page numbers in the following passage are Heylyn's and refer to this book.
2. Ten commandments.
3. Officers of the law courts.

An English usurer. From John Blaxton, *The English Usurer* (1634).

borne (202). No man to speak or talk of pleasures (272), or any other worldly matter (275).

Most magisterially determined! Indeed, more like a Jewish Rabbin[4] than a Christian Doctor! Yet Jewish and Rabbinical though his doctrine were, it carried a fair face and show of piety, at least in the opinion of the common people and such who stood not to examine the true grounds thereof, but took it up on the appearance. * * * In which it is most strange to see how suddenly men were induced not only to give way unto it, but without more ado to abet the same, till in the end, and that in very little time, it grew the most bewitching error, the most popular deceit, that ever had been set on foot in the Church of England. * * * And though they failed of that applauded parity which they so much aimed at in the advancing of their Elderships,[5] yet hoped they without more ado to bring all higher powers whatever into an equal rank with the common people in the observance of their Jew Sabbatarian rigors.

4. Rabbi.
5. He refers primarily to contemporary Presbyterians, who preferred more democratic Elderships to the hierarchical system of Bishoprics in the Church of England.

*   *   *

So that we may perceive by this that their intent from the beginning was to cry down the holy days as superstitious popish ordinances, that so their new-found Sabbath being placed alone (and Sabbath now it must be called) might become more eminent. Nor were the other, though more private, effects thereof of less dangerous nature, the people being so ensnared with these new devices and passed with rigors more than Jewish that certainly they are in as bad condition as were the Israelites of old when they were captivated and kept under by the Scribes and Pharisees. * * * That which most of all affects me is that a gentlewoman at whose house I lay in Leicester, the late Northern Progress *anno* 1634,[6] expressed a great desire to see the king and queen, who were then both there. And when I proffered her my service to satisfy that loyal longing, she thanked me but refused the favor because it was the Sabbath Day. Unto so strange a bondage are the people brought that, as before I said, a greater never was imposed on the Jews themselves.

SIR SIMONDS D'EWES

[Parliamentary Debate on Usury, April 19, 1571]†

Mr Molley, first learnedly and artificially[1] making an introduction to the matter, showed what it might be thought on for any man to endeavor the defense of that which every preacher at all times, following the letter of the Book, did speak against. Yet, saith he, it is convenient and being in some sort used it is not repugnant to the word of God. Experience hath proved the great mischief which doth grow by reason of excessive taking, to the destruction of young gentlemen and otherwise, infinitely; but the mischief is of the excess, not otherwise. Since to take reasonably, or so that both parties might do good, was not hurtful, for to have any man lend his money without any commodity—hardly should you bring that to pass. And since every man is not an occupier[2] who hath money, and

---

6. Every summer, the court would go on progress through towns and country estates of the realm. As one of the court chaplains, author Heylyn participated.
† From *The Journals of All the Parliaments during the Reign of Queen Elizabeth* (London, 1682), pp. 171–73, the extensive debate that accompanied the second reading of a proposed bill against usury in the House of Commons. The law that resulted specified that loans charging more than 10 percent interest were usurious and illegal.
1. With artifice.
2. Trader or money dealer.

some which have not money may yet have skill to use money, except you would hinder good trades, [without usury] bargaining and contracting cannot be. God did not so hate it that He did utterly forbid it, but to the Jews amongst themselves only, for that He willed they should lend as brethren together; for unto all others they were at large, and therefore to this day they are the greatest usurers in the world. But be it, as indeed it is, evil, and that men are men, no saints to do all these things perfectly, uprightly and brotherly; yet *ex duobus malis minus malum eligendum*; and better may it be borne to permit a little than utterly to take away and prohibit traffic,[3] which hardly may be maintained generally without this.

* * *

Doctor Wilson, Master of the Requests, said that in a matter of so great weight he could not shortly speak, and acknowledging that he had thoroughly studied the matter, desired the patience of the House. And first he endeavored to prove that the common state may be without usury; then he showed how even men that have been ignorant of God or His laws, finding the evils thereof by their laws, redressed it and utterly prohibited the use thereof: as the Athenians caused all the writings taken for interest money to be burnt, and the like did Lycurgus[4] by a law which he made, and seeing the fire he said he never saw so fair a flame as those books yielded.

* * *

In Italy, quoth [Dr. Wilson], a great known usurer being dead, the curate denied him the common place of burial. His friends made suit; the priest would not hear. In fine, the suitors bethought them of a policy to bring it to pass that he might be buried in the church, which was this: the parson of the church did accustomably use to carry his books daily from his house to the church on his ass; and the ass by often going needed not to be driven but, knowing his journey as soon as he was laden, would of himself go to the church door. They desired the parson [that] his ass might carry the dead body, and where it should stay[5] the body to be buried. To so fond a request the priest agreed. The body was laid on the ass, who, feeling a greater burden than he was used to bear, did run towards the town, never staying until he came to the common place of execution.

This tale merrily told, he again entered to his matter, and proved the condemnation of usury and usurers by the Nicene[6] and divers

---

3. Trade. "*Ex duobus . . . eligendum*": of two evils the lesser evil should be chosen (Latin).
4. Lawgiver of ancient Sparta.
5. Stop.
6. The first worldwide council of the Christian Church, held in 325 C.E.

other councils. He showed that the divines do call usury a spider, a canker, an aspis,[7] a serpent, and a devil. He showed how in nature the offences of homicide and usury are to be compared, and by examples proved the ruins of divers commonwealths when such practices for gain are suffered, as that of the commonwealth of Rome, etc.

*   *   *

Mr. Bell said this matter, being so ample, had occasioned much speech and was for cunning men a fit theme to show their wits and skills upon. Yet, said he, it stands doubtful what usury is; we have no true definition of it, and in our laws we have little written thereon.

EDWARD NICHOLAS

An Apology for the Honorable Nation of the Jews†

The crying sins of our nation do call for vengeance, which we have just cause to expect unless we meet God by repentance and satisfaction of the oppressed.

*   *   *

The sin principally intended here is the strict and cruel laws now in force against the most honorable nation of the world, the nation of the Jews, a people chosen by God, as appears by the many and large expressions of His favor to them, styling them His gems, His firstborn, a precious people above all peoples of the earth, a kingdom of priests, an holy people unto himself. And further saith they are His own servants, and should not be in bondage to any being— only to serve six years and the seventh to go out free, and in the year of Jubilee every man was to return to his inheritance. But above all, that privilege of theirs, the benefit whereof hath an influence on all the faithful and redounds to their happiness, "That in thee and thy seed shall all the nations of the earth be blessed." So strong an obligation are we bound in to them through God's mercy.

And now let all the faithful servants of God take to their considerations how great endurings that honorable nation hath suffered, what bloody slaughters have been made of them in London, in the North Country of England, and divers other parts of this kingdom, and how they have been proscribed and banished this kingdom and

---

7. Highly poisonous snake (asp).
† From *An Apology for the Honorable Nation of the Jews and All the Sons of Israel* (London: John Field, 1648), pp. 3–15. The word "Apology" here means *defense*. This tract was published in connection with the English parliament's debates over the proposal that the Jews, who had been formally expelled in 1290, be allowed to re-settle in England.

denied that commerce allowed to all others, even to barbarous infidels. So that the transcendency of this sin is not to be paralleled.

* * *

'Tis objected the great guilt that lies on the Jews for crucifying Christ, and that therefore and for refusing the Gospel, they are rejected of God, so unworthy of favor, assistance, and compassion herein desired. In answer, though this be imputed to the whole nation, yet it is apparent in the gospel that that action was done by the elders, chief priests, and scribes—His doctrine reproving their hypocrisy and laziness and pride that they wrought a faction against Him—and not that the whole nation were guilty. For the people erewhile brought Him into the city crying "Hosanna!"

* * *

I style them honorable, though it may seem ridiculous to their enemies and the ignorant; yet I may truly say they are of the highest and most honorable descent of any nobility in any country of the world, being ennobled by God himself, and the reason given—which must be most righteous—not for anything in them, or for their multitude, but because God set His love upon them. We see prince's favorites are much courted; there's much more reason that God's favor should attract a greater respect to these sons of Israel than they have. God made good His promises made to Abraham, Isaac, and Jacob, who descended from Sem,[1] the choice and beloved seed. The works and wonders God showed in their deliverance out of Egypt, honoring them with His presence and leading them by a pillar of a cloud by day and a pillar of fire by night. Why should then the great princes and nobles of the world so much magnify themselves for their ancient and honorable descent, whereas the Jews were God's chosen people and beloved, and descended from the most holy men of God?

* * *

I humbly offer this Apology with these considerations to the whole kingdom of England, from the highest to the lowest, that as God hath exceedingly blamed this kingdom above others especially in this, that it hath been almost one hundred years the chief bulwark for defense of the truth and retreat of the afflicted in Europe, so now that we all show ourselves compassionate and helpers of the afflicted Jews, and pray that the same authority that proceeded against them formerly, that now the same power and authority will repeal those severe laws made against them, that our receiving them again and giving them all possible satisfaction and restoring them to commerce in this kingdom may be exemplary to other nations that have done them and continue to do them wrong. Till

---

1. Shem, eldest of the three sons of Noah, who, according to Genesis 10, repopulated the earth after the flood.

which time (God putting their tears into His bottle) God will charge their sufferings upon us and will avenge them on their persecutors.

And what I have now written was not upon any man's motion of the Jews' nation,[2] but a thing that I have long and deeply revolved within my heart, but truly and indeed, my endeavors are for the glory of God, the comfort of those His afflicted people, the love of my own sweet native country of England, and the freeing of my own soul in the day of account. For I thought myself obliged in conscience to publish my conceptions herein, and furthermore do most earnestly pray that the potent parties may no longer continue in division but denying all counsels of the flesh, the acquiring of honors and all self-ends, may ingenuously confess themselves and their failings one to another, and dealing with lenity one towards another, and humbled before Jehovah, may obtain remission of our sins and miseries, and a blessing from God be showered down upon us, which God almighty of His infinite mercy grant.

2. Any Jew's initiative.

CRITICISM

NICHOLAS ROWE

[Remarks on *The Merchant of Venice*]†

* * *

[Shakespeare's] clowns, without which character there was hardly
any play writ in that time, are all very entertaining. And I believe
Thersites in *Troilus and Cressida* and Apemantus in *Timon* [*of
Athens*] will be allowed to be masterpieces of ill nature and satyrical
snarling. To these I might add that incomparable character of Shylock the Jew in *The Merchant of Venice*; but though we have seen
that play received and acted as a comedy and the part of the Jew
performed by an excellent comedian, yet I cannot but think it was
designed tragically by the author. There appears in it such a deadly
spirit of revenge, such a savage fierceness and fellness,[1] and such a
bloody designation of cruelty and mischief, as cannot agree either
with the style or characters of comedy.

The play itself, take it all together, seems to me to be one of the
most finished of any of Shakespeare's. The tale, indeed, in that part
relating to the caskets and the extravagant and unusual kind of
bond given by Antonio, is a little too much removed from the rules
of probability. But taking the fact for granted, we must allow it to
be very beautifully written. There is something in the friendship of
Antonio to Bassanio very great, generous, and tender. The whole
fourth act, supposing, as I said, the fact to be probable, is extremely
fine. But there are two passages that deserve a particular notice.
The first is what Portia says in praise of mercy, page 577,[2] and the
other one the power of music, page 587.

* * *

WILLIAM HAZLITT

The Merchant of Venice‡

This is a play that in spite of the change of manners and prejudices
still holds undisputed possession of the stage. Shakespear's[1] malig-

† From "Some Account of the Life &c. of Mr. William Shakespeare." *The Works of Mr.
  William Shakespeare*. 6 vols., ed. Nicholas Rowe (London: Jacob Tonson, 1709), 1: xix–xx.
1. Cruelty, severity [*Editor*].
2. Page numbers are to the passages in Rowe's edition.
‡ From *Lectures on the Literature of the Age of Elizabeth* (1820; rpt. London: George Bell
  and Sons, 1897), pp. 189–95.
1. "Shakespear" was a common spelling of Shakespeare's name in the nineteenth century
  [*Editor*].

nant has outlived Mr. Cumberland's benevolent Jew.[2] In proportion as Shylock has ceased to be a popular bugbear, "baited with the rabble's curse," he becomes a half-favourite with the philosophical part of the audience, who are disposed to think that Jewish revenge is at least as good as Christian injuries. Shylock is *a good hater*; "a man no less sinned against than sinning." If he carries his revenge too far, yet he has strong grounds for "the lodged hate he bears Antonio," which he explains with equal force of eloquence and reason. He seems the depositary of the vengeance of his race; and though the long habit of brooding over daily insults and injuries has crusted over his temper with inveterate misanthropy, and hardened him against the contempt of mankind, this adds but little to the triumphant pretensions of his enemies. There is a strong, quick, and deep sense of justice mixed up with the gall and bitterness of his resentment. The constant apprehension of being burnt alive, plundered, banished, reviled, and trampled on, might be supposed to sour the most forbearing nature, and to take something from that "milk of human kindness," with which his persecutors contemplated his indignities. The desire of revenge is almost inseparable from the sense of wrong; and we can hardly help sympathising with the proud spirit, hid beneath his "Jewish gaberdine," stung to madness by repeated undeserved provocations, and labouring to throw off the load of obloquy and oppression heaped upon him and all his tribe by one desperate act of "lawful" revenge, till the ferociousness of the means by which he is to execute his purpose, and the pertinacity with which he adheres to it, turn us against him; but even at last, when disappointed of the sanguinary revenge with which he had glutted his hopes, and exposed to beggary and contempt by the letter of the law on which he had insisted with so little remorse, we pity him and think him hardly dealt with by his judges. In all his answers and retorts upon his adversaries, he has the best not only of the argument but of the question, reasoning on their own principles and practice. They are so far from allowing of any measure of equal dealing, of common justice or humanity between themselves and the Jew, that even when they come to ask a favour of him, and Shylock reminds them that on such a day they spit upon him, another spurned him, another called him dog, and for these courtesies they request he'll lend them so much money, Antonio, his old enemy, instead of any acknowledgment of the shrewdness and justice of his remonstrance, which would have been preposterous in a respectable Catholic merchant in those times, threatens him with a repetition of the same treatment—

2. Richard Cumberland wrote *The Jew*, a sentimentalized update of *The Merchant of Venice* that was successfully staged in 1795. [*Editor*].

I am as like to call thee so again,
To spit on thee again, to spurn thee too.[3]

After this, the appeal to the Jew's mercy, as if there were any common principle of right and wrong between them, is the rankest hypocrisy or the blindest prejudice; and the Jew's answer to one of Antonio's friends, who asks him what his pound of forfeit flesh is good for, is irresistible—"To bait fish withal."

*   *   *

The whole of the trial-scene, both before and after the entrance of Portia, is a master-piece of dramatic skill. The legal acuteness, the passionate declamations, the sound maxims of jurisprudence, the wit and irony interspersed in it, the fluctuations of hope and fear in the different persons, and the completeness and suddenness of the catastrophe, cannot be surpassed. Shylock, who is his own counsel, defends himself well, and is triumphant on all the general topics that are urged against him, and only fails through a legal flaw.

*   *   *

The keenness of his revenge awakes all his faculties; and he beats back all opposition to his purpose, whether grave or gay, whether of wit or argument, with an equal degree of earnestness and self-possession. His character is displayed as distinctly in other less prominent parts of the play, and we may collect from a few sentences the history of his life—his descent and origin, his thrift and domestic economy, his affection for his daughter, whom he loves next to his wealth, his courtship and his first present to Leah his wife! "I would not have given it" (the ring which he first gave her) "for a wilderness of monkeys!"[4] What a fine Hebraism is implied in this expression!

Portia is not a very great favourite with us; neither are we in love with her maid, Nerissa. Portia has a certain degree of affectation and pedantry about her, which is very unusual in Shakespear's women, but which perhaps was a proper qualification for the office of a "civil doctor," which she undertakes and executes so successfully. The speech about Mercy is very well; but there are a thousand finer ones in Shakespear. We do not admire the scene of the caskets: and object entirely to the Black Prince, Morocchius.[5] We should like Jessica better if she had not deceived and robbed her father, and Lorenzo, if he had not married a Jewess, though he thinks he has a right to wrong a Jew. The dialogue between this newly-married couple by moonlight, beginning "On such a night," &c., is

3. 1.3.
4. 3.1.
5. The prince of Morocco [Editor].

a collection of classical elegancies. Launcelot, the Jew's man, is an honest fellow. The dilemma in which he describes himself placed between his "conscience and the fiend," the one of which advises him to run away from his master's service and the other to stay in it, is exquisitely humorous.

Gratiano is a very admirable subordinate character. He is the jester of the piece: yet one speech of his, in his own defence, contains a whole volume of wisdom.

> ANTONIO. I hold the world but as the world, Gratiano,
> A stage, where every man must play his part;
> And mine a sad one.
>   GRATIANO.   Let me play the fool.
> With mirth and laughter let old wrinkles come;
> And let my liver rather heat with wine,
> Than my heart cool with mortifying groans.
> Why should a man, whose blood is warm within,
> Sit like his grandsire cut in alabaster?
> Sleep when he wakes? and creep into the jaundice
> By being peevish? I tell thee what, Antonio—
> I love thee, and it is my love that speaks;—
> There are a sort of men, whose visages
> Do cream and mantle like a standing pond:
> And do a wilful stillness entertain,
> With purpose to be dress'd in an opinion
> Of wisdom, gravity, profound conceit;
> As who should say, *I am Sir Oracle,*
> *And when I ope my lips, let no dog bark!*
> O my Antonio, I do know of these,
> That therefore only are reputed wise,
> For saying nothing; when, I'm very sure,
> If they should speak, would almost damn those ears,
> Which hearing them, would call their brothers fools.
> I'll tell thee more of this another time:
> But fish not with this melancholy bait,
> For this fool-gudgeon, this opinion.[6]

Gratiano's speech on the philosophy of love, and the effect of habit in taking off the force of passion, is as full of spirit and good sense. The graceful winding-up of this play in the fifth act, after the tragic business is despatched, is one of the happiest instances of Shakespear's knowledge of the principles of the drama. We do not mean the pretended quarrel between Portia and Nerissa and their husbands about the rings, which is amusing enough, but the conversation just before and after the return of Portia to her own

6. 1.1.

house, beginning, "How sweet the moonlight sleeps upon this bank," and ending, "Peace! how the moon sleeps with Endymion, and would not be awaked." There is a number of beautiful thoughts crowded into that short space, and linked together by the most natural transitions.

When we first went to see Mr. Kean[7] in Shylock, we expected to see, what we had been used to see, a decrepit old man, bent with age and ugly with mental deformity, grinning with deadly malice, with the venom of his heart congealed in the expression of his countenance, sullen, morose, gloomy, inflexible, brooding over one idea, that of his hatred, and fixed on one unalterable purpose, that of his revenge. We were disappointed, because we had taken our idea from other actors, not from the play. There is no proof there that Shylock is old, but a single line, "Bassanio and *old* Shylock, both stand forth,"—which does not imply that he is infirm with age—and the circumstance that he has a daughter marriageable, which does not imply that he is old at all. It would be too much to say that his body should be made crooked and deformed to answer to his mind, which is bowed down and warped with prejudices and passion. That he has but one idea, is not true; he has more ideas than any other person in the piece; and if he is intense and inveterate in the pursuit of his purpose, he shows the utmost elasticity, vigour, and presence of mind, in the means of attaining it. But so rooted was our habitual impression of the part from seeing it caricatured in the representation, that it was only from a careful perusal of the play itself that we saw our error. The stage is not in general the best place to study our author's characters in. It is too often filled with traditional common-place conceptions of the part, handed down from sire to son, and suited to the taste of *the great vulgar and the small*.—" 'Tis an unweeded garden—things rank and gross do merely gender in it!"[8] If a man of genius comes once in an age to clear away the rubbish, to make it fruitful and wholesome, they cry, " 'Tis a bad school: it may be like nature, it may be like Shakespear, but it is not like us." Admirable critics!

7. Edmund Kean, the most stellar of early-nineteenth-century British Shakespearean actors (see Lelyveld essay, pp. 219–25) [*Editor*].
8. Slight misquotation of *Hamlet* 1.2.135–37 [*Editor*].

Portia, by J. W. Wright, from Mrs. Anna Jameson, *The Heroines of Shakespeare* (1832; rpt. 1898), p. 39.

MRS. ANNA JAMESON

Portia†

* * *

It is singular, that hitherto no critical justice has been done to the character of Portia; it is yet more wonderful, that one of the finest writers on the eternal subject of Shakspeare and his perfections, should accuse Portia of pedantry and affectation, and confess she is not a great favorite of his—a confession quite worthy of him, who avers his predilection for servant-maids, and his preference of the Fannies and the Pamelas over the Clementinas and Clarissas.[1] Schlegel, who has given several pages to a rapturous eulogy on the Merchant of Venice, simply designates Portia as a "rich, beautiful, clever heiress:"—whether the fault lie in the writer or translator, I do protest against the word clever.[2] Portia *clever!* what an epithet to apply to this heavenly compound of talent, feeling, wisdom, beauty, and gentleness! * * *

* * *

These and other critics have been apparently so dazzled and engrossed by the amazing character of Shylock, that Portia has received less than justice at their hands; while the fact is, that Shylock is not a finer or more finished character in his way, than Portia is in hers. These two splendid figures are worthy of each other; worthy of being placed together within the same rich framework of enchanting poetry, and glorious and graceful forms. She hangs beside the terrible, inexorable Jew, the brilliant lights of her character set off by the shadowy power of his, like a magnificent beauty-breathing Titian by the side of a gorgeous Rembrandt.

Portia is endued with her own share of those delightful qualities, which Shakspeare has lavished on many of his female characters; but besides the dignity, the sweetness, and tenderness which should distinguish her sex generally, she is individualized by qualities peculiar to herself; by her high mental powers, her enthusiasm of temperament, her decision of purpose, and her buoyancy of spirit. These are innate; she has other distinguishing qualities more external, and which are the result of the circumstances in which she is placed. Thus she is the heiress of a princely name and countless wealth; a train of obedient pleasures have ever waited round her; and from infancy she has breathed an atmosphere redolent of

† From *The Heroines of Shakespeare* (1832; rpt. Philadelphia: John E. Potter and Co., 1898), pp. 39–46.
1. *Hazlitt's Essays*, vol. ii., p. 167.
2. I am informed that the original German word is *geistreiche*, literally, *rich in soul or spirit*, a just and beautiful epithet.

perfume and blandishment. Accordingly there is a commanding grace, a high-bred, airy elegance, a spirit of magnificence in all that she does and says, as one to whom splendor had been familiar from her very birth. She treads as though her footsteps had been among marble palaces, beneath roofs of fretted gold, o'er cedar floors and pavements of jasper and porphyry—amid gardens full of statues, and flowers, and fountains, and haunting music. She is full of penetrative wisdom, and genuine tenderness, and lively wit; but as she has never known want, or grief, or fear, or disappointment, her wisdom is without a touch of the sombre or the sad; her affections are all mixed up with faith, hope and joy; and her wit has not a particle of malevolence or causticity.

It is well known that the Merchant of Venice is founded on two different tales; and in weaving together his double plot in so masterly a manner, Shakespeare has rejected altogether the character of the astutious lady of Belmont with her magic potions, who figures in the Italian novel. With yet more refinement, he has thrown out all the licentious part of the story, which some of his contemporary dramatists would have seized on with avidity, and made the best or the worst of it possible; and he has substituted the trial of the caskets from another source.[3] We are not told expressly where Belmont is situated; but as Bassanio takes ship to go thither from Venice, and as we find them afterwards ordering horses from Belmont to Padua, we will imagine Portia's hereditary palace as standing on some lovely promontory between Venice and Trieste, overlooking the blue Adriatic, with the Friuli mountains or the Euganean hills for its background, such as we often see in one of Claude's or Poussin's[4] elysian landscapes. In a scene, in a home like this, Shakspeare, having first exorcised the original possessor, has placed his Portia: and so endowed her, that all the wild, strange, and moving circumstances of the story, become natural, probable, and necessary in connection with her. That such a woman should be chosen by the solving of an enigma, is not surprising: herself and all around her, the scene, the country, the age in which she is placed, breathe of poetry, romance and enchantment.

> From the four quarters of the earth they come
> To kiss this shrine, this mortal breathing saint.
> The Hyrcanian desert, and the vasty wilds
> Of wild Arabia, are as thoroughfares now,
> For princes to come view fair Portia;

3. In the "Mercatante di Venezia" of Ser. Giovanni, we have the whole story of Antonio and Bassanio, and part of the story, but not the character, of Portia. The incident of the caskets is from the Gesta Romanorum.
4. Claude Lorrain and Nicolas Poussin were celebrated French landscape artists of the seventeenth century [*Editor*].

> The watery kingdom, whose ambitious head
> Spits in the face of heaven is no bar
> To stop the foreign spirits; but they come
> As o'er a brook to see fair Portia.

The sudden plan which she forms for the release of her husband's friend, her disguise, and her deportment as the young and learned doctor, would appear forced and improbable in any other woman; but in Portia are the simple and natural result of her character.[5] The quickness with which she perceives the legal advantage which may be taken of the circumstances; the spirit of adventure with which she engages in the masquerading, and the decision, firmness, and intelligence with which she executes her generous purpose, are all in perfect keeping, and nothing appears forced— nothing as introduced merely for theatrical effect.

But all the finest parts of Portia's character are brought to bear in the trial scene. There she shines forth all her divine self. Her intellectual powers, her elevated sense of religion, her high honorable principles, her best feelings as a woman, are all displayed. She maintains at first a calm self-command, as one sure of carrying her point in the end; yet the painful heart-thrilling uncertainty in which she keeps the whole court, until suspense verges upon agony, is not contrived for effect merely; it is necessary and inevitable. She has two objects in view; to deliver her husband's friend, and to maintain her husband's honor by the discharge of his just debt, though paid out of her own wealth ten times over. It is evident that she would rather owe the safety of Antonio to anything rather than the legal quibble with which her cousin Bellario has armed her, and which she reserves as a last resource. Thus all the speeches addressed to Shylock in the first instance, are either direct or indirect experiments on his temper and feelings. She must be understood from the beginning to the end, as examining with intense anxiety the effect of her own words on his mind and countenance; as watching for that relenting spirit, which she hopes to awaken either by reason or persuasion. She begins by an appeal to his mercy, in that matchless piece of eloquence, which, with an irresistible and solemn pathos, falls upon the heart like "gentle dew from heaven;"—but in vain; for that blessed dew drops not more fruitless and unfelt on the parched sand of the desert, than do these heavenly words upon the ear of Shylock. She next attacks his avarice:

> Shylock, there's *thrice* thy money offered thee!

---

5. In that age, delicate points of law were not determined by the ordinary judges of the provinces, but by doctors of law, who were called from Bologna, Padua, and other places celebrated for their legal colleges.

Then she appeals, in the same breath, both to his avarice and his pity

> Be merciful!
> Take thrice thy money.   Bid me tear the bond.

All that she says afterwards—her strong expressions, which are calculated to strike a shuddering horror through the nerves—the reflections she interposes—her delays and circumlocution to give time for any latent feeling of commiseration to display itself—all, all are premeditated and tend in the same manner to the object she has in view. Thus—

> You must prepare your bosom for his knife.

> Therefore lay bear your bosom!

These two speeches, though addressed apparently to Antonio, are spoken *at* Shylock, and are evidently intended to penetrate *his* bosom. In the same spirit she asks for the balance to weigh the pound of flesh; and entreats of Shylock to have a surgeon ready—

> Have by some surgeon, Shylock, on your charge,
> To stop his wounds, lest he do bleed to death!
> SHYLOCK. Is it so nominated in the bond?
> PORTIA. It is not so expressed—but what of that?
> 'T were good you do so much, for *charity*.

So unwilling is her sanguine and generous spirit to resign all hope, or to believe that humanity is absolutely extinct in the bosom of the Jew, that she calls on Antonio, as a last resource, to speak for himself. His gentle, yet manly resignation—the deep pathos of his farewell, and the affectionate allusion to herself in his last address to Bassanio—

> Commend me to your honorable wife;
> Say how I lov'd you, speak me fair in death, &c.

are well calculated to swell that emotion, which through the whole scene must have been laboring suppressed within her heart.

At length the crisis arrives, for patience and womanhood can endure no longer; and when Shylock, carrying his savage bent "to the last hour of act," springs on his victim—"A sentence! come, prepare!" then the smothered scorn, indignation, and disgust, burst forth with an impetuosity which interferes with the judicial solemnity she had at first affected—particularly in the speech—

> Therefore, prepare thee to cut off the flesh.
> Shed thou no blood; nor cut thou less, nor more,
> But just the pound of flesh; if thou tak'st more,

Or less than a just pound,—be it but so much
As makes it light, or heavy, in the substance,
Or the division of the twentieth part
Of one poor scruple; nay, if the scale do turn
But in the estimation of a hair,—
Thou diest, and all thy goods are confiscate.

But she afterwards recovers her propriety, and triumphs with a cooler scorn and a more self-possessed exultation.

It is clear that, to feel the full force and dramatic beauty of this marvellous scene, we must go along with Portia as well as with Shylock; we must understand her concealed purpose, keep in mind her noble motives, and pursue in our fancy the under current of feeling, working in her mind throughout. The terror and the power of Shylock's character,—his deadly and inexorable malice,—would be too oppressive; the pain and pity too intolerable, and the horror of the possible issue too overwhelming, but for the intellectual relief afforded by this double source of interest and contemplation.

* * *

HEINRICH HEINE

[Jessica and Portia]†

Jessica

When I saw this piece played in Drury Lane there stood behind me in the box a pale British beauty who, at the end of the fourth act, wept passionately, and many times cried out, "The poor man is wronged!" It was a countenance of noblest Grecian cut, and the eyes were large and black. I have never been able to forget them, those great black eyes which wept for Shylock!

When I think of those tears I must include the *Merchant of Venice* among the tragedies, although the frame of the work is a composition of laughing masks and sunny faces, satyr forms and amorets,[1] as though the poet meant to make a comedy. Shakespeare perhaps intended originally to please the mob, to represent a thorough going wehr-wolf, a hated fabulous being who yearns for blood, and pays for it with daughter and with ducats, and is over and above laughed to scorn. But the genius of the poet, the spirit of

---

† From "Shakespeare's Maidens and Women" (originally published in 1838), *The Works of Heinrich Heine*, trans. Charles Godfrey Leland, 12 vols. (London: William Heinemann, 1906), pp. 377–400. Heine himself was a convert from Judaism to Christianity. Translator's notes are omitted here.
1. Cupids [*Editor*].

Jessica, by Sir Samuel Luke Fildes. From *The Graphic Gallery of Shakespeare's Heroines* (1896).

the wide world which ruled in him, was ever stronger than his own will, and so it came to pass that he in Shylock, despite the glaring grotesqueness, expressed the justification of an unfortunate sect which was oppressed by providence, from inscrutable motives, with the hatred of the lower and higher class, and which did not always return this hate with love.

But what do I say? The genius of Shakespeare rises still higher over the petty strife of two religious sects, and his drama shows us neither Jews nor Christians, but oppressors and oppressed, and the madly agonised cries of exultation of the latter when they can repay their arrears of injuries with interest. There is not in this play the least trace of difference in religion, and Shakespeare sets forth in Shylock a man whom nature bade hate his enemies, just as he in Antonio and his friends by no means expresses the disciples of that divine doctrine which commands us to love our enemies. When Shylock says to the man who would borrow money of him:—

> "Signor Antonio, many a time and oft,
> In the Rialto, you have rated me
> About my monies and my usances:
> Still have I borne it with a patient shrug;
> For suff'rance is the badge of all our tribe:
> You call me misbeliever, cut-throat dog,
> And spit upon my Jewish gaberdine,
> And all for use of that which is mine own.
> Well, then, it now appears you need my help:
> Go to, then; you come to me, and you say,
> 'Shylock, we would have monies:'—you say so;
> You, that did void your rheum upon my beard,
> And foot me, as you spurn a stranger cur
> Over your threshold: monies is your suit.
> What should I say to you? Should I not say
> 'Hath a dog money? Is it possible,
> A cur can lend three thousand ducats?' or
> Shall I bend low, and in a bondman's key,
> With 'bated breath and whisp'ring humbleness,
> Say this,—
> 'Fair sir, you spit on me on Wednesday last;
> You spurn'd me such a day; another time
> You call'd me dog; and for these courtesies
> I'll lend you thus much monies?'"[2]

To which Antonio replies:—

> "I am as like to call thee so again,
> To spit on thee again, to spurn thee too."

2. *Merchant of Venice*, act i. sc. 3.

Where is the Christian love in this? Truly Shakespeare would have written a satire against Christianity if he had made it consist of those characters who are the enemies of Shylock, but who are hardly worthy to unlace his shoes. The bankrupt Antonio is a weak creature without energy, without strength of hatred, and as little of love, a melancholy worm-heart whose flesh is really worth nothing save "to bait fish withal." He does not repay the swindled Jew the three thousand ducats. Nor does Bassanio repay him—this man is, as an English critic calls him, a real fortune-hunter; he borrows money to make a display so as to win a rich wife and a fat bridal portion, for as he says to his friend:—

> " 'Tis not unknown to you, Antonio,
> How much I have disabled mine estate,
> By something showing a more swelling port
> Than my faint means would grant continuance:
> Nor do I now make moan to be abridg'd
> From such a noble rate; but my chief care
> Is, to come fairly off from the great debts,
> Wherein my time, something too prodigal,
> Hath left me gag'd. To you, Antonio,
> I owe the most, in money and in love;
> And from your love I have a warranty
> To unburthen all my plots and purposes
> How to get clear of all the debts I owe."[3]

As for Lorenzo, he is the accomplice of a most infamous theft, and according to the laws of Prussia he would have been branded, set in the pillory, and condemned to fifteen years' imprisonment, notwithstanding his susceptibility to the beauties of nature, landscapes by moonlight, and music. As for the other noble Venetians who appear as allies of Antonio, they do not seem to have any special antipathy to money, and when their poor friend is in difficulties they have nothing for him but words or minted air. * * * Much as we must hate Shylock we can hardly take it amiss of him that he despises this folk a little, as he well may do. * * *

*   *   *

No, Shylock loves money, but there are things which he loves more, among others his daughter, "Jessica, my child." Though he curses her in the greatest passion of wrath, and would fain see her dead at his feet, with the jewels in her ears and with the ducats in her coffin, he still loves her more than all ducats and jewels. Excluded from public life and Christian society, and forced into the narrow consolation of domestic happiness, there remain to the poor Jew only family feelings, and these come forth from him with

3. *Merchant of Venice*, act i. sc. 1.

the most touching tenderness. The turquoise, the ring which his wife Leah once gave him, he would not exchange for "a wilderness of monkeys." When in the judgment scene Bassanio speaks thus to Antonio:—

> Antonio, I am married to a wife
> Which is as dear to me as life itself;
> But life itself, my wife, and all the world,
> Are not with me esteem'd above thy life:
> I would lose all, ay, sacrifice them all
> Here to this devil, to deliver you.

To which Gratiano adds:—

> I have a wife, whom, I protest, I love:
> I would she were in heaven, so she could
> Entreat some power to change this currish Jew.[4]

Then there awakes in Shylock a dreadful apprehension as to the fate of his daughter, married among men who will sacrifice their wives for their friends, and aside, not aloud, he says to himself:—

> These be the Christian husbands! I have a daughter;
> Would any of the stock of Barrabas
> Had been her husband, rather than a Christian![5]

This passage—this casual word—is the basis of the condemnation which we must pronounce of the fair Jessica. It was not an unloving father whom she robbed and abandoned. Shameful deceit! She even makes common cause with the enemies of Shylock, and when they at Belmont say all manner of evil things of him, Jessica does not cast down her eyes, nor do her lips grow white—no, Jessica herself says the worst things of her father. Atrocious wickedness! She has no feeling, only a love of what is remarkable and romantic. She is wearied and *ennuyée* in the closely shut "honourable" house of the stern and bitter Jew, which at last appears to her to be a hell. Her frivolous heart was all too easily attracted by the lively notes of the drum, and the wry-necked fife. Did Shakespeare here mean to sketch a Jewess? Indeed no; what he depicts is only a daughter of Eve, one of those beautiful birds, who, when they are fledged, fly away from the paternal nest to the beloved man. So Desdemona followed the Moor, so Imogene Posthumus.[6] That is woman's way. We may remark in Jessica a certain timid shame which she cannot overcome when she must put on a boy's dress. It may be that in this we recognise the remarkable

4. *Merchant of Venice*, act iv. sc. 1.
5. *Merchant of Venice*, act iv. sc. 1.
6. Desdemona remained true to the Moor Othello in Shakespeare's *Othello*; Imogen followed her beloved Posthumus in Shakespeare's *Cymbeline* [Editor].

chastity which is peculiar to her race, and which gives its daughters such a wonderfully lovely charm. The chastity of the Jews is perhaps the result of an opposition which they always maintained against that Oriental religion of sense and sensuality which once flourished among their neighbors the Egyptians, Phœnicians, Assyrians, and Babylonians in rankest luxuriance, and which in continual transformation has survived to the present day. The Jews are a chaste, temperate, I might say an abstract race, and in purity of morals they are most nearly allied to the Germanic races. The chastity of the women among Jews and Germans is perhaps of no real value in itself, but its manifestation makes the most fascinating, charmingly sweet, and deeply moving impression. It is touching even to tears when we read that after the defeat of the Cimbri and Teutones, the women begged Marius not to give them over to the soldiery, but to make them slaves in the temple of Vesta.[7]

It is indeed wonderful what a deep elective affinity prevails between both races, Jews and Germans. This chosen alliance did not originate in a historical course, because the great family chronicle of the Jews, or the Bible, was used by the whole Germanic world, nor because both races were from early times foes to the Romans, and were thereby naturally allies; it has a deeper ground, the two being so much alike that one might regard primæval Palestine as an Oriental Germany, just as one might regard the Germany of to-day as the home of the Holy Word, for the mother-soil of prophetdom, for the citadel of the Holy Spirit.

*   *   *

Portia

*   *   *

* * * What [Mrs. Jameson] says of Portia, as opposed to Shylock, is not only beautiful but true.[8] Should we take the latter, according to the usual conception, as the representative of the stern, earnest, art-detesting representative of Judea, Portia, on the contrary, appears to us as setting forth that after-blossoming of Greek spirit which spread forth its delicious perfume in the sixteenth century from Italy all over the world, and which we love and esteem to-day as the Renaissance. Portia is also the type of gay prosperity in antithesis to the gloomy adversity which Shylock presents. How blooming, rose-like, pure ringing, is her every thought and saying, how glowing with joy her every word, how beautiful all the figures

---

7. Reference to the defeat of Germanic tribes by the Romans under the leadership of Marius in 101 B.C.E. As slaves in the temple of Vesta, whose priestesses were virgins, the captured women would be safe from sexual predation [Editor].
8. See Mrs. Anna Jameson on Portia, pp. 141–45 [Editor].

of her phrases, which are mostly from the mythology. And how dismal, sharp, pinching, and ugly are, on the contrary, the thoughts and utterances of Shylock, who employs only similes from the Old Testament. His wit is cramped and corroding, he seeks his metaphors amid the most repulsive subjects, and even his words are discords squeezed together, shrill, hissing, and whirring. As the people, so their homes. When we see how the servant of Jehovah will not endure an image of either God or man in his "honourable house," and even closes its ears—the windows—lest the sounds of heathenish masquerading should pierce therein, and then see on the contrary the costly and exquisitely tasteful villegiatura-life[9] in the beautiful palace of Belmont, where all is light and music, where among pictures, marble statues, and high laurel-trees, the elegantly clad wooers wander and discuss enigmas of love, while through and amid all this splendour fair Signora Portia gleams like a goddess whose sunny locks—

Hang on her temples like a golden fleece.[1]

By such a contrast the two chief personages of the drama are so individualised that one might swear they were not the feigned fantasies of a poet, but real people and of woman born. Yes, they seem to us to be even more living than the common creatures of the world, for neither time nor death have part in them, and in their veins runs immortal blood, that of undying poetry. * * *

* * *

I at least, a wandering hunter of dreams, looked around me on the Rialto to see if I could find Shylock. I had something to tell him which would have pleased him; which was, that his cousin Monsieur de Shylock in Paris[2] had become the greatest baron of all Christendom, and received from their Catholic Majesties the Order of Isabella, which was originally instituted to celebrate the expulsion of Jews and Moors from Spain. But I found him not on the Rialto, so I determined to look for my old acquaintance in the Synagogue.

* * *

But while looking round for old Shylock and passing in careful review all the pale suffering faces of the Jews, I made a discovery which I—more is the pity!—cannot suppress. I had the same day visited the madhouse of San Carlo, and now it occurred to me in the Synagogue that there glimmered in the glances of the Jews the

9. Life in a country villa [Editor].
1. Merchant of Venice, act i. sc. 1.
2. Probable reference to Baron Lionel de Rothschild, a member of the internationally prominent Jewish banking family, who received the Catholic Order of Isabella in 1835 [Editor].

same dreadful, half staring, half unsteady, half crafty, half stupid expression which I had previously seen in the eyes of the lunatics in San Carlo. This indescribable, perplexing look did not so much indicate absence of mind as rather the supremacy of a fixed idea. Has perhaps the faith in that extra-mundane thunder-god whom Moses preached, become the fixed idea of a whole race, so that, though they have for two thousand years suffered from it in strait-jackets and shower-baths, yet for all that will not give it up—like that lunatic lawyer whom I saw in San Carlo, who would not be persuaded but what the sun was an English cheese, the rays of which were long red maggots, and that one of these worm-rays was eating away his brain.

I will here by no means deny the value of that fixed idea, but I will only say that those who have it are much too weak to manage it, and therefore being oppressed by it have become incurable. What tremendous martyrdom have they suffered from it! what greater martyrdoms await them in future! I shudder at the thought, and an infinite pity ripples through my heart. * * *

* * *

SIGMUND FREUD

The Theme of the Three Caskets†

I

Two scenes from Shakespeare, one from a comedy and the other from a tragedy, have lately given me occasion for posing and solving a small problem.

The first of these scenes is the suitors' choice between the three caskets in *The Merchant of Venice*. The fair and wise Portia is bound at her father's bidding to take as her husband only that one of her suitors who chooses the right casket from among the three before him. The three caskets are of gold, silver and lead: the right casket is the one that contains her portrait. Two suitors have already departed unsuccessful: they have chosen gold and silver. Bassanio, the third, decides in favour of lead; thereby he wins the bride, whose affection was already his before the trial of fortune. Each of the suitors gives reasons for his choice in a speech in

---

† From "The Theme of the Three Caskets" (1913) in *The Standard Edition of the Complete Psychological Works of Sigmund Freud*, trans. James Strachey, 12 (London: Hogarth Press, 1958), pp. 291–300. Copyright © The Institute of Psycho-Analysis and The Hogarth Press. Reprinted by permission of The Random House Group Ltd. Notes and comments in brackets are those of Freud's editors.

which he praises the metal he prefers and depreciates the other two. The most difficult task thus falls to the share of the fortunate third suitor; what he finds to say in glorification of lead as against gold and silver is little and has a forced ring. If in psycho-analytic practice we were confronted with such a speech, we should suspect that there were concealed motives behind the unsatisfying reasons produced.

Shakespeare did not himself invent this oracle of the choice of a casket; he took it from a tale in the *Gesta Romanorum*,[1] in which a girl has to make the same choice to win the Emperor's son.[2] Here too the third metal, lead, is the bringer of fortune. It is not hard to guess that we have here an ancient theme, which requires to be interpreted, accounted for and traced back to its origin. A first conjecture as to the meaning of this choice between gold, silver and lead is quickly confirmed by a statement of Stucken's,[3] who has made a study of the same material over a wide field. He writes: "The identity of Portia's three suitors is clear from their choice: the Prince of Morocco chooses the gold casket—he is the sun; the Prince of Arragon chooses the silver casket—he is the moon; Bassanio chooses the leaden casket—he is the star youth." In support of this explanation he cites an episode from the Estonian folk-epic "Kalewipoeg", in which the three suitors appear undisguisedly as the sun, moon and star youths (the last being "the Pole-star's eldest boy") and once again the bride falls to the lot of the third.

Thus our little problem has led us to an astral myth! The only pity is that with this explanation we are not at the end of the matter. The question is not exhausted, for we do not share the belief of some investigators that myths were read in the heavens and brought down to earth; we are more inclined to judge with Otto Rank[4] that they were projected on to the heavens after having arisen elsewhere under purely human conditions. It is in this human content that our interest lies.

Let us look once more at our material. In the Estonian epic, just as in the tale from the *Gesta Romanorum*, the subject is a girl choosing between three suitors; in the scene from *The Merchant of Venice* the subject is apparently the same, but at the same time something appears in it that is in the nature of an inversion of the theme: a *man* chooses between three—caskets. If what we were concerned with were a dream, it would occur to us at once that caskets are also women, symbols of what is essential in woman, and therefore of a woman herself—like coffers, boxes, cases, baskets,

1. [A mediaeval collection of stories of unknown authorship.]
2. Brandes (1896).
3. Stucken (1907, 655).
4. Rank (1909, 8 ff.).

154   SIGMUND FREUD

and so on.[5] If we boldly assume that there are symbolic sub-
stitutions of the same kind in myths as well, then the casket scene
in *The Merchant of Venice* really becomes the inversion we suspected. With a wave of the wand, as though we were in a fairy tale,
we have stripped the astral garment from our theme; and now we
see that the theme is a human one, *a man's choice between three
women*.

This same content, however, is to be found in another scene of
Shakespeare's, in one of his most powerfully moving dramas; not
the choice of a bride this time, yet linked by many hidden similarities to the choice of the casket in *The Merchant of Venice*. The old
King Lear resolves to divide his kingdom while he is still alive
among his three daughters, in proportion to the amount of love
that each of them expresses for him. The two elder ones, Goneril
and Regan, exhaust themselves in asseverations and laudations of
their love for him; the third, Cordelia, refuses to do so. He should
have recognized the unassuming, speechless love of his third
daughter and rewarded it, but he does not recognize it. He disowns
Cordelia, and divides the kingdom between the other two, to his
own and the general ruin. Is not this once more the scene of a
choice between three women, of whom the youngest is the best,
the most excellent one?

There will at once occur to us other scenes from myths, fairy
tales and literature, with the same situation as their content. The
shepherd Paris has to choose between three goddesses, of whom he
declares the third to be the most beautiful. Cinderella, again, is a
youngest daughter, who is preferred by the prince to her two elder
sisters. Psyche, in Apuleius's story, is the youngest and fairest of
three sisters. Psyche is, on the one hand, revered as Aphrodite in
human form; on the other, she is treated by that goddess as Cinderella was treated by her stepmother and is set the task of sorting
a heap of mixed seeds, which she accomplishes with the help of
small creatures (doves in the case of Cinderella, ants in the case of
Psyche).[6] Anyone who cared to make a wider survey of the material
would undoubtedly discover other versions of the same theme preserving the same essential features.

Let us be content with Cordelia, Aphrodite, Cinderella and Psyche. In all the stories the three women, of whom the third is the
most excellent one, must surely be regarded as in some way alike if
they are represented as sisters. (We must not be led astray by the
fact that Lear's choice is between three *daughters*; this may mean
nothing more than that he has to be represented as an old man. An

5. [See *The Interpretation of Dreams* (1900a), Standard Ed., 5, 354.]
6. I have to thank Dr. Otto Rank for calling my attention to these similarities. [Cf. a reference to this in Chapter XII of *Group Psychology* (1921c), Standard Ed., 18, 136.]

old man cannot very well choose between three women in any other way. Thus they become his daughters.)

But who are these three sisters and why must the choice fall on the third? If we could answer this question, we should be in possession of the interpretation we are seeking. We have once already made use of an application of psycho-analytic technique, when we explained the three caskets symbolically as three women. If we have the courage to proceed in the same way, we shall be setting foot on a path which will lead us first to something unexpected and incomprehensible, but which will perhaps, by a devious route, bring us to a goal.

It must strike us that this excellent third woman has in several instances certain peculiar qualities besides her beauty. They are qualities that seem to be tending towards some kind of unity; we must certainly not expect to find them equally well marked in every example. Cordelia makes herself unrecognizable, inconspicuous like lead, she remains dumb, she "loves and is silent"[7] Cinderella hides so that she cannot be found. We may perhaps be allowed to equate concealment and dumbness. These would of course be only two instances out of the five we have picked out. But there is an intimation of the same thing to be found, curiously enough, in two other cases. We have decided to compare Cordelia, with her obstinate refusal, to lead. In Bassanio's short speech while he is choosing the casket, he says of lead (without in any way leading up to the remark):

"Thy paleness[8] moves me more than eloquence."

That is to say: "Thy plainness moves me more than the blatant nature of the other two." Gold and silver are "loud"; lead is dumb—in fact like Cordelia, who "loves and is silent".[9]

In the ancient Greek accounts of the Judgement of Paris, nothing is said of any such reticence on the part of Aphrodite. Each of the three goddesses speaks to the youth and tries to win him by promises. But, oddly enough, in a quite modern handling of the same scene this characteristic of the third one which has struck us makes its appearance again. In the libretto of Offenbach's La Belle Hélène, Paris, after telling of the solicitations of the other two goddesses, describes Aphrodite's behaviour in this competition for the beauty-prize:

7. [From an aside of Cordelia's, Act I, Scene I.]
8. 'Plainness' according to another reading.
9. In Schlegel's translation this allusion is quite lost; indeed, it is given the opposite meaning: "Dein schlichtes Wesen spricht beredt mich an." ["Thy plainness speaks to me with eloquence."]

La troisième, ah! la troisième . . .
La troisième ne dit rien.
Elle eut le prix tout de même . . .[1]

If we decide to regard the peculiarities of our "third one" as concentrated in her "dumbness", then psycho-analysis will tell us that in dreams dumbness is a common representation of death.[2]

More than ten years ago a highly intelligent man told me a dream which he wanted to use as evidence of the telepathic nature of dreams. In it he saw an absent friend from whom he had received no news for a very long time, and reproached him energetically for his silence. The friend made no reply. It afterwards turned out that he had met his death by suicide at about the time of the dream. Let us leave the problem of telepathy on one side:[3] there seems, however, not to be any doubt that here the dumbness in the dream represented death. Hiding and being unfindable—a thing which confronts the prince in the fairy tale of Cinderella three times, is another unmistakable symbol of death in dreams; so, too, is a marked pallor, of which the "paleness" of the lead in one reading of Shakespeare's text is a reminder.[4] It would be very much easier for us to transpose these interpretations from the language of dreams to the mode of expression used in the myth that is now under consideration if we could make it seem probable that dumbness must be interpreted as a sign of being dead in productions other than dreams.

At this point I will single out the ninth story in Grimm's *Fairy Tales*, which bears the title "The Twelve Brothers".[5] A king and a queen have twelve children, all boys. The king declares that if the thirteenth child is a girl, the boys will have to die. In expectation of her birth he has twelve coffins made. With their mother's help the twelve sons take refuge in a hidden wood, and swear death to any girl they may meet. A girl is born, grows up, and learns one day from her mother that she has had twelve brothers. She decides to seek them out, and in the wood she finds the youngest; he recognizes her, but is anxious to hide her on account of the brothers' oath. The sister says: "I will gladly die, if by so doing I can save my twelve brothers." The brothers welcome her affectionately, however, and she stays with them and looks after their house for them.

---

1. [Literally: "The third one, ah! the third one . . . the third one said nothing. She won the prize all the same."—The quotation is from Act I, Scene 7, of Meilhac and Halévy's libretto. In the German version used by Freud "the third one" *"blieb stumm"*—"remained dumb".]
2. In Stekel's *Sprache des Traumes*, too, dumbness is mentioned among the "death" symbols (1911a, 351). [Cf. *The Interpretation of Dreams* (1900a), *Standard Ed.*, 5, 357.]
3. [Cf. Freud's later paper on "Dreams and Telepathy" (1922a).]
4. Stekel (1911a), loc. cit.
5. ["Die zwölf Brüder." Grimm, 1918, 1, 42.]

In a little garden beside the house grow twelve lilies. The girl picks them and gives one to each brother. At that moment the brothers are changed into ravens, and disappear, together with the house and garden. (Ravens are spirit-birds; the killing of the twelve brothers by their sister is represented by the picking of the flowers, just as it is at the beginning of the story by the coffins and the disappearance of the brothers.) The girl, who is once more ready to save her brothers from death, is now told that as a condition she must be dumb for seven years, and not speak a single word. She submits to the test, which brings her herself into mortal danger. She herself, that is, dies for her brothers, as she promised to do before she met them. By remaining dumb she succeeds at last in setting the ravens free.

In the story of "The Six Swans"[6] the brothers who are changed into birds are set free in exactly the same way—they are restored to life by their sister's dumbness. The girl has made a firm resolve to free her brothers, "even if it should cost her her life"; and once again (being the wife of the king) she risks her own life because she refuses to give up her dumbness in order to defend herself against evil accusations.

It would certainly be possible to collect further evidence from fairy tales that dumbness is to be understood as representing death. These indications would lead us to conclude that the third one of the sisters between whom the choice is made is a dead woman. But she may be something else as well—namely, Death itself, the Goddess of Death. Thanks to a displacement that is far from infrequent, the qualities that a deity imparts to men are ascribed to the deity himself. Such a displacement will surprise us least of all in relation to the Goddess of Death, since in modern versions and representations, which these stories would thus be forestalling, Death itself is nothing other than a dead man.

But if the third of the sisters is the Goddess of Death, the sisters are known to us. They are the Fates, the Moerae, the Parcae or the Norns, the third of whom is called Atropos, the inexorable.

II

We will for the time being put aside the task of inserting the interpretation that we have found into our myth, and listen to what the mythologists have to teach us about the role and origin of the Fates.[7]

The earliest Greek mythology (in Homer) only knew a single Moira, personifying inevitable fate. The further development of this

6. ["Die sechs Schwäne." Grimm, 1918, 1, 217. (No. 49.)]
7. What follows is taken from Roscher's lexicon [1884–1937], under the relevant headings.

one Moera into a company of three (or less often two) sister-goddesses probably came about on the basis of other divine figures to which the Moerae were closely related—the Graces and the Horae [the Seasons].

The Horae were originally goddesses of the waters of the sky, dispensing rain and dew, and of the clouds from which rain falls; and, since the clouds were conceived of as something that has been spun, it came about that these goddesses were looked upon as spinners, an attribute that then became attached to the Moerae. In the sun-favoured Mediterranean lands it is the rain on which the fertility of the soil depends, and thus the Horae became vegetation goddesses. The beauty of flowers and the abundance of fruit was their doing, and they were accredited with a wealth of agreeable and charming traits. They became the divine representatives of the Seasons, and it is possibly owing to this connection that there were three of them, if the sacred nature of the number three is not a sufficient explanation. For the peoples of antiquity at first distinguished only three seasons: winter, spring and summer. Autumn was only added in late Graeco-Roman times, after which the Horae were often represented in art as four in number.

The Horae retained their relation to time. Later they presided over the times of day, as they did at first over the times of the year; and at last their name came to be merely a designation of the hours (*heure*, *ora*). The Norns of German mythology are akin to the Horae and the Moerae and exhibit this time-signification in their names.[8] It was inevitable, however, that a deeper view should come to be taken of the essential nature of these deities, and that their essence should be transposed on to the regularity with which the seasons change. The Horae thus became the guardians of natural law and of the divine Order which causes the same thing to recur in Nature in an unalterable sequence.

This discovery of Nature reacted on the conception of human life. The nature-myth changed into a human myth: the weather-goddesses became goddesses of Fate. But this aspect of the Horae found expression only in the Moerae, who watch over the necessary ordering of human life as inexorably as do the Horae over the regular order of nature. The ineluctable severity of Law and its relation to death and dissolution, which had been avoided in the charming figures of the Horae, were now stamped upon the Moerae, as though men had only perceived the full seriousness of natural law when they had to submit their own selves to it.

The names of the three spinners, too, have been significantly explained by mythologists. Lachesis, the name of the second, seems

8. [Their names may be rendered: "What was," "What is," "What shall be."]

to denote "the accidental that is included in the regularity of destiny"[9]—or, as we should say, "experience"; just as Atropos stands for "the ineluctable"—Death. Clotho[1] would then be left to mean the innate disposition with its fateful implications.

But now it is time to return to the theme which we are trying to interpret—the theme of the choice between three sisters. We shall be deeply disappointed to discover how unintelligible the situations under review become and what contradictions of their apparent content result, if we apply to them the interpretation that we have found. On our supposition the third of the sisters is the Goddess of Death, Death itself. But in the Judgement of Paris she is the Goddess of Love, in the tale of Apuleius she is someone comparable to the goddess for her beauty, in *The Merchant of Venice* she is the fairest and wisest of women, in *King Lear* she is the one loyal daughter. We may ask whether there can be a more complete contradiction. Perhaps, improbable though it may seem, there is a still more complete one lying close at hand. Indeed, there certainly is; since, whenever our theme occurs, the choice between the women is free, and yet it falls on death. For, after all, no one chooses death, and it is only by a fatality that one falls a victim to it.

However, contradictions of a certain kind—replacements by the precise opposite—offer no serious difficulty to the work of analytic interpretation. We shall not appeal here to the fact that contraries are so often represented by one and the same element in the modes of expression used by the unconscious, as for instance in dreams.[2] But we shall remember that there are motive forces in mental life which bring about replacement by the opposite in the form of what is known as reaction-formation; and it is precisely in the revelation of such hidden forces as these that we look for the reward of this enquiry. The Moerae were created as a result of a discovery that warned man that he too is a part of nature and therefore subject to the immutable law of death. Something in man was bound to struggle against this subjection, for it is only with extreme unwillingness that he gives up his claim to an exceptional position. Man, as we know, makes use of his imaginative activity in order to satisfy the wishes that reality does not satisfy. So his imagination rebelled against the recognition of the truth embodied in the myth of the Moerae, and constructed instead the myth derived from it, in which the Goddess of Death was replaced by the Goddess of Love and by what was equivalent to her in human shape. The third of the sisters was no longer Death; she was the fairest, best, most desirable and most lovable of women. Nor was this substitution in any

9. Roscher [ibid.], quoting Preller, ed. Robert (1894).
1. The youngest of the three Fates [*Editor*].
2. [Cf. *The Interpretation of Dreams* (1900a), *Standard Ed.*, 4, 318.]

way technically difficult: it was prepared for by an ancient ambivalence, it was carried out along a primaeval line of connection which
could not long have been forgotten. The Goddess of Love herself,
who now took the place of the Goddess of Death, had once been
identical with her. Even the Greek Aphrodite had not wholly relin-
quished her connection with the underworld, although she had
long surrendered her chthonic role to other divine figures, to Perse-
phone, or to the tri-form Artemis-Hecate. The great Mother-
goddesses of the oriental peoples, however, all seem to have been
both creators and destroyers—both goddesses of life and fertility
and goddesses of death. Thus the replacement by a wishful opposite in our theme harks back to a primaeval identity.

The same consideration answers the question how the feature of
a choice came into the myth of the three sisters. Here again there
has been a wishful reversal. Choice stands in the place of necessity,
of destiny. In this way man overcomes death, which he has recognized intellectually. No greater triumph of wish-fulfilment is conceivable. A choice is made where in reality there is obedience to a
compulsion; and what is chosen is not a figure of terror, but the
fairest and most desirable of women.

On closer inspection we observe, to be sure, that the original
myth is not so thoroughly distorted that traces of it do not show
through and betray its presence. The free choice between the three
sisters is, properly speaking, no free choice, for it must necessarily
fall on the third if every kind of evil is not to come about, as it does
in *King Lear*. The fairest and best of women, who has taken the
place of the Death-goddess, has kept certain characteristics that
border on the uncanny, so that from them we have been able to
guess at what lies beneath.

* * *

Works Cited

Brandes, G. (1896) *William Shakespeare*. Paris, Leipzig, Munich.
Freud, S. (1953–74) *Standard Edition of the Complete Psychological Works*, ed. and trans.
   James Strachey, *et al*. 24 vols. London: Hogarth Press.
Grimm, J. and W. (1918) *Die Märchen der Brüder Grimm* (complete edition). Leipzig.
Rank, O. (1907) *Der Künstler, Ansätze zu einer Sexualpsychologie*. Leipzig and Vienna.
Roscher, W. H., ed. (1884–1937) *Ausfürliches Lexikon der griechischen und römischen
   Mythologie*. Leipzig.
Stekel, W. (1911) *Die Sprache des Traumes*. Wiesbaden.

G. WILSON KNIGHT

[The Music of *The Merchant of Venice*]†

* * *

The merchant-theme is developed further in *The Merchant of Venice*. In no play of this period is there so clear and significant a contrast between the tempests of tragedy and the music of romance. The play opens with a fine description of Antonio's argosies:

SALARINO.[1] Your mind is tossing on the ocean;
  There, where your argosies with portly sail,
  Like signiors and rich burghers on the flood,
  Or, as it were, the pageants of the sea,
  Do overpeer the petty traffickers,
  That curtsy to them, do them reverence,
  As they fly by them with their woven wings.
SALANIO. Believe me, sir, had I such venture forth,
  The better part of my affections would
  Be with my hopes abroad. I should be still
  Plucking the grass, to know where sits the wind,
  Peering in maps for ports, and piers, and roads;
  And every object that might make me fear
  Misfortune to my ventures, out of doubt
  Would make me sad.
SALARINO.   My wind cooling my broth
  Would blow me to an ague, when I thought
  What harm a wind too great at sea might do.
  I should not see the sandy hour-glass run,
  But I should think of shallows and of flats,
  And see my wealthy Andrew dock'd in sand,
  Vailing her high top lower than her ribs
  To kiss her burial. Should I go to church,
  And see the holy edifice of stone,
  And not bethink me straight of dangerous rocks,
  Which, touching but my gentle vessel's side,
  Would scatter all her spices on the stream,
  Enrobe the roaring waters with my silks,
  And, in a word, but even now worth this,
  And now worth nothing? Shall I have the thought
  To think on this; and shall I lack the thought,
  That such a thing bechanc'd would make me sad?

---

† From *The Shakespearian Tempest* (London: Oxford University Press, 1932), pp. 127–37. Copyright © 1932. Reprinted with the permission of Oxford University Press.
1. In most modern editions the names Salarino and Salanio are regularized to Salerio and Solanio. See the discussion of names on p. 77 [*Editor*].

> But tell not me; I know, Antonio
> Is sad to think upon his merchandise.   (I. i. 8)

Notice how the sea is impregnated with melancholy suggestion. So is it in another passage, referring to human enthusiasm and its all-too-quick extinction:

> How like a younker or a prodigal
> The scarfed bark puts from her native bay,
> Hugg'd and embraced by the strumpet wind!
> How like the prodigal doth she return,
> With over-weather'd ribs and ragged sails,
> Lean, rent, and beggar'd by the strumpet wind!   (II. vi. 14)

Such is a true Shakespearian image of life's voyages. We see how universal is the content of our "bark" and "tempest" passages.

Throughout this play we must observe the opposition of sea tragedy and romance, which opposition is more powerfully and exactly significant here than in any other of these plays. The tempest-music opposition is indeed more essentially dramatic here than in our former plays: the two impressions oppose each other almost like dramatic persons. From Venice and Antonio's melancholy we are taken eastward over seas to Love's magic land, Belmont. Bassanio tells Antonio of the rich Portia—we may remember that love itself is a kind of "riches"—and her home across the sea:

> Nor is the wide world ignorant of her worth,
> For the four winds blow in from every coast
> Renowned suitors, and her sunny locks
> Hang on her temples like a Golden Fleece;
> Which makes her seat of Belmont Colchos' strond,
> And many Jasons come in quest of her.   (I. i. 167)

Bassanio's quest is a "sea" adventure. But we may also note that Bassanio's journey separates him from his lover, Antonio. The farewell is described (II. viii). We may, too, observe a Venice-Belmont contrast. Venice is, of all towns, most closely associated with the sea, even interwoven with it; and Belmont suggests a more airy height, a finer element. Venice is the scene of tragedy, Belmont of love. The one is overcast with gloom—we may note that even the masque never actually comes off; the other is a land of music, love, and "holy crosses". Morocco later repeats the idea expressed by Bassanio in his "Jason" speech:

> The Hyrcanian deserts and the vasty wilds
> Of wide Arabia are as throughfares now
> For princes to come view fair Portia:
> The watery kingdom, whose ambitious head

> Spits in the face of heaven, is no bar
> To stop the foreign spirits, but they come,
> As o'er a brook, to see fair Portia.   (II. vii. 41)

* * * Antonio undertakes the venture for love's merchandise. He loves Bassanio, and his risk is wholly a merchant's venture for the sake of love; his love for Bassanio, Bassanio's for Portia. The gold of love is finely associated and yet strongly contrasted with love's gold in the Casket scene. Morocco's Arragon's, and Bassanio's speeches on the gold, silver, and lead caskets are most significant. This play is full of "riches" imagery. Such ornament

> is but the guiled shore
> To a most dangerous sea; the beauteous scarf
> Veiling an Indian beauty.   (III. ii. 97)

Again the Siren idea, here given in terms of an "Indian beauty". Though this may at first suggest "Indian" to have a wholly derogatory sense, we may compare the lover who "sees Helen's beauty in a brow of Egypt" (*A Midsummer Night's Dream*, v. i. 11). And we remember Cleopatra. Such passages suggest, partly at least, the mystery and glamour of the East, the dangerous Indian shores of fairyland, that fairyland's too often untrustworthy and cheating lure. So merchandise, gold and silver caskets, Portia's ring, all the usual associations interthread our texture. But here they are unusually powerful, both actualized and dramatically active. Imagery is becoming the very plot itself. Twenty merchants (III. ii. 282) have attempted to placate Shylock. Antonio is "a royal merchant" (III. ii. 242); Portia's boundless wealth is emphasized again and again; riches are scattered over the play. Shylock himself loses both his loved daughter and vast riches, "ducats", jewels, his "turquoise". Love and riches are ever close. The play is full of ducats and wealth. Shylock rates his ducats and jewels above his daughter, strongly as he loves her; but Bassanio's and Portia's love is finely shown as being of an integrity that sees through the superficial brilliance of gold to the true worth within: hence Bassanio's choice of the leaden casket. These caskets are intensely symbolical. As in *Timon*, the spiritual gold of true love is contrasted with the outward gilding which decorates the false.

And there is music. Belmont is the home of love and music:

> Let music sound while he doth make his choice;
> Then, if he lose, he makes a swan-like end,
> Fading in music: that the comparison
> May stand more proper, my eye shall be the stream
> And watery death-bed for him. He may win;
> And what is music then? Then music is

> Even as the flourish when true subjects bow
> To a new-crowned monarch: such it is
> As are those dulcet sounds in break of day
> That creep into the dreaming bridegroom's ear
> And summon him to marriage.   (III. ii. 43)

A lovely speech, rich in typical suggestion. We should note the
death and music association, the eye-stream comparison, and the
"watery death-bed": death by water made sweet in music, like
Ophelia's death or like the music in which the tragedy of *Othello*
dissolves in beauty. And, after the "death" thought, the victory of
love: love "crowned" like a king, the music that awakes the sleeper,
bidding him take his happiness. So Hermoine "awakes" to music in
The Winter's Tale. The purely imaginative order reflects the
progress later developed from the Tragedies to the Final Plays. So
here there is a song, "Tell me, where is fancy bred?", and music,
and Bassanio wins his joy. He is like Hercules rescuing his lady
from "the sea-monster" (III. ii. 55–8); and if we remember that both
the sea and all fierce beasts are equally symbols of mortal terror in
Shakespeare we may understand the terrific significance of sea-
monsters here and elsewhere, notably in *Lear*.

But Bassanio's joy is short-lived. Throughout we fear the sinister
forces of tempest on which the action depends. We know, like Shylock, that the sea is dangerous:

> . . . he hath an argosy bound to Tripolis, another to the Indies;
> I understand, moreover, upon the Rialto, he hath a third at
> Mexico, a fourth for England, and other ventures he hath,
> squandered abroad. But ships are but boards, sailors but men:
> there be land-rats and water-rats, water-thieves and land-
> thieves, I mean pirates, and then there is the peril of waters,
> winds, and rock. . . . (I. iii. 18)

Fears are justified:

> I reason'd with a Frenchman yesterday,
> Who told me, in the narrow seas that part
> The French and English, there miscarried
> A vessel of our country richly fraught.   (II. viii. 27)

Again,

> SALANIO. Now, what news on the Rialto?
> SALARINO. Why, yet it lives there unchecked that Antonio hath
> a ship of rich lading wrecked on the narrow seas; the Good-
> wins, I think they call the place; a very dangerous flat and
> fatal, where the carcases of many a tall ship lie buried. . . .
>   (III. i. 1)

Tubal, who "spoke with some of the sailors that escaped the wreck" (III. i. 109), tells Shylock that Antonio "hath an argosy cast away, coming from Tripolis" (III. i. 105). All Antonio's ships have failed:

> But is it true, Salerio?
> Have all his ventures fail'd? What, not one hit?
> From Tripolis, from Mexico, and England,
> From Lisbon, Barbary, and India?
> And not one vessel 'scape the dreadful touch
> Of merchant-marring rocks?   (III. ii. 269)

"Twenty merchants" (III. ii. 282) sue on Antonio's behalf. But Shylock is firm. Tempests have leagued with Shylock, both equally forces of tragedy to be set against love, music, and Portia.

It is significant that Shylock hates festive music:

> Lock up my doors: and when you hear the drum
> And the vile squealing of the wry-neck'd fife,
> Clamber not you up to the casements then,
> Nor thrust your head into the public street
> To gaze on Christian fools with varnished faces,
> But stop my house's ears, I mean my casements;
> Let not the sound of shallow foppery enter
> My sober house.   (II. v. 29)

He "has no mind of feasting forth". He is to be contrasted with music and feasting. His "music" phrases are naturally hostile: witness his other words about when the "bagpipe sings i' the nose" (IV. i. 49) and its unpleasant effects. Now Shylock himself is like a "tempest". He is the tragedy-force in the play. "The very tyranny and rage" of his "spirit" (IV. i. 13) is a typical tempest impression recalling the music in *Love's Labour's Lost* that could "ravish savage ears and plant in tyrants mild humility" (*Love's Labour's Lost*, IV. iii. 348). The "current" of his cruelty is "unfeeling" (IV. i. 63–4). Again,

> I pray you, think you question with the Jew:
> You may as well go stand upon the beach
> And bid the main flood bate his usual height;
> You may as well use question with the wolf
> Why he hath made the ewe bleat for the lamb;
> You may as well forbid the mountain pines
> To wag their high tops and to make no noise,
> When they are fretted with the gusts of heaven;
> You may as well do any thing most hard,
> As seek to soften that—than which what's harder?—
> His Jewish heart.   (IV. i. 70)

"Tops" is a usual word in tempest passages, applied both to waves and mountain-trees. "Pines" are important in such passages. Here

we should observe also (i) the sea, (ii) the wolf, and (iii) the winds:
all associated with human cruelty, and the forces of tragedy. Here
the wolf, thus enclosed by the other two, stresses the association.
Elsewhere Shylock is powerfully compared to a wolf in a speech
which vividly outlines the Shakespearian intuition of the beast in
man:

> O, be thou damn'd, inexecrable dog!
> And for thy life let justice be accused.
> Thou almost makest me waver in my faith
> To hold opinion with Pythagoras,
> That souls of animals infuse themselves
> Into the trunks of men: thy currish spirit
> Govern'd a wolf, who, hang'd for human slaughter,
> Even from the gallows did his fell soul fleet,
> And, whilst thou lay'st in thy unhallow'd dam
> Infused itself in thee; for thy desires
> Are wolvish, bloody, starved and ravenous.
>
>   (IV. i. 128)

This play as certainly as, and more tragically than, the Induction to
The Taming of the Shrew, sets the beast in man against love and
music. The tempest-beast association is always important. And here
both are clearly to be related to Shylock and tragedy.

Tragedy in the form of merchant-marring tempests breaks into
the music of Bassanio's joy at the moment of his love-success at
Belmont. But Portia, love's queen, descends from the fairyland of
music and love, Belmont, into the turmoil and dust of human conflict and cruelty at Venice. She is as a being from a different world.
We may observe that she, like Shakespeare's other heroines, is often associated directly with thoughts of divinity. Here, we have Portia's lovely Mercy speech, and her pretended pilgrimage, reminding
us of Helena in *All's Well*. So she takes arms against the tragic
forces of tempest and wins.

We are finally brought back to Belmont, where again we find romance and music. Jessica and Lorenzo make love by moonlight:

> The moon shines bright; in such a night as this
> When the sweet wind did gently kiss the trees
> And they did make no noise, in such a night
> Troilus methinks mounted the Troyan walls
> And sigh'd his soul toward the Grecian tents,
> Where Cressid lay that night.   (V. i. 1)

Soft airs and love: a usual association, most notable of all in *Antony
and Cleopatra* and *Cymbeline*. Themselves happy, these lovers yet
image love's tragedies: Troilus sighing his soul out to the gentle sigh

of the wind, Thisbe who "saw the lion's shadow" and "ran dismay'd away" (V. i. 8), and finally, Dido, parted by cruel waters from her lover:

> In such a night
> Stood Dido with a willow in her hand
> Upon the wild sea-banks, and waft her love
> To come again to Carthage.   (V. i. 9)

A typical thought of love parted by water; and an inverse of our other sea-shore and love image, wherein love beckons across dangerous seas. The triple imagery is again important: (i) "wind" and "sighs", (ii) the "lion", and (iii) the "sea"—an almost exact repetition of our sea-beast-wind association just observed. Here it is less tempestuous, the beast nobler. Twice the "beast" is thus sandwiched between "sea" and "wind", which, being the main elements of our "tempest" symbol, here point clearly to the close beast-tempest association. Lorenzo calls for music to be brought forth "into the air". Then,

LORENZO. How sweet the moonlight sleeps upon this bank!
   Here will we sit and let the sounds of music
   Creep in our ears: soft stillness and the night
   Become the touches of sweet harmony.
   Sit, Jessica: look, how the floor of heaven
   Is thick inlaid with patines of bright gold:
   There's not the smallest orb which thou behold'st,
   But in his motion like an angel sings,
   Still quiring to the young-ey'd cherubins:
   Such harmony is in immortal souls;
   But, whilst this muddy vesture of decay
   Doth grossly close it in, we cannot hear it.
          Enter Musician.
   Come, ho! and wake Diana with a hymn:
   With sweetest touches pierce your mistress' ear,
   And draw her home with music
          [*Music*]
JESSICA. I am never merry when I hear sweet music.
LORENZO. The reason is, your spirits are attentive:
   For do but note a wild and wanton herd,
   Or race of youthful and unhandled colts,
   Fetching mad bounds, bellowing, and neighing loud,
   Which is the hot condition of their blood:
   If they but hear perchance a trumpet sound,
   Or any air of music touch their ears,
   You shall perceive them make a mutual stand,
   Their savage eyes turn'd to a modest gaze
   By the sweet power of music: therefore the poet

Did feign that Orpheus drew trees, stones, and floods;
Since nought so stockish, hard, and full of rage,
But music for the time doth change his nature.
The man that hath no music in himself,
Nor is not mov'd with concord of sweet sounds,
Is fit for treasons, stratagems, and spoils;
The motions of his spirit are dull as night,
And his affections dark as Erebus:
Let no such man be trusted.—Mark the music.

(v. i. 54)

Here we should observe the association of music, stillness, the moon, and love: all are elsewhere important. Stars, too, are a development of the moon idea and blend with jewel and gold imagery: "patines of bright gold". We remember the "gold candles" of Sonnet XXI. * * * See, too, how the "music of the spheres" mentioned also in *Twelfth Night* and *Pericles*, there, too, with love suggestion, is here quaintly and beautifully taken from its Ptolemaic context and given a Copernican significance. This spheral music is heard only by "immortal souls"—we may thus note its aptness in the paradisal vision of *Pericles*—but the universal harmony is blurred to mortal understanding. Here Portia, love's queen, is to be drawn home "with music". But Jessica is made sad by the too-great sweetness of music: we might compare Sonnet VIII. * * * Music thus charms the wildness of animals, a music-beast opposition; and music, similarly, can draw "trees, stones, and floods". Notice the tree-tempest association: it is often important. And a man who has not "music" in him is apt to disintegrate states: since music is equally suggestive of personal love or political concord. His soul is "dull as night" and "dark as Erebus": hence the "darkness" in connexion with conspiracy or murder in *Julius Caesar* and *Macbeth*. Music, stars, moonlight, and love are thus set against tempests, wild beasts, and dark conspiracy. We must ever observe the universal imagery of star, moon, and sun which blends with love and music.

So Portia returns. And in this final scene of love's victory over tragedy we should not be surprised that the melancholy Antonio, too, finds his way to Belmont, and that victorious love in Portia's person brings news of his ships' miraculous survival:

Antonio, you are welcome;
And I have better news in store for you
Than you expect: unseal this letter soon;
There you shall find three of your argosies
Are richly come to harbour suddenly:
You shall not know by what strange accident
I chanced on this letter.

(v. i. 273)

Antonio risked all material merchandise, even the rich merchandise of his own life, for Bassanio, for love. Love's prize, in turn, gives him back his ships. It is the conquest of romance over tragedy, music and love's gold over tempests. No play more perfectly illustrates the Shakesperian feeling for merchants, riches, gold, tempests, and music entwined and interactive. These elements are here most concretely embodied in the plot, in the action. Imaginative forces conflict, and the plot is made to suit them. The play is thus highly charged with poetic power from start to finish.

* * *

BARBARA K. LEWALSKI

Biblical Allusion and Allegory in *The Merchant of Venice*†

* * *

The allegorical aspects of *The Merchant of Venice* can, I believe, be greatly illuminated by the medieval allegorical method exemplified by Dante. Indeed, though it omits *MV*, a recent study by Bernard Spivack has persuasively argued the utility of the Dante comparison in comprehending the allegorical origins and characteristics of many Shakespearian villains.[1] In contrast to personification allegory wherein a particular is created to embody an insensible, Dante's symbolic method causes a particular real situation to suggest a meaning or meanings beyond itself. In *MV* Shakespeare, like Dante, is ultimately concerned with the nature of the Christian life, though as a dramatist he is fully as interested in the way in which the allegorical dimensions enrich the particular instance as in the use of the particular to point to higher levels of meaning. The various dimensions of allegorical significance in *MV*, though not consistently maintained throughout the play and not susceptible of analysis with schematic rigor, are generally analogous to Dante's four levels of allegorical meaning: a literal or story level; an allegorical significance concerned with truths relating to humanity as a whole and to Christ as head of humanity; a moral or tropological level dealing with factors in the moral development of the individual; and an anagogical significance treating the ultimate

---

† From "Biblical Allusion and Allegory in *The Merchant of Venice*," *Shakespeare Quarterly* 13 (1962): 328–43. Copyright © Folger Shakespeare Library. Reprinted with the permission of The Johns Hopkins University Press.
1. *Shakespeare and the Allegory of Evil: The History of a Metaphor in Relation to His Major Villains* (N. Y., 1958), pp. 50–99.

reality, the Heavenly City.[2] Moreover, comprehension of the play's allegorical meanings leads to a recognition of its fundamental unity, discrediting the common critical view that it is a hotchpotch which developed contrary to Shakespeare's conscious intention.

The use of Biblical allusion to point to such allegorical meanings must now be illustrated in relation to the various parts of the work.

Antonio and Shylock

At what would correspond in medieval terminology to the "moral" level, the play is concerned to explore and define Christian love and its various antitheses.[3] As revealed in the action, Christian love involves both giving and forgiving: it demands an attitude of carelessness regarding the things of this world founded upon a trust in God's providence; an attitude of self-forgetfulness and humility founded upon recognition of man's common sinfulness; a readiness to give and risk everything, possessions and person, for the sake of love; and a willingness to forgive injuries and to love enemies. In all but the last respect, Antonio is presented throughout the play as the very embodiment of Christian love, and Shylock functions as one (but not the only) antithesis to it.

Antonio's practice of Christian love is indicated throughout the play under the metaphor of "venturing", and the action begins with the use of this metaphor in a mock test of his attitude toward wealth and worldly goods. The key scripture text opposing love of this world to the Christian love of God and neighbor is Matt. vi. 19–21, 31–33:

> Lay not up treasures for your selves upon the earth, where the moth and canker corrupt, & where theeves dig through, and steale. / But lay up treasures for your selves in heaven. . . . / For where your treasure is, there will your heart be also / . . . . Therefore take no thought, saying, what shall we eate? or what shall we drink? or wherewith shall we be clothed? / . . . But seeke ye first the kingdome of God, and his righteousnesse, & all these things shalbe ministred unto you.[4]

2. H. Flanders Dunbar, *Symbolism in Medieval Thought* (New Haven, 1929), pp. 19, 497. Cf. Dante, "Letter to Can Grande della Scala", in *Dante's Eleven Letters*, ed. G. R. Carpenter (N. Y., 1892).

3. Many critics have suggested that the play is essentially concerned with the contrast and evaluation of certain moral values—such as money, love, and friendship; appearance and reality; true love and fancy; mercy and justice; generosity and possessiveness; the usury of commerce and the usury of love. See J. R. Brown, "Introduction," *The Merchant of Venice*, Arden edition (London, 1955), pp. xxxvii–lviii; M. C. Bradbrook, *Shakespeare and Elizabethan Poetry* (London, 1951), pp. 170–79; Cary B. Graham, "Standards of Value in the *Merchant of Venice*", *Shakespeare Quarterly*, IV (N. Y., 1953), 145–51; C. R. Baskervill, "Bassanio as an Ideal Lover", *Manly Anniversary Studies*, pp. 90–103. All these, however, may be subsumed under the central concern, Christian Love.

4. Unless otherwise indicated, scripture quotations are from the *Geneva Bible* (London,

In language directly alluding to this passage, Salario suggests that Antonio's melancholy may result from worry about his "ventures" at sea: "Your mind is tossing on the ocean, / There where your argosies [are]", and Solanio continues in this vein: "had I such venture forth, / The better part of my affections would / Be with my hopes abroad" (I. i. 8–9, 15–17).[5] Gratiano repeats the charge— "You have too much respect upon the world. / They lose it that do buy it with much care" (I. i. 74–75)—a speech also recalling Matt. xvi. 25–26, "Whosoever will save his life, shall lose it. . . . / For what shall it profite a man, though he should winne the whole worlde, if he lose his owne soule?" Yet the validity of Antonio's disclaimer, "I hold the world but as the world Gratiano" (I. i. 77)— that is, as the world deserves to be held—is soon evident: his sadness is due not to worldly concern but to the imminent parting with his beloved friend Bassanio. After witnessing this parting Salerio testifies, "I think he only loves the world for him" (II. viii. 50).

Gratiano's second playful charge, that Antonio's melancholy may be a pose to feed his self-importance, to seem a "Sir Oracle" with a wise and grave demeanor (I. i. 88–102), recalls the passage in I Cor. xiii. 4–5 where Paul characterizes Christian love in terms of humility and self-forgetfulness: "Love suffereth long: it is bountifull: love envieth not: love doth not boast it selfe: it is not puffed up. / It disdaineth not: it seeketh not her owne things." But this charge against Antonio is quickly dismissed by Bassanio as "an infinite deal of nothing" (I. i. 114–18).

The quality of Antonio's love is then shown in the positive forms of charity and benevolence, according to the following requirements of scripture:

> Give to every man that asketh of thee: and of him that taketh away thy goods, aske them not againe. / And if ye lende to them of whom yee hope to receive, what thanke shal ye have? for even the sinners lend to sinners, to receive the like. / Wherefore . . . doe good, & lend, looking for nothing againe, and your reward shall be great (Luke vi. 30, 34–35).

1584; 1st ed., 1560). Richmond Noble, *Shakespeare's Biblical Knowledge* (London, 1935), notes that all of Shakespeare's Biblical allusions are drawn from one or more of the following versions—*Geneva, Geneva-Tomson* (1st ed., 1576), and the *Bishops Bible* (1st ed., 1568), and that the first two, being quartos, had the widest circulation during the period. For this play, the Geneva renderings seem on the whole closest, though occasionally the phraseology suggests that of the *Bishops Bible*, which Shakespeare may have recalled from the church services.

5. In these speeches they testify to their own failure to come up to the standard of Christian perfection achieved by Antonio. Shylock's later speech concerning Antonio's "sufficiency" also alludes to the imagery of this Biblical passage in describing the transiency of worldly goods: "Ships are but boards, sailors but men, there be land-rats, and water-rats, water-thieves and land-thieves" (I. iii. 19–21).

> Greater love then this hath no man, then any man bestoweth
> his life for his friendes (John xv. 13).

Though his first loan to Bassanio has not been repaid, Antonio is
willing to "venture" again for his friend "My purse, my person, my
extremest means" (I. i. 138), even to the pledge of a pound of his
flesh. And when this pledge (and with it his life) is forfeit, he can
still release Bassanio from debt: "debts are clear'd between you and
I" (III. ii. 317). Furthermore, Antonio lends money in the community at large without seeking interest, and often aids victims of Shylock's usurious practices (I. iii. 39–40; III. iii. 22–23).

Shylock's "thrift" poses the precise contrast to Antonio's "ventures". His is the worldliness of niggardly prudence, well-
characterized by his avowed motto, "Fast bind, fast find,— / A
proverb never stale in thrifty mind" (II. v. 53–54). He locks up
house and stores before departing, he begrudges food and maintenance to his servant Launcelot, he demands usurious "assurance"
before lending money. This concern with the world poisons all his
relations with others and even his love for Jessica: the confused
cries, "My daughter! O my ducats! O my daughter!" after Jessica's
departure (II. viii. 15), reveal, not his lack of love for his daughter,
but his laughable and pitiable inability to determine what he loves
most. Shylock also manifests pride and self-righteousness. He
scorns Antonio's "low simplicity" in lending money gratis (I. iii.
38–39), despises the "prodigal" Bassanio for giving feasts (II. v. 15),
and considers the "shallow fopp'ry" of the Christian maskers a de-
filement of his "sober house" (II. v. 35–36).

The moral contrast of Shylock and Antonio is more complex with
reference to that most difficult injunction of the Sermon on the
Mount—forgiveness of injuries and love of enemies. Recollection
of this demand should go far to resolve the question as to whether
an Elizabethan audience would regard Shylock's grievances as genuine:[6] presumably an audience which could perceive the Biblical
standard operating throughout the play would also see its relevance
here. The text is Matt. v. 39, 44–47):

> Resist not evill: but whosoever shall smite thee on thy right
> cheeke, turn to him the other also / . . . . Love your enemies:
> bless them that curse you: do good to them that hate you, and

6. For the argument that Shylock could have been nothing but a monster and comic butt
to an Elizabethan audience steeped in antisemitism, see E. E. Stoll, *Shakespeare Studies*
(N. Y., 1927), pp. 255–336. This argument has been challenged on the ground that
there was little ordinary antisemitism in England in Shakespeare's time, because few
Jews resided there, and also on the ground that Shylock is, for a part of the play at least,
made human, complex, and somewhat sympathetic. See H. R. Walley, "Shakespeare's
Portrayal of Shylock", *The Parrott Presentation Volume* (Princeton, N. J., 1935), pp.
211–42, and J. L. Cardozo, *The Contemporary Jew in Elizabethan Drama* (Amsterdam,
1926).

pray for them which hurt you, and persecute you. / That ye may be the children of your Father that is in heaven: for hee maketh his sunne to arise on the evill, & the good, and sendeth raine on the just, and unjust. / For if ye love them, which love you, what reward shall you have? Doe not the Publicanes even the same? / And if ye be friendly to your brethren onely, what singular thing doe ye? doe not even the Publicanes likewise?

Antonio at the outset of the play is rather in the position of the publican described as friendly to his brethren only—he loves and forgives Bassanio beyond all measure, but hates and reviles Shylock.[7] For evidence of this we have not only Shylock's indictment, "You call me misbeliever, cut-throat dog, / And spet upon my Jewish gaberdine, / . . . And foot me as you spurn a stranger cur" (I. iii. 106–107, 113), but also Antonio's angry reply promising continuation of such treatment: "I am as like to call thee so again, / To spet on thee again, to spurn thee too" (I. iii. 125–26). Indeed, the moral tension of the play is lost if we do not see that Shylock, having been the object of great wrongs, must make a difficult choice between forgiveness and revenge—and that Antonio later finds himself in precisely the same situation.

Ironically, Shylock poses at first as the more "Christian" of the two in that, after detailing his wrongs, he explicitly proposes to turn the other cheek—to "Forget the shames that you have stain'd me with, / Supply your present wants, and take no doit / Of usance for my moneys" (I. iii. 135–37). Of course it is merely pretence: Shylock had declared for revenge at the first sight of Antonio (I. iii. 41–42), and, according to Jessica's later report, he eagerly planned for the forfeit of Antonio's flesh long before the bond came due (III. ii. 283–87). And in this fixed commitment to revenge, this mockery of forgiveness, lies I believe the reason for the often-deplored change from the "human" Shylock of the earlier scenes to the "monster" of Act IV. At the level of the moral allegory Shylock undergoes (rather like Milton's Satan) the progressive deterioration of evil; he turns by his own choice into the cur that he has been called—"Thou call'dst me dog before thou hadst a cause, / But since I am a dog, beware my fangs" (III. iii. 6–7). Conversely, Antonio in the trial scene suffers hatred and injury but foregoes revenge and rancor, manifesting a genuine spirit of forgiveness—for Shylock's forced conversion is not revenge, as will be seen. Thus, his chief deficiency surmounted, Antonio becomes finally a perfect embodiment of Christian love.

7. Hence Shylock's reference to Antonio as a "Fawning publican" may allude to the passage cited above (Matt. v. 47) as well as, more obviously, to the parable of the Pharisee and the Publican.

The Shylock-Antonio opposition functions also at what the medieval theorists would call the "allegorical" level; in these terms it symbolizes the confrontation of Judaism and Christianity as theological systems—the Old Law and the New—and also as historic societies. In their first encounter, Shylock's reference to Antonio as a "fawning publican" and to himself as a member of the "sacred nation" (I. iii. 36,43) introduces an important aspect of this contrast. The reference is of course to the parable of the Pharisee and the Publican (Luke xviii. 9–13) which was spoken "unto certayne which trusted in themselves, that they were ryghteous, and despised other".[8] Shylock's words are evidently intended to suggest the Pharisee's prayer, "God I thank thee that I am not as other menne are, extorcioners, unjust, adulterers, or as this Publicane. / I fast twyce in the weeke, I geve tythe of al that I posesse", and his scornful reference to Antonio's "low simplicity" relates Antonio to the Publican who prayed with humble faith, "God be merciful to me a sinner". The contemporary interpretation of this parable is suggested in Tomson's note:[9] "Two things especially make our prayers voyde and of none effect: confidence of our owne ryghteousnesse, and the contempts of other. . . . we [are] despised of God, as proude & arrogant, if we put never so little trust in our owne workes before God." Through this allusion, then, the emphasis of the Old Law upon perfect legal righteousness is opposed to the tenet of the New Law that righteousness is impossible to fallen man and must be replaced by faith—an opposition which will be further discussed with reference to the trial scene.

Also in this first encounter between Antonio and Shylock, the argument about usury contrasts Old Law and New in terms resembling those frequently found in contemporary polemic addressed to the usury question. Appealing to the Old Testament, Shylock sets forth an analogy between Jacob's breeding of ewes and rams and the breeding of money to produce interest.[1] Antonio, denying the analogy with the query, "is your gold and silver ewes and rams?" echoes the commonplace Christian argument (based upon Aristotle)[2] that to take interest is to "breed" barren metal, which is unnatural. Antonio's remark, "If thou wilt lend this money, lend it not / As to thy friends, for when did friendship take / A breed for barren metal of his friend? / But lend it rather to thine enemy" (I. iii.

---

8. *Bishops Bible* (London, 1572).
9. *The New Testament*. . . . Englished by L. Tomson (London, 1599).
1. Again they refer to their characteristic metaphors: Shylock argues that Jacob's trick to win the sheep from Laban (Gen. xxx. 31–43) was justifiable "thrift", whereas Antonio (citing a later verse, Gen. xxxi. 9, referring the trick to God's inspiration) declares that it was rather a "venture . . . / A thing not in his power to bring to pass, / But sway'd and fashion'd by the hand of heaven."
2. *Politics*, I.10.1258[b]. 1–8. Cf. Francis Bacon, "Of Usury", *Essays* (1625), "They say . . . it is against Nature, for *Money* to beget *Money*."

127–30), prescribes Shylock's course of action according to the dictum of the Old Law—"Unto a stranger thou mayest lend upon usury, but unto thy brother thou shalt not lend upon usury" (Deut. xxiii. 20). However, according to most exegetes, the Gospel demanded a revision of this rule. Aquinas declares, "The Jews were forbidden to take usury from their brethren, i.e., from other Jews. By this we are given to understand that to take usury from any man is evil simply, because we ought to treat every man as our neighbor and brother, especially in the state of the Gospel, whereto all are called."[3] Furthermore, the Sermon on the Mount was thought to forbid usury absolutely by the words, "Lend, looking for nothing againe", a text which is glossed as follows in the Geneva Bible— lend, "not only not hoping for profite, but to lose ye stocke, and principall, for as much as Christ bindeth him selfe to repaie the whole with a most liberall interest."

At this same encounter, Shylock's pretense of following the Christian prescription regarding forgiveness of injuries again contrasts Old Law and New as theological systems, for it recalls the fact that Christ in the Sermon on the Mount twice opposed the Christian standard to the Old Law's demand for strict justice: "Ye have heard that it hath bene saide, An eye for an eye, & a tooth for a tooth. /[4] But I say unto you, Resist not evill: but whosoever shall smite thee on thy right cheeke, turne to him the other also / . . . . Ye have hearde that it hath bene saide, Thou shalt love thy neighbour, & hate thine enemie. / But I say unto you, Love your enemies" (Matt. v. 38–39, 43–44). Later, some of the language of the trial scene alludes again to the differing demands of the two dispensations with regard to forgiveness of enemies:

> Bass: Do all men kill the things they do not love?
> Shy: Hates any man the thing he would not kill?
> Bass: Every offense is not a hate at first!
> Shy: What! wouldst thou have a serpent sting thee twice?
>
> (IV. i. 66–69)

And the Duke reiterates this opposition almost too pointedly when he tenders Shylock the mercy of the Christian court, observing that Shylock could recognize from this "the difference of our spirit" (IV. i. 364).

This allegorical dimension encompasses also the historical expe-

---

3. *Summa Theologica* II–II, Ques. 78, Art. I, in *The Political Ideas of St. Thomas Aquinas*, ed. Dino Bigongiari (N. Y., 1953), p. 149. As R. H. Tawney points out in *Religion and the Rise of Capitalism* (N. Y., 1953), p. 135, the arguments of the schoolmen were in constant circulation during the sixteenth century, and the medieval view regarding usury was maintained by an overwhelming proportion of Elizabethan writers on the subject (pp. 128–49). See Sir Thomas Wilson, *Discourse upon Usury* (1572), Miles Mosse, *The Arraignment and Conviction of Usurie* (1595), H. Smith, *Examination of Usury* (1591).

4. Christ refers to Exod. xxi. 24; Levit. xxiv. 20; Deut. xix. 21.

rience of the two societies, Jewish and Christian. After Jessica's departure, Shylock explicitly assumes unto himself the sufferings of his race: "The curse never fell upon our nation till now, I never felt it till now (III. i. 76–78). This curse is that pronounced upon Jerusalem itself—"Behold, your habitation shalbe left unto you desolate" (Matt. xxiii. 38). First Shylock's servant Launcelot leaves the "rich Jew" to serve the poor Bassanio; then his daughter Jessica[5] "gilds" herself with her Father's ducats and flees with her "unthrift" Christian lover; and finally, all of Shylock's goods and his very life are forfeit to the state. Shylock's passionate outcries against Antonio (III. i. 48 ff.) also take on larger than personal significance: they record the sufferings of his entire race in an alien Christian society—"he hath disgrac'd me . . . laugh'd at my losses, mock'd at my gains, scorned my nation, thwarted my bargains, cooled my friends, heated mine enemies—and what's his reason? I am a Jew!" This is followed by the eloquent plea for recognition of the common humanity Jew shares with Christian, "Hath not a Jew eyes? . . .", and it concludes with the telling observation that despite the Christian's professions about "humility" and turning the other cheek, in practice he is quick to revenge himself upon the Jew. The taunts of Salario, Solanio, and Gratiano throughout the play give some substantiation to these charges.

Yet overlaying this animosity are several allusions to Shylock's future conversion, suggesting the Christian expectation of the final, pre-millennial conversion of the Jews. The first such reference occurs, most appropriately, just after Shylock's feigned offer to forego usury and forgive injury. Antonio salutes Shylock's departure with the words, "Hie thee gentle Jew"—probably carrying a pun on gentle-gentile—and then prophesies, "The Hebrew will turn Christian, he grows kind" (I. iii. 173–74). "Kind" in this context implies both "natural" (in foregoing unnatural interest) and "charitable"; thus Antonio suggests that voluntary adoption of these fundamental Christian principles would lead to the conversion of the Jew. The second

---

5. It has been plausibly argued that Jessica's name derives from the Hebrew Jesca, a form of Iscah, daughter of Haran (Gen. xi. 29), glossed by Elizabethean commentators as "she that looketh out" (Gollancz, p. 42, G. L. Kittredge ed., *Merchant of Venice*, Ginn, 1945, p. ix). A direct play upon this name seems to occur in II. v. 31–32, where Shylock directs Jessica, "Clamber not you up to the casements then / Nor thrust your head into the public street", and Launcelot prompts her to "look out at window for all this" (II. v. 40) to see Lorenzo. Her departure thus signifies a breaking out of the ghetto, a voluntary abandonment of Old Law for New. This significance is continued in III. v. 1–5, when Launcelot quips that Jessica will be damned since (according to Mosaic Law, Exod. xx. 5) the "sins of the father are to be laid upon the children", and she replies (II. 17–18), "I shall be sav'd by my husband"—reecting Paul's promise in the New Law, I Cor. vii. 14, "the unbeleeving wife is sanctified by the husband". Shylock's name is probably taken from Shalach, translated by "cormorant" (Levit. xi. 17, Deut. xiv. 17)—an epithet often applied to usurers in Elizabethan English. The name "Tubal", taken from Tubal Cain (Gen. x. 2, 6) is glossed in Elizabethan Bibles as meaning "worldly possessions, a bird's nest of the world" (Gollancz, pp. 40–41; Kittredge, p. ix).

prediction occurs in Lorenzo's declaration, "If e'er the Jew her father come to heaven, / It will be for his gentle daughter's sake" (II. iv. 33–34)—again with the pun on gentle-gentile. As Shylock's daughter and as a voluntary convert to Christianity, Jessica may figure forth the filial relationship of the New Dispensation to the Old, and Lorenzo's prediction may carry an allusion to Paul's prophecy that the Jews will ultimately be saved through the agency of the Gentiles.[6] At any rate, the final conversion of the Jews is symbolized in just such terms in the trial scene: because Antonio is able to rise at last to the demands of Christian love, Shylock is not destroyed, but, albeit rather harshly, converted. Interestingly enough, however, even after Portia's speeches at the trial have reminded Antonio and the court of the Christian principles they profess, Gratiano yet persists in demanding revenge. This incident serves as a thematic counterpoint to the opposition of Old Law and New, suggesting the disposition of Christians themselves to live rather according to the Old Law than the New. Such a counterpoint is developed at various points throughout the play—in Antonio's initial enmity to Shylock, in the jeers of the minor figures, in Shylock's statements likening his revenge to the customary vengeful practices of the Christians and his claim to a pound of flesh to their slave trade in human flesh (IV. i. 90–100). Thus the play does not present arbitrary, black-and-white moral estimates of human groups, but takes into account the shadings and complexities of the real world.

As Shylock and Antonio embody the theological conflicts and historical interrelationships of Old Law and New, so do they also reflect, from time to time, the ultimate sources of their principles in a further allegorical significance. Antonio, who assumes the debts of others (rescuing Bassanio, the self-confessed "Prodigal", from a debt due under the law) reflects on occasion the role of Christ satisfying the claim of Divine Justice by assuming the sins of mankind. The scripture phrase which Antonio's deed immediately brings to mind points the analogy directly: "This is my commandement, that ye love one another, *as I have loved you.* /[7] Greater love hath no man than this, that a man lay down his life for his friends" (John xv. 12–13). And Shylock, demanding the "bond" which is due him under the law, reflects the role of the devil, to whom the entire human race is in bondage through sin—an analogy which Portia makes explicit when she terms his hold upon Antonio a "state of hellish cruelty". The dilemma which that delightful malaprop Launcelot experiences with regard to leaving Shylock, whom he terms the "devil incarnation" (II. ii. 1–30), springs directly from the implications of this analogy. According to I Pet. xii. 18–19, one must serve even a bad master "for conscience toward God": thus Launcelot's conscience bids him stay and the fiend bids him go. But on the other hand, to serve the devil is obviously damnation; so he concludes, "in my conscience, my conscience is but a kind of hard conscience to offer to counsel me to stay with the Jew", and determines flight. Similarly, Jessica declares, "Our house is hell" (II. iii. 2), thus placing her departure in the context of a flight from the devil to salvation. As E. E. Stoll points out,[8] the identification of Jew and Devil is repeated nine times in the play, and was a commonplace of medieval and Elizabethan antisemitic literature. Yet it seems to function here less to heap opprobrium upon the Jew than to suggest the ultimate source of the principles of revenge and hatred which Shylock seeks to justify out of the Law. Again the meaning is clarified by a Biblical quotation—Christ's use of the same identification in denouncing the Jews for their refusal to believe in him and their attempts to kill him—"Ye are of your father the devill, and the lustes of your father ye will doe: Hee hath bene a murtherer from the beginning" (John viii. 44).

Bassanio and the Caskets

The story of Bassanio and the casket choice also appears to incorporate a "moral" and an "allegorical" meaning. At the moral level, the incident explores the implications of Christian love in the romantic relationship, whereas Antonio's story deals with Christian love in terms of friendship and social intercourse. Morocco, in renouncing the leaden casket because it does not offer "fair advantages", and in choosing the gold which promises "what many men desire", exemplifies the confusion of love with external shows:[9] like most of the world, he values Portia not for herself but for her beauty and wealth. However, the death's head within the golden casket indicates the common mortality to which all such accidents as wealth and beauty are finally subject. Aragon, by contrast, represents love of self so strong that it precludes any other love. He renounces the gold because he considers himself superior to the common multitude whom it attracts; he disdains the lead as not "fair" enough to deserve his hazard; and in choosing the silver which promises "as much as he deserves" he declares boldly, "I will assume desert" (II. ix. 51). But the blinking idiot in the casket testifies to the folly of him who supposes that love can be bargained

---

8. *Shakespeare Studies*, pp. 270–71.
9. Morocco amusingly displays the illogic in his own position. He begs that he be not judged by his tawny complexion but rather by his valor and inner worth (II. i. 1–12), and then argues that the picture symbolic of Portia could be fittingly placed only in a golden casket (II. vii. 48–55).

for in the pitiful coin of human merit. Bassanio, on the other hand, chooses the lead casket which warns, "Who chooseth me, must give and hazard all he hath" (II. ix. 21)—thus signifying his acceptance of the self-abnegation, risk, and venture set up throughout the play as characteristics of true Christian love. And the metaphor of the "venture" is constantly used with reference to Bassanio and Portia just as it is with Antonio. Bassanio proposes to venture like a Jason for the golden fleece of Portia's sunny locks (I. i. 169–77), and, though Portia complains that it is hard to be subject to the lottery of the caskets, she accepts the premise that this hazard will reveal her true lover (I. ii. 12–34; III. ii. 41). Finally, when Bassanio goes forth to choose she likens his venture, upon which her own fate depends, to that of Hercules striving to rescue Hesione from the sea-monster:[1] "I stand for sacrifice, / The rest aloof are the Dardanian wives, / With bleared visages come forth to view / The issue of th'exploit: go Hercules" (III. ii. 57–60).

At the "allegorical" level, the caskets signify Everyman's choice of the paths to spiritual life or death. This analogy is explicitly developed in the "Moral" appended to the casket story in the *Gesta Romanorum* which is almost certainly Shakespeare's source for this incident.[2] In the *Gesta* the casket choice tests the worthiness of a maiden (the soul) to wed the son of an Emperor (Christ). The moral declares, "The Emperour sheweth this Mayden three vessells, that is to say, God putteth before man life & death, good and evill, & which of these he chooseth hee shall obtaine."[3] This passage contains a reference to Deut. xxx. 15–20, wherein Moses warns, after delivering the commandments to the Jews:

> Beholde, I have set before thee this day life and good, death and evill . . . But if thine heart turne away, so that thou wilt not obey, but shalt be seduced and woorship other gods, and serve them, / I pronounce unto you this day, that ye shall surely perish. . . . / Therefore chuse life, that both thou and thy seede may live. / By loving the Lord thy God, by obeying his voyce, and by cleaving unto hym: For he is thy life, & the length of thy dayes: that thou mayest dwell in the lande which the Lord sware unto thy fathers.

As a note in the Bishops Bible indicates, the last promise was taken to refer not only to the "land of Chanaan, but also the heavenly inheritance, whereof the other was a figure". That Shakespeare in-

---

1. Interestingly, Morocco also compares the casket choice to an exploit of Hercules, but not to one fairly testing strength and true worth, as does Portia. Rather, he sees it as a dice game wherein by pure chance Hercules might lose out to his valet (II. l. 31–34).
2. A selection of stories from the *Gesta* was printed in English translation by Richard Robinson in 1577 and again in 1595. See Arden *MV*, pp. xxxii, 172–74.
3. Arden *MV*, p. 174.

tended to recall this Biblical allusion so pointed in the *Gesta*, and thus to make the caskets symbolize the great choices of spiritual life and death, is evident by the constant references in the lovers' conversation to "life" and "death" just before Bassanio's venture. Bassanio declares, "Let me choose, / For as I am, I live upon the rack"; Portia continues the "rack" metaphor, urging, "Confess and live", a phrase which Bassanio immediately transposes to "Confess and Love" (III. ii. 24–35). When he goes forth to venture, Portia calls for music to celebrate whichever result, death or life, will attend his choice: "If he lose he makes a swan-like end, / Fading in music" into the "wat'ry deathbed" of her tears. If he win, music will celebrate his Hercules-like victory and the life of both—"Live thou, I live". That the casket choice represents Everyman's choice among values is further emphasized by the multitude at Portia's door: some of them refuse to choose (like the inhabitants of the vestibule of Hell in Dante); others choose wrongly and, having demonstrated by this that they are already wedded to false values, are forbidden to make another marriage. Furthermore, Antonio's action in making possible Bassanio's successful venture reflects the role of Christ in making possible for the true Christian the choice of spiritual life, the love of God.

The meaning of the symbolic caskets is further illuminated by James v. 2–3: "Your riches are corrupt: and your garments are motheaten. / Your golde and silver is cankred, and the rust of them shall be a witness against you."[4] Morocco, the pagan, with his boasts of bravery in battle and of the love of the "best-regarded virgins of our clime", with his sensuous imagery and dashing superlatives (II. i. 1–38) is a fit type of worldliness, Mammon. The warning of the death's head is that such a life is spiritual death: "Many a man his life hath sold / But my outside to behold,— Gilded tombs do worms infold." Aragon, the Spaniard—the very embodiment of Pride according to the Elizabeth caricature—is the type of Pharisaical self-righteousness: his sonorously complacent language about the "barbarous multitudes" and the faults of others (II. ix. 19–52) rather suggests the "sounding brasse" and "tinckling cymbale" of Paul's image (I Cor. xiii. 1), and certainly recalls the Pharisee's prayer. But through its first line, "The fire seven times tried this", the scroll refers Aragon to the twelfth Psalm,[5] which denounces vanity and proud speaking. It then refers to the casket as merely "silver'd o'er"—thus suggesting Christ's comparison of the

---

4. The same imagery appears in Matt. vi. 25, the passage alluded to in testing Antonio's contempt for worldly goods (pp. 168–69 above).
5. Psalter for the *Book of Common Prayer*, in *Bishops Bible*, 1584, verses 3, 7: "The Lorde shal roote out al deceptful lippes: and the tongue that speaketh proude thinges / . . . . The woordes of the Lord are pure woordes: even as the silver whiche from the earth is tryed, and purified seven times in the fyre."

scribes and pharisees to "whited sepulchres" (Matt. xxiii. 27). Also, the blinking idiot within the casket mutely testifies that since all men are sinners pharisaical pride is folly.[6] This defeat and lessoning of Morocco and Aragon foreshadows the defeat and conversion of Shylock, for he represents in somewhat different guise these same antichristian values of worldliness and self-righteousness.[7]

Bassanio's choice of the lead casket is the choice of life, the love of God. The use of romantic love as a symbol for divine love is of course a commonplace in mystical literature, deriving chiefly from the example of the Song of Solomon, which was understood to treat, as the caption in the Bishops Bible expresses it, "The familiar talke and mystical communication of the spiritual love between Jesus Christe and his Churche". Bassanio's meditation on the caskets (III. ii. 73–107) symbolically suggests his understanding and renunciation of the two kinds of "Ornament" which oppose this love: his description of the silver as "thou common drudge between man and man" suggests his knowledge of the pretense of righteousness with which men generally cover their vices when presenting themselves to others, and the skull image which he uses in denouncing the gold indicates his awareness of the transience and corruptibility of worldly goods. Also clarifying the significance of Bassanio's choice is Portia's remark, "I stand for sacrifice", made in relation to her Hercules-Hesione simile as she sends Bassanio forth to choose (III. ii. 57). The word "stand" is ambiguous, suggesting at once that she occupies the position of a sacrificial victim whose life must be saved by another, but also that she "represents" sacrifice—the very core of Christian love. The exact counterpart of Portia's remark, both in form and ambiguity of meaning, is Shylock's later comment, "I stand for judgement. . . . I stand here for law" (IV. i. 103, 142).

The Trial

The trial scene climaxes the action at all the levels of meaning that have been established. As has been suggested, it portrays at the moral level Shylock's degradation to a cur and a monster through his commitment to revenge, and by contrast, Antonio's attainment of the fullness of Christian love through his abjuration of revenge. Allegorically, the scene develops the sharpest opposition of Old

---

6. The *Gesta*'s moral points to the same meanings though the inscriptions on the caskets are somewhat different: the gold is said to represent "worldly men, both mightie men & riche, which outwardly shine in riches and pomps of this world", the silver stands for "some Justices & wise men of this world which shine in faire speach but within they be full of wormes and earth"—as were the whited sepulchres (Arden *MV*, Appendix V, p. 174; Cf. Matt. xxiii. 24).

7. Aragon's appeal to Portia after his defeat, "Did I deserve no more than a fool's head? / Is that my prize? are my deserts no better" (II. ix. 59–60), foreshadows Portia's role in the trial scene as opponent and judge of the claim based upon righteousness.

Law and New in terms of their respective theological principles,
Justice and Mercy, Righteousness and Faith; it culminates in the final defeat of the Old Law and the symbolic conversion of the Jew.

Throughout the first portion of Act IV, until Portia begins the
dramatic reversal with the words. "Tarry a little, there is something
else—" (IV. i. 301), the action is simply a debate between Old Law
and New in terms of Justice and Mercy—but that debate is carried
forth in a dual frame of reference. The phrase in the Lord's Prayer
rendered by both the Bishops and the Geneva Bibles as "Forgeve us
our dettes, as we forgeve our detters", is alluded to twice in this
scene, making the debtor's trial in the court of Venice a precise
analogue of the sinner's trial in the court of Heaven. The Duke in-
quires of Shylock, "How shalt thou hope for mercy rend'ring
none?" (IV. i. 88), and Portia reiterates, "Though justice be thy
plea, consider this, / That in the course of justice, none of us /
Should see salvation: we do pray for mercy, / And that same prayer,
doth teach us all to render / The deeds of mercy" (IV. i. 194–98). In
his *Exposition of the Lord's Prayer* a contemporary clergyman,
William Perkins,[8] works out a similar analogy: "For even as a debt
doth binde a man, either to make satisfaction, or els to goe to
prison: so our sinnes bindes us either to satisfie Gods justice, or
else to suffer eternall damnation." Shylock is referred for this analogy not only to the Lord's Prayer but also to his own tradition: Portia's language (IV. i. 180 ff.) echoes also certain Old Testament
psalmists and prophets whose pleas for God's mercy were explained
by Christian exegetes as admissions of the inadequacies of the Law
and testimonies of the need for Christ.[9] For example the striking
image, "Mercy . . . droppeth as a gentle rain from Heaven upon the
place beneath", echoes Ecclesaisticus xxv. 19, "O how fayre a thyng
is mercy in the tyme of anguish and trouble: it is lyke a cloud of
rayne that commeth in the tyme of drought." This reference should
also remind Shylock of the remarkable parallel to the Lord's Prayer
contained in a passage following close upon this one: "He that
seeketh vengeance, shall finde vengeance of the Lord. . . . / Forgeve
thy neyghbour the hurt that he hath donne thee, and so shal thy
sinnes be forgeven thee also when thou prayest / . . . . He that
sheweth no mercie to a man which is lyke himselfe, how dare he
aske forgevenesse of his sinnes" (Ecclus. xxiii. 1–24).[1]

Through these allusions, Antonio's predicament in the courtroom

---

8. Cambridge, 1605, p. 410.
9. See Psalms 103, 136, 143. With reference to such passages, Henrie Bullinger declares
(*Fiftie Godlie and Learned Sermons*, trans. H. I., London, 1587, p. 403), "The ancient
Saints which lived under the old testament, did not seeke for righteousness and salvation in the works of the lawe, but in him which is the perfectnes and ende of the law,
even Christ Jesus."
1. *Bishops Bible*.

of Venice is made to suggest traditional literary and iconographical presentations of the "Parliament of Heaven" in which fallen man was judged. Both sides agree that Antonio's bond (like the sinner's) is forfeit according to the law, and that the law of Venice (like that of God) cannot be abrogated. Shylock constantly threatens, "If you deny me, fie upon your law" (IV. i. 101), and Portia concurs, "there is no power in Venice / Can alter a decree established" (IV. i. 214–15). The only question then is whether the law must be applied with strictest justice, or whether mercy may somehow temper it. In the traditional allegory of the Parliament of Heaven,[2] Justice and Mercy, as the two principal of the four "daughters" of God, debate over the judgement to be meted out to man; Launcelot Andrewes in his version of the debate[3] aligns these figures with the Old Law and the New respectively—"Righteousnesse, she was where the Law was (for, that, the *rule of righteousnesse*) where the Covenant of the Old Testament was, *doe this and live* (the very voyce of Justice)", whereas "The Gentiles they claim by *Mercy*, that is their virtue." So in the trial scene Shylock as the embodiment of the Old Law represents Justice: "I stand for Judgment. . . . I stand here for Law" (IV. i. 103, 142), whereas Portia identifies herself with that "Quality of Mercy" enthroned by the New Law. Also, another conception of the Heavenly Court is superadded to this by means of several references during the trial to Shylock as Devil (IV. i. 213, 283). The scene takes on something of the significance of the trial described in the medieval drama, the *Processus Belial*, in which the Devil claims by justice the souls of mankind due him under the law, and the Virgin Mary intercedes for man by appealing to the Mercy of God.[4]

In either formulation, the demands of Justice and Mercy are reconciled only through the sacrifice of Christ, who satisfies the demands of justice by assuming the debts of mankind, and thus makes mercy possible. Therefore it is not surprising that the courtroom scene also evokes something of the crucifixion scene—as the moment of reconciling these opposed forces, as the time of defeat for the Old Law, as the prime example of Christian Love and the object of Christian Faith. Both plot situation and language suggest a typical killing of Christ by the Jew. Antonio, baring his breast to shed his blood for the debt of another, continues the identification with Christ occasionally suggested at other points in the play. Shylock's cry, "My deeds upon my head" (IV. i. 202) clearly suggests the assumption of guilt by the Jews at Christ's crucifixion—"His blood be on us, and on our children" (Matt. xxvii. 25)—and his later re-

---

2. For a resumé of this tradition see Samuel C. Chew, *The Virtues Reconciled* (Toronto, 147).
3. "Christmas, 1616", *XCVI Sermons*, 3rd Edn. (London, 1635), p. 104.
4. See John D. Rea, "Shylock and the *Processus Belial*" *PQ*, VIII (Oct., 1929), 311–13.

mark, "I have a daughter— / Would any of the stock of Barrabas / Had been her husband, rather than a Christian" (IV. i. 291–93) recalls the Jews' choice of the murderer Barrabas over Christ as the prisoner to be released at Passover (Matt. xxvii. 16–21). A similar fusion of the symbols of debtor's court and crucifixion occurs in a Christmas sermon by Launcelot Andrewes on Gal. iii. 4–5:

> If one be in debt and danger of the *Law*, to have a *Brother* of the same bloud . . . will little avail him, except he will also come *under the Law*, that is, become his Surety, and undertake for him. And such was our estate. As debtors we were, by vertue of . . . the *handwriting* that was against us. Which was our *Bond*, and we had forfeited it. . . . Therefore Hee became bound for us also, entred bond anew, took on Him, not only our *Nature*, but our *Debt*. . . . The debt of a Capitall Law is Death.[5]

Throughout the action thus far described, Shylock has persistantly denied pleas to temper justice with mercy—to forgive part of the debt, to accept three times the value of the debt rather than the pound of flesh, or even to supply a doctor "for charity" to stop Antonio's wounds. His perversity is rooted in his explicit denial of any need to "deserve" God's mercy by showing mercy to others, for he arrogates to himself the perfect righteousness which is the standard of the Old Law—"What judgment shall I dread doing no wrong?" (IV.i.89). Accordingly, after Portia's "Tarry a little", the action of the scene works out a systematic destruction of that claim of righteousness, using the laws of Venice as symbol. Shylock is shown first that he can claim nothing by the law: his claim upon Antonio's flesh is disallowed by the merest technicality. This reflects the Christian doctrine that although perfect performance of the Law would indeed merit salvation, in fact fallen man could never perfectly observe it, any more than Shylock could take Antonio's flesh without drawing blood. According to Paul, Romans iii. 9–12, "all, both Jewes and Gentiles are under sinne, / . . . There is none righteous, no not one. / . . . there is none that doth good, no not one. / Therefore by the workes of the Law shal no flesh be justified in his sight". Next, Shylock is shown that in claiming the Law he not only gains nothing, but stands to lose all that he possesses and even life itself. He becomes subject to what Paul terms the "curse" of the Law, since he is unable to fulfill its conditions: "For as many as are of the workes of the Lawe, are under the curse: for it is written, Cursed is every man that continueth not in all things, which are written in the booke of the Lawe, to do them" (Gal. iii. 10).

The names applied to and assumed by Portia during the trial reinforce these meanings. When Portia gives judgment at first in Shy-

5. "Christmas 1609", *XCVI Sermons*, p. 28.

lock's favor, he cries out, "A Daniel come to judgment: yea, a Daniel! / O wise young judge", in obvious reference to the apocryphal Book of Susanna, wherein the young Daniel confounded the accusors of Susanna, upholding thereby the justice of the Law. The name, Daniel, which means in Hebrew, "The Judge of the Lord", was glossed in the Elizabethan Bibles as "The Judgment of God".[6] But the name carries other implications as well, which Shylock ironically forgets. Portia has assumed the name "Balthasar" for the purposes of her disguise, and the name given to the prophet Daniel in the Book of Daniel is Baltassar—a similarity hardly accidental.[7] According to Christian exegetes, Daniel in this book foreshadows the Christian tradition by his explicit denial of any claim upon God by righteousness, and his humble appeal for mercy: "O my God, encline thyne eare, & hearken, open thyne eyes, beholde howe we be desolated . . . for we doo not present our prayers before thee in our owne righteousnesse, but in thy great mercies" (Daniel ix.18).[8] These implications greatly enrich the irony when Gratiano flings the title back in Shylock's face—"A second Daniel, a Daniel, Jew" (IV. i. 329).

Shylock's "forced conversion" (a gratuitous addition made by Shakespeare to the source story in *II Pecorone*) must be viewed in the context of the symbolic action thus far described. Now that Shylock's claim to legal righteousness has been totally destroyed, he is made to accept the only alternative to it, faith in Christ. Paul declares (Gal. ii. 16), "A man is not justified by the workes of the Lawe, but by the fayth of Jesus Christ", and a note in the *Bishops Bible* explains, "Christ hath fulfylled the whole lawe, and therefore who so ever beleeveth in him, is counted just before God, as wel as he had fulfylled ye whole law him selfe." Thus the stipulation for Shylock's conversion, though it of course assumes the truth of Christianity, is not antisemitic revenge: it simply compels Shylock to avow what his own experience in the trial scene has fully "demonstrated"—that the Law leads only to death and destruction, that faith in Christ must supplant human righteousness. In this connection it ought to be noted that Shylock's pecuniary punishment under the laws of Venice precisely parallels the conditions im-

---

6. See glossary, *Geneva Bible*.
7. The slight variation may be due to imperfect memory: the king whom Daniel served was named Balthasar.
8. *Bishops Bible*. A note on this passage declares that it shows how "the godly flee only unto gods mercies and renounce theyr owne workes when they seeke for remission of their sinnes." Cf. Bullinger, *Fiftie Sermons*, p. 434: "And although they did not so usually call upon God as wee at this day doe, through the mediatour and intercessour Christe Jesus . . . yet were they not utterly ignorant of the mediatour, for whose sake they were heard of the Lord. Daniel in the ninth Chapter of his prophecie maketh his prayer, and desireth to bee hearde of God for the Lordes sake, that is, for the promised Christ his sake."

posed upon a Jewish convert to Christianity throughout most of Europe and also in England during the Middle Ages and after. All his property and goods, as the ill-gotten gain of usury, were forfeit to the state upon his conversion, but he was customarily allotted some proportion (often half) of his former goods for his maintenance, or else given a stipend or some other means of support.[9]

There is some evidence that Shylock himself in this scene recognizes the logic which demands his conversion, though understandably he finds this too painful to admit explicitly. His incredulous question "Is that the law" (IV. i. 309) when he finds the law invoked against him, shows a new and overwhelming consciousness of the defects of legalism. Also, he does not protest the condition that he become a Christian as he protested the judgment (soon reversed) which would seize all his property: his brief "I am content" suggests, I believe, not mean-spiritedness but weary acknowledgement of the fact that he can no longer make his stand upon the discredited Law.

Indeed, Portia's final tactic—that of permitting the Law to demonstrate its own destructiveness—seems a working out of Paul's metaphor of the Law as a "Schoolemaster to bring us to Christ, that we might be made righteous by faith" (Gal. iii. 24). The metaphor was utilized by all the major Christian theological traditions, and received much the same interpretation in all of them:

> The law was our pedagogue in Christ. . . . So also did he [God] wish to give such a law as men by their own forces could not fulfill, so that, while presuming on their own powers, they might find themselves to be sinners, and, being humbled, might have recourse to the help of grace. (Aquinas)[1]

> Another use of the law is . . . to reveale unto a man his sinne, his blindnes, his misery, his impietie, ignorance, hatred and contempt of God, death, hel, the judgment and deserved wrath of God to the end that God might bridle and beate down this monster and this madde beaste (I meane the presumption of *mans* own righteousness) . . . [and drive] them to Christ. (Luther)[2]

> Some . . . from too much confidence either in their own strength or in their own righteousness, are unfit to receive the

9. James Parkes, *The Jew in the Medieval Community* (London, 1938), pp. 101–46; Michael Adler, *Jews of Medieval England* (London, 1939), pp. 280–334; Cecil Roth, *A History of the Jews in England* (Oxford, 1949), p. 96.
1. *Summa Theologica*, II.I. Ques. 98. Art. 2, in *Basic Writings*, ed. Anton Pegis (N. Y., 1944), p. 809.
2. *A Commentarie of M. Doctor Martin Luther upon the Epistle of S. Paul to the Galathians* (London, Thomas Vautroullier, 1575), n.p.

grace of Christ till they have first been stripped of every thing. The law, therefore, reduces them to humility by a knowledge of their own misery, that thus they may be prepared to pray for that of which they before supposed themselves not destitute. (Calvin)[3]

And, from the contemporary sermon literature the following commentaries are typical:

The law . . . was given because of transgression. . . . out of the which they might learn the will of God, what sin, right, or unright is; and to know themselves, to go into themselves, and to consider, how that the holy works which God requireth are not in their own power; for the which cause all the world have great need of a mediator. . . . Thus was the law our schoolmaster unto Christ. (Myles Coverdale)[4]

The law . . . shewes us our sinnes, and that without remedy: it shewes us the damnation that is due unto us: and by this meanes, it makes us despaire of salvation in respect of our selves: & thus it inforceth us to seeke for helpe out of our selves in Christ. The law is then our schoolemaster not by the plaine teaching, but by stripes and corrections. (Perkins)[5]

Thus Shylock, as representative of his entire race, having refused the earlier opportunity to embrace voluntarily the principles of Christianity, must undergo in the trial scene the harsh "Schoolmastership" of the Law, in order to be brought to faith in Christ.

The Ring Episode and Belmont

The ring episode is, in a sense, a comic parody of the trial scene—it provides a means whereby Bassanio may make at least token fulfillment of his offer to give "life itself, my wife, and all the world" (IV. i. 280) to deliver Antonio. The ring is the token of his possession of Portia and all Belmont: in offering it Portia declared, "This house, these servants, and this same myself / Are yours . . . I give them with this ring, / Which when you part from, lose, or give away, / Let it presage the ruin of your love, / And be my vantage to exclaim on you" (III. ii. 170–174). So that in giving the ring to the "lawyer" Balthasar—which he does only at Antonio's bidding—Bas-

3. *Institutes of the Christian Religion*, II, chap. 7, trans. John Allen (Philadelphia, Pa., 1936), I, 388.
4. "The Old Faith", trans. by Myles Coverdale from H. Bullinger. 1547, *Writings and Translations*, ed. George Pearson (Cambridge, 1844), pp. 42–43.
5. *A Commentarie, or Exposition upon the first five chapters of the Epistle to Galatians* (London, 1617), p. 200. See also, John Donne, Sermon 17, *Sermons*, ed. E. Simpson and G. Potter, VI (Berkeley, Calif., 1953), 334–45; John Colet, *An Exposition of St. Paul's Epistle to the Romans*, 1497, trans. J. H. Lupton (London, 1873), pp. 1–18.

sanio surrenders his "claim" to all these gifts, even to Portia's person, and is therefore taunted at his return with her alleged infidelity. But Belmont is the land of the spirit, not the letter, and therefore after Bassanio has been allowed for a moment to feel his loss, the whole crisis dissolves in laughter and amazement as Antonio again binds himself (his soul this time the forfeit) for Bassanio's future fidelity, and Portia reveals her own part in the affair. At the moral level, this pledge and counter pledge by Bassanio and Antonio continue the "venture" metaphor and further exemplify the willingness to give all for love. At the allegorical level, despite the lighthearted treatment, Bassanio's comic "trial" suggests the "judgment" awaiting the Christian soul as it presents its final account and is found deficient. But Love, finally, is the fulfillment of the Law and covers all defects—Bassanio's (Everyman's) love in giving up everything, in token at least, for Antonio, and Antonio's (Christ's) love toward him and further pledge in his behalf.

Belmont functions chiefly at the anagogical level (if one may invoke the term): it figures forth the Heavenly City. Jessica points to this analogy explicitly—"It is very meet / The Lord Bassanio live an upright life / For having such a blessing in his lady, / He finds the joys of heaven here on earth" (III. v. 67–70). Here Gentile and Jew, Lorenzo and Jessica, are united in each other's arms, talking of the music of the spheres:

> How sweet the moonlight sleeps upon this bank!
>
> . . . .
>   Look how the floor of heaven
> Is thick inlaid with patens of bright gold,
> There's not the smallest orb which thou behold'st
> But in his motion like an angel sings,
> Still quiring to the young-eye'd cherubins;
> Such harmony is in immortal souls   (V. i. 54, 58–63)

And Portia's allusion upon returning, "Peace!—how the moon sleeps with Endymion, / And would not be awak'd" (V. i. 108–109) also suggests eternity, for Diana, enamoured of Endymion's beauty, caused him to sleep forever on Mount Latmos. In Belmont all losses are restored and sorrows end: Bassanio wins again his lady and all Belmont; Antonio is given a letter signifying that three of his argosies are returned to port richly laden; and Lorenzo receives the deed naming him Shylock's future heir. Lorenzo's exclamation, "Fair ladies, you drop manna in the way of starving people", together with the reference to "patens" in the passage quoted above, sets up an implied metaphor of the heavenly communion. Here all who have cast their bread upon the waters in the "ventures" of Christian love receive the reward promised:

Whoever shall forsake houses, or brethren, or sisters, or father, or mother, or wife, or children, or landes, for my names sake, hee shal receive an hundreth folde more, and shal inherite everlasting life (Matt. xix. 29).

LAWRENCE DANSON

[Platonic Doctrine and the Music of Act 5]†

* * *

* * * Alone with Jessica again, Lorenzo begins by reestablishing for the audience a nocturnal perception of the scene—and in such a way as to make us ever grateful for the technological poverty of the Shakespearean stage:

> How sweet the moonlight sleeps upon this bank!
> Here will we sit, and let the sounds of music
> Creep in our ears—soft stillness and the night
> Become the touches of sweet harmony:
> Sit Jessica,—
>
> (5.1.54–58)

And because Jessica is a newcomer, and because he loves her, Lorenzo tells Jessica about the musical wonders of this peaceful night:

> look how the floor of heaven
> Is thick inlaid with patens of bright gold:
> There's not the smallest orb which thou behold'st
> But in his motion like an angel sings,
> Still quiring to the young-ey'd cherubins;
> Such harmony is in immortal souls,
> But whilst this muddy vesture of decay
> Doth grossly close it in, we cannot hear it.
>
> (5.1.58–65)

Lorenzo's pedagogical tact is demonstrated as much by what he does not say as by what he does. The modern scholar can direct us to various sources for the ideas contained in Lorenzo's speech. But within the play itself the venerable traditions that validate the speech are felt in the very gravity and clarity of the speech's manner.

Still, since the modern reader or auditor is even less familiar with these ideas than is Jessica, some guidance is in order. Beginning with the lexical: though most of the recent editions widely used by

---

† From *The Harmonies of* The Merchant of Venice (New Haven and London: Yale University Press, 1978), pp. 185–89. Reprinted by permission of Yale University Press.

students gloss the word "patens" in such a way as to leave them merely decorative blotches against the night sky, the word has, in fact, a specifically sacramental association.[1] These "patens of bright gold" to which Lorenzo likens the stars refer (as the note in the Arden edition explains) to "shallow dishes, as used in the celebration of the Holy Communion." We will also want to know that a congeries of ideas with good pagan foundations is made explicitly Christian in Lorenzo's version. Cicero's influential *Somnium Scipionis* (as it is preserved in Macrobius' commentary) talks about heavenly music; but for man's inability to hear that music, Cicero explains that we are deafened "like those who live too near the cataracts of the Nile."[2] Lorenzo, however, alludes to "man's fallen state: our senses are clogged by the grossness of our flesh" (Heninger, p. 5); and thus, while enclosed in the muddy vesture of mortality, we retain only an intimation of the celestial music accessible to the pure spirit.

When Jessica, with (I take it) a newcomer's insecurity, confesses "I am never merry when I hear sweet music"—and Lorenzo replies reassuringly, "The reason is your spirits are attentive"—it is worth knowing that her properly attuned listening attitude reflects the widely known doctrine of Boethius. According to Boethius, whose *De Institutione Musica* "remained an unquestioned authority on the music of Antiquity and on music in general for a thousand years after its composition in the early sixth century," there are three interrelated types of music: *musica mundana*, *musica humana*, and *musica instrumentalis*.[3] The first term refers to the music produced by the wondrous order of the cosmos itself; the second, "human music," is " 'that which unites the incorporeal activity of the reason with the body . . . a certain mutual adaptation and as it were tempering of high and low sounds into a single consonance' " (Hollander, p. 25). Where there is *musica humana*, there is in the individual a harmonious blending of soul and body, reason and passion; and that personal harmony is analogous to the harmony of the cosmos (at one extreme) and the tuning of the strings of a musical instrument (at the other extreme).

We are likely to think of "human music" as being an attribute

1. Here are the footnotes provided for the reader in some widely accepted collected editions: The Signet Shakespeare: *patens* = "tiles"; Hardin Craig / David Bevington: "thin, circular plates of metal"; Pelican: "metal plates or tiling"; Riverside: "metal plates or discs." A welcome exception is W. Moelwyn Merchant's edition for the New Penguin Shakespeare; *patens* is there glossed as "the dish, of silver or gold, from which the consecrated bread of the eucharist is served." The suppression of the sacramental associations of the word, in a passage too likely to be dismissed as just so much pretty "poetry" in any case, is a serious one.
2. Quoted in S. K. Heninger, Jr., *Touches of Sweet Harmony: Pythagorean Cosmology and Renaissance Poetics* (San Marino, California, 1974), p. 5. I am indebted to Heninger for other parts of this discussion.
3. I quote Hollander, *The Untuning of the Sky* (Princeton, New Jersey, 1961), p. 25.

only of the emotions; its relation to the *reason* should therefore be stressed. In the Boethian system, the effects of music are moral and intellectual.

> The origin of music, Boethius tells us in *De Arithmetica*, is God Himself, and his means of creating it is exemplarism from the unchanging laws of number in His mind. From these laws are drawn the relations of the elements, of the seasons, and of the stars . . . and by means of these laws, *the intellectual role of . . . music* is to lead man's mind from the deceiving senses back to certain *knowledge.*[4]

Therefore, in *The Merchant of Venice*, music properly accompanies Bassanio's casket-choice; it properly is called upon to draw home Portia and Nerissa; and it properly suggests itself as the accompaniment to the tripartite dance of gracious giving that unites Bassanio, Portia, and Antonio. And, of course, it confirms the difference between the play's two merchants: Antonio, who is out-of-tune as the play opens but is attuned when he extends his love beyond the circle of his friends; and Shylock, who wilfully prefers his silent entombment in the flesh.

The intellectual history of the ideas out of which Lorenzo's speech on celestial music is made—its Platonic and Pythagorean bases, its Roman and Christian elaborations, its presence in the works of Shakespeare's contemporaries: this history, embarrassingly rich, is of intrinsic interest. But it is not necessary to dwell on it in order to appreciate the speech, so tactful is Lorenzo's pedagogy. Of the moral effects of musical harmony, for instance, Lorenzo says that there is

> naught so stockish, hard, and full of rage
> But music for the time doth change his nature,—
> The man that hath no music in himself,
> Nor is not moved with concord of sweet sounds,
> Is fit for treasons, stratagems, and spoils;
> The motions of his spirit are dull as night,
> And his affections dark as Erebus:
> Let no such man be trusted.
>
> (5.1.81–88)

Lorenzo's treatment of music's role in human and in cosmic nature is at once description and demonstration: it enacts its meanings. It leaves us, as audience, as it does Jessica, prepared to "mark the music."

*   *   *

4. David S. Chamberlain, "Philosophy of Music in the *Consolatio* of Boethius," *Speculum*, 45 (1970): 81. This worthwhile addition to the account available in Hollander was brought to my attention by Professor D. W. Robertson, Jr.; my italics.

Edwin Booth as Shylock (1870). From the Walter Hampden Memorial Library at The Players, New York.

DEREK COHEN

Shylock and the Idea of the Jew†

Current criticism notwithstanding, *The Merchant of Venice* seems to me a profoundly and crudely anti-Semitic play. The debate about its implications has usually been between inexpert Jewish readers and spectators who discern an anti-Semitic core and literary critics (many of them Jews) who defensively maintain that the Shakespearean subtlety of mind transcends anti-Semitism. The critics' arguments, by now familiar, center on the subject of Shylock's essential humanity, point to the imperfections of the Christians, and remind us that Shakespeare was writing in a period when there were so few Jews in England that it didn't matter anyway (or, alternatively, that because there were so few Jews in England Shakespeare had probably never met one, so he didn't really know what he was doing). Where I believe the defensive arguments go wrong is in their heavy concentration on the character of Shylock; they overlook the more encompassing attempt of the play to offer a total poetic image of the Jew. It is all very well for John Russell Brown to say *The Merchant of Venice* is not anti-Jewish, and that "there are only two slurs on Jews in general";[1] but this kind of assertion, a common enough one in criticism of the play, cannot account for the fear and shame that Jewish audiences and readers have always felt from the moment of Shylock's entrance to his final exit. I wish to argue that these feelings are justified and that such an intuitive response is more natural than the critical sophistries whose purpose is to exonerate Shakespeare from the charge of anti-Semitism. Although few writers on the subject are prepared to concede as much, it is quite possible that Shakespeare didn't give a damn about Jews or about insulting England's minuscule Jewish community, and that, if he did finally humanize his Jew, he did so simply to enrich his drama. It is, of course, interesting to speculate on whether Shakespeare was an anti-Semite, but we cannot rise beyond speculation on this point.

The image of Jewishness which *The Merchant of Venice* presents is contrasted with the image of Christianity to which it is made referable and which ultimately encompasses and overwhelms it. Though it is simplistic to say that the play equates Jewishness with

† From *Major Literary Characters: Shylock*, ed. Harold Bloom (New York and Philadelphia: Chelsea House, 1991), pp. 305–316. Originally published in Derek Cohen, *Shakespearean Motives*, (London: Macmillan, 1988), pp. 104–18. Reprinted by permission of Palgrave Macmillan.
1. Introduction, *The Merchant of Venice*. The Arden Edition (London: Methuen, 1964), p. xxxix.

evil and Christianity with goodness, it is surely reasonable to see a moral relationship between the insistent equation of the *idea* of Jewishness with acquisitive and material values while the *idea* of Christianity is linked to the values of mercy and love. In this chapter I wish first of all to demonstrate that *The Merchant of Venice* is an anti-Semitic play by examining the image of Jewishness which it presents and by placing that image in the contrasting context of Christianity to which it is automatically made referable. Secondly, I wish to examine the paradox which follows from my assertion of the anti-Semitic nature of the play—that is, the way in which Shylock is humanized in his final scene and made simultaneously both the villain of the drama and its unfortunate victim.

Let us first ask what is meant by anti-Semitism when that term is applied to a work of art. Leo Kirschbaum suggests that it is a "wholly irrational prejudice against Jews in general, noting it would be difficult to accuse any of the Christian characters in *The Merchant of Venice* of such a vice."[2] This seems to be John Russell Brown's view as well; he perceives the play's only anti-Semitic remarks to be Launcelot's statement "my master's a very Jew" (II. ii. 100) and Antonio's comment about Shylock's "Jewish heart" (IV. i. 80).[3] While generally acceptable, Kirschbaum's definition seems to me to err in its use of the term irrational. Prejudice is almost always rationalized, and it is rationalized by reference to history and mythology. Jews have been hated for a number of reasons, the most potent among them that they were the killers of Jesus Christ.

I would define an anti-Semitic work of art as one that portrays Jews in a way that makes them objects of antipathy to readers and spectators—objects of scorn, hatred, laughter, or contempt. A careful balance is needed to advance this definition, since it might seem to preclude the possibility of an artist's presenting any Jewish character in negative terms without incurring the charge of anti-Semitism. Obviously, Jews must be allowed to have their faults in art as they do in life. In my view, a work of art becomes anti-Semitic not by virtue of its portrayal of an individual Jew in uncomplimentary terms but solely by its association of negative racial characteristics with the term Jewish or with Jewish characters generally. What we must do, then, is look at the way the word *Jew* is used and how Jews are portrayed in *The Merchant of Venice* as a whole.

The word *Jew* is used 58 times in *The Merchant of Venice*. Variants of the word like *Jewess, Jews, Jew's,* and *Jewish* are used 14 times;

---

2. Leo Kirschbaum, *Character and Characterization in Shakespeare* (Detroit: Wayne State University Press, 1962), p. 19.
3. Bernard Grebanier, interestingly enough, agrees that the play is not anti-Semitic, but contains instances of anti-Semitism. He remarks that Gratiano "is the only character in the entire play who can be accused of anti-Semitism" [*The Truth about Shylock* (New York: Random House, 1962), p. 300].

Hebrew is used twice. There are, then, 74 direct uses of *Jew* and unambiguously related words in the play. Since it will readily be acknowledged that Shakespeare understood the dramatic and rhetorical power of iteration, it must follow that there is a deliberate reason for the frequency of the word in the play. And as in all of Shakespeare's plays, the reason is to surround and inform the repeated term with associations which come more and more easily to mind as it is used. A word apparently used neutrally in the early moments of a play gains significance as it is used over and over; it becomes a term with connotations that infuse it with additional meaning.

The word *Jew* has no neutral connotations in drama. Unlike, say, the word *blood* in *Richard II* or *Macbeth*—where the connotations deepen in proportion not merely to the frequency with which the word is uttered but to the poetic significance of the passages in which it is employed—*Jew* has strongly negative implications in *The Merchant of Venice*. It is surely significant that Shylock is addressed as "Shylock" only seventeen times in the play. On all other occasions he is called "Jew" and is referred to as "the Jew". Even when he and Antonio are presumed to be on an equal footing, Shylock is referred to as the Jew while Antonio is referred to by name. For example, in the putatively disinterested letter written by the learned doctor Bellario to commend Balthazar/Portia, there is the phrase "*I acquainted him with the cause in controversy between the Jew and Antonio . . .*" (IV. i. 153–54). Similarly, in the court scene Portia calls Shylock by his name only twice; for the rest of the scene she calls him Jew to his face. The reason for this discrimination is, of course, to set Shylock apart from the other characters. This it successfully does. Calling the play's villain by a name which generalizes him while at the same time ostensibly defining his essence is, in a sense, to depersonalize him. As in our own daily life, where terms like *bourgeois*, *communist* and *fascist* conveniently efface the humanness and individuality of those to whom they are applied, the constant reference to Shylock's "thingness" succeeds in depriving him of his humanity while it simultaneously justifies the hostility of his enemies. The word *Jew* has for centuries conjured up associations of foreignness in the minds of non-Jews. When it is repeatedly used with reference to the bloodthirsty villain of the play, its intention is unmistakable. And the more often it is used, the more difficult it becomes for the audience to see it as a neutral word. Even if John Russell Brown is right, then, in pointing out that there are only two overtly anti-Semitic uses of the word in the play, it will surely be seen that overt anti-Semitism very early becomes unnecessary. Each time that *Jew* is used by any of Shylock's enemies, there is a deeply anti-Jewish implication already and automatically assumed.

In Act I, scene iii, after the bond has been struck, Antonio turns to the departing Shylock and murmurs, "Hie thee gentle Jew. / The Hebrew will turn Christian, he grows kind" (173–74). The lines themselves seem inoffensive, but let us examine the words and the gestures they imply. Shylock has left the stage and Antonio is commenting on the bond that has just been sealed. It is impossible to ignore the mocking tone of Antonio's words and the fact that the scorn they express is directed toward Shylock's Jewishness as much as toward Shylock himself. Surely, too, the elevation of one religion over another is accomplished only at the expense of the religion deemed inferior. To imply that Shylock is so improved (however ironically this is meant) that he verges on becoming Christian is an expression of amused superiority to Jews. The relatively mild anti-Semitism implicit in this passage is significant, both because it is so common in the play and because it leads with the inexorable logic of historical truth to the more fierce and destructive kind of anti-Semitism, borne of fear, that surfaces when the object of it gains ascendancy. While Shylock the Jew is still regarded as a nasty but harmless smudge on the landscape, he is grudgingly accorded some human potential by the Christians; once he becomes a threat to their happiness, however, the quality in him which is initially disdained—his Jewishness—becomes the very cynosure of fear and loathing.

In its early stages, for example, the play makes only light-hearted connections between the Jew and the Devil: as the connections are more and more validated by Shylock's behavior, however, they become charged with meaning. When Launcelot, that dismal clown, is caught in the contortions of indecision as he debates with himself the pros and cons of leaving Shylock's service, he gives the association of Jew and Devil clear expression:

> Certainly, my conscience will serve me to run from this Jew my master . . . to be rul'd by my conscience, I should stay with the Jew my master, who (God bless the mark) is a kind of devil; and to run away from the Jew, I should be rul'd by the fiend, who (saving your reverence) is the devil himself. Certainly the Jew is the very devil incarnation, and in my conscience, my conscience is but a kind of hard conscience, to offer to counsel me to stay with the Jew.
>
> (II. ii. 1–28)

Significant here is the almost obsessive repetition of "the Jew". In the immediate context the phrase has a neat dramatic ambiguity; it refers explicitly to Shylock, but by avoiding the use of his name it also refers more generally to the concept of the Jew. The ambiguity of the phrase makes the demonic association applicable to Jews generally.

That Launcelot's description is anti-Jewish more than simply anti-Shylock is to be seen in the fact that the view of the Jew it presents is in accord with the anti-Semitic portrayal of Jews from the Middle Ages on. Launcelot's image of the Jew as the Devil incarnate conforms to a common medieval notion. It is expressed in Chaucer and much early English drama, and it is given powerful theological support by Luther, who warns the Christian world that "next to the devil thou hast no enemy more cruel, more venemous and violent than a true Jew."[4] That a fool like Launcelot should take the assertion a step further and see the Jew as the Devil himself is only to be expected. And that the play should show, as its final discovery, that Shylock is only a devil *manqué* is merely to lend further support to Luther's influential asseveration.

A less mythological but more colourful and dramatically effective anti-Jewish association is forged by the frequent and almost casually employed metaphor of Jew as dog. The play is replete with dialogue describing Shylock in these terms. In the mouth of Solanio, for example, the connection is explicit: "I never heard a passion so confus'd, / So strange, outrageous, and so variable / As the dog Jew did utter in the streets" (II. viii. 12–14). I do not believe that it is going too far to suggest that in this passage the word *strange* carries a host of anti-Semitic reverberations. It recalls to the traditional anti-Semitic memory the foreign and, to the ignorant, frightening Jewish rituals of mourning—rituals which in anti-Semitic literature have been redolent with implications of the slaughter of Christian children and the drinking of their blood. With this report of Shylock's rage and grief comes a massive turning point in the play. The once verminous Jew is implicitly transformed into a fearful force.

To this argument I must relate a point about a passage hardly noticed in the critical literature on the play. Having bemoaned his losses and decided to take his revenge, Shylock turns to Tubal and tells him to get an officer to arrest Antonio. "I will have the heart of him if he forfeit, for were he out of Venice I can make what merchandise I will. Go, Tubal," he says, "and meet me at our synagogue,—go good Tubal,—at our synagogue, Tubal" (III. i. 119–20). This collusive and sinister request to meet at the synagogue has always seemed to me to be the most deeply anti-Semitic remark in the play. It is ugly and pernicious precisely because it is indirect. What is the word synagogue supposed to mean in the context? Shylock has just determined to cut the heart out of the finest man in Venice; worse yet, the knowledge that he is legally entitled to do so brings him solace in his grief. Now what might an Elizabethan have

---

4. Lucy S. Dawidowicz, *The War against the Jews 1933–1945* (New York: Holt, Rinehart & Winston, 1975), p. 29.

thought the synagogue really was? Is it possible that he thought
it merely a place where Jews prayed? Is it not more likely that he
thought it a mysterious place where strange and terrible rituals
were enacted? Whatever Shakespeare himself might have thought,
the lines convey the notion that Shylock is repairing to his place of
worship immediately after learning that he can now legally murder
the good Antonio. Bloodletting and religious worship are brought
into a very ugly and insidious conjunction.

Slightly earlier Tubal is observed approaching. Solanio remarks,
"Here comes another of the tribe,—a third cannot be match'd, unless the devil himself turn Jew" (III. i. 70–71). Incredible as it may
seem, this line has been used to demonstrate that the play is not
anti-Semitic, because Shylock and Tubal alone among the Jews are
so bad as to be like devils. What the lines more probably mean is
that these two villains are the worst Jews around, and that as the
worst of a very bad lot they must be pretty bad.

In her study of the origins of modern German anti-Semitism
Lucy Dawidowicz discerns two irreconcilable images of Jews in
anti-Semitic literature,

> . . . both inherited from the recent and medieval treasury of
> anti-Semitism. One was the image of the Jew as vermin, to be
> rubbed out by the heel of the boot, to be exterminated. The
> other was the image of the Jew as the mythic omnipotent
> super-adversary, against whom war on the greatest scale had to
> be conducted. The Jew was, on the one hand, a germ, a bacil-
> lus, to be killed without conscience. On the other hand, he
> was, in the phrase Hitler repeatedly used . . . the "mortal en-
> emy" (*Todfiend*) to be killed in self-defense.[5]

The Christians in *The Merchant of Venice* initially see Shylock in
terms of the first image. He is a dog to be spurned and spat upon.
His Jewish gaberdine and his Jewish habits of usury mark him as a
cur to be kicked and abused. (Is it likely that Antonio would enjoy
the same license to kick a rich Christian moneylender with impunity?) As Shylock gains in power, however, the image of him as a
cur changes to an image of him as a potent diabolical force. In Antonio's eyes Shylock's lust for blood takes on the motive energy of
Satanic evil, impervious to reason or humanity.

> I pray you think you question with the Jew,—
> You may as well go stand upon the beach
> And bid the main flood bate his usual height,
> You may as well use question with the wolf,
> Why he hath made the ewe bleat for the lamb:

5. Dawidowicz, p. 222.

You may as well forbid the mountain pines
To wag their high tops, and to make no noise
Whey they are fretten with the gusts of heaven:
You may as well do anything most hard
As seek to soften that—than which what's harder?—
His Jewish heart!   (IV. i. 70–80)

In this speech Shylock, is utterly "the Jew"—the embodiment of his species. And the Jew's Jewish heart is wholly obdurate. He is a force of evil as strong as nature itself. No longer a dog to be controlled by beating and kicking, he has become an untamable wolf, an inferno of evil and hatred. The logical conclusion of sentiments like these, surely, is that the Jew must be kept down. Once he is up, his instinct is to kill and ravage. Indeed, Shylock has said as much himself: "Thou call'dst me dog before thou hadst a cause, / But since I am a dog, beware my fangs" (III. iii. 7–8). If the play defines Christianity as synonymous with tolerance and kindness and forgiveness, it defines Jewishness in opposite terms. The symbol of evil in *The Merchant of Venice* is Jewishness, and Jewishness is represented by the Jew.

The counterargument to the charge that Shakespeare is guilty of anti-Semitism has always depended upon the demonstration that the portrait of Shylock is, ultimately, a deeply humane one—that Shylock's arguments against the Christians are unassailable and that his position in the Christian world has resulted from that world's treatment of him. This view, romantic in inception, still persists in the minds of a large number of critics and directors. From such authors as John Palmer and Harold Goddard one gets the image of a Shylock who carries with him the Jewish heritage of suffering and persecution, Shylock as bearer of the pain of the ages. This Shylock is religious and dignified, wronged by the world he inhabits, a man of whom the Jewish people can justly be proud and in whose vengeful intentions they may recognize a poetic righting of the wrongs of Jewish history.[6] That Jews have themselves recognized such a Shylock in Shakespeare's play is borne out in the self-conscious effusions of Heinrich Heine, for whom the Jewish moneylender possessed "a breast that held in it all the martyrdom . . . [of] a whole tortured people."[7]

The usual alternative to this view is that of the critics who see Shylock as no more than a stereotyped villain. For these critics, what his sympathizers regard as Shakespeare's plea for Shylock's es-

6. John Palmer, *Political and Comic Characters of Shakespeare* (London: Macmillan, 1962), pp. 401–39; Harold C. Goddard, *The Meaning of Shakespeare* (University of Chicago Press, 1960), pp. 81–116.
7. Quoted by Lawrence Danson, *The Harmonies of* The Merchant of Venice (New Haven and London: Yale University Press, 1978), p. 130.

sential humanity (the "Hath not a Jew eyes" speech [III. i. 52ff.])
is nothing more than a justification for revenge. These critics cir-
cumvent the charge that Shakespeare is anti-Semitic by arguing
that Shylock is not so much a Jew as a carryover from the old
morality plays. Albert Wertheim, for example, asserts that "Shylock
is a stylized and conventional comic villain and no more meant to
be a realistic portrayal of a Jew than Shakespeare's Aaron is meant
to be a realistic Moor."[8] John P. Sisk confidently declares that
"Kittredge was mainly right in his contention that the play is not
an anti-Semitic document."[9] These views are determinedly anti-
sentimental and usefully balance the oversensitive opposing position. Their mainstay is dramatic precedent, from which can be
deduced the similarities between Shylock and the stereotypical
comic villain of earlier dramatic modes. Toby Lelyveld notes striking resemblances between Shylock and the Pantalone figure of
commedia dell' arte, for example: "In physical appearance, mannerisms and the situations in which he is placed, Shylock is so like his
Italian prototype that his characterization, at least superficially,
presents no new aspects save that of its Jewishness."[1]

What the two critical opinions have in common is their determination to defend Shakespeare from the charge of anti-Semitism—
but from opposite sides of the fence. Shylock is either a better man
than we might be disposed to believe or he is not really human.[2]
The latter reading seems to me to be closer to what the play presents. It is undoubtedly true that Shylock's "humanity" has frequently been given full—even excessive—play in the theatre. But it
is always useful to bear in mind that he is the play's villain. All his
words, even the most convincingly aggrieved among them, are the
words of a cold, heartless killer and should therefore be regarded
skeptically. Shylock is untouched by the plight of those around him,
and he plots the ruthless murder of Antonio. Pity for him therefore
strikes me as grossly misplaced, and the view of him as the embodiment of wickedness seems dramatically correct. His argument that
he is like other men and that he is vengeful only because he has
been wronged by them is a violent corruption of the true state of
things. Shylock is cruel and monstrous and utterly unlike other
men in their capacity for love, fellowship, and sympathy. Consider
his remark that he would not have exchanged the ring his daughter
stole for a wilderness of monkeys. Rather than redeeming him, as

8. Albert Wertheim, "The Treatment of Shylock and Thematic Integrity in *The Merchant of Venice*," *Shakespeare Studies*, 6 (1970): 75.
9. John P. Sisk, "Bondage and Release in *The Merchant of Venice*", *Shakespeare Quarterly* 20 (1969): 217.
1. Toby Lelyveld, *Shylock on the Stage* (Cleveland: Press of Western Reserve University, 1960), p. 8.
2. A fuller analysis of these two critical readings is provided in Danson, pp. 126–39.

Kirschbaum points out, it only makes him the worse; by demonstrating that he is capable of sentiment and aware of love, it "blackens by contrast his inhumanity all the more".[3] As a sincerely expressed emotion the line is out of character. It is the only reference to his wife in the play, and, if we are to take his treatment of Jessica as an indication of his treatment of those he professes to hold dear, we may reasonably conclude that it is a heartfelt expression not of love but of sentimental self-pity. Shylock is, in short, a complete and unredeemed villain whose wickedness is a primary trait. It is a trait, moreover, that is reinforced by the fact of his Jewishness, which, to make the wickedness so much the worse, is presented as synonymous with it.

And yet, although Shylock is the villain of the play, the critics who have been made uneasy by the characterization of his evil have sensed a dimension of pathos, a quality of humanity, that is part of the play. Audiences and readers have usually found themselves pitying Shylock in the end, even though the play's other characters, having demolished him, hardly give the wicked Jew a second thought. The Christians fail to see the humanity of Shylock, not because they are less sensitive than readers and spectators, but because that humanity emerges only in the end, during the court scene when they are understandably caught up in the atmosphere of happiness that surrounds Antonio's release from death. Audiences and readers, whose attention is likely to be equally shared by Antonio and Shylock, are more aware of what is happening to Shylock. They are therefore aware of the change that is forced upon him. To them he is more than simply an undone villain. He is a suffering human being.

Shylock becomes a pitiable character only during his last appearance in the court of Venice. It is here that he is humanized—during a scene in which he is usually silent. Ironically, it is not in his pleadings or self-justifications that Shylock becomes a sympathetic figure, but in his still and silent transformation from a crowing blood-hungry monster into a quiescent victim whose fate lies in the hands of those he had attempted to destroy. How this transmogrification is accomplished is, perhaps, best explained by Gordon Craig's exquisitely simple observation about the chief character of The Bells. Craig remarked that "no matter who the human being may be, and what his crime, the sorrow which he suffers must appeal to our hearts . . ."[4] This observation helps explain why the scene of the reversal which turns aside the impending catastrophe of The Merchant of Venice does not leave the audience with feelings

3. Kirschbaum, p. 26.
4. Gordon Craig, "Irving's Masterpiece—'The Bells,'" Laurel British Drama: The Nineteenth Century, ed. Robert Corrigan (New York: Dell, 1967), p. 119.

of unmixed delight in the way that the reversals of the more conventional comedies do. The reversal of *The Merchant of Venice* defies a basic premise of the normal moral logic of drama. Instead of merely enjoying the overthrow of an unmitigated villain, we find ourselves pitying him. The conclusion of the play is thus a triumph of ambiguity: Shakespeare has sustained the moral argument which dictates Shylock's undoing while simultaneously compelling us to react to an emotional level more compassionate than intellectual.

If it is true that Jewishness in the play is equated with wickedness, it is surely unlikely that Shylock's elaborate rationalizations of his behaviour are intended to render him as sympathetic. Embedded in the lengthy speeches of self-justification are statements of fact that ring truer to Shylock's motives than the passages in which he identifies himself as wrongly and malevolently persecuted. In his first encounter with Antonio, for example, Shylock explains in a deeply felt aside why he hates the Christian merchant: "I hate him for he is a Christian: / But more, for that in low simplicity / He lends out money gratis, and brings down / The rate of usance here with us in Venice" (I. iii. 37–40). It is only as an afterthought that he ponders the larger question of Antonio's hatred of the Jews. The chief reason Shylock gives for hating Antonio—and he announces it as the chief reason—is directly related to his avarice in money matters.

Almost all of Shylock's speeches can convincingly be interpreted in this light. When he speaks, Shylock is a sarcastic character both in the literal sense of flesh-rending and in the modern sense of sneering. For example, when he describes the bloody agreement as a "merry bond", the word *merry* becomes charged with a sinister ambiguity. Until the scene of his undoing, Shylock's character is dominated by the traits usual to Elizabethan comic villains. He is a hellish creature, a discontented soul whose vilifying of others marks him as the embodiment of malevolence and misanthropy. After Jessica's escape Shylock is seen vituperating his daughter, not mourning her, bemoaning the loss of his money as much as the loss of his child. His affirmations of his common humanity with the Christians, particularly in the "Hath not a Jew eyes" speech, are above all meant to justify his thirst for revenge. His allegations that Antonio has disgraced him, laughed at him, and scorned his nation only because he is a Jew are lopsided. He is abused chiefly because he is a devil. The fact of his Jewishness only offers his abusers an explanation for his diabolical nature; it does not offer them the pretext to torment an innocent man. His speech of wheedling self-exculpation is surely intended to be regarded in the way that beleaguered tenants today might regard the whine of their wealthy landlord: "Hath not a landlord eyes? Hath not a landlord organs, di-

mensions, senses, affections, passions?" Instead of eliciting sympathy for an underdog, Shakespeare intended the speech to elicit
detestation for one in a privileged and powerful position who know-
ingly and deliberately abases himself in a plea for unmerited sympathy.

Furthermore, in answer to the tradition which defends Shylock
on the grounds that Shakespeare gave him a sympathetic, self-
protecting speech, we need to be reminded that the assertions it
contains are dependent upon a demonstrable falsehood. The climax
of Shylock's speech, its cutting edge, is his confident cry that his revenge is justified by Christian precedent: "If a Jew wrong a Christian, what is his humility? Revenge! If a Christian wrong a Jew,
what should his sufference be by Christian example?—why revenge!" (III. i. 62–64). In fact what happens is that in return for
the crime which Shylock commits against Antonio, he is offered
not revenge but mercy—harshly given perhaps, but mercy nonetheless—and this in circumstances where revenge would be morally
and legally sanctioned. The director who causes this speech to be
uttered as a genuine defense of its speaker is thus ignoring one of
the play's most tangible morals.

Until the court scene, Shylock remains a readily understood and
easily identified villain. His dominant characteristics are the negative qualities normally associated with vice figures. Sympathy for
him before the reversal therefore does violence to the dramatic purpose of the play. Completely in the ascendancy, he has power and
the law itself on his side. When sympathy finally becomes right and
proper, it transcends the narrow bounds of religion and stereotype.
When finally we are made to pity Shylock, we do not pity a wrong-
fully persecuted member of an oppressed minority. Instead we pity
a justly condemned and justly punished villain. A potential murderer has been caught, is brought to justice, and is duly and appropriately sentenced. The pity we are moved to feel is as natural and
inevitable as the great loathing we were made to feel formerly. It results simply from the sympathy that we are likely to admit at any
sight of human suffering, no matter how well deserved it may be.

In the court scene the presence of Portia stands as a direct assurance that Antonio will not die. While we remain conscious of
Shylock's evil intentions, then, our judgement of him is tempered
by our privileged awareness of his ultimate impotence. In other
words, although we might despise Shylock, we do not fear him.
This distinction is critical to an understanding of his character and
of Shakespeare's intentions, and it helps explain the readiness with
which we are able to extend sympathy to the villain.

The chief explanation, however, goes somewhat deeper. It is simultaneously psychological and dramatic. It is psychological to the

extent that we are willy-nilly affected by the sight of Shylock in pain. It is dramatic to the extent that the scene is so arranged as to dramatize in the subtlest possible way the manifestation of that pain. Shylock remains onstage while his erstwhile victims are restored to prosperity by Portia. The publication of Antonio's rescue and of Shylock's punishment takes ninety-six lines, from Portia's "Tarry a little, there is something else . . ." (IV. i. 301) to Gratiano's gleeful "Had I been judge, thou shouldst have had ten more, / To bring thee to the gallows, not to the font" (ll. 395–96). During this period—about five minutes—Shylock is transformed from a villain into a victim.

In part the inversion is achieved by use of the established fool, Gratiano, who, by trumpeting the victory of the Christians, assumes Shylock's earlier role as one who enjoys another's pain. Gratiano is a character who talks too much, who suspects silence, who prefers to play the fool. His joy in Shylock's downfall becomes sadistic and self-serving. Interestingly, it is not shared in quite so voluble a fashion by the other Christian characters. Portia has done all the work, and yet it is Gratiano—whose real contribution to the scene is to announce Portia's success and to excoriate the Jew—who cries at Shylock "Now, infidel, I have you on the hip" (l. 334). Until this point in the play Shylock has been vicious and sadistic, nastily rubbing his hands in anticipation of a bloody revenge, thriving on the smell of the blood he is about to taste. Now that role is taken from him by Gratiano, on whom it sits unattractively. The failure of his friends to participate in this orgy of revenge suggests that their feelings are more those of relief at Antonio's release than of lust for Shylock's blood.

As the tables are turned upon him, Shylock gradually and unexpectedly reveals a new dimension of himself, and the farcical pleasure we have been led to expect is subverted by his surprising response to defeat. He reveals a capacity for pain and suffering. As a would-be murderer, Shylock gets at least what he deserves. As a human being asking for mercy, he receives, and possibly merits, sympathy. Shylock recognizes instantly that he has been undone. Once Portia reminds him that the bond does not allow him to shed one drop of blood, his orgy is over and he says little during the scene of dénouement. "Is that the law?" he lamely asks. Five lines later, he is ready to take his money and leave the court with whatever remaining dignity is permitted him. But an easy egress is not to be his. He is made to face the consequences of his evil. Portia's addresses to Shylock during the confrontation are disguised exhortations to him to suffer for the wrong he has done. She forces him to acknowledge her triumph and his defeat: "Tarry a little" (l. 301); "Soft . . . soft, no haste!" (ll. 316–17); "Why doth the Jew pause?"

(l. 331); "Therefore prepare thee to cut" (l. 320); "Tarry Jew" (l. 343); "Art thou contented Jew? What dost thou say?" (l. 388). Shylock is made to stand silently, receiving and accepting mercy and some restitution from Antonio; he is compelled to bear, not the stings of revenge upon himself, but the sharper stings of a forgiveness that he is incapable of giving. His humiliation lies in his inability to refuse the gift of life from one whose life he maliciously sought. When he requests leave to go from the court, the change that has come over him is total. He is no longer a figure of vice, and he has not become a figure of fun (except, perhaps, to Gratiano). He is a lonely, deprived, and defeated creature feeling pain. The fact that he has caused his own downfall does not diminish the sympathy felt for him now, in part because of the protraction of his undoing, and in part because of the dramatic effect of the change in him. The suddenness of the alteration of his character forces a comparison between what he once was and what he has become. And where dramatic energy is its own virtue, the visible eradication of that energy is a source of pathos.

In this scene the word *Jew* has been used like a blunt instrument by Portia and Gratiano. Now, being used against one who has become a victim, the former associations of the word are thrown into question. Portia's persistence in doing to the Jew as he would have done to Antonio has a strangely bitter effect. She hunts him when he is down; she throws the law in his teeth with a righteousness that seems repulsive to us primarily because we have long been aware that Antonio was ultimately invulnerable. Having removed Shylock's sting, she is determined to break his wings in the bargain. In this determination, she is unlike her somewhat dull but more humane husband, who is prepared to pay Shylock the money owed him and to allow him to leave. Portia's stance is beyond legal questioning, of course. What gives us pause is the doggedness with which she exacts justice. Shylock is ruined by adversity and leaves the stage without even the strength to curse his foes: "I pray you give me leave to go from hence, / I am not well" (ll. 391–92). He communicates his pain by his powerlessness, and the recognition of this pain stirs the audience.

In a brief space, in which his silence replaces his usual verbosity, Shylock is transformed. A villain is shown to be more than merely villainous. Shylock is shown to be more than merely the Jew. He is shown to possess a normal, unheroic desire to live at any cost. The scene of undoing is an ironic realization of Shylock's previously histrionic pleas for understanding. We now see something that formerly there was no reason to believe: that if you prick him, Shylock bleeds.

By endowing Shylock with humanity in the end Shakespeare

would seem to have contradicted the dominating impression of the play, in which the fierce diabolism of the Jew is affirmed in so many ways. And indeed, the contradiction is there. Having described a character who is defined by an almost otherwordly evil, whose life is one unremitting quest for an unjust vengeance, it seems inconsistent to allow that he is capable of normal human feelings. The Jew has been used to instruct the audience and the play's Christians about the potential and essential evil of his race; he has been used to show that a Jew with power is a terrible thing to behold, is capable of the vilest sort of destruction. And the play has demonstrated in the person of his daughter that the only good Jew is a Christian. The contradiction emerges almost in spite of Shakespeare's anti-Semitic design. He has shown on the one hand, by the creation of a powerful and dominant dramatic image, that the Jew is inhuman. But he seems to have been compelled on the other hand to acknowledge that the Jew is also a human being.

The most troubling aspect of the contradictory element of *The Merchant of Venice* is this: if Shakespeare knew that Jews were human beings like other people—and the conclusion of the play suggests that he did—and if he knew that they were not *merely* carriers of evil but human creatures with human strengths and weaknesses, then the play as a whole is a betrayal of the truth. To have used it as a means for eliciting feelings of loathing for Jews, while simultaneously recognizing that its portrayal of the race it vilifies is inaccurate or, possibly, not the whole truth, is profoundly troubling. It is as though *The Merchant of Venice* is an anti-Semitic play written by an author who is not an anti-Semite—but an author who has been willing to use the cruel stereotypes of that ideology for mercenary and artistic purposes.

LAURENCE LERNER

Wilhelm S and Shylock†

Who is the mysterious dramatist who has shot to world-wide fame in our century because of his political relevance? His plays were performed before the incipiently fascist public in France and the actually fascist public in Germany during the 1930s, and he was acclaimed for his vigorous portrayal of the dangers of mob rule and the need for strong leadership, as well as for his awareness of the ineradicable enmity between Christian generosity and the Jewish

---

† From *Shakespeare Survey* 48 (Cambridge: Cambridge University Press, 1995), pp. 61–68. Reprinted by permission of Cambridge University Press.

fixation on money. At some point during the war he appears to have moved to England, since he wrote a film script for Laurence Olivier depicting the courage and resourcefulness of the English when fighting on the continent, and was much praised for his patriotism. After the war, his series of plays on English history showed the desirability of hereditary monarchy and the dangers of civil war; but after the student uprisings of 1968 he appears to have treated revolution much more sympathetically. His taste for a deliberately antiquated style and archaic diction lends (paradoxically) a sharpness to his critique of contemporary politics; his passion for anonymity and seclusion has kept biographers guessing, and has fascinated the public; and his obvious wanderlust has enabled him to exert an influence in every major country in the world.

There is some uncertainty even about his name: it has come to us in various spellings, and there are even theories that this was not his name at all, but that of an actor whom the dramatist used to disguise his true identity. Since in this essay I intend to discuss the anti-Semitic play he wrote when in Nazi Germany, I shall use the German form of his given name, and avoid all orthographical controversy by abbreviating his surname: I shall call him Wilhelm S. Although we cannot be sure that he was actually German, there is no doubt about the great success he enjoyed there. He was congratulated for his awareness of Nordic profundity, and for the Nordic traits in the characterization of Hamlet: the tendency to muse about life and its meaning, and the melancholy with which he responds to the death of his father and the marriage of his mother. One critic saw these Nordic traits as interacting with other, more Latinate ("westisch") traits in Hamlet, and attributed the mixture to a corresponding interaction in the dramatist himself. Since biographical information about S is so hard to come by, this claim can hardly be tested.[1]

But the play which particularly led Nazi Germany to congratulate S for his understanding of racial psychology was *The Merchant of Venice*, in which he rewrote the old folk-tale of the Jew who lent three thousand ducats to a Christian merchant in return for a "merry bond" by which, if the money was not repaid in time, he would be entitled to a pound of the debtor's flesh. The grotesque power of this anti-Semitic story obviously appealed to the German

1. Alex Niederstenbruch, "Einige Gedanken zur rassischen Betrachtung von S's Hamlet", *Zeitschrift für neusprachlichen Unterricht* 41 (1942): 31–33. This and all other German passages are translated by me. For a valuable bibliography of discussions of S in Germany in the 1930s, see Ruth Freifrau von Ledebuhr, "Der deutsche Geist und S: Anmerkungen zur S-Rezeption 1933–45," in *Wissenschaft und Nazionalsozialismus* (Herausgeber: R. Geissler and W. Popp, 1988). I have also used Werner Habicht, "S and Theatre Politics in the Third Reich", in *The Play out of Context*, ed. Scolnicov and Holland (1989); and *S im dritten Reich* by Georg Zähringer (Magisterarbeit: Universität München, 1988).

audience because of its brilliant portrayal of the racial characteristics of the Eastern Jew, and the contrast with the nobility of the
Christian merchant, "the royal merchant who loved money not for
its own sake but in order to help his friends, who in order to put it
in the service of life is willing to renounce everything. He keeps his
word and is ready to carry it out to the bitter end."[2]

That the play contains one apparently philo-semitic speech, the
well-known self-defence "Hath not a Jew eyes . . .", need not worry
us: the Nordic reader, who shares S's insights into racial psychology, will not err in reading the play, but will realize that this torrent
of words is judged and refuted by Antonio, who expresses the poet's
own opinion in his speech in the trial scene asserting that reasoning with the Jew is as futile as trying to alter nature:

> You may as well do anything most hard
> As seek to soften that—than which what's harder?—
> His Jewish heart.   (4.1.77–79)

We know today, in the light of racial biology, that Shylock is mistaken in his claim that a Jew is human like the rest of us (or them),
since "der Jude eben rassenbiologisch ein anderer, artfremder
Mensch für uns ist": that is, he is "biologically distinct" and so
alienated from us—a point made by the Duke when he speaks of
"the difference of our spirit".[3]

There is an ideological as well as a racial dimension to the contrast between Shylock and the Christians, which can be interestingly formulated as that between justice and the rule of law:

> Rationalism and technical formalism are constitutive elements
> of every modern system of law. S's parody is not quite directed
> at these, but should be seen rather as an attack on that ideol-
> ogy of the rule (or the reliability) of law which submits so fully
> to these technical elements in law that it allows the just deci-
> sion to yield without struggle to the calculable one. It justifies
> itself by claiming that it is more important to put an end to
> struggle than to put a just end to it; that the existence of a le-
> gal system is more important than its justice; and that the rule
> of law has as its prime duty the bringing about of peace. Ac-
> cording to this concept (which, I add in parenthesis, is very
> like the rules by which the police work in our society) peace
> depends on security and is independent of justice. One only
> needs to attend to the meaning of these words in terms of for-
> eign politics and national rights to realise what view of law is
> here in question: it is that of western positivism, the politics of

2. Dr Karl Pempelfort, "Er besteht auf seinem Schein", *Königsberger Tageblatt*, 31 March
   1935; reprinted in Joseph Wulf, *Theater und Film im dritten Reich* (1964), p. 257.
3. Gregor Schwartz-Bostunitsch, "Shylock und wir", *Der Weltkampf*, 17 (1940): 17.

the status-quo, or bourgeois security . . . in the legal consciousness of the Old Testament and of Jewry the element of
security is of special importance. In the figure of Shylock this
connexion is vividly expressed.[4]

This seems a very perceptive reading of *The Merchant of Venice*:
precisely this contrast is dealt with in the exchange between Bassanio and "Balthazar", in which Bassanio begs:

> Wrest once the law to your authority.
> To do a great right, do a little wrong,
> And curb this cruel devil of his will. (4.1.212–14)

—and Portia, as Balthazar, replies:

> It must not be. There is no power in Venice
> Can alter a decree establishèd:
> 'Twill be recorded for a precedent,
> And many an error by the same example
> Will rush into the state. It cannot be. (4.1.215–19)

—asserting in other words that the most important thing in law is
its reliability, that the rule of law must not be overturned in the interests of justice ("a great right") because—the classic objection of
the legalist—it would set a precedent. Shylock too asserted the
same contrast:

> The pound of flesh which I demand of him
> Is dearly bought. 'Tis mine, and I will have it.
> If you deny me, fie upon your law:
> There is no force in the decree of Venice. (4.1.98–101)

That is to say, it is not the task of the court to pass judgement on
the law, but to enforce it. And Shylock sees too that this conception
of law is the basis of property: that is why he draws the parallel with
slavery. His sarcastic suggestion about the "purchased slaves"—"Let
them be free, marry them to your heirs"—could be paraphrased (if
we remove the sarcasm) as "let justice override legality", and he
correctly indicates that this is out of the question by giving the conventional reply: "The slaves are ours." Is it not therefore correct to
describe Shylock's view of law as positivist, as based on bourgeois
security and the status quo?

Even the love story of S's play can be given a racial interpretation. The annual lecture for 1937 to the German Association for
the study of Wilhelm S (yes, he was sufficiently celebrated to have
his own Association) was delivered by a Eugenicist, "someone who
has inquired what conception of love and marriage will be suitable

---

4. Wilhelm Grewe, "Shylock, oder die Parodie der Rechtssicherheit", *Deutsche Volkstum*,
18 (1936): 77–79.

or necessary to improve the stock of a people, someone who has further inquired what kind of girls and women the young men of a people ought to incline to in order to beget a more effective, more handsome and nobler posterity". The lecturer concluded that Portia was just the ticket: she shows the needed "mixture of reserve, strong feeling and clarity of mind, along with a talent for the masterful assurance that belongs to an inherently aristocratic being. We cannot doubt that she will develop into a truly Germanic mistress of the house (Hausherrin germanischer Prägung)".[5] It is hard to believe, after all this, that *The Merchant of Venice* has also been performed in Israel (though we must add that it has not always been popular there). Did the Israelis not realize what they were doing, when they put on this anti-Semitic play before their own people? Or were they so committed to a non-political aestheticism that they allowed the dramatic genius of S to override his ideology?

Particularly interesting is the production in 1936, when Israel was still Palestine, because after it took place the theatre organized a public debate, in which author, theatre and director were put on trial, accused of producing "a play in which [they] involved an anti-Jewish theme without being informed enough to treat the subject".[6]

I can find no evidence that Wilhelm S, world traveller though he has since become, came to Palestine for this "trial", so he was no doubt represented by proxy. Play and production were attacked both for what they said and for what they did not say: for attributing to Shylock a spirit of revenge wholly alien to the Jews, "in whom an ancient spiritual culture is coupled with the long experience of humiliation and suffering", and for not admitting that the responsibility for turning Jews into usurers rested with Christian society, "because you never let us survive in any other way: you have turned us into usurers and profiteers". I shall return shortly to this objection.

But first I wish to perform a thought-experiment. Let us imagine that so little is known about S not because he has kept himself hidden but because he lived a long time ago; that he did not write *The Merchant of Venice* as an act of homage to Nazi ideology, but that it was written in a quite different time and place, and was appropriated by the Nazis. What difference would this make? Obviously it would introduce a historical factor. It would enable us to ask whether the Nazi interpreters were distorting the play to fit their

5. Hans F. K. Günther, "S's Mädchen und Frauen" (Vortrag vor der deutschen S-Gesellschaft), *S-Jahrbuch*, 75 (1937): 85, 104.
6. Ya'akov Fikhman, quoted in Avraham Oz, "Transformations of Authenticity", *S-Jahrbuch* (1983): 169.

own ideology, or whether the distant age in which S wrote (say three or four centuries ago) shared their anti-Semitic assumption.

And instead of being impressed with the enterprise shown by S in writing in so many countries and so many different political situations, we shall now say that it was the various countries and societies that were enterprising, helping themselves to his plays and interpreting them as they wished or felt compelled to. We shall then find ourselves asking whether interpreting an old play is fundamentally different from writing a new one. To some the difference will seem obvious; but to some schools of criticism now flourishing (represented, say, by Stanley Fish or Terence Hawkes) there will be no significant difference: for if the meaning of a text is constituted entirely by an interpretive community, if we can attribute no qualities to the text itself but only to the way it is read, then there can be no appeal to an author living in the past, outside of the community of readers. This view is now so influential that it is worth pausing to discuss it, since it is central to my thought experiment.

I choose Terence Hawkes as the representative of this position, which he sets forth with great vigour in *That Shakespeherian Rag* and *Meaning by Shakespeare*. The two books maintain that "great" works of art have "no claim to existence 'in themselves' ", and that we should study the ways in which they have been "worked upon . . . as part of the struggle for cultural meaning".[7] As an example of how he applies his claim that "meaning is made rather than found" we can look at his discussion of Nedar, a character who is mentioned but does not appear in *A Midsummer Night's Dream* (Helena is Nedar's daughter). The witty changes that Hawkes rings on Nedar's name culminate in the claim that she should be regarded as a woman, Helena's mother rather than her father, "not because Nedar necessarily *is* female, but because, in twentieth-century terms, the suggestion that she could be unseats a number of presuppositions investing the play, and demonstrates an indeterminacy, an undecidability, that is a feature of all texts".[8]

Now since we do not know whether Nedar is male or female (the phrase "old Nedar's daughter" allows, as Hawkes rightly points out, either meaning) the play can be said to license the claim that she is female, and the fact that previous commentators have seen "her" as male certainly confirms the view that we have here "a struggle for cultural meaning". But that kind of indeterminacy cannot possibly be seen as "a feature of all texts". The existence of some indeterminate elements does not show that all elements are indeterminate, it

7. Terence Hawkes, *That Shakespeherian Rag: Essays on a Critical Process* (London 1986), p. 123.
8. Hawkes, *Meaning by Shakespeare* (London and New York 1992), p. 39.

rather reminds us how determinate others are. To claim that "in twentieth-century terms" Shylock should be turned into a woman would raise very different issues—and much more resistance.

The twentieth-century issue I am here concerned with, however, is not gender but prejudice. Wilhelm S offers us an anti-Semitic *Merchant of Venice*, and we, reacting like good liberals, are upset by it. My "thought experiment" was a way of asking how important is the difference between writing an anti-Semitic play, and offering an anti-Semitic interpretation of a play written in 1597. According to the theory that meaning is made rather than found, there can be no difference; and in that case, treating *The Merchant of Venice* as if it was written by Wilhelm S in Nazi Germany is not the (ingenious or tiresome) gimmick which my readers have no doubt assumed it to be, but indistinguishable from the normal study of Shakespeare.

It will now be clear that I believe they *are* distinguishable, and appealing to history is the obvious way to distinguish them. But, as we are all aware nowadays, to appeal to the thought system of sixteenth-century England as a guide to correct understanding of S's plays soon raises problems. The appeal to history can alter our reading of a text only if some kind of direct access to the past is possible; if it produces the same kind of arguments as already rage about the plays, we may find ourselves reasoning in a circle.

And if we do appeal to history we shall soon find that German critics in the 1930s anticipated us, and were prepared to defend *their* reading on historical grounds:

> *The Merchant of Venice* is not the tragedy of Shylock, as was believed by the sentimental sympathy of the 19th Century, which, closely related to semitic ways of thinking, thought that higher justice sided with the Jew, downtrodden and spat upon, and wanted to reopen the trial to Shylock and decide it in favour of the enemy of the Christians. The play begins with Antonio's puzzling and unhealthy melancholy, and ends in complete serenity. The concluding scene in Belmont follows consistently from the preceding struggles and decisions, as the Empire is the consequence of the return of the Jews to the Church. The so-called Jewish tragedy is an enchanting comedy of incomparable political power and beauty, transfigured by theology. The prominent use of music should be explained by the fact that great music is to be seen as part of a great political system. The final scene is not to be understood as lyrical in the way bourgeois moonlight romanticism is lyrical, but in its connexion with heavenly matters and eternal glory, with peace as the final goal of all politics in accordance with essential human nature, with the libera securitas et secura tranquillitas, the union of nature and grace symbolised by the wedding of

Portia and Bassanio, the transfiguration of the body and the harmony of blessed spirits.[9]

Clemens Lang here is (almost) impeccably historical. He abuses the sentimental sympathy of the nineteenth century in a way that has been a commonplace since Irving Babbitt and T. S. Eliot, adding, however, one detail that sticks out like a sore thumb: the assertion that this sentimentality is closely related to a Jewish way of thinking ("semitische Geisteart"). If, as his hostile critics have sometimes suggested, Eliot would have liked to say that too, at least he never did; but it is not difficult to guess where Lang got the idea. The view that *The Merchant of Venice* is the tragedy of Shylock was put forward by Heine in *Shakespeares Mädchen und Frauen* in a memorable and eloquent paragraph:

> When I saw this play produced in Drury Lane, there was a beautiful pale British woman standing behind me in the box, who wept copiously at the end of the fourth act, and cried out several times "The poor man is wronged!" [The exclamation is in English in the original]. She had a face of the noblest Grecian profile, and her eyes were large and black. I have never been able to forget them, those large black eyes which wept over Shylock!
>
> And when I think about those tears, I have to count *The Merchant of Venice* among the tragedies, although the framework of the play is decorated with the liveliest masques, images of satyrs and cupids, and although the poet actually wanted to give us a comedy . . .[1]

Even though Heine, in an elegant touch, is careful to attribute the exclamation to a pale and beautiful young woman "vom edelsten griechischen Schnitt", the conclusion that the play is the tragedy of Shylock belongs to Heine himself, and to Clemens Lang, writing in the 1930s, it is an example of the "semitische Geistesart". Of course Lang has generalized wildly in attributing not just this interpretation of *The Merchant of Venice* but the whole of the "sentimentalisches Mitleid des neunzehnten Jahrhunderts" to the Jewish way of thinking; and each of the passages I have quoted from the Nazi critics contains a similar touch of wanton anti-Semitic generalization that can be removed with greater or less damage to the main argument. In the case of Günther's lecture, for instance, the restatement of the wedding celebrations that normally end a romantic comedy in terms of eugenics is merely quaint to the

9. Clemens Lang, "S's Kaufmann von Venedig—die Tragödie des Juden Shylock", *Deutsches Volkstum* (1933): 962–65.
1. Heinrich Heine, "S's Mädchen und Frauen" (1838), *Sämtliche Werke* (Winkler Verlag, München, 1972), vol. 3, p. 652.

Shakespeare critic, but alarmingly important to the historian of Nazism. In the case of Lang, the damage done by removing the anti-Semitic digression is negligible, and his main argument is an account of Renaissance political thinking that the majority of historical scholars would find quite acceptable, even perceptive. "Shakespeare carries on tiptoe his burden of Renaissance thought", says Philip Brockbank of this play,[2] and though Lang's formulation ("Die angebliche jüdische Tragödie ist eine bezaubernde Komödie von unvergleichlicher politischer Kraft und theologisch verlkärter Schönheit") may be less elegant, his point is essentially the same. The analogy with music (seeing both human society and God's universe as a harmony), and the claim that the play is a romantic comedy whose conclusion is meant to emerge from the resolution of earlier conflicts: all this is what any responsible literary historian would tell us. S is a playwright who loves to build wholes out of contrasting and interrelating parts, and Heine's humane and sympathetic interpretation would make nonsense of the whole of the last act: to attribute a sour taste to the serene ending of this enchanting comedy would be merely perverse.

Does this mean that the W S of our thought experiment, who wrote 400 years ago, clearly wrote an anti-Semitic play? If we can establish that Elizabethan society was anti-Semitic, then since the play is by an Elizabethan it too must be anti-Semitic. That is precisely the kind of simplistic argument that the New Historicism has set out to subvert. If historical scholarship is a matter of uncovering the tensions and contradictions of past societies, then literary history must expect to find these tensions reproduced in the texts produced by those societies. And even if we claim to find in the homilies and sermons of Renaissance England a clear attempt to pin down these shifting contradictions in unambiguous assertions, we can still say (with the New Historicism) that to read such homilies in depth is to see that the pinning down does not ever quite succeed, or (with the more traditional literary critic) that whatever may happen in sermons, drama does not pin down, and to reduce *The Merchant of Venice* (or any other play by W S) to a homily is to ignore what makes it a great play, even what makes it a play.

I return now to the "trial" of the play after it was produced in Palestine in 1936. The prosecution charged that the play failed to admit that the responsibility for turning Jews into usurers rested with Christian society "because you never let us survive in any other way: you have turned us into usurers and profiteers". This is the most interesting form of the indictment I have come across,

---

2. Philip Brockbank, "S and the Fashion of these Times", *Shakespeare Survey 16* (1963): 40.

since it raises the question of what a play can and cannot say. Certainly there is no awareness *in Shylock* that Christian society is responsible for forcing him into a degrading profession; on the contrary, he seems to embrace it with gusto, citing his Old Testament precedents for "thrift" with a chuckle of pleasure:

> When Jacob grazed his uncle Laban's sheep—
> This Jacob from our holy Abram was,
> As his wise mother wrought in his behalf,
> The third possessor; ay, he was the third—   (1.3.70–73)

Shylock is pleased both at his own knowledge of Scripture and at the way it confirms him in his profession; and he then proceeds to tell a story that demonstrates Jacob's thrift and shrewdness, concluding, in reply to Antonio's objection (a medieval commonplace) "Is your gold and silver ewes and rams?", with a further chuckle at his own financial acumen: "I cannot tell, I make it breed as fast." Shylock, clearly, is a moneylender to the core.

But is that incompatible with the view that society is responsible? Once the Jews have been driven into money-lending, there is no reason why they shouldn't do it well, and even enjoy doing it. Awareness of the social explanation does not need to be part of the consciousness of the individual money-lender.

Does it then need to be part of the consciousness of the play? That is trickier. Certainly it does not need to be explicitly said in the play: for that purpose we would need a chorus, or a perceptive observer among the characters who would point out (cynically or sorrowfully or even appreciatively) the mechanisms in Venetian society that were keeping Shylock down. That would be one kind of play, but not the only kind, and not the kind that S writes.

But are there not subtler ways of conveying such awareness? One suggestion that has often been popular with directors and critics is that Shylock really meant the bond to be a merry one, and was only goaded into revenge by his daughter's elopement. Tyrone Guthrie, who also (in 1959) produced the play in Israel, held this view:

> It is my view that Shakespeare's portrait is not anti-semitic, that the pound of flesh wager was entered upon as a jest, and only turns to vengeance after Shylock has been robbed and his daughter abducted by young Venetians of Antonio's set.[3]

This is attractive, not only to liberal critics but also to directors, since it suggests a tableau that was introduced notably by Henry Irving in his Lyceum production, and has often been repeated, the return of Shylock at the end of Act 2 Scene 6 to find the house

---

3. Tyrone Guthrie, *In Various Directions: A View of Theatre* (1965); quoted by Oz, "Transformations of Authenticity", p. 172.

empty, his daughter gone, and (perhaps) the shutters flapping in mockery.[4] But attractive as it is, this interpretation seems refuted by the text for two reasons: first, that Shylock's aside on his first appearance ("I hate him for he is a Christian") suggests that the bitter hostility to Antonio was there from the beginning, and second that Jessica tells us quite explicitly "When I was with him" (that is, before the elopement)

> I have heard him swear
> To Tubal and to Cush, his countrymen,
> That he would rather have Antonio's flesh
> Than twenty times the value of the sum . . .
>
> (3.2.282–85)

Yet although this disposes of Guthrie's reading, it does contain a tiny verbal detail that reveals a good deal about how Venetian society treated Shylock: that is Jessica's use of "his". Tubal and Cush were, after all, her countrymen too, but she has now identified herself completely with the Christian shutting out of Shylock. The ease with which Jessica changes sides, like her stealing of his ring and selling it for a monkey, aligns her with Christian exclusiveness and frivolity, and if we had pointed it out to Heine's "schöne blasse Brittin" it would surely have strengthened her feeling that the poor man is wronged.

Not of course that we need hunt for such tiny verbal details in order to see how Venetian society excluded Shylock. It mocked him, cruelly and grossly: most famously in the parody by Solanio and Salerio of his grief when his daughter has run away:

> I never heard a passion so confused,
> So strange, outrageous, and so variable
> As the dog Jew did utter in the streets.
> "My daughter! O, my ducats! O, my daughter!
> Fled with a Christian! O, my Christian ducats!
> A sealèd bag, two sealèd bags of ducats,
> Of double ducats, stol'n from me by my daughter!"
>
> (2.8.12–18)

Mockery as crude as this would goad anyone to wanting his pound of flesh. It does not matter that Shylock doesn't hear this speech, just as it doesn't matter that he doesn't hear his daughter say "his countrymen": he must have caught that tone in her voice when she was still with him, and he must have heard mockery like Solanio's a hundred times ("Many a time and off / On the Rialto you have rated me"). This is a glimpse of the endemic anti-

---

4. John Gross, *Shylock: Four Hundred Years in the Life of a Legend* (London, 1992), discusses this, amid much else of relevance to the present essay.

Semitism of the Venetians, and can easily be interpreted as an explanation for Shylock's lodged hate and certain loathing of Antonio.

But it is also a comic speech, which must have been thoroughly enjoyed by the original audience. The alliteration of ducats and daughter is brilliant: the two losses are, to him, equivalent, and the equivalence is reproduced in the signifiers. The same effect recurs in more complex form in "double ducats", where the relation between form and meaning becomes a kind of tautology: money is twice as important as people realize, and to express this we use both the word "double", and an act of doubling. The speech is a perfect mimesis of the fury of the comic villain whose thoughts are fixated on money.

Mimesis? Or caricature? A representation of the crude greed of the Jewish usurer, or of the crudity with which the Venetians perceive him? Is the speech anti-Semitic, or a representation of anti-Semitism? Again, this raises the question of what dramatic representation can and cannot do. The question whether the play shows any awareness of the social explanation for Shylock's greed is unanswerable, because plays do not show that kind of awareness directly. A play is a representation of social behaviour, not an explanation of it. Of course representation can imply explanation (ideology, as the point might now be put, is unavoidable), but not in any simple, monocausal fashion: explanation results from the interaction between play and audience, and the audience will decide whether anti-Semitism is being expressed or caricatured—not because all meaning is indeterminate, but because audiences fit meaning into an ideological framework. The original audience may have identified with Solanio and roared with delight—both original audiences, Shakespeare's Elizabethans and Wilhelm S's Nazis. But a different audience (you and I, reader) will laugh uneasily, or feel indignant, or praise the author for his exposure of Solanio's crude mockery. And audiences are not uniform: there could have been someone in 1597, and there almost certainly was someone in 1939, who had a Jewish friend, or for any reason felt uneasy about the ideological demands made on him, who did not laugh either. It is even possible that Shakespeare did not laugh.

Edmund Kean as Shylock (1814). From the Hiram Stead Collection of the
New York Public Library.

TOBY LELYVELD

[Edmund Kean as Shylock]†

Edmund Kean was responsible for a number of significant innova-
tions in acting that were subsequently incorporated into stage
convention. His influence was felt during the years, early in the
nineteenth century, when he shone as the brightest star in the theatrical firmament. Kean was the first to break with the tradition
that made of Shylock a preposterous fiend. Macklin had built his
reputation almost entirely on a conception of a stormy and diabolical Shylock, and although the veteran had been dead for almost
two decades, the memory of his portrayal was kept green by the
rank and file of actors who continued to find in *The Merchant of
Venice* a rewarding role.

It took courage and imagination to dress Shylock in a black wig
and to remold him so that his character would conform to his new
appearance. It required an interpretation that would infuse credibly
human qualities into what had become a mythical figure. Kean succeeded in accomplishing this. An actor's performance stands or
falls with the support it receives from an audience, and the encour-
agement that Kean sought when he first presented his version of
Shylock in London in 1814 came in surprising measure.

There was little justification for the hopefulness with which an
actor normally undertakes a new role, when Kean first appeared as
Shylock at the Drury Lane. A number of contemporary accounts report how only one rehearsal had been scheduled, the morning of
the performance. Kean's portrayal had left the manager not only
doubtful but disapproving. The actor had been assured that his
characterization would not do, and now he was relying on his public to support him—the scant public that had witnessed not a single
happy venture at the Drury Lane during the entire season. Kean
did not have the benefits of a carefully analyzed production that
would integrate his interpretation with that of the other members
of the cast. When his fellow-actors heard that he intended to play
Shylock in a new manner, they were not only unprepared to support him, but were entirely hostile to him and to his proposed in-
novations, whatever they might be. The chief credit for the support
of Kean's extraordinary performance goes, therefore, to the handful
of spectators who first witnessed it.

The mode of acting that Garrick had established half a century
earlier was characterized by polish and smoothness. Its techniques

† From *Shylock on the Stage* (Cleveland, Ohio: Western Reserve University Press, 1960),
pp. 39–47. Reprinted by permissioon of the Western Reserve Historical Society.

were possibly a vast improvement over the bombastic methods of the early eighteenth century, but Garrick's acting style made little distinction between the forceful and quiet, and it conveyed but little depth of character. When Kean first began to be noticed in 1814, it was to a considerable extent, for his energetic and sober portrayal. What was called demonstrative and passionate in his acting would undoubtedly now be considered extravagant and frantic. Nevertheless, he developed a style of acting that was known as "romantic" and it found adherents in such later practitioners as Junius Brutus Booth and Edwin Forrest.

Kean was only twenty-seven when he appeared as Shylock in that historic performance of January 26, 1814. Virtually unknown, wretchedly poor after years of hardship and privation, he staked his future on what he was convinced was the only valid delineation of Shakespeare's Jew. He was far from being a novice; the role of Shylock was not new to him. At the age of eleven, he had been featured as Edmund Craig, "the infant prodigy", and had astounded his listeners with dramatic readings. In this youthful repertory he included a recital of the complete text of *The Merchant of Venice*. The year prior to his Drury Lane debut, he had toured the provinces with a company and played the traditional Shylock over an extended period. We get some inkling of the demands made upon actors during this period, when we find Kean, on one occasion, billed as a dancer in a new *pas de deux* immediately following his Shylock appearance.[1] He had been brought up on a regimen of comedy, opera, farce and pantomime, in addition to tragedy—the one medium in which he demonstrated true skill. By 1814, he might well have grown stale in the Shylock role. Only a true artist could have conceived a fresh and original reworking of the character after so many years of routine acquaintance with the part.

The 1814 theatrical season was, as we have already noted, conspicuously unsuccessful, and performances at the Drury Lane were poorly attended. Kean found himself, during this period, in severe financial straits. He had never been free of the enveloping shadow of poverty. Hunger and poverty had hung about him as closely as the black cape he constantly wore to hide the meagerness of his person. The long, vain quest for approval and patronage, the memory of a miserable childhood, several years of which had been spent with his legs in straightening irons, the humiliation of being the bastard child of an erratic mother—these are not the ingredients of self-confidence—but they did much to give Kean insight and sympathy. He was willing to see in Shylock what no one but Shakespeare had seen—the tragedy of a man. For the rest, what was

1. In a benefit performance for Kean in Totnes, August 6, 1813.

called a vigorous and brilliant performance was, in reality, a do-or-die struggle for existence. It was a matter of making a spectacular showing for once, or of ending a miserable career forever. His conviction must have been great indeed.

Kean, at this time, was small and thin, with an intense face and piercing eyes. An 1814 engraving shows his Shylock as a strong, handsome man with a short, trim beard, a cross on his left sleeve, and in his right hand, a butcher's knife.[2] Innumerable references have been made to Kean's bold use of a black wig for Shylock. This innovation may have been due simply to the fact that Kean's status at the Drury Lane was so precarious that he had to provide his own wig and costume.[3] It was no secret that the theatre had sustained 135 nights of continued losses and could not afford the expense of dressing the play adequately. We have no information that Kean owned a red wig at this time. He must have worn one during his earlier Shylock days in the provinces, but his frequent trips to the pawnshop raise a question as to the extent of his wardrobe in 1814.

The outstanding actor of the day was John Philip Kemble. Kemble had adapted *The Merchant of Venice* for the modern stage in 1795 and had been the first to mount it with historical accuracy. A colored engraving that was issued five years before Kean's Drury Lane appearance, shows Kemble as Shylock in a skull cap, long robe, long black hair and a short, matching underchin beard.[4] An absence of comment on Kemble's use of a black beard leads us to suspect that this was an artist's conception and that he must have worn the kind of beard that was conventionally used for Shylock. The excitement over Kean's use of a black beard came too soon after this for Kemble's similar make-up to have passed unnoticed. Kemble's neatly dressed Shylock had provoked some criticism; several reviewers did not consider him qualified by appearance to play the role.[5] In an attempt at realism, no doubt, he spoke Shylock's lines with a foreign accent and he encountered some disapproval because he "either growled in the same unvaried tone of utterance, or attempting to rise above himself like the winding of 10,000 Jacks."[6]

In the edition of the play that was revised by Kemble[7] "and now published as it is performed at the Theatre Royal, London . . . price

2. Stead Collection.
3. "After dinner, Kean prepared for the awful evening. His stock of 'properties' was very scanty. He tied up his wig and collar . . . an old pair of black silk stockings, in a pocket handkerchief. . . ." B. W. Proctor, *The Life of Edmund Kean*, (London, 1835) vol. II, p. 35.
4. Stead Collection.
5. Timothy Plain, *Letters Respecting the Performances at the Theatre Royal* (Edinburgh, 1800), p. 55.
6. *Ibid.*
7. Printed for John Miller, 1814.

one shilling and sold in the theatres" there are occasional Shylock
speeches that are italicized for emphasis. Among these we find:

> *Hath a dog money? Is it possible*
> *A cur can lend three thousand ducats?*
>
> . . .
>
> *Fair sir, you spit on me on Wednesday last;*
> *You spurn'd me such a day; another time*
> *You call'd me dog; and for these courtesies*
> *I'll lend you thus much monies?*

The absence, on the other hand, of any edifying markings in the
"To bait fish withal" speech, the passionate "Why, there, there,
there, there! A diamond gone . . ." or anywhere in the trial scene,
leaves us uninformed as to Kemble's reading.

Kean seems to have borrowed little from Kemble. He had been
acclaimed for his ability to mimic Garrick's acting. As a boy he had
appeared with the great Kemble and with Mrs. Siddons. If these associations inspired him at all, it was doubtless in a negative way.
Kemble's technique had been characterized by its artificiality; Kean
was to become noted for his sincerity. There was nothing lachry-
mose in Kean's style. He did not rely on declamatory powers. His
great contribution to the theatrical development of *The Merchant
of Venice* was in the degree to which he intellectualized his acting
of Shylock.

When William Hazlitt recalled his first impressions of Kean's
Shylock, not only did his description suggest the freshness and energy of the actor's portrayal, but it cast a backward glance at the
delineation of earlier actors who had followed in the tradition of
Macklin's Jew.

> When first we went to see Mr. Kean in Shylock, we expected to
> see what we had been used to see, a decrepit old man, bent
> with age and ugly with mental deformity, grinning with deadly
> malice, with the venom of his heart congealed in the expres-
> sion of his countenance, sullen, morose, gloomy, inflexible,
> brooding over one idea, that of his hatred, and fixed on one
> unalterable purpose, that of his revenge. We were disap-
> pointed, because we had taken our idea from other actors, not
> from the play . . . a man of genius comes once in an age to
> clear away the rubbish, to make it fruitful and wholesome. . . .[8]

It was Kean's performance in 1817 that inspired Hazlitt[9] to take
out of its original context the phrase "no less sinned against than
sinning" and to apply it to Shylock.

---

8. William Hazlitt, *Characters of Shakespeare's Plays* (New York, 1845), p. 178f.
9. *Ibid.*, p. 174.

Kean's Shylock did more than evoke sympathy; it startled his spectators. The first evidence of approval that Kean received came when his sparse audience of fifty burst into hearty applause following the line in his opening scene, "I will be assured I may."[1] The response must indeed have been balm to his soul. Dr. Drury reported that he could scarcely hold his breath when Kean first came on the stage as Shylock. "But directly you took your position," he later told the actor, "and leaned upon your cane, I saw that it was right."[2] Kean was, in fact, considered by many to be one of the best pantomime actors of his day.

In his interpretation of the Jacob and Laban speech, Kean played for time; Shylock had not yet hit on his scheme for vengeance. Toward the close of his speech to Antonio, he delivered the line, "you call'd me dog . . . ," with a voice of terrible passion, recovering himself just in time, and concluding with seemingly profound obsequiousness on "and for these courtesies I'll lend you thus much monies?". Here another enthusiastic outburst from the audience further dispelled his doubts as to the effectiveness of his interpretation.[3] He gained confidence, and with the acclaim he received for the fierce energy in the "Hath not a Jew eyes?" speech, he entered upon his kingship.

Hawkins describes the slightly deprecating manner in which Kean said "I am a Jew." Shylock's unmitigated miseries seemed to pass away in a moment when he reflected that the dignity of his race must not be hurt by his exciting commiseration in a Christian.[4] But it was in the scene with Tubal that Kean made his greatest impression. It is said that he raged like a lion. With the lines, "I would that my daughter were dead at my foot . . . ," we are told that Kean

> . . . started back, as with a revulsion of paternal feeling from the horrible image his avarice had conjured up, and borrowing a negative from the next inquiry ("no news of them"?), gasped an agonising "No, no, no."[5]

The writer calls the spirit of this scene "the alternation of the two passions of anguished avarice and hopeful revenge."[6]

Many observers expressed the opinion that Kean's acting in the trial scene was anti-climactic compared with the overwhelming effectiveness of his scene with Tubal. A contemporary biographical study points to Kean's delineation here as a defect in characteriza-

---

1. William Shakespeare, *The Merchant of Venice*, ed. Henry Irving and Frank A. Marshall (New York, 1890), vol. III, footnote to Act I, Scene 3.
2. Proctor, *op. cit.*, vol. II, p. 37.
3. Irving and Marshall, *op. cit.*, vol. III, footnote to Act I, Scene 3.
4. Frederick W. Hawkins, *The Life of Edmund Kean* (London, 1869), vol. I, p. 150.
5. W. J. Fox, "W. C. Macready," *The People's Journal* (London, December 12, 1846).
6. *Ibid.*

tion, describing it as a picture of a man stung into rage, rather than the impersonation of the spirit of hatred.[7] But this is a comment of one who had come to accept the long-standardized personification of a vengeful Shylock as being the only valid one. On the other hand, Horace Howard Furness recalls his father's admiration of Kean in this scene; particularly for the

> . . . prolonged, grating, gutteral tone of utter contempt with which Kean's Shylock told Gratiano "Till thou canst rail this seal from off my bond. . . ."[8]

Gould illustrates Kean's powerful acting by the way in which his "Nay, take my life and all . . ." changed, by the pathos of his voice, the audience's hatred of Shylock, to one of pity.[9] We are told that Kean's entire appearance seemed to change with Shylock's last speeches. The pause in "I am—content," as if it almost choked him to bring out the last word; the partial bowing down of his seemingly inflexible will in "I pray you give me leave to go from hence, I am not well;" the horror of his countenance when he was told of his enforced conversion to Christianity; the combined scorn and pity with which he regarded the ribald Gratiano; his final exit, as he took with him the full measure of the audience's sympathy.[1]

The Theatrical Observer responded negatively to Kean's final exit as Shylock. It considered that Shylock should be

> . . . so completely overwhelmed . . . that he ought to represent the mind in calm though bitter anguish. This style . . . loses all effect on the stage, by circumstances of the only power of expression to indicate this state of feeling, lying in the features . . . the perfect stillness of the frame, the clenched hands, and downcast eyes.[2]

In this criticism, there is revealed Kean's sympathetic, and even compassionate treatment of Shylock. For the first time, the stage-Jew was taking on human form, and for the first time the audience was able to appreciate it.

During the early days of Kean's career, he was plagued by a fear of losing his voice. Several accounts describe the way in which he dashed from the stage to dressing room between the scenes on that famous opening night, eating oranges, in the hope that his voice would hold out. But what his voice lacked in durability was more than compensated in tonal quality. The use of conversational tones

7. Proctor, *op. cit.*, vol. II, p. 46f.
8. William Shakespeare, *The Merchant of Venice*, Horace Howard Furness, New Variorum edition (Philadelphia, 1895), p. 207.
9. Thomas R. Gould, *The Tragedian* (New York, 1868) p. 74.
1. Hawkins, *op. cit.*, vol. I, p. 152.
2. February 15, 1825.

on the stage is a modern practice of the natural school of acting. In the early nineteenth century, actors employed an orotund method of delivery, sustaining their words in a singing manner. In this style, Kean was a virtuoso.

In a valuable study of Kean's voice, William Gardiner tells us:

> Musically speaking, he is the best orator, who, to his natural speaking voice, unites the upper and lower voices, that is, the *voce de testa* and the *voce de petto*. Mr. Kean possesses these qualifications in the highest degree. He has at his command the greatest number of effects, having a range of tones from F below the line to F above it . . . the natural key of his voice being that of B-flat. . . . His hard gutteral tone upon G is as piercing as the third string of a violoncello; whilst his mezzo and pianissimo expressions are as soft as from the voice of a woman. He has three distinct sets of tones; as if he occasionally played upon a flute, clarionet [sic], and bassoon, which he uses as the passion dictates . . . his notes are of the most touching and persuading kind, often springing from the harmonies of his natural voice, which he elicits with exquisite delicacy. . . . But the same voice, when moved with a ruder stroke, gave the yell and choked utterance of a savage.

His tones of furious passion are deep-seated in the chest, like those of the lion and tiger; and it is his mastery over these instinctive tones by which he so powerfully moved his audience. At times he vomits a torrent of words in a breath, yet avails himself of all the advantages of deliberation. His pauses give a grandeur to his performance, and speak more than words themselves.[3]

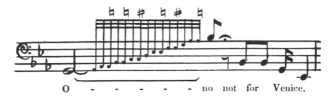

3. William Gardiner, *The Music of Nature* (Boston, 1837), p. 58f.

JAMES SHAPIRO

[Circumcision and the "Pound of Flesh"]†

* * *

Those watching or reading *The Merchant of Venice* are often curious about what part of Antonio's body Shylock has in mind when they learn of Shylock's desire to exact "an equal pound" of Antonio's "fair flesh, to be cut off and taken" in that "part" of his body that "pleaseth" the Jew. Those all too familiar with the plot may forget that it is not until the trial scene in act 4 that this riddle is solved and we learn that Shylock intends to cut from Antonio's "breast" near his heart.[1] Or partially solved. Why, one wonders, is Antonio's breast the spot most pleasing to Shylock? And why, for the sake of accuracy, wouldn't Shylock cut out rather than "cut off" a pound of flesh if it were to come from "nearest" Antonio's

The pound of flesh. Geraldine James, Leigh Lawson, and Dustin Hoffman in the Peter Hall production. Haymarket Theatre, 1989. Courtesy of Dominic Photography.

† From *Shakespeare and the Jews* (New York: Columbia University Press, 1996), pp. 121–30. Reprinted by permission of Columbia University Press.
1. Shakespeare, *The Merchant of Venice*, 1.3.146–48, and 4.1.249. The first hint appears in act 3, when Shylock says to Tubal, "I will have the heart of him if he forfeit" (3.1.119–20).

"heart"? Moreover, why don't we learn of this crucial detail until Shylock's final appearance in the play?

It is not immediately clear how for an Elizabethan audience an allusion to a Jew cutting off a man's "fair flesh" would invoke images of a threat to the victim's heart, especially when one calls to mind the identification of Jews as circumcisors and emasculators. On a philological level, too, the choice of the word *flesh* here carries with it the strong possibility that Shylock has a different part of Antonio's anatomy in mind. In the late sixteenth century the word *flesh* was consistently used, especially in the Bible, in place of *penis*. Readers of the Geneva Bible would know from examples like Genesis 17.11 that God had commanded Abraham to "circumcise the foreskin of your flesh," and that discussions of sexuality and disease in Leviticus always use the word *flesh* when speaking of the penis.[2]

Not surprisingly, popular writers took advantage of the punning opportunities made available by this euphemism. Shortly before writing *The Merchant of Venice* Shakespeare himself had played on the sexual possibilities of *flesh* in *Romeo and Juliet*. In the opening scene of that play the servant Samson, boasting of his sexual prowess, tells Gregory: "Me [the maids] shall feel while I am able to stand, and 'tis known I am a pretty piece of flesh." Playing on the contrast between erect flesh and flaccid fish, Gregory responds: " 'Tis well thou art not fish." Mercutio returns to the same tired joke about the loss of tumescence when he says of Romeo's melancholy: "O flesh, flesh, how art thou fishified."[3] *The Merchant of Venice* is similarly replete with bad jokes about trimmed male genitals. As noted above, Antonio in the court scene speaks of himself as "a tainted wether" best suited to suffer the exaction of Shylock's cut.[4] In addition, Salerio's jibe about Jessica having Shylock's

2. "Whosoever hath an issue from his flesh is unclean because of his issue," Leviticus 15.2. Biblical anthropologists have traced the practice of using the euphemism *basar* (flesh) when referring to the penis to the priestly redactors (rather than the Jahwist, who did not use this euphemism). See Howard Eilberg-Schwartz, *The Savage in Judaism: An Anthropology of Israelite Religion and Ancient Judaism* (Bloomington: Indiana University Press, 1990), pp. 170–71.

3. Shakespeare, *Romeo and Juliet*, 1.1.29–30, and 2.4.37.

4. Shakespeare, *The Merchant of Venice*, 4.1.113. Antonio's next lines—"the weakest kind of fruit / Drops earliest to the ground, and so let me" (4.1.114–15)—may connect back to the recurrent biblical identification of fruit trees with circumcision. In his chapter on "Uncircumcised Fruit Trees," Howard Eilberg-Schwartz notes the frequent comparison in biblical literature between "fruit trees and male organs" (p. 149; see, for example, Leviticus 19.23–25), and concludes that "the symbolic equation of an uncircumcised male and a young fruit tree rests on two, and possibly three, associations. The fruit of a juvenile tree is proscribed like the foreskin of the male organ. Furthermore, a male who is uncircumcised and not part of the covenantal community is infertile like an immature fruit tree. Finally, this symbolic equation may draw part of its plausibility from an analogy between circumcision and pruning," Eilberg-Schwartz, *The Savage in Judaism*, p. 152. See, too, his "People of the Body: The Problem of the Body for the People of the Book," *Journal of the History of Sexuality* 2 (1991), pp. 1–24.

"stones," that is, testicles, "upon her" and Gratiano's tasteless joke about "mar[ring] the young clerk's pen" (i.e., penis) offer two other instances from the play of men's obsessive anxiety about castrating cuts.[5] It should also be noted that in Elizabethan England such a cut was not merely the stuff of jokes. As a deterrent to crime, convicted male felons were told at their sentencing to prepare to be "hanged by the neck, and being alive cut down, and your privy members to be cut off, and your bowels to be taken out of your belly and there burned, you being alive."[6]

Scholars have long recognized that Shakespeare drew upon a well established tradition in his retelling the story of the pound of flesh. Among the printed sources Shakespeare may have looked at were Giovanni Fiorentino's *Il Pecorone* and Alexander Silvayn's *The Orator*. Other scholars have uncovered a range of analogues and antecedents, including popular English ballads like "Gernatus the Jew" and medieval works like the *Cursor Mundi* that bear a strong resemblance to Shakespeare's plot. Surprisingly little attention has been paid, however, to what part of the body the pound of flesh is taken from in these sources and analogues. In fact, when Shakespeare came to one of the main sources that we are pretty confident he consulted, Silvayn's *The Orator*, he would have read about a Jew who wonders if he "should cut of his [Christian victim's] privy members, supposing that the same would altogether weigh a just pound?" Before turning to this story and its curious reception, I want to consider another first, one that is even more revealing about the significance of the pound of flesh: Gregorio Leti's *The Life of Pope Sixtus the Fifth*.

Leti was a popular Italian historian, born in the early seventeenth century, who left Italy and took up residence in Northern Europe after converting to Protestantism. For a brief period in the early 1680s he lived and wrote in England. Although there are no recorded performances of *The Merchant of Venice* during his stay there, Leti may well have become familiar with the printed text of Shakespeare's play in the course of the extensive research he undertook on Elizabethan England.[7] The earliest edition of his biography of Sixtus V, first published in Lausanne in 1669, omits any reference to the celebrated pound of flesh story; the anecdote was

---

5. Shakespeare, *The Merchant of Venice*, 2.8.22, 5.1.237.

6. As cited in J. H. Baker, "Criminal Courts and Procedure at Common Law, 1550–1800," in *Crimes in England, 1550–1800*, ed. J. S. Cockburn (Princeton: Princeton University Press, 1977), p. 42.

7. Before he had to leave in 1683—having run afoul of the Duke of York and England's Catholic community—Leti had even been elected to the Royal Society and asked by Charles II to write a history of England from its origins to the Restoration. See the introduction to Nati Krivatsy, *Bibliography of the Works of Gregorio Leti* (Newcastle, Delaware: Oak Knoll Books, 1982).

only introduced in the revised version, published in Amsterdam after Leti's visit to England,[8] which may suggest that Leti drew on English sources for this addition.

After 1754, when Ellis Farneworth translated Leti's story,[9] those unable to read the Italian original could learn how in the days of Queen Elizabeth I it was "reported in Rome" that the great English naval hero, Sir Francis Drake, "had taken and plundered St. Domingo, in Hispaniola, and carried off an immense booty. This account came in a private letter to Paul Secchi, a very considerable merchant in the city, who had large concerns in those parts, which he had insured." Leti then relates that Secchi then "sent for the insurer, Sampson Ceneda, a Jew, and acquainted him with it. The Jew, whose interest it was to have such a report thought false, gave many reasons why it could not possibly be true and, at last, worked himself up into such a passion, that he said, 'I'll lay you a pound of my flesh it is a lie.' " Secchi replied, "If you like it, I'll lay you a thousand crowns against a pound of your flesh, that it's true." The Jew accepted the wager, and articles were immediately executed betwixt them, the substance of which was "that if Secchi won, he should himself cut the flesh, with a sharp knife, from whatever part of the Jew's body he pleased."

Leti then relates that "the truth of the account" of Drake's attack "was soon after confirmed by other advices from the West Indies," which threw the Jew "almost into distraction, especially when he was informed that Secchi had solemnly sworn [that] he would compel him to the exact literal performance of his contract, and was determined to cut a pound of flesh from that part of his body which it is not necessary to mention." We move here from a cut "from whatever part of the Jew's body he pleased" to the more precisely defined "part of his body which it is not necessary to mention." The original Italian version conveys even more strongly a sense that only modesty prevents specifying that Secchi's intended cut will come from the unmentionable genitals of the Jew (*"e che la modestia non vuo che io nomine"*).[1] The circumcised Jew faces a bit more surgery than he reckoned for.

The rest of the story should be familiar to anyone who has read Shakespeare's play, except, of course, that this time it is the Christian who is intent on cutting the flesh of the Jew. The Governor of Rome referred the tricky case to the authority of Pope Sixtus V, who tells Secchi that he must fulfill the contract and "cut a pound of flesh

8. Gregorio Leti, *Vita di Sisto V*, 3 vols. (Amsterdam, 1693), vol. 3, pp. 134ff. Since the first English translation of Leti's biography—*The Life of Pope Sixtus the Vth* (London, 1704)—was based on the 1669 text, it does not contain the pound of flesh story.
9. Gregorio Leti, *The Life of Pope Sixtus the Fifth*, trans. Ellis Farneworth (London, 1754). A subsequent edition of this translation was published in Dublin in 1766.
1. Leti, *Vita di Sisto V* (1693), vol. 3, p. 136.

from any part you please, of the Jew's body. We would advise you, however, to be very careful; for if you cut but a scruple, or a grain, more or less than your due, you shall certainly be hanged. Go, and bring hither a knife and a pair of scales, and let it be done in our presence." This verdict led both Secchi and the Jew to agree to tear up the contract, though the affair was not fully settled until Sixtus V fined both of them harshly to serve as an example to others.[2]

Farneworth, in a note appended to his translation, states the obvious: the "scene betwixt Shylock and Antonio in Shakespeare's *Merchant of Venice* seems to be borrowed from this story, though the poet has inverted the persons and decently enough altered some of the circumstances."[3] Farneworth's comment that Shakespeare "decently enough . . . altered some of the circumstances" presumably alludes to the threatened castration of the Jew. And while we don't know why Leti in the version of the story has "inverted the persons," there is little likelihood that he did it out of love of the Jews. In his book on Great Britain published in England shortly before his departure, Leti reveals his familiarity with London Jewry, describes the services at the Bevis Marks Synogogue in London in somewhat mocking terms, and makes fun of the ridiculous gestures of the Jewish worshippers.[4] We can only speculate about the original source of Leti's seventeenth-century story. Did it antedate Shakespeare's play, and was Shakespeare familiar with versions in which the Jew was the victim? Or did it emerge out of a tradition that was itself influenced by *The Merchant of Venice*? Did turning the tables and having the Christians threaten to castrate or symbolically recircumcise the Jew ultimately prove more satisfying to Christian readers?

Farneworth's translation of Leti's story made a strong impression on eighteenth-century English interpreters of *The Merchant of Venice*. Edmond Malone reproduced this passage in his influential edition of Shakespeare's works in 1790,[5] and David Erskine Baker, though he does not acknowledge his source, wrote that Shakespeare's story "is built on a real fact which happened in some part of Italy, with this difference indeed, that the intended cruelty was

---

2. And, conveniently, to pay for a hospital that he had recently founded. See Leti, *Sixtus the Fifth*, trans. Farneworth, pp. 293–95.

3. Leti, *Sixtus the Fifth*, trans. Farneworth, p. 293, n. 19.

4. Leti writes of their "gesti ridicolosissimi." For his remarks about London's Jews, see Leti, *Del Teatro Brittanico o Vero Historia dello Stato, Antico e Presente . . . della Grande Brettagna*, 2 vols. (London, 1683), esp. vol. 1, pp. 251–52, 549–50, as cited in Jonathan I. Israel, "Gregorio Leti (1631–1701) and the Dutch Sephardi Elite at the Close of the Seventeenth Century," in *Jewish History: Essays in Honour of Chimen Abramsky*, ed. Ada Rapoport-Albert and Steven J. Zipperstein (London: Peter Halban, 1988), p. 269.

5. Edmond Malone, *The Plays and Poems of William Shakespeare* (London, 1790), vol. 3, pp. 111–13.

really on the side of the Christian, the Jew being the happy delinquent who fell beneath his rigid and barbarous resentment." Tellingly, he adds that "popular prejudice, however, vindicates our author in the alteration he had made. And the delightful manner in which he has availed himself of the general character of the Jews, the very quintessence of which he has enriched his Shylock with, makes more than amends for his deviating from a matter of fact which he was by no means obliged to adhere to."[6] Again, we are left with a set of difficult choices: is it "popular prejudice" that "vindicates" Shakespeare reassigning the "intended cruelty" to Shylock? Or is it Shakespeare's play that by the late eighteenth-century is influential enough to perpetuate and channel this "popular prejudice"?

Familiarity with this inverted version of the pound of flesh story was given even broader circulation by Maria Edgeworth in her novel *Harrington*, where she allows the Jew, Mr. Montenero, to present what he believes to be the historically accurate version of the facts in his response to Harrington, who had recently attended a performance of Shakespeare's *Merchant of Venice*. Edgeworth, too, sees the issue of "popular prejudice" as a central one, and has Mr. Montenero politely acknowledge that while "as a dramatic poet, it was" Shakespeare's "business . . . to take advantage of the popular prejudice as a *power*," nonetheless "we Jews must feel it peculiarly hard, that the truth of the story should have been completely sacrificed to fiction, so that the characters were not only misrepresented, but reversed." Harrington "did not know to what Mr. Montenero meant to allude." He politely tried to "pass it off with a slight bow of general acquiescence," before Mr. Montenero went on to explain that in "the true story, from which Shakespeare took the plot of *The Merchant of Venice*, it was a Christian who acted the part of the Jew, and the Jew that of the Christian. It was a Christian who insisted upon having the pound of flesh from next the Jew's heart." Seeing how struck Harrington is by this revelation, Mr. Montenero magnanimously offers that "perhaps his was only the Jewish version of the story, and he quickly went on to another subject." Edgeworth adds her own authority to Montenero's when she provides a footnote to the words "true story" directing readers to "Steevens' Life of Sixtus V and Malone's Shakespeare," where the Farneworth translation appears. Strikingly, though, at the very moment that she insists on the original version, Edgeworth herself either misremembers or swerves away

6. David Erskine Baker, *Biographia Dramatica or a Companion to the Playhouse Containing Historical and Critical Memoirs*, 3 vols. (London, 1812), vol. 3, p. 34. First published in 1782.

from a key features of Leti's "true story" in favor of Shakespeare's version of the events when she substitutes the words "having the pound of flesh from next the Jew's heart" for Farneworth's translation of Leti's original: "from that part of his body which it is not necessary to mention."[7]

Once nineteenth-century Shakespearean source-hunters like Francis Douce and James Orchard Halliwell-Phillipps pointed out that Leti's version could not have antedated Shakespeare's play, and, moreover, that this episode in Sixtus V's life was probably fictional, interest in Leti's narrative rapidly declined. H. H. Furness, in his still influential variorum edition of *The Merchant of Venice*, includes Farneworth's translation but then invokes the authority of those who dismiss it as a source. And though he quotes Farneworth's observation that Shakespeare's plot "is taken from this incident," he cuts off the quotation at the point where it leads Farneworth to point out that Shakespeare has also made the Jew the victim and left out indecent details.[8] Interest in pure sources— rather than near contemporary versions that might cast light on various aspects of the story—has been influential enough in Shakespeare studies in this century to account for the virtual disappearance of Leti's story from editions or even from collections of Shakespeare's sources.[9] Nowadays, Leti's version is no longer cited, mentioned, or even known to most Shakespeareans.

When we turn to Alexander Silvayn's *The Orator*, which these same source-hunters agree is one of Shakespeare's primary sources for the pound of flesh plot, we find a clear precedent for the argument that a Jew considers the possibility of castrating the Christian. The ninety-fifth declamation of *The Orator*, translated into English in 1596 shortly before the composition of *The Merchant*, describes "a Jew, who would for his debt have a pound of the flesh of a Christian."[1] In his appeal to the judge's sentence that he "cut a just pound of the Christian flesh, and if he cut either more or less, then his own head should be smitten off," the Jew insists that in the original agreement the Christian was to hand over the said pound:

> Neither am I to take that which he oweth me, but he is to deliver it me. And especially because no man knoweth better than he where the same may be spared to the least hurt of his person, for I might take it in such a place as he might thereby happen to lose his life. What a matter were it then if I should

7. Edgeworth, *Harrington*, p. 96.
8. Furness, ed., *The Merchant of Venice, A New Variorum Edition*, pp. 295ff.
9. For one of the few twentieth-century citations of Leti's story in relationship to Shakespeare's play, see Berta Viktoria Wenger, "Shylocks Pfund Fleish," *Shakespeare Jahrbuch* 65 (1929), esp. pp. 148–50.
1. Bullough, *Sources*, vol. 1, p. 483.

cut of his privy members, supposing that the same would altogether weigh a just pound?[2]

While Shakespeare's eighteenth-century editors included this source in unadulterated form,[3] a century later it would be partially suppressed, apparently proving too obscene for Furness to reprint in unexpurgated form. In a strange act of textual castration and substitution, Furness alters the line to read "what a matter were it then, if I should cut of his [head], supposing that the same would weigh a just pound.[4] This makes little sense, no matter how light-headed the victim might be, since in the next sentence the Jew continues, "Or else his head, should I be suffered to cut it off, although it were with the danger of mine own life,"[5] and in the sentence after that wonders if his victim's "nose, lips, his ears, and. . . . eyes . . . make of them altogether a pound."[6] Furness's textual intervention immediately influenced subsequent editions of the play; a year after his edition was published, for example, Homer B. Sprague wrote "head" (without brackets) in his popular school edition of the play.[7] The bowdlerization of this source, and the lack of interest in Leti, have effectively deflected critical attention away from aspects of the play that touch upon ritual Jewish practices.

The Circumcision of the Heart

> Why this bond is forfeit,
> And lawfully by this the Jew may claim
> A pound of flesh, to be by him cut off
> Nearest the merchant's heart.
> —*The Merchant of Venice*, 4.1.227–30

When Paul declares that "the circumcision is of the heart" and is "in the spirit, not in the letters," we are presented with a double displacement: of the physical by the spiritual and of the circumcision of the flesh by the circumcision of the heart. Elizabethan commentators were well aware that Paul's metaphorical treatment of circumcision builds upon a preexisting tradition in the Old Testament, expressed particularly in Deuteronomy 10.16 and 30.6: "Circumcise the foreskin of your heart," and "The Lord thy God will circumcise thine heart."[8] Mornay, in Sidney's translation, also notes

2. Bullough, *Sources*, vol. 1, p. 484. In other sources the cutting is to be done to the eyes (as in Anthony Munday's *Zeluto*), or is left ambiguous or unspecified, in the words of Fiorentino's *Il Pecorone* (1558), "wheresoever he pleases."
3. Malone, ed., *Plays and Poems of Shakespeare*, vol. 3, p. 114.
4. Furness, ed., *The Merchant of Venice, A New Variorum Edition*, pp. 311–12.
5. Bullough, *Sources*, vol. 1, p. 484.
6. Furness, ed., *The Merchant of Venice, A New Variorum Edition*, p. 312.
7. Sprague, ed., *The Merchant of Venice* (New York: Silver, Burdett, 1889).
8. See Willet's gloss on this passage in *Hexapla*. Elizabethan editions of the Bible constantly read Pauline doctrine back into the Old Testament passages. Thus, for example,

that when the Old Testament prophets "rebuke us, they call us not simply uncircumcised, but uncircumcised of heart or lips,"[9] and Peter Martyr simply confirms that "Paul borrowed" this "phrase touching the circumcision of the heart . . . out of the Old Testament."[1]

Hugo Grotius understood that this substitution of heart for flesh neatly defined the relationship between Christian fellowship and the genealogical Judaism it replaced, since the Covenant "should be common to all people." He even argued that the Old Testament prophets recognized this "mystical and more excellent signification contained" in "the precept of circumcision," since they in fact "command the circumcision of the heart, which all the commandments of Jesus aim at."[2] John Donne is particularly eloquent on this symbolic displacement: "The principal dignity of this circumcision was that it . . . prefigured, it directed to that circumcision of the heart." For Donne, "Jewish circumcision were an absurd and unreasonable thing if it did not intimate and figure the circumcision of the heart."[3]

The unexplained displacement of Shylock's cut from Antonio's "flesh" upward to his heart is now considerably clearer. Viewed in light of this familiar exegetical tradition, Shylock's decision to exact his pound of flesh from near Antonio's heart can be seen as the height of the literalism that informs all his actions in the play, a literalism that when imitated by Portia leads to his demise. Also echoing through the trial scene of *The Merchant* are the words of Galatians 6.13: "For they themselves which are circumcised keep not the Law, but desire to have you circumcised, that they might rejoice in your flesh," that is to say (as the gloss to this line in the Geneva Bible puts it), "that they have made you Jews." Shylock will cut his Christian adversary in that part of the body where the Christians believe themselves to be truly circumcised: the heart. Shylock's threat gives a wonderfully ironic twist to the commentary on Paul's Romans that "he is the Jew indeed . . . who cuts off all superfluities and pollutions which are spiritually though not literally meant by the law of circumcision."[4] Psychoanalytically inclined readers will immediately recognize how closely the terms of this

---

the Bishops' Bible gloss explains: "That is, let all your affections be cut off. He showeth in these words the end of circumcision"; and "Cut off all your evil affections."

9. Mornay, *Trewnesse of the Christian Religion*, pp. 581–82.

1. Peter Martyr [Vermigli], *Most Learned and Fruitfull Commentaries of D. Peter Martir Vermilius, Florentine . . . Upon the Epistle of S. Paul to the Romanes* (London, 1568), p. 49v. Andrew Willet also cites the prophet Jeremiah, who proclaims that "all the nations are uncircumcised, and all the house of Israel are uncircumcised in the heart" (9.26).

2. Hugo Grotius, *True Religion Explained and Defended* (London, 1632), p. 274.

3. Donne, *Sermons*, vol. 6, p. 193.

4. Henry Hammond, *A Paraphrase and Annotations Upon All the Books of the New Testament* (London, 1653), p. 475.

Pauline displacement correspond to the unconscious substitution central to Freud's secular theories. Theodore Reik, a disciple of Freud's, interpreted Shylock's bond in just these terms, arguing first that the "condition that he can cut a pound of flesh 'in what part of your body pleaseth me' " is "a substitute expression of castration." Reik adds that when it is later decided that "the cut should be made from the breast, analytic interpretation will easily understand the mechanism of distortion that operates here and displaces the performance from a part of the body below to above."[5]

In repudiating circumcision, Paul's sought to redirect the Covenant, sever the genealogical bond of Judaism, distinguish Jew from Christian, true Jew from false Jew, and the spirit from the flesh (while retaining in a metaphorical sense the sexuality attendant on the flesh). Yet his actual remarks about circumcision are enigmatic and confusing. It is only mild consolation that they proved no less puzzling to the sixteenth-century theologians who tried to untangle the various levels of Paul's literal and symbolic displacements. Take, for example, the Geneva Bible's gloss to Romans, which reaches new depths of convolution in its attempt to iron out these difficulties by asserting that "Paul useth oftentimes to set the letter against the spirit. But in this place the circumcision which is according to the letter is the cutting off of the foreskin. But the circumcision of the spirit is the circumcision of the heart. That is to say, the spiritual end of the ceremony is true holiness and righteousness, whereby the people of God is known from profane and heathenish men." In their frustration, Paul's interpreters often turned against one another. Andrew Willet, for example, chastised Origen for misreading Paul and "thus distinguishing the circumcision of the flesh; that because there is some part of the flesh cut off and lost, some part remaineth still. The lost and cut off part (saith he) hath a resemblance of that flesh, whereof it is said, all flesh is grass. The other part which remaineth is a figure of that flesh, whereof the Scripture speaketh, all flesh shall see the salutation of God." Willet is sensitive to Origen's conflation of the two kinds of circumcision here, spiritual and fleshly—"Origen confoundeth the circumcision of the flesh and the spirit, making them all one"—but it is hard to see how to maintain hard and fast divisions when, on the one hand, commentators drive a wedge between the spiritual

---

5. For this psychoanalyst (who had first witnessed Shakespeare's play as a young boy at the turn of the century in antisemitic Vienna), only "one step is needed to reach the concept that to the Gentile of medieval times the Jew unconsciously typified the castrator because he circumcised male children." The "Jew thus appeared to Gentiles as a dangerous figure with whom the threat of castration originated." Theodore Reik, "Psychoanalytic Experiences in Life, Literature, and Music," in *The Search Within* (New York: Farrar, Strauss and Cudahy, 1956), pp. 358–59; first printed as "Jessica, My Child," *American Imago* 8 (1951), pp. 3–27.

and the physical, while, on the other, they show how even in the Old Testament circumcision was used both literally and metaphorically. For Willet, then, the correct interpretation, and one that seems to require a bit of mental gymnastics, requires that we think not of the circumcision of the flesh and the circumcision of the heart "as though there were two kinds of circumcisions" but as "two parts of one and the same circumcision which are sometimes joined together, both the inward and the outward."[6]

Uncircumcision

If the distinction between inward and outward circumcision were not confusing enough, Paul further complicated matters by introducing the concept of reverse, or *un*circumcision. Even if a faithful Christian were circumcised in the heart, what if one's body still carried (as Paul's did) the stigmatical mark that revealed to the world that one was born a Jew? The seventeenth-century Scottish preacher John Weemse recognized that the early Christians were embarrassed by this Judaical scar: "When they were converted from Judaism to Christianity there were some of them so ashamed of their Judaism that they could not behold it; they took it as a blot to their Christianity."[7] Uncircumcision, then, was the undoing of the seemingly irreversible physical act that had been accomplished through the observance of Jewish law, and it was a topic that Paul would return to obsessively (in large part because it was a pressing issue within the new Christian communities he was addressing). Paul asks in Romans "if the uncircumcision keep the ordinances of the Law, shall not his uncircumcision be counted for circumcision? And shall not uncircumcision which is by nature (if it keep the Law) condemn thee, which by the letter and circumcision art a transgressor of the Law?"[8] In Galatians he writes in a similar vein that "in Jesus Christ neither circumcision availeth anything" nor "uncircumcision, but faith, which worketh by love."[9] His remarks in Corinthians on the irrelevance of this mark are even more forceful: "Is any man called being circumcised? Let him not gather his

6. Willet, *Hexapla*, pp. 130–31.
7. Weemse, *The Christian Synagogue*, vol. 1, p. 127. There is considerable medical evidence for uncircumcision or reverse circumcision as far back as classical antiquity. See, for example, J. P. Rubin, "Celsus' decircumcision operation: medical and historical implications," *Urology* 16 (1980), p. 121; and B. O. Rogers, "History of External Genital Surgery," in *Plastic and Reconstruction Surgery of the Genital Area*, ed. C. E. Horton (Boston: Little, Brown, & Co., 1973), pp. 3–47. Willard E. Goodwin's "Circumcision: A Technique for Plastic Reconstruction of a Prepuce After Circumcision," *Journal of Urology* 144 (1990), pp. 1203–05, offers a helpful overview of both the history of and the procedures for reversing circumcision.
8. Romans, 2.26–27.
9. Galatians, 5.6. He would return to this idea again shortly, when he states that "in Christ Jesus neither circumcision availeth any thing, nor uncircumcision, but a new creature" (Galatians, 6.15).

circumcision. Is any called uncircumcised? Let him not be circumcised. Circumcision is nothing, and uncircumcision is nothing, but
the keeping of the commandments of God."[1]

Paul's shifts between literal and figurative uncircumcision in
these key passages are dizzying, and the commentators had to
scramble to keep up with him. Thomas Godwyn voices the question
that must have been on many readers' minds: "Here it may be
demanded how it is possible for a man, after once he hath been
marked with the sign of circumcision, to blot out that character
and become uncircumcised?"[2] He is responding to Paul's warning
that one should not "gather" or reverse one's circumcision. The
gloss to this line in the Geneva Bible also takes Paul in the most literal sense imaginable, explaining that this "gathering" is accomplished with "the help of a surgeon" who undoes the effect of the
cutting of the foreskin by "drawing the skin with an instrument, to
make it to cover the nut" or glans of the penis. The Geneva Bible
even directs readers to the medical source for this procedure, the
seventh book of Celsus's *De Medicina*.[3] Other writers explained
that Paul forbids this literal uncircumcision in his letter to the
Corinthians "because some that were converted to Christianity
from Judaism did so renounce all their Judaical rites that they used
means to attract the preputia again, which was an act of too much
superstition and curiosity, and so is censured here."[4] It also needs

1. Corinthians, 7.18–19.
2. Thomas Godwyn, *Moses and Aaron: Civil and Ecclesiastical Rites Used by the Ancient Hebrewes*, 4th ed. (London, 1631), p. 242.
3. The same information was also made available in the margin of the Geneva Bible, where Elizabethans, who had no need of this procedure themselves, were nonetheless informed that "the surgeon by art draweth out the skin to cover the part circumcised." The Geneva Bible also cross-references 1 Maccabees 1.16, which describes how the Jews followed the "fashions of the heathen" and "made themselves uncircumcised, and for-sook the holy Covenant." The table of contents to the 1589 Geneva Bible (which use-fully cites all biblical passages that mention circumcision) cites this passage as one in which the "Jews did uncircumcise themselves, and became apostates," indicating that the act carried with it associations of abandoning one religion for another.
   Those curious enough to follow up the medical reference would have read in the Latin text of A. Cornelius Celsus (the first English translation, from which I quote, was not published until 1756) that this procedure requires that "under the circle of the glans, the skin" is "to be separated by a knife from the inner part of the penis." Celsus explains that this "is not very painful, because the extremity being loosened, it may be drawn backwards by the hand, as far as the pubes; and no hemorrhage follows upon it." Next, the "skin being disengaged, is extended again over the glans; then it is bathed with plenty of cold water, and a plaister put round it of efficacy in repelling an inflammation." Celsus offers as postoperative advice that "the patient is to fast, till he almost be over-come with hunger, lest a full diet should perhaps cause an erection of that part." Finally, when "the inflammation is gone, it ought to be bound up from the pubes to the circle of the glans; and a plaister being first laid on the glans, the skin ought to be brought over it" (A. Cornelius Celsus, *Of Medicine. In Eight Books*, trans. James Greive [London, 1756], pp. 438–39).
4. Hammond, *A Paraphrase*, p. 565. Hammond also describes the "practice of some Jews, who under the Egyptian tyranny first, then under Antiochus, and lastly under the Ro-mans, being oppressed for being Jews, of which their circumcision was an evidence, used means by some medicinal applications to get a new praeputium. And these were called by the Talmudists *mishuchim*" (I transliterate the Hebrew here). Following the

to be stressed here that, uncircumcision, like circumcision, was understood by Paul's commentators to operate both spiritually and literally; Andrew Willet reminds his readers that "as there are two
kinds of circumcision, so there is also a twofold uncircumcision,
"an uncircumcision of the heart, and another of the flesh."

The belief that one could be uncircumcised, could have one's ir-
reducible Jewish identity replaced with a Christian one, is also a
fantasy that powerfully shapes the final confrontation between Shylock and Antonio in *The Merchant of Venice*. Antonio's consummate
revenge upon his circumcised adversary, whose actions symbolically
threaten to transform not just his physical but his religious identity,
is to ask of the court a punishment that precisely reverses what
Shylock had in mind for him. When Antonio demands that Shylock
"presently become a Christian," a demand to which the Duke readily agrees, the "christ'ning" that Shylock is to receive will metaphorically uncircumcise him. The new covenant has superseded the old,
as the sacrament of baptism, which has replaced circumcision,
turns Jew into Christian.[5] In his commentary on Romans Peter
Martyr offers up a summary of Paul's treatment of the Jews that
ironically foreshadows Antonio's victory over Shylock at the end of
the trial scene: "In civil judgments, when any is to be condemned
which is in any dignity or magistrateship, he is first deprived of his
dignity or office, and then afterward condemned. So the apostle
first depriveth the Jews of the true Jewishness, and of the true circumcision, and then afterward condemneth them."[6]

Antonio and Shylock, who fiercely insist on how different they are
from each other, to the last seek out ways of preserving that difference through symbolic acts that convert their adversary into their
own kind. Paradoxically, though, these symbolic acts—a threatened
circumcision of the heart and a baptism that figuratively uncircum-
cises—would have the opposite effect, erasing, rather than preserving, the literal or figurative boundaries that distinguish merchant
from Jew.[7] It is just this fear of unexpected and unsatisfying transfor-

---

Geneva Bible gloss, Hammond cites as a medical authority "the famous Physician" Celsus, and, unusually, also invokes Talmudic antecedents, citing Rabbi "Aleai of Achan,"
who "made himself a praeputium."

5. Shakespeare, *The Merchant of Venice*, 4.1.383, 4.1.394. Cf. Reik, who argues that if
"Shylock insists upon cutting out a pound of flesh from Antonio's breast, it is as if he demanded that the Gentile be made a Jew if he cannot pay back the three thousand ducats
at the fixed time. Otherwise put: Antonio should submit to the religious ritual of circumcision." In addition, at "the end of the 'comedy' Antonio demands that Shylock
should 'presently become a Christian.' If this is the justified amends the Jew has to make
for his earlier condition, it would be according to poetic justice that the Jew be forced to
become a Christian after he had insisted that his opponent should become a Jew" (*The
Search Within*, pp. 358–59).

6. Martyr, *Most Learned and Fruitfull Commentaries*, p. 48r.

7. See the fascinating discussion of the philosophical implications of Shylock's circumcising cut in Stanley Cavell, *The Claims of Reason: Wittgenstein, Skepticism, Morality, and
Tragedy* [(New York: Oxford University Press, 1979), pp. 479–81]. Marjorie Garber notes

mation that makes *The Merchant of Venice* so unsettling a comedy, and that renders the even more deeply submerged and shadowy charge of ritual murder such a potent one. The desire to allay such fears produces a fantasy ending in which the circumcising Jew is metamorphosed through conversion into a gentle Christian. While this resolution can only be sustained through legal force in the play (Shylock's alternative, after all, is to be executed), its power was sufficiently strong for this spectacle of conversion to be reenacted in a number of English churches in late-sixteenth- and early-seventeenth-century England, as a handful of Jews were led to the baptismal font.

STEPHEN ORGEL

[Shylocks in Shakespeare's England]†

* * *

But what kind of Jew is Shylock? Barabas is identifiable as a reprehensible Jew simply from his name, that of the biblical thief released instead of Jesus. Shakespeare's other Jews, too, have immediately recognizable biblical names: Leah, Tubal, Chus (or Cush in the Authorized Version); but Shylock and Jessica come from another onomastic world entirely. Commentators since the eighteenth century have been baffled by Shylock's name, and have attempted to rationalize it by deriving it from Shiloh, a word for the Messiah, or from a genealogy in Genesis where the name Shelah is found, or from a pamphlet entitled *Caleb Shillocke his prophecy, or the Jew's Prediction* which, since it was published in 1607, is more likely to derive from Shakespeare's Shylock than Shylock from it. The point of all this critical energy is to avoid the awkward fact that Shylock is, quite simply, an English name—this was first pointed out in 1849 by M. A. Lower, who found a power of attorney granted to a Sir Richard Shylok of Hoo, Sussex, in 1435. Subsequent commentators looking for keys to Shakespeare dismissed Sir Richard Shylok because he had no evident connection with either Shakespeare or usury, as if he were the only person in England who ever bore that surname. But Sir

---

that both "Reik and Cavell predicate their insights upon an assumption of doubling or twinship, a moment of perceptual equipoise that enforces the disconcerting confusion of identities. . . . Cavell, with 'skepticism with respect to other minds' and the epistemological uncertainty of identity. Each reader appropriates Shylock's scene, persuasively, to his own theoretical project, and finds the twinship of Shylock and Antonio in the courtroom a theatrical hypostasis, an onstage crux that reifies his own perceptions" (Garber, p. 187, n. 63). See also Marc Shell, *Money, Language, and Thought* (Berkeley: University of California Press, 1982), pp. 47–83.

† From *Imagining Shakespeare: A History of Texts and Visions* (Houndmills, Basingstoke, Hampshire: Palgrave Macmillan, 2003), pp. 151–55. Reprinted by permission of Palgrave Macmillan.

Richard Shylok had ancestors, and siblings, and relatives, and descendants; and over several hundred years there were other Shylock families who were not related to him. The surname Shylock appears in the hundreds rolls, and the name had been, since Saxon times, a native one. It means white haired, and is the same name as its more common English equivalents Whitlock and Whitehead. The original name is still in use: there is a Christopher Shylock currently living in London, and the Shylock Beauty Salon may be found in Sydney. Shylock is not some form of a biblical name; in Shakespeare's time it was clearly and unambiguously English.

As for Jessica, it too is not a biblical name, though unlike Shylock, it is also not English. It might be like Sidney's Pamela, an invented name that has passed into the culture. Pamela, however, reveals its sources easily: all honey, or sweetness, or melody. Jessica is less easy to locate. It might conceivably be intended as a female diminutive of the name of David's father Jesse, which would be appropriate because Jesse means "wealth"; but there is no reason whatever to believe that Shakespeare knew any Hebrew or was being advised by someone who did. Attempts to extract Jessica more directly from the Old Testament are even more farfetched. They depend on a brief genealogy of Abraham's family in Genesis 11.29, in which a daughter is mentioned whose name is given in the Geneva Bible as Iscah and in the Bishops' Bible as Jisca, and who is never referred to again. But surely in the world of Leah, Tubal and Cush, this is clutching at straws: Jessica is in fact a common enough name in Scotland, a diminutive of the woman's name Jessie. If Shakespeare knew any Jessicas they were Scottish.

What does this mean? To begin with, it may reveal more about us than about Shakespeare. There are many parallels. The Navarre of *Love's Labour's Lost* includes Nathaniel and Costard (the most English of apples); all the Athenian workmen in *A Midsummer Night's Dream* have English names—Snout, Bottom, Snug, Quince, Flute, Starveling; the Mediterranean duchy of Illyria is home to the relentlessly English Sir Toby Belch and Sir Andrew Aguecheek; the servants in the Verona of *Romeo and Juliet* are Sampson, Gregory, Peter and Abraham (and no critic to my knowledge has ever claimed that Sampson and Abraham were Jews); the villain in *Much Ado About Nothing*, a world of Pedros, Leonatos, Claudios, Borachios, is Don John. Shakespeare often wanted his clowns and grotesques to be recognizably English—why is only Shylock's name a problem?

Where do we go from there? If I were hunting for the real Shylock of Shakespeare's imagination, I would look not in Old Testament genealogies but in the continuing Elizabethan debates on banking and interest—for example, in Thomas Wilson's *Discourse Upon Usury* (1572), and more particularly in R. H. Tawney's masterful long introduction to the 1925 edition. The Shylocks of Shakespeare's world were absolutely ubiquitous; but by the end of the sixteenth century they began to be localized in a few groups: goldsmiths, mercers, and most visibly of all, scriveners, who combined the functions of accountant and legal adviser. None of these had anything to do with Jews—the association of Jews with usury in England was entirely conventional. Wilson, on the contrary, is convinced that the rise of usury was precisely a function of Protestantism, of Reformation morality and the abandonment of canon law. As Tawney says, "Calvin approached [economic life] as a man of affairs, who assumed, as the starting point of his social theory, capital, credit, large-scale enterprise,"[1] and therefore sanctioned the taking of interest on loans.

So one way to play Shylock "authentically" would be as one of the Puritan moneylenders of Shakespeare's London, for whom the Old Testament rhetoric would be entirely in character, and the Jewishness a moral comment on the profession. I am not, however, looking for a "real" Shylock, I am simply following out the implications of his English name. What about the fact that he is a Jew: what would an authentic Jew be like for Shakespeare's stage? To begin with, not a lower-class Londoner or an east European refugee with a yarmulke, but Spanish or Portuguese: such figures carried with them, as in the Lopez case, the villainous subtext of Jesuit subversion. James Shapiro cites a wonderfully paranoid passage from William Prynne that makes the point: "If extraordinary care be not taken . . . under pretext of Jews, we shall have many hundreds of Jesuits, Popish priests, and friars come over freely into England from Portugal, Spain, Rome, Italy, and other places, under the title, habit, and disguise of Jews."[2] The Jew is the mask of the papist—we return to Macklin's red skullcap.

To play Shylock as a Renaissance Spaniard would not, of course, have much resonance for a modern audience. To play him as a modern Latino, however, would make a striking kind of sense for American audiences: Shylock, after all, is not an outsider, any more than Latinos are in American society. He is as Venetian as the Christians are, but he is part of an underclass, marginalized within the society. Latinos are not associated with money in our culture, but a production might make real capital out of that. After all, if, as Antonio says, there are Christian moneylenders who charge no interest, then why are Bassanio and Antonio involved with Shylock at all? But the point is surely that Bassanio has already gone to all the classy mainline banks, and none of them will give him the time of day—Antonio is

1. Thomas Wilson, *A Discourse Upon Usury* (London: Bell, 1925), p. 111.
2. James Shapiro, *Shakespeare and the Jews* (New York: Columbia University Press, 1996), p. 27.

obviously a bad risk, and his emissary is an even worse one. So he ends up with Shylock—that means, let's say, in our American production, that he ends up at a barrio bank. The Latino banker also sees perfectly well that Antonio and Bassanio are a bad investment, but he never gets any business from the Anglo community, and he thinks that if he does a favor for Antonio perhaps that will get him some clout in the mainstream financial world—at least Antonio will be in his debt, owe him some favors. So he makes the loan, with a jokey stipulation substituting a body part for his usual interest—a joke, that is, that precludes his charging interest. And then he gets completely screwed by the Anglo world he is trying to become a part of, losing not just his money but his daughter to the Anglos, and he goes crazy and gets very vindictive. That would be, for us, a quite comprehensible psychological scenario.

But as I have already suggested, there is another side to Shylock, and to the Jew figure, for the Elizabethans, and that is his Old Testament component. Jews have a special status theologically: they are neither heathens nor heretics, categorically different from pagans and Moslems because they were God's chosen people, and in them Renaissance Christianity saw its own past. The conversion of the Jews was a holy mission, because it would mark the historical completion of Christ's work—the Turks were to be destroyed, but the Jews had to be converted. Coryate expresses the cultural ambivalence very clearly, observing from his Venetian experience that "our English proverbe: To looke like a Jewe (whereby is meant sometimes a weather beaten warp-faced fellow, sometimes a phreneticke and lunaticke person, sometimes one discontented) is not true. For indeed I noted some of them to be most elegant and sweet featured persons, which gave me occasion the more to lament their religion."[3] And for Christians who saw the church as corrupt, or as having fallen away from its proper function and its original purity, the Jews represented a tradition to be embraced and returned to, a way of starting afresh. Various radical Protestant sects used the Jews as a model, both for the ordering of society and for their rhetoric; and there is a lot in Shylock's language that recalls Puritan ways of speaking and arguing. Such sects quite explicitly emulated Judaism, calling their priests rabbis and using Hebrew—Jonson satirizes the practice with Rabbi Zeal-of-the-Land Busy in *Bartholomew Fair*. In 1655 Cromwell convened the Whitehall Conference to discuss formally readmitting the Jews to England—they had been formally expelled in 1290. There were even negotiations to sell the decaying St Paul's Cathedral to the Jewish community as a great central synagogue, and while the Whitehall Conference

---

3. *Crudities* (London, 1611), p. 231.

ended inconclusively, the government granted various privileges to resident Jews, though it stopped short of allowing them to be naturalized. They were technically "denizens," legally resident in the society but not finally integrated into it.

Shylock can be seen as a kind of Puritan. Shakespeare is not at all sympathetic to the Puritan cause, but his distaste for it is not a distaste for foreigners. Shylock is very deeply part of Venetian society; he expresses a good deal of its deepest nature. The success of both Antonio's love for Bassanio and Bassanio's love for Portia depends not only on Shylock's capital, but on his willingness to see it used merely to enable a Venetian romance. This helps to explain the strange ambivalence Shakespeare exhibits about this villain; and it also helps to explain why he is unwilling to destroy or expel him after the trial scene, but wants to incorporate him into the Christian world, to force him to convert. He is an essential part of Venice, which is to say, of England. Hence the most striking point about him, his English name: there is Shakespeare's ambivalence epitomised. Just what kind of subversion does this figure represent? All those pleasure-loving types in the play are Italians, but for an Elizabethan audience, Shylock is one of us.

*   *   *

CHARLES EDELMAN

[The Shakespeares as Money-lenders]†

*   *   *

The way Shakespeare employs the words "usance" and "usurer" in *The Merchant of Venice* epitomizes what was a major public debate of Elizabethan England, for although Elizabethan writers were, as Danson says, "unanimous in their condemnation of the practice of usury"[1] they were anything but unanimous in defining it. As Norman Jones writes in his endlessly fascinating book, *God and the Moneylenders*, "all good Christians agreed that usury was wrong, but they could not agree on what it was and when it occurred."[2]

Until 1545, any charging of interest was considered usury, and hence illegal, with the obvious effect of keeping interest rates extremely high. In response, Henry VIII's 1545 statute defined the of-

---

† From "Which Is the Jew That Shakespeare Knew?: Shylock on the Elizabethan Stage," *Shakespeare Survey* 52, Special issue on Shakespeare and the Globe, ed. Stanley Wells (Cambridge: Cambridge University Press, 1999), pp. 103–104. Reprinted by permission of Cambridge University Press.

1. Lawrence Danson, "The Problem of Shylock", in *Major Literary Characters: Shylock*, ed. Harold Bloom (New York, 1991), p. 273.

2. Norman Jones, *God and the Moneylenders* (London, 1989), p. 24.

fence as interest in excess of 10 per cent, although most loans were for periods much shorter than a year, so the nominal annual interest was actually far higher. Enforcement proved very difficult, however, and rates remained high, so the lawmakers did what they always do when they cannot regulate something—they outlaw it again. In 1552 Henry VIII's statute was repealed and replaced by total prohibition, with the same effect as that other well-known prohibition, so in 1571, a year after one John Shakespeare of Stratford was fined 40 shillings for charging an astonishing £20 interest for a *one-month* £80 loan,[3] Elizabeth's parliament, after extensive debate, restored the legal limit at 10 percent, whatever the term of the loan was. (If there was a *New York Daily News* in those days, it would have reported that "Johnny Gloves" was busted for nailing his customers on a "vig" of six points a week.)[4]

In reading *God and the Moneylenders* and Laura Caroline Stevenson's *Praise and Paradox: Merchants and Craftsmen in Elizabethan Popular Literature*, one learns that writers such as Miles Mosse, who saw usury as the charging of any interest, rather than excessive interest, were what we would call today the extreme right wing, or even a "lunatic fringe".[5] Still, interest rates, like taxes, are always too high, so we might easily assume that many in Shakespeare's audience would have known the difficulty of repaying a loan, and would have seen Shylock as a usurer. But for every borrower there is a lender, and there were no banks or credit unions then—ordinary people who needed money borrowed from a neighbour or acquaintance, or found an acquaintance to act as broker to negotiate the loan with someone else. Given the diverse social makeup of the Elizabethan theatre-going public, it is quite probable that some in the audience, since they were engaged in the practice themselves, believed that lending money at the going market rate, or receiving a commission for arranging a loan, was a socially useful and even honourable thing to do. *One* member of the original audience at *The Merchant of Venice* would surely have thought so, presuming he was not acting a part on stage—the play's author.

It has been established beyond doubt that like his father, William

---

3. S. Schoenbaum, *Shakespeare's Lives*, new edn. (Oxford, 1991), 562–63; E. A. J. Honigmann, " 'There is a World Elsewhere', William Shakespeare, Businessman", in *Images of Shakespeare: Proceedings of the Third Congress of the International Shakespeare Association*, 1986, ed. Werner Habicht, D. J. Palmer, Roger Pringle (Newark, 1986), p. 40; see also D. L. Thomas and N. E. Evans, "John Shakespeare in The Exchequer", *Shakespeare Quarterly*, 35 (1984), 314–18.

4. According to the *Wall Street Journal*, as cited in *The New Dictionary of American Slang*, ed. Robert L. Chapman (London, 1986), "vig" or "vigorish"—the extortionate interest charged by criminal loan sharks—would be about 180 per cent per year, or 15 per cent per month. John Shakespeare charged double that.

5. Laura Caroline Stevenson, *Praise and Paradox: Merchants and Craftsmen in Elizabethan Popular Literature* (Cambridge, 1984). Mosse's *Arraignment and Conviction of Usurie*, 1595, receives ample discussion in N. Jones, pp. 144 ff.

Shakespeare loaned out, at interest, what were sizable sums of money, and he was prepared to sue when he was not paid back. He also, as the Quiney correspondence shows, acted as a broker on occasion, arranging loans of what would be, as E. A. J. Honigmann notes, "five-figure" sums today.[6] When Antonio says

> Shylock, albeit I neither lend nor borrow
> By taking nor by giving of excess

> (I. 3. 59–60)

would not the play's author have expected, even wanted, at least someone in the audience, in those very inflationary times, to ask what Antonio was doing with a shirt on his back?

* * *

WALTER COHEN

[*The Merchant of Venice* and Proto-capitalism]†

* * *

Critics who have studied *The Merchant of Venice* against the background of English history have justifiably seen Shylock, and especially his lending habits, as the embodiment of capitalism.[1] The last third of the sixteenth century witnessed a sequence of denunciations of the spread of usury. In *The Speculation of Vsurie*, published during the year Shakespeare's play may first have been performed, Thomas Bell expresses a typical sense of outrage. "Now, now is nothing more frequent with the rich men of this world, than to writhe about the neckes of their poore neighbours, and to impouerish them with the filthie lucre of Usurie."[2] Behind this fear lay the transition to capitalism: the rise of banking; the increasing need for credit in industrial enterprises; and the growing threat of indebtedness facing both aristocratic landlords and, above all, small, independent producers, who could easily decline to working-class status.[3] Although the lower classes were the main victims, it may be

---

6. Honigmann, "World Elsewhere", pp. 41–5; see also his *Shakespeare's Impact on his Contemporaries* (London, 1982), pp. 8–14.

† From *ELH* 49 (1982): 765–89. Reprinted by permission of The John Hopkins University Press.

1. John W. Draper, "Usury in *The Merchant of Venice*," *Modern Philology*, 33 (1935), 37–47; E. C. Pettet, "*The Merchant of Venice* and the Problem of Usury," *Essays and Studies*, 31 (1945), 19–33; and Paul N. Siegel, "Shylock, the Elizabethan Puritan, and Our Own World," in *Shakespeare in His Time and Ours* (Notre Dame: U of Notre Dame P, 1968).

2. Thomas Bell, *The Speculation of Vsurie* (London, 1596), A2r. For similar statements, see Thomas Lodge, *An Alarum Against Vsurers* (London, 1584), Elr, and Roger Fenton, *A Treatise of Vsurie* (London, 1611), Blr.

3. R. H. Tawney, Introd. to *A Discourse upon Usury by Way of Dialogue and Orations, for the Better Variety and More Delight of All Those That Shall Read this Treatise* (1572), by

as inadequate to describe opposition to usury in Shakespeare or elsewhere as popular in character, as it is misleading to argue that "Elizabethan drama, even in its higher ranges, was not the expression of a 'class' culture at all."[4] Rather, we are confronted with the hegemonic position of the nobility, whose interests the ideology ultimately served. Artisans and peasant smallholders might fall into the proletariat, but once the majority of the traditional ruling class had adapted to capitalism, the issue of usury faded away.

This had not occurred by 1600, however, and *The Merchant of Venice* offers a number of specific parallels to the antiusury campaign[5] most notably in its contrasts between usury and assistance to the poor, and between usurers and merchants. Miles Mosse, for example, laments that "lending upon *vsurie* is growne so common and usuall among men, as that free lending to the needie is utterly overthrowne."[6] The distinction between merchants and usurers, also of medieval origin, could be drawn on the grounds that only the former operated for mutual benefit, as opposed to self-interest. Or it might be argued, in language recalling Shakespeare's high valuation of "venturing," that the usurer does not, like "the merchant that crosse the seas, adventure," receiving instead a guaranteed return on his money.[7]

A number of dubious consequences follow from concentrating too narrowly on the English background of *The Merchant of Venice*, however. From such a perspective, the play as a whole seems unproblematic, noneconomic issues unimportant, and related matters like Shylock's religion or the Italian setting irrelevant.[8] Even explicitly economic concerns do not make adequate sense. An emphasis on the difference between trade and usury might imply that Antonio and his creator are resolutely medieval anticapitalists.[9] But not

---

Thomas Wilson (New York: Harcourt Brace, [1925]), pp. 1–172. See also Lawrence Stone, *The Crisis of the Aristocracy, 1558–1641* (Oxford: Clarendon Press, 1965), pp. 158, 183, and 541–43.

4. L. C. Knights, *Drama and Society in the Age of Jonson* (London: Chatto and Windus, 1937), p. 11. The same assumption governs Knights's comments on usury, pp. 127–30, 164–68, and passim.

5. Some of these are pointed out by Draper, pp. 45–46, and Pettet, pp. 26–27.

6. Miles Mosse, *The Arraignment and Conviction of Vsurie* (London, 1595), C3v. See also H. A. [Henry Arthington?], *Provision for the Poore, Now in Penurie* (London, 1597), C2v, and Philip Caesar, *A General Discovrse Against the Damnable Sect of Vsvrers* (London, 1578), the title page of which refers to "these / later daies, in which, Charitie being ba- / nished, Couetousnes hath got- / ten the vpper hande."

7. *The Death of Vsvry, or the Disgrace of Vsvrers* (London, 1594), E1r. The contrary valuation of merchant and usurer may also be found in Nicolas Sanders, *A Briefe Treatise of Vsvrie* (Lovanii, 1568), D1r, and in Lodge and Thomas Greene's *A Looking Glasse for London and England* (1590), ed. Tetsumaro Hayashi (Metuchen, NJ: The Scarecrow Press, 1970), I.iii. and III.i. A sympathetic view of merchants is taken for granted—a position impossible at the time with regard to usurers—in John Browne, *The Merchants Avizo* (London, 1591), and in *A True Report of Sir Anthony Shierlies Iourney* (London, 1600).

8. Draper, pp. 46–47; Pettet, pp. 19, 29, and 32; and Siegel, "Shylock," pp. 249 and 252.

9. Draper, p. 39, and Pettet, pp. 19, 22, 23, 27, and 29.

Laurence Olivier, with Jeremy Brett as Bassanio (1970).

only do Shakespeare's other plays of the 1590's show few signs of hostility to capitalism, *The Merchant of Venice* itself is quite obviously procapitalist, at least as far as commerce is concerned. It would be more accurate to say that Shakespeare is criticizing merely the worst aspects of an emerging economic system, rather than the system itself. In this respect, moreover, he deviates from the antiusury tracts and from English reality alike. Writers of the period register both the medieval ambivalence about merchants and the indisputable contemporary fact that merchants were the leading usurers: suspicion of Italian traders ran particularly high.[1] It may be that Shakespeare intends a covert parallel between Shylock and Antonio. Yet no manipulation will convert a comedy in which there are no merchant-usurers and in which the only usurer is a Jew into a faithful representation of British economic life.

Similar trouble arises with Shylock, whom critics have at times allegorically Anglicized as a grasping Puritan.[2] The identification is unconvincing, however, partly because it is just as easy to transform him into a Catholic[3] and, more generally, because he is too complex and contradictory to fit neatly the stereotype of Puritan thrift. It is also unclear what kind of capitalist Shylock is. The crisis of the play arises not from his insistence on usury, but from his refusal of it. The contrast is between usury, which is immoral because it computes a charge above the principal from the moment of the loan, and interest, which is perfectly acceptable because it "is never due but from the appointed day of payment forward."[4] Antonio immediately recognizes that Shylock's proposal falls primarily into the latter category, and he responds appropriately, if naively: "Content in faith, I'll seal to such a bond, / And say there is much kindness in the Jew."[5]

In addition, the penalty for default on the bond is closer to folklore than to capitalism: stipulation for a pound of flesh, after all, is hardly what one would expect from *homo economicus*. To be sure, Shakespeare is literalizing the traditional metaphorical view of usurers.[6]

---

1. Bell, B4v and C3v, is again representative. Medieval attitudes toward merchants are surveyed by Tawney, *Religion and the Rise of Capitalism: A Historical Study*, Holland Memorial Lectures, 1922 (New York: New American Library, 1954), pp. 20–39. *A Discovery of the Great Subtiltie and Wonderful Wisedom of the Italians* (London, 1591), Blr, partly attributes Italy's success in economically exploiting other nations to the country's vigorous trade.
2. Siegel, "Shylock," and A. A. Smirnov, *Shakespeare: A Marxist Interpretation* (New York: Critics Group, 1936), p. 35.
3. Danson, pp. 78–80, and T.A., *The Massacre of Money* (London, 1602), C2v.
4. Mosse, F2r. Tawney, *Religion*, pp. 43–44, elaborates on this point, and W. H. Auden, *The Dyer's Hand and Other Essays* (New York: Vintage, 1968), pp. 227–28, notes that Shylock does not demand usury.
5. The Arden edition of *The Merchant of Venice*, ed. Brown (London: Methuen, 1955), I. iii. 148–49. Subsequent references are noted in the text.
6. Barber, p. 169; *Whartons Dreame* (London, 1578), A3r; and for a striking theatrical anticipation, Robert Wilson, *The Three Ladies of London (1581)*, ed. John S. Farmer (The Tudor Facsimile Texts, 1911), D4v.

Moreover, Shylock's desire for revenge is both motivated by economics and possessed of a large degree of economic logic (e.g., I. iii. 39–40; and III. i. 49, and 117–18). But when the grasping moneylender refuses to relent in return for any repayment—"No not for Venice"—he goes beyond the bounds of rationality and against the practices of a ruthless modern businessman (IV. i. 226).[7] In short, although it is proper to view *The Merchant of Venice* as a critique of early British capitalism, that approach fails even to account for all of the purely economic issues in the work. Can tolerable sense be made of the play's economics, or was Shakespeare merely being fanciful? To answer these questions, we need to take seriously the Venetian setting of the action.

To the English, and particularly to Londoners, Venice represented a more advanced stage of the commercial development they themselves were experiencing. G. K. Hunter's telling remark about the predilections of the Jacobean theater—"Italy became important to the English dramatists only when 'Italy' was revealed as an aspect of England"—already applies in part to *The Merchant of Venice*.[8] Yet Venetian reality during Shakespeare's lifetime contradicted almost point for point its portrayal in the play. Not only did the government bar Jewish usurers from the city, it also forced the Jewish community to staff and finance low-interest, nonprofit lending institutions that served the Christian poor. Funding was primarily derived from the involuntary donations of Jewish merchants active in the Levantine trade. The Jews of Venice thus contributed to the early development of capitalism not as usurers but as merchants involved in an international, trans-European economic network. Ironically, elsewhere in the Veneto, the public Christian banks on which the Jewish loan-houses of Venice were modeled drew most of their assets from interest-bearing deposits by the late sixteenth century.[9]

From a longer historical view of Italy and Venice, however, *The*

7. Stephen J. Greenblatt, "Marlowe, Marx, and Anti-Semitism," *Critical Inquiry*, 5 (1978), 291–307, emphasizes Shylock's irrationality, even madness. My discussion of *The Merchant of Venice* is generally indebted to this essay.

8. "English Folly and Italian Vice: The Moral Landscape of John Marston," in *Jacobean Theatre*, ed. John Russell Brown and Bernard Harris, Stratford-upon-Avon Studies, No. 1 (London: Edward Arnold, 1960), p. 95. For reservations about conflating late Elizabethan and Jacobean Italianism, see pp. 91–94. For comments on Venetian trade, see Robert Johnson's translation of Giovanni Botero, *Relations of the Most Famous Kingdoms and Common-weales thorovgh the World* (London, 1611), Gg2v–Gg3v, and George Sandys, *A Relation of a Iourney* (London, 1615), Blr.

9. Brian Pullan, *Rich and Poor in Renaissance Venice: The Social Institutions of a Catholic State, to 1620* (Oxford: Basil Blackwell, 1971), pp. 538–621, and Fernand Braudel, *The Mediterranean and the Mediterranean World in the Age of Philip II*, trans. Siân Reynolds (London: Collins, 1973), II, 817 and 823. Fynes Moryson, *Shakespeare's Europe: A Survey of the Conditions of Europe at the End of the Sixteenth Century; Being Unpublished Chapters of Fynes Moryson's "Itinerary" (1617)*, ed. Charles Hughes, 2nd ed. (1903; rpt. New York: Benjamin Blom, 1967), p. 488, gives a reasonably accurate picture of the position of Italian Jews.

Merchant of Venice assumes a recognizable relationship to reality. Between the twelfth and the early fourteenth centuries in Italy, international merchant-usurers were often required by the church to make testamentary restitution of their profits from moneylending. Thereafter, this occupation decomposed into its constituent parts. Without changing their financial transactions, the merchants experienced a sharp rise in status, eventually evolving into the great philanthropical merchant princes of the Renaissance. The other descendants of the earlier merchant-usurers, the small, local usurer-pawnbrokers, suffered a corresponding decline in social position. This latter group, the main victim of ecclesiastical action against usury in the fifteenth and sixteenth centuries, increasingly consisted of immigrant Jews.[1]

Jewish moneylenders benefited the Venetian Republic in two principal ways. They provided a reliable, lucrative source of tax revenues and forced loans to finance the state's military preparations; and they also drove down interest rates for private citizens, rich and poor, underselling the Christian usurers, whom, consequently, they gradually replaced. The Christian banks referred to above, founded beginning in the late fifteenth century, were designed not only to assist the poor but also to eliminate Jewish moneylenders by providing cheaper credit. Although never established in Venice itself, the *Monti di Pietá*, as they were called, were soon widespread in the cities and towns of the Republican mainland. They rarely succeeded in completely replacing Jewish pawnbrokers, however.[2]

This, then, is the other, Italian historical background to *The Merchant of Venice*. None of Shakespeare's probable sources refers to any prior enmity between merchant and usurer, much less to a comparable motive for the antagonism. English discussions of Italy, on the other hand, regularly mention both Jewish usury and Venetian charity,[3] while Bell, among others, speaks of the *mons pietatis*, a bank where the poor can "borrow money in their neede, and not bee oppressed with usury."[4] From this point of view, the hostility between Antonio, the open-handed Christian merchant, and Shylock, the tight-fisted Jewish usurer, represents not the conflict be-

---

1. Benjamin N. Nelson, "The Usurer and the Merchant Prince: Italian Businessmen and the Ecclesiastical Law of Restitution, 1100–1550," *Journal of Economic History*, Supp. 7 (1947), 104–22, an essay deeply aware of the parallels to *The Merchant of Venice*.
2. Pullan, pp. 431–537.
3. Wylliam Thomas, *The Historye of Italye* (London, 1549), U4v–X1r, Y2v, and Y3v; Lewes Lewkenor's translation of Gasparo Contarini, *The Commonwealth and Gouernment of Venice* (London, 1599), T2r; and Moryson, *An Itinerary* (London, 1617), H1v–H2r.
4. D4v. See also Fenton, P4v, and, for background, Tawney, Introd., pp. 125–27, and *Religion*, p. 53; Draper, pp. 45–46; and Nelson, *The Idea of Usury: From Tribal Brotherhood to Universal Otherhood*, 2nd ed. (Chicago: Univ. of Chicago Press, 1969), p. 73 n. 2. Greenblatt seems to be the only critic to suggest a parallel between Antonio and the Monti di Pietà.

tween declining feudalism and rising capitalism, but its opposite. It may be seen as a special instance of the struggle, widespread in Europe, between Jewish quasifeudal fiscalism and native bourgeois mercantilism, in which the indigenous forces usually prevailed.[5] Both the characterization and the outcome of *The Merchant of Venice* mark Antonio as the harbinger of modern capitalism. By guaranteeing an honorable reputation as well as a secure and absolute title to private property, the exemption of the Italian merchant-financier from the stigma of usury provided a necessary spur to the expansion of the new system.[6] Shylock, by contrast, is a figure from the past: marginal, diabolical, irrational, archaic, medieval. Shakespeare's Jacobean tragic villains—Iago, Edmund, Macbeth, and Augustus—are all younger men bent on destroying their elders. Shylock is almost the reverse, an old man with obsolete values trying to arrest the course of history.[7]

Obviously, however, the use of Italian materials in *The Merchant of Venice*, for all its historicity, remains deeply ideological in the bad sense, primarily because of the anti-Semitic distinction between vindictive Jewish usurer and charitable Christian merchant.[8] Shylock's defense of usury is not so strong as it could have been,[9] nor was Shakespeare's preference for an Italian merchant over a Jewish usurer universally shared at the time.[1] Indeed, the very contrast between the two occupations may be seen as a false dichotomy, faithful to the Renaissance Italian merchant's understanding of himself but not to the reality that self-conception was designed to justify.

We can understand the apparently contradictory implications of British and Italian economic history for *The Merchant of Venice* as a response to the intractability of contemporary life. The form of the play results from an ideological reworking of reality designed to produce precisely the intellectual and structural pattern described at the beginning of this discussion. The duality we have observed, especially in Shylock, is absolutely necessary to this end. Briefly stated, in *The Merchant of Venice* English history evokes fears of capitalism, and Italian history allays those fears. One is the prob-

---

5. For fiscalism versus mercantilism, see Immanuel Wallerstein, *The Modern World-System: Capitalist Agriculture and the Origins of the European World-Economy in the Sixteenth Century* (New York: Academic Press, 1974), pp. 137–38 and 149. For possible problems with this hypothesis, as applied to Italy, see Pullan, p. 451. Greenblatt employs Wallerstein's paradigm to help explain *The Merchant of Venice*, but he does not seem aware that his argument consequently contradicts the position of those scholars, whom he also cites, who rely on the antiusury tracts. See his n. 5.

6. Nelson, "The Usurer and the Merchant Prince," 120–22.

7. For similar perceptions, see Barber, p. 191, and Frye, p. 98.

8. Curiously, Brown, Introd. to his edition of *The Merchant of Venice*, p. xxxix, denies that the play is anti-Semitic.

9. Danson, pp. 148–50, argues that Shakespeare allows Shylock a fairly strong case but Draper, pp. 43–44, seems more persuasive in taking the opposite position.

1. See, for example, *Three Ladies*, D3v.

lem, the other the solution, the act of incorporation, of transcendence, toward which the play strives.

*   *   *

KAREN NEWMAN

Portia's Ring: Unruly Women and Structures of Exchange in *The Merchant of Venice*†

The merchant of Shakespeare's title is ambiguous; it applies literally to Antonio, but also characterizes Shylock, and indeed all the play's action, not only the "bond" plot, but the love plot as well. The exchange of goods, whether they be "rich lading wrack'd on the narrow seas" (III.i.3) or women, characterizes the play's action. Readers have often remarked the language of commerce that characterizes the Venetian world of the Rialto where even a church, "the holy edifice of stone," would remind Christian merchants "of dangerous rocks, / Which touching but my gentle vessel's side / Would scatter all her spices on the stream, / Enrobe the roaring waters with my skills" (I.i.30–34).[1] Here the feminine personification of merchant ship as woman wounded figures both the commodification of woman and her violation. Belmont seems at first to be presented quite differently—talk there is of love, sexuality, familial relationships seemingly free from Venetian economic motives and aims.[2] Portia's suitors are judged not on the basis of their wealth or goods, but in terms of personal and moral qualities, and it must be said, racial prejudice.[3]

But as many readers have noted, any simple binary opposition between Belmont and Venice is misleading, for the aristocratic country life of Belmont shares much with commercial Venice: the matter and mottoes of the caskets suggest commercial values, and Portia's father's will rules her choice of husbands. Though venturing at Belmont is admittedly idealized—Bassanio's quest of Portia is likened to Jason's voy-

---

† From *Shakespeare Quarterly* 38 (1987): 19–33. Copyright © Folger Shakespeare Library. Reprinted by permission of The Johns Hopkins University Press.

1. *The Merchant of Venice*, The Arden Shakespeare, ed. John Russell Brown (1955; rpt. London: Methuen, 1977). All future references are to the Arden edition.
2. Lawrence Danson and other readers have noted "the play's unusually prominent series of binary relationships," *The Harmonies of* The Merchant of Venice (New Haven: Yale Univ. Press, 1978), p. 10.
3. I have chosen deliberately to leave Shylock out of my reading of *The Merchant of Venice* in order to disturb readings of the play that center their interpretive gestures on the Jew. I recognize the suggestive possibilities, however, of readings such as Marianne Novy's which link Shylock and Portia as outsiders by virtue respectively of their race and sex, *Love's Argument: Gender Relations in Shakespeare* (Chapel Hill: Univ. of North Carolina Press, 1984), pp. 64 ff.

age, thus endowing it with a mythical dimension,[4] and Portia's father's will, through the mottoes, criticizes rather than endorses commercial values—what is important is the *structure* of exchange itself which characterizes both the economic transactions of Venice and the love relationships forged at Belmont. Venice and Belmont are throughout the play compared and contrasted, but the syntax of exchange itself functions in both locales; indeed, it seems universal.

Before considering structures of exchange in Shakespeare's play, I would like to look in some detail at the status of exchange in anthropology. In his *Essai sur le don*, Marcel Mauss describes and analyzes one of the most remarkable features of primitive societies: the extent to which exchange—giving, receiving, and reciprocating gifts—dominates social intercourse.[5] Gift-giving is significant according to Mauss because it establishes and expresses social bonds between the partners of an exchange. In the cultures that Mauss describes, "food, women, children, possessions, charms, land, labour, services, religious offices, rank" circulate in exchange.[6] By offering a gift, the giver solicits friendship, establishes a relationship, perhaps seeks a reward. Gift-giving can be competitive—its "underlying motives are competition, rivalry, show and a desire for greatness and wealth."[7] Acceptance of a gift creates a reciprocal relationship by implying a willingness to return a gift, so by giving a gift that cannot be reciprocated, either because of its kind or its excess, the giver can humiliate the receiver. Perhaps the most striking anthropological example of such gift-giving is the so-called Big Man of highland New Guinea who is assigned in adolescence a *buanyin* or exchange partner, and, apparently against indigenous norms of social behavior, is trained to an entire system of exchange and gift-giving in excess of what can be reciprocated. Such behavior results in prestige and power.

Claude Lévi-Strauss reworks Mauss's theory of the gift in his *Elementary Structures of Kinship* by proposing that marriage is the most fundamental form of gift exchange, and women the most basic of gifts. In studying the function and origins of exogamy, Lévi-Strauss argues that incest taboos and other rules prohibiting sexual relations and marriage between family members insure alliances and relationships among men:

---

4. See Elizabeth Sklar's interesting comparison of Bassanio and Jason in "Bassanio's Golden Fleece," *Texas Studies in Literature and Language*, 18 (1976): 500–509.
5. I am 'indebted to Gayle' Rubin's discussion of Mauss in "The Traffic in Women: Notes on the 'Political Economy' of Sex," *Toward an Anthropology of Women*, ed. Rayna Reiter (New York: Monthly Review, 1975). I also thank Lynda Boose whose careful reading of this paper and its anthropological frame steered me to the specific analogy between Portia and the Big Man which I develop here.
6. *Essai sur le don*, trans: Ian Cunnison (rpt. New York: W. W. Norton & Co., 1967), pp. 11–12.
7. Mauss, p. 26.

> The prohibition of incest is less a rule prohibiting marriage with the mother, sister, or daughter, than a rule obliging the mother, sister, or daughter to be given to others. It is the supreme rule of the gift. . . .[8]

Gift-giving, then, for Mauss and Lévi-Strauss, establishes social bonds and is a strategy of power. For Lévi-Strauss, however, such bonds and strategies are gender specific: they are exercised by and forged between and among men by means of the exchange of women:

> The total relationship of exchange which constitutes marriage is not established between a man and a woman . . . but between two groups of men, and the woman figures only as one of the objects in the exchange, not as one of the partners. . . .
>
> (p. 115)

> Exchange—and consequently the rule of exogamy which expresses it—has in itself a social value. It provides the means of binding men together, and of superimposing upon the natural links of kinship the henceforth artificial links . . . of alliance governed by rule. . . . It provides the fundamental and immutable rule ensuring the existence of the group as a group.
>
> (pp. 480–81)

For Lévi-Strauss, the exchange of women is at the origin of social life. His androcentric analysis seeks to authorize the exchange of women and the male bonds it constitutes by claiming that culture depends upon such ties. Feminists have pointed out two related consequences of Lévi-Strauss's claims. On the one hand, the seeming centrality of the woman as desired object is a mystification: she is a pseudo-center, a prize the winning of which instead of forging a male/female relation, serves rather to secure male bonds.[9] Others have looked not so much at the woman in this system of exchange, but at the male bonds it establishes. The French psychoanalyst Luce Irigaray postulates that if, as Lévi-Strauss claims,

> the exchanges which organize patriarchal societies take place exclusively between men, . . . [and if] women, signs, goods, money, pass from man to man or risk . . . slipping into incestuous and endogamous relations which would paralyze all social and economic intercourse, . . . [then] the very possibility of the socio-cultural order would entail homosexuality. Homosexuality would be the law that regulates the socio-cultural economy.[1]

8. *The Elementary Structures of Kinship*, ed. Rodney Needham (Boston: Beacon Press, 1969), p. 481.
9. See Julia Kristeva, *Texte du roman* (The Hague: Mouton, 1970), pp. 160, 60.
1. *Ce sexe qui n'en est pas un* (Paris: Les éditions de Minuit, 1977), p. 189, my translation. Also available in English translation, *This Sex Which is Not One*, trans. Catherine Porter with Carolyn Burke (Ithaca: Cornell Univ. Press, 1985).

Irigaray's use of the French conditional, *exigerait* and *serait*, translated here as "would entail" and "would be," and her stipulation that homosexual relations *per se* are prohibited because they risk short-circuiting the very systems of exchange that produce male bonds, suggest her polemical purpose in positing homosexuality as "the law that regulates the socio-cultural economy." Irigaray eroticizes the ties between men Lévi-Strauss describes in order to suggest a continuum—which she expresses by her pun, "hom(m)osexualité"[2]—that encompasses an entire range of male relations from the homoerotic to the competitive to the commercial. Recently Eve Sedgwick has made the perspectives first conceptualized by Kristeva and Irigaray available to the Anglo-American reader by appropriating the term "homosocial" from the social sciences to describe "the whole spectrum of bonds between men, including friendship, mentorship, rivalry, institutional subordination, homosexual genitality, and economic exchange—within which the various forms of the traffic in women take place."[3]

The Merchant of Venice would seem to offer an exemplary case not only of Lévi-Strauss's exchange system but also of the French feminist critique of that system. The exchange of Portia from her father via the caskets to Bassanio is the *ur*-exchange upon which the "main" bond plot is based: it produces Bassanio's request for money from Antonio and in turn the bond between Antonio and Shylock. Though the disposition of Portia by her father's will, and the financial arrangements between Bassanio and Antonio that permit Bassanio's courtship, lead to heterosexual marriage, the traffic in women paradoxically promotes and secures homosocial relations between men. Read from within such a system, Portia's seeming centrality is a mystification, a pseudo-center, for woman in this series of transactions, to repeat Lévi-Strauss's phrase, "figures only as one of the objects in the exchange, not as one of the partners." The feminist rereading of Lévi-Strauss also provides another angle from which to read the *Merchant*'s much-debated male relationship. Commentators have often remarked Shakespeare's introduction of the theme of friendship, a shift from the paternal/filial relationship of *Il Pecorone* usually recognized as the *Merchant*'s primary source. But the relationship between Antonio and Bassanio has been interpreted not only as a version of idealized Renaissance friendship,

---

2. Irigaray, p. 168. I am grateful to Jonathan Goldberg for reminding me of this orthographic play.
3. "Sexualism and the Citizen of the World: Wycherley, Sterne and Male Homosocial Desire," *Critical Inquiry*, 11 (1984), 227. For a more extended discussion, including a fine chapter on the sonnets, see her *Between Men: English Literature and Male Homosocial Desire* (New York: Columbia Univ. Press, 1985). See also Lars Engle, " 'Thrift is Blessing': Exchange and Explanation in *The Merchant of Venice*," *Shakespeare Quarterly*, 37 (1986): 20–37, for a discussion of Sedgwick's work in relation to the *Merchant*.

but also as homoerotic.[4] Certainly textual evidence suggests the difficulty in distinguishing between the erotic and the platonic in Antonio's relations with Bassanio. Instead of choosing one interpretation over another, idealized male friendship or homosexuality, Irigaray's reading of Lévi-Strauss allows us to recognize in Antonio's relationship with Bassanio a homosocial bond, a continuum of male relations which the exchange of women entails.

Some anthropologists have challenged not the phallocentrism of Lévi-Strauss's claim that exogamous marriage and the exchange of women is a necessary condition for the formation of social groups and ultimately of culture, but his theory of kinship itself. Pierre Bourdieu, for example, adduces instances of parallel cousin marriage from nomadic and gatherer groups which refute the structuralist interpretation of kinship as a rule-governed *system*, arguing instead that kin relationships are social *practices* that produce and reproduce historically specific social relations. In the cultures Bourdieu examines, for example, women often take part in the choice of a spouse for their children: how marriages are made and what they do "depend on the aims or collective strategies of the group involved" and are not constitutive *per se* of male bonds or of culture.[5] But Bourdieu's ungendered social science vocabulary ("the collective strategies of the group involved") glosses over the significant fact that these aims and strategies inevitably allot women secondary status, for it is always the bride, and never the groom, who is an object of exchange among family groups and the means whereby social relations are reproduced. However they may disagree about the reasons for and results of kinship "rules" or "practices," in both Lévi-Strauss's structural anthropology and Bourdieu's functionalist analysis, women figure as capital, as objects of exchange among men.

But the "traffic in women" is neither a universal law on which culture depends, as Lévi-Strauss would have it, nor simply a means of producing and reproducing generalized "social relations," as Bourdieu claims: Kristeva's and Irigaray's analysis of exchange exposes it as a strategy for insuring hierarchical gender relations. The

4. Recent critics who explain Antonio's melancholy as a loss of friendship include Leonard Tenenhouse, "The Counterfeit Order of *The Merchant of Venice*," in *Representing Shakespeare: New Psychoanalytic Essays*, eds. Murray M. Schwartz and Coppélia Kahn (Baltimore: Johns Hopkins Univ. Press, 1980), pp. 57–66, and Keith Geary, "The Nature of Portia's Victory: Turning to Men in 'The Merchant of Venice,' " *Shakespeare Survey*, 37 (1984): 55–68. Graham Midgley, "*The Merchant of Venice*: A Reconsideration," *Essays in Criticism*, 10 (1960), 119–33; W. H. Auden, "Brothers and Others," *The Dyer's Hand and Other Essays* (New York: Random House, 1962); Lawrence W. Hyman, "The Rival Lovers in *The Merchant of Venice*," *SQ*, 21 (1970): 109–16; and W. Thomas MacCary, *Friends and Lovers: The Phenomenology of Desire: Shakespearean Comedy* (New York: Columbia Univ. Press, 1985), claim a homoerotic impulse in Antonio's attachment.
5. *Outline of a Theory of Practice*, trans. Richard Nice, Studies in Social Anthropology, No. 16 (Cambridge: Cambridge Univ. Press, 1977), p. 58.

exchange of women produces and reproduces what Gayle Rubin has termed a "sex/gender system" in which the traffic in women is only part of an entire system of

> sexual access, genealogical statuses, lineage names and ancestors, rights and *people*—men, women and children—in concrete systems of social relationships. . . . "Exchange of women" is a shorthand for expressing that the social relations of a kinship system specify that men have certain rights in their female kin, and that women do not have the same rights either to themselves or to their male kin.
>
> (p. 177)

Such a sex/gender system functioned historically in early modern England where marriage, among the elite at least, was primarily a commercial transaction determined by questions of dowry, familial alliances, land ownership, and inheritance.[6] Daughters were pawns in the political and social maneuvers of their families, particularly their male kin.[7] Marriage contracts and settlements, familiar letters and wills, conduct books and sermons alike recognize in marriage an economic transaction based on the exchange of gifts—women, cash, annuities, rents, land.[8] Divines preached sermons with such titles as "A Good Wife Gods Gift"; women were explicitly commodified, as in John Wing's exemplary exhortation, in his treatise on marriage, that men seek wives not in the devil's place—playhouses, may games, dance matches—but in God's house, since

> [a]ll men love in merchandizing for any commodity, to goe as neere the *welhead* as they can, to such as *make the commodities themselves*, and from whose hands they *doe originally* come.[9]

The commercial language to describe love relationships common in Elizabethan love poetry and in *The Merchant of Venice* displays not only the economic determinants of marriage in Elizabethan society, but England's economic climate more generally—its developing cap-

6. Lawrence Stone, *The Family, Sex and Marriage in England 1500–1800* (New York: Harper & Row, 1977).
7. See Lisa Jardine, *Still Harping on Daughters: Women and Drama in the Age of Shakespeare* (Brighton: Harvester Press; Totowa, N.J.: Barnes & Noble, 1983), chap. 3.
8. See E. T., *The Lawes Resolution of Women's Rights: or the Lawes Provision for Women* (London, 1632), also known as *The Woman's Lawyer*, which gathers together in one volume contemporary laws about women, property, and marriage. In Bk. II, chap. xxxii, there is an extended discussion specifically of the "condiments of love," that is, the gifts given at marriage. In his recent essay on exchange in the *Merchant*, Lars Engle (see note 3 above) claims Portia's name suggests the marriage portion, a common means of relieving debt in early modern England. Though it is conceivable that an audience might hear "Portia" as an aural pun on "portion," the name is not etymologically related to the Latin *portio, -onis*, a share, part, proportion, but the Latin *porcus*, pig, and the Roman clan, the Porcii, breeders of pigs.
9. *The Crowne Conjugall or the Spouse Royal* (London, 1632), sig. K2ʳ.

italist economy characterized by the growth and expansion of urban centers, particularly London; the rise of banking and overseas trade; and industrial growth with its concomitant need for credit and large amounts of capital.[1] Such changes, as Walter Cohen has demonstrated, inevitably generated anxiety that readers of *The Merchant of Venice* have recognized in the tension Shakespeare created between trade and usury, and in the ultimate triumph of Antonio and his incorporation into Belmont's world of aristocratic, landed values.[2]

The exchange of gifts dominated not only kinship relations, but power relations as well. Gift-giving was a significant aspect of Elizabethan and Jacobean social intercourse, as demonstrated by royal prestation and patronage, and by the New Year's gift rolls, account books, and records of aristocratic families who vie with one another in their generosity to the monarch in quest of favor.[3] Not only the monarch and the aristocracy, but the gentry and the middling sort—all took part in these systems of exchange. Even the poorest families participated in such exchange systems: observers describe the custom in English villages of placing a basin in the church at weddings, into which guests placed gifts to help to establish the newly formed family in the community.[4] In the 1620s and 30s, gift-giving declined and signalled the alienation of the aristocracy, gentry, and urban elite from the court.[5]

In III.ii, of *The Merchant of Venice*, Portia offers her love to Bassanio in a speech that epitomizes the Elizabethan sex/gender system:

> You see me Lord Bassanio where I stand,
> Such as I am; though for myself alone
> I would not be ambitious in my wish
> To wish myself much better, yet for you,
> I would be trebled twenty times myself,
> A thousand times more fair, ten thousand times more rich,
> That only to stand high in your account,

1. See R. H. Tawney, *Religion and the Rise of Capitalism* (New York: Penguin Books, 1947); Christopher Hill, *The Century of Revolution: 1603–1714* (New York: Norton, 1982); Lawrence Stone, *The Crisis of the Aristocracy, 1558–1641* (Oxford: Clarendon Press, 1965), and Keith Wrightson, *English Society 1580–1680* (New Brunswick, N.J.: Rutgers Univ. Press, 1982), pp. 122–48.
2. See Walter Cohen's admirable "*The Merchant of Venice* and the Possibilities of Historical Criticism," *ELH*, 49 (1983): 765–89, which appears in part in his recent book, *Drama of a Nation: Public Theater in Renaissance England and Spain* (Ithaca and London: Cornell Univ. Press, 1985).
3. See particularly Wallace T. MacCaffrey, "Place and Patronage in Elizabethan Politics," *Elizabethan Government and Society*, eds. S. T. Bindoff, J. Hurstfield, and C. H. Williams (London: Univ. of London, The Athlone Press, 1961), pp. 97–125. For a discussion of prestation and literary fictions in Elizabethan culture, see Louis Adrian Montrose, "Gifts and Reasons: The Contexts of Peele's *Araygnement of Paris*," *ELH*, 47 (1980): 433–61.
4. See William Vaughan, *The Golden Grove* (London, 1600), sig. M8^r.
5. For a more detailed account of Jacobean gift-giving, see Coppélia Kahn's " 'Magic of bounty': *Timon of Athens*, Jacobean Patronage, and Maternal Power," especially pp. 41 ff., in *Shakespeare Quarterly* 38 (1987): 34–57.

I might in virtues, beauties, livings, friends
Exceed account: but the full sum of me
Is sum of something: which to term in gross,
Is an unlesson'd girl, unschool'd, unpractised,
Happy in this, she is not yet so old
But she may learn: happier than this,
She is not bred so dull but she can learn;
Happiest of all, is that her gentle spirit
Commits itself to yours to be directed,
As from her lord, her governor, her king.
Myself, and what is mine, to you and yours
Is now converted. But now I was the lord
Of this fair mansion, master of my servants,
Queen o'er myself: and even now, but now,
This house, these servants, and this same myself
Are yours,—my lord's!—I give them with this ring. . . .
                                              (III.ii.149–71)

This speech begins with what we might term an affective paradox.
Portia presents herself to Bassanio using the first person in an en-
gagingly personal, if highly rhetorical, manner: "Such as I am." But
her account of herself, as my own dead metaphor suggests, illustrates the exchange between the erotic and the economic that
characterizes the play's representation of human relations. The
rhetorical distance created by the mercantile metaphor shifts the
speech from her personal commitment to a more formal bond
marked by the giving of her ring, and that move is signaled by the
shift to the third person ("an unlesson'd girl . . . she"). Portia objec-
tifies herself and thereby suppresses her own agency in bestowing
herself on Bassanio. The passives are striking—she casts herself
grammatically in the role of object "to be directed"; she and all she
owns "is converted" to Bassanio by an unstated agent. Perhaps the
most marked stylistic feature of these lines is the repeated use of
now which signals both temporal shifts and, more importantly, a
moment of conversion. The rhetorical balance of line 166 is arrested by the caesura and the *now* of line 167 which insists on the
present moment of commitment to Bassanio. The "but now" that
follows refers back in time, emphasizing Portia's prior role as "lord"
of Belmont, a role that she yields to Bassanio with her vow "I give
them with this ring"; the moment of fealty is underscored by the repeated "even now, but now" in line 169.

The governing analogy in Portia's speech is the Renaissance political commonplace that figures marriage and the family as a kingdom in small, a microcosm ruled over by the husband.[6] Portia's

6. Kenneth Burke calls this figure the " 'noblest synecdoche,' the perfect paradigm or
   prototype for all lesser usages, [which] is found in metaphysical doctrines proclaiming the

Graziano giving Portia the ring. Illustration by Gordon Browne. From *The Works of Shakespeare*, ed. Henry Irving and Frank A. Marshall (1888), vol. 3.

speech figures woman as microcosm to man's macrocosm and as subject to his sovereignty. Portia ratifies this prenuptial contract with Bassanio by pledging her ring, which here represents the codified, hierarchical relation of men and women in the Elizabethan sex/gender system in which a woman's husband is "her lord, her governor, her king."[7] The ring is a visual sign of her vow of love and submission to Bassanio; it is a representation of Portia's acceptance of Elizabethan marriage which was characterized by women's subjection, their loss of legal rights, and their status as goods or chattel. It signifies her place in a rigidly defined hierarchy of male power and privilege; and her declaration of love at first seems to exemplify her acquiescence to woman's place in such a system.

But Portia's declaration of love veers away in its final lines from

identity of 'microcosm' and 'macrocosm.' In such doctrines, where the individual is treated as a replica of the universe, and vice versa, we have the ideal synecdoche. . . ." *A Grammar of Motives and A Rhetoric of Motives* (Cleveland: Meridian, 1962), p. 508.

7. For a contemporary discussion of the giving of rings, see Henry Swinburne, *Treatise of Spousals or Matrimonial Contracts* (London, 1686), but written and published much earlier; see also Anne Parten, "Re-establishing sexual order: The Ring episode in *The Merchant of Venice*," *Selected Papers of the West Virginia Shakespeare and Renaissance Association*, 6 (1976), 27–34. Parten also remarks this link between Portia's ring and her submission. Engle, cited above, claims that Portia's actions in the final acts represent "her triumphant manipulation of homosocial exchange" and her "absolute mastery" (p. 37). Not only the historical and cultural position of women in early modern England, but also the generic boundaries of comedy seem to me to preclude such optimism. We can, however, claim resistance, a dislocation of the structures of exchange.

the exchange system the preceding lines affirm. Having moved through past time to the present of Portia's pledge and gift of her ring, the speech ends in the future, with a projected loss and its aftermath, with Portia's "vantage to exclaim on" Bassanio:

> I give them with this ring,
> Which when you part from, lose, or give away,
> Let it presage the ruin of your love,
> And be my vantage to exclaim on you.
>
> (ll. 171–74)

Here Portia is the gift-giver, and it is worth remembering Mauss's description of gift-giving in the New Guinea highlands in which an aspiring "Big Man" gives more than can be reciprocated and in so doing wins prestige and power. Portia gives more than Bassanio can ever reciprocate, first to him, then to Antonio, and finally to Venice itself in her actions in the trial which allow the city to preserve both its law and its precious Christian citizen. In giving more than can be reciprocated, Portia short-circuits the system of exchange and the male bonds it creates, winning her husband away from the arms of Antonio.[8]

Contemporary conduct books and advice about choosing a wife illustrate the dangers of marriage to a woman of higher social status or of greater wealth. Though by law such a marriage makes the husband master of his wife and her goods, in practice contemporary sources suggest unequal marriages often resulted in domination by the wife.[9] Some writers and Puritan divines even claimed that women purposely married younger men, men of lower rank or of less wealth, so as to rule them.[1] Marriage handbooks and sermons all exhort women to submit to their husbands, regardless of disparity in rank or fortune, as in this representative example from Daniel Tuvill's *St. Pauls Threefold Cord*:

> Yea, though there were never so great a disproportion betwixt them in state and condition; as say the wife were a Princesse, the husband but a pesant, she must be yet in conjugall respects as a hand-mayd unto him; he must not be as a servant unto her. . . . And this subjection is so necessary, that without it the world could not long subsist; yea nature herselfe would suddenly be dissolved. . . .[2]

8. For a discussion of "negative usury" or "giving more than you get," see Henry Berger, Jr., "Marriage and Mercifixion in *The Merchant of Venice*," *SQ* (1981), 155–62. Some readers have argued that Portia must redeem Antonio who "may make impossible the marriage union Portia seeks," Marc Shell, "The Wether and the Ewe: Verbal Usury in *The Merchant of Venice*," *Kenyon Review*, I (1979), 65–92; see also Engle, cited in note 3 above, p. 253.
9. Cf. Bartholomew Battus, *The Christian Mans Closet*, trans. William Lowth (London, 1581), Bk. II.
1. William Gouge, *Of Domesticall Duties* (London, 1634), sig. T2^r.
2. (London, 1635), sigs. B4^v–B5^v.

The vehemence and fear of chaos and disorder Tuvill betrays are characteristic and imply a growing need in the Stuart period to shore up eroding class and gender hierarchies.

Bassanio's answer to Portia's pledge of love implicitly recognizes such a disparity and its effect by metaphorically making her the master:

> Madam, you have bereft me of all words,
> Only my blood speaks to you in my veins,
> And there is such confusion in my powers,
> As after some oration fairly spoke
> By a beloved prince, there doth appear
> Among the buzzing pleased multitude,
> Where every something being blent together,
> Turns to a wild of nothing, save of joy
> Express'd, and not express'd: but when this ring
> Parts from this finger, then parts life from hence,—
> O then be bold to say Bassanio's dead!
>
> (III.ii.175–85)

Bassanio's heavily marked epic simile is anomalous in Shakespearean comedy. It echoes the first and perhaps most famous Virgilian simile of the *Aeneid*, when Neptune's effect in quelling the storm inspired by Juno is compared to that of "a man remarkable / for righteousness and service" for whom the people "are silent and stand attentively; and he controls their passion by his words and cools their spirits."[3] Shakespeare translates the Virgilian simile into his own romantic context in which the speaker's words, instead of having a quieting effect on heart and mind, create a Petrarchan paradox: blood that speaks, but a lover silenced. And in keeping with Petrarchan conventions, Bassanio's comparison figures Portia as dominating and distant—that is, as a prince. Renaissance rhetoricians such as Wilson and Puttenham define figurative language as *translation*, "an inuersion of sence by transport"[4]—a kind of figurative exchange which disturbs normal communication and makes unexpected connections.[5] Poets use tropes so that "the hearer is ledde by cogitation vppon rehearsall of a Metaphore, and thinketh more by remembraunce of a worde translated, then is there expressely spoken: or else because the

---

3. Virgil knew the simile from the end of Hesiod's prologue to the *Theogony*, but Shakespeare would only have known it, of course, through Virgil.
4. Puttenham, *The Arte of English Poesie* (1589), in *English Literary Criticism: The Renaissance*, ed. O. B. Hardison, Jr. (London: Peter Owen, 1967), p. 177.
5. Compare Lévi-Strauss's discussion of language and the emergence of symbolic thought in the final pages of *Elementary Structures*: "But woman could never become just a sign and nothing more, since even in a man's world she is still a person, and since in so far as she is defined as a sign she must be recognized as a generator of signs. In the matrimonial dialogue of men, woman is never purely what is spoken about; for if women in general represent a certain category of signs, destined to a certain kind of communication, each woman preserves a particular value. . . . In contrast to words, which have wholly become signs, woman has remained at once a sign and a value," (p. 496).

whole matter seemeth by a similitude to be opened. . . ."[6] Bassanio's political simile with its Virgilian intertextual exchange "disguises" Portia as a man and prefigures her masculine role in the trial scene where she insures the Venetian republic by reconciling the principle of equity with the rigor of the law.

We should also remember that Portia, whom Bassanio earlier describes as "nothing undervalu'd / To Cato's daughter, Brutus' Portia" (I. i. 165–66), is named after her classical ancestor who describes herself in *Julius Caesar* as "A woman well-reputed, Cato's daughter. / Think you I am no stronger than my sex, / Being so fathered and so husbanded?" (II. i. 295–97). That Portia was renowned in antiquity for sharing the political ideals of her father and husband, and Shakespeare represents her commitment to political action by her insistence, as Plutarch had recorded, on knowing of the plot to murder Caesar and by her taking part in the conference of Republicans at Antium. The *Merchant*'s Portia resembles her classical namesake and her figural persona ("beloved prince") by entering the male lists of law and politics. Far from simply exemplifying the Elizabethan sex/gender system of exchange, the *Merchant* short-circuits the exchange, mocking its authorized social structure and hierarchical gender relations.

For Portia's ring, we should remember, does not remain on Bassanio's finger, and *his* gift of the ring to Balthazar does indeed give Portia "vantage to exclaim." The gift of Portia's ring shifts the figurative ground of her speech from synecdoche to metonymy.[7] Her lines first figure the ring as a part of her which she gives as a sign of the whole to Bassanio; in the final lines, however, the prefigured loss of the ring signals not substitution, but contiguity, metonymic relations. By following the movements of her ring, we may discover something about how the play both enacts and interrogates Elizabethan structures of figural and sexual exchange. Objects, like words, change their meaning in different contexts; as things pass from hand to hand, they accumulate meanings from the process of exchange itself. Bassanio gives away his ring in payment for services rendered and in doing so transgresses his pledge to Portia. When it begins its metonymic travels from Bassanio to the young doctor, the ring picks up new meanings which contradict its status as a sign of male possession, fidelity, and values;[8] it moves from Bassanio to Balthazar to Portia to Antonio and back to Bassanio again and the very multiplicity of exchanges undermines its prior signification. The

6. Thomas Wilson, *The Arte of Rhetorique* (1560), in Hardison, p. 42.
7. See Burke's account of metonymy, the basic strategy of which is to convey an "incorporeal or intangible state in terms of the corporeal or tangible" (p. 506; see note 6, above, p. 260).
8. This is also the case with the play's other lost ring given as a prenuptial pledge, from Leah to Shylock, which Jessica gives to one of Antonio's creditors for a monkey.

ring also makes a figural progress; in Renaissance rhetorical terms it
is transmuted, "which is, when a word hath a proper signification of
the [sic] owne, and being referred to an other thing, hath an other
meaning."[9] Portia's ring becomes a sign of hierarchy subverted by
establishing contiguities in which the constituent parts have shifting
sexual and syntactic positions. By opening out the metonymic chain
to include Balthazar, Bassanio opens his marriage to forces of disorder, to bisexuality, equality between the sexes, and linguistic equivalence in opposition to the decorous world of Renaissance marriage
represented by the love pledges in III.ii. Bassanio gives his ring to an
"unruly woman," that is, to a woman who steps outside her role and
function as subservient, a woman who dresses like a man, who em-
barks upon behavior ill-suited to her "weaker" intellect, a woman
who argues the law.[1]

In her fine essay, "Women on Top: Symbolic Sexual Inversion and Political Disorder in Early Modern Europe," Natalie
Zemon Davis details the ways in which women's disorderliness
manifested itself in England and Europe during this period. Davis
observes that anthropologists generally agree that forms of sexual inversion—switches in sex roles, topsy turvy, and images of the world
turned upside down, "the topos of the woman on top"—

> like other rites and ceremonies of reversal, are ultimately
> sources of order and stability in hierarchical society. They can
> clarify the structure by the process of reversing it. They can
> provide an expression of, and safety valve for, conflicts within
> the system. They can correct and relieve the system when it
> has become authoritarian. But, so it is argued, they do not
> question the basic order of the society itself. They can renew
> the system, but they cannot change it.[2]

Many feminist critics have agreed with such judgments in their
readings of Shakespeare's comedies of sexual inversion. They argue
that such play, usually in the service of courtship, is ultimately conservative, leading to conventional gender roles and patriarchal marriage.[3] Portia, we are told, in giving up her disguise and returning

9. Wilson, in Hardison, p. 45.
1. Lisa Jardine discusses the significance of Portia's "arguing the law," in "Cultural Confusion and Shakespeare's Learned Heroines: These are old paradoxes," in *Shakespeare
   Quarterly* 38 (1987): 1–18.
2. *Society and Culture in Early Modern France* (1965; rpt. Stanford: Stanford Univ. Press,
   1975), p. 130. Davis refers to the work of several anthropologists including Gluckman,
   Turner, Bateson, Flügel, Delcourt, and Meslin.
3. See, for example, Clara Claiborne Park, "As We Like It: How A Girl Can Be Smart and
   Still Popular," in *The Woman's Part: Feminist Criticism of Shakespeare*, eds. Carolyn
   Ruth Swift Lenz, Gayle Greene, and Carol Thomas Neely (Urbana: Univ. of Illinois
   Press, 1980), pp. 100–116; Irene Dash, *Wooing, Wedding and Power: Women in Shake-
   speare's Plays* (New York: Columbia Univ. Press, 1981), and more recently, Peter Erick-
   son's *Patriarchal Structures in Shakespeare's Drama* (Berkeley and London: Univ. of
   California Press, 1985). Compare Richard Horwich who claims that the ring trick is "a

Bassanio's ring, returns to "unthreatening 'femininity.' "[4] But Davis herself disputes the interpretation of sexual inversion as simply a safety mechanism. She points out first that historians of early modern Europe are likely to find inversion and reversals less in prescribed rites than in popular festivities and carnival. Cultural play with the concept of the unruly woman, she argues, was a multivalent image which "could undermine as well as reinforce traditional hierarchical formations." Davis adduces examples of comic and festive inversion that carried over into political action, that provided not only release, but also represented efforts or provided the means whereby the distribution of power in society was questioned and changed. And, I would add, inversion affects not only the distribution of power but also perhaps structures of exchange themselves that historically have insured male hegemony and patriarchal power. Sexual inversion and play with the *topos* of the woman on top offered an alternative mode of conceiving family structure and gender behavior within that structure.

When Bassanio leaves for Venice to aid his friend, Portia evokes the conventional ideal of a Renaissance lady: she promises "My maid Nerissa, and myself meantime / Will live as maids and widows" (III. ii. 308–309); to Lorenzo she claims they will live in a monastery to fulfill a vow "to live in prayer and contemplation," behavior which conforms to the Renaissance ideal of womanhood: chaste, silent, and obedient. Shakespeare evokes here the accepted codes of feminine behavior in his culture, thereby distancing the action from the codes of dramatic comedy that permit masculine disguise, female dominance, and linguistic power. Portia evokes the ideal of a proper Renaissance lady and then transgresses it; she becomes an unruly woman.

The common remedies for the weaker sex's disorderliness were, even among the humanists such as Vives, Erasmus, and More, religious training to make her modest and humble, education of a restricted kind designed not to inflame her imagination but to acquaint her with her moral duty, and honest work of a sort appropriate to female capabilities. Transgression of the traditional expectations for women's behavior brought down wrath such as John Knox's *The First Blast of the Trvmpet Against the Monstrvovs Regiment of Women*:

> . . . the holie ghoste doth manifestlie expresse, saying: I suffer not that woman vsurpe authoritie aboue man: he sayth not, I will not, that woman vsurpe authoritie aboue her husband, but

---

device by which she may exercise her free will"; it restores "what from the start she complained of lacking—the power of choice," "Riddle and Dilemma in *The Merchant of Venice*," *Studies in English Literature*, 18 (1977): 199.
4. Parten, "Re-establishing sexual order," p. 32.

he nameth man in generall, taking frome her all power and au-
thoritie, to speake, to reason, to interprete, or to teache, but
principallie to rule or to iudge in the assemblie of men. . . . [A]
woman promoted to sit in the seate of God, that is, to teache, to
iudge, or to reigne aboue man, is a monstre in nature, contu-
melie to God, and a thing most repugnāt to his will ād ordināce.[5]

It might be argued that the excess of Knox's attack, directed specifically against Mary Tudor, reflects his own rather than widely held
views. But even humanist writers sympathetic to the cause of
women's education assume the propriety of Knox's claims, if not his
rhetoric. They exclude women from the public arena and assume
the necessity of their silence.[6] Leonardo Bruni, for example, warns
that "rhetoric in all its forms—public discussion, forensic argument,
logical fence, and the like—lies absolutely outside the province of
women."[7] When Portia takes off for Venice dressed as a man, she
looses her tongue in public talk on subjects ill-suited to the ladylike
conduct she posits as a model and does exactly those things Knox
and others violently attacked. She engages, that is, in productive labor reserved for men, and not insignificantly, in linguistic labor, in a
profession the successful practice of which depends on a knowledge
of history and precedent, on logic and reasoning, and on rhetoric, all
areas of education traditionally denied to women.

Portia's manner of winning her case, her "integrative solution" as
it has been called, deserves consideration. Her defense depends on
a verbal quibble,[8] a characteristic linguistic strategy of Shakespearean clowns which allows them to express ideologically subversive or contradictory attitudes or ideas. Indeed, in the Merchant,
Launcelot Gobbo uses the quibble for just such purposes. His
wordplay around the command to come to dinner at III.v.43, and
his earlier play with Jessica on damnation (III. v. 4–7), give a double perspective to serious issues in the play, issues of social and

5. (London, 1558), sigs. 16ᵛ–17ʳ.
6. On the position of the learned lady in the Renaissance, see Lisa Jardine, " 'O decus Ital-
   iae virgo,' or the myth of the learned lady in the Renaissance," Historical Journal, 28
   (1985): 799–819, as well as the opening pages of her essay in Shakespeare Quarterly 38
   (1987): 1–98.
7. De Studiis et litteris, trans. William H. Woodward in Vittorino de Feltre and Other Humanist Educators (Cambridge, 1897), pp. 124, 126, quoted in Constance Jordan, "Fem-
   inism and The Humanists: The Case of Sir Thomas Elyot's Defence of Good Women,"
   Renaissance Quarterly, 36 (1983): 181–201. See also Vives's discussion of women and
   eloquence in Foster Watson, ed., Vives and the Renascence Education of Women (New
   York: Longmans, Green, & Co., 1912), pp. 48–56, and More's letters, quoted in Watson,
   esp. pp. 179 ff. Similar exhortations can be found in Protestant tracts.
8. O. Hood Phillips observes that Portia's solution would never have succeeded in court in
   Shakespeare and The Lawyers (London: Methuen, 1972), pp. 91–118. Bullough claims
   on the basis of Mosaic Law that "the separation of flesh and blood is less of a quibble
   than critics have thought," Narrative and Dramatic Sources of Shakespeare, I (London:
   Routledge and Kegan Paul; New York: Columbia Univ. Press, 1957), p. 448.

Christian hierarchy and the like.[9] Portia and Launcelot Gobbo, woman and servant, are linked by this shared verbal strategy which allows them seemingly at least to reconcile irreconcilable perspectives and to challenge the play's overall mimetic design. They represent the "other" in the play, those marginal groups that are oppressed under the Elizabethan class/gender system, but whose presence paradoxically is needed to insure its existence. Their playful, quibbling misuse of language veils their subversive linguistic power. Portia's wise quibble saves the Venetian republic by enabling the Duke to follow the letter of the law *and* to save Antonio, to satisfy the opposing viewpoints represented by the Old and New law, by Shylock and Antonio. In another register, as Walter Cohen has pointed out, it unites the bourgeois values of self-interest with those of the traditional landed gentry, an imaginary literary solution to ideological conflicts manifest in late sixteenth-century England (pp. 776 ff.). But Portia's linguistic play here and in the final scene, like Launcelot Gobbo's, resists the social, sexual, and political system of which she is a part and provides a means for interrogating its distribution of power along gender lines.

The *Merchant of Venice* does not end with Portia's success in the courtroom; after her winning defense of Antonio, Portia asks Bassanio to return her ring, knowing, as her husband puts it, that "There's more depends on this than the value."[1] We know this ring symbolizes the bargain of faith in patriarchal marriage Portia and Bassanio have made in III.ii. By obeying Antonio's exhortation and giving his ring to Balthazar, Bassanio affirms homosocial bonds— the exchange of women, here represented by Portia's ring, sustains relations between men. But Balthazar is, of course, Portia in disguise (and Portia, we should not forget, was played by a boy, so that literally all the love relations in the play are homosocial). When Portia laughs at the thought of "old swearing / That they did give the rings away to men; / But we'll outface them and outswear them too" (IV. ii. 15–17), she keeps her promise. In losing their rings and breaking their promises to Portia and Nerissa, Bassanio and Gratiano seem paradoxically to lose the male privileges the exchange of women and the rings insured. When in the final act Portia returns her ring to her husband via Antonio, its multiple metonymic travels

---

9. See Cohen, pp. 779–81, cited in note 2 above, p. 255, and Robert Weimann's discussion of inversion and wordplay in *Shakespeare and the Popular Tradition in the Theatre*, ed. Robert Schwartz (Baltimore: Johns Hopkins Univ. Press, 1978), esp. pp. 39–48, 120–50.

1. See Murray Biggs's "A Neurotic Portia," *ShS*, 25 (1977): 153–59, which recognizes from an opposite perspective the meaning of Portia's request: "she, perversely, asks for Bassanio's wedding ring. It is her one fall from heavenly grace." For a heavily psychoanalytic reading of Portia's behavior and her quest for mastery, see Vera Jiji, "Portia Revisited: The Influence of Unconscious Factors Upon Theme and Characterization in *The Merchant of Venice*," *Literature and Psychology*, 26 (1975): 5–15.

have changed it. The ring no longer represents the traditional relationship it figured in III.ii. On its figural as well as literal progress,
it accumulates other meanings and associations: cuckoldry and
thus female unruliness, female genitalia, woman's changeable nature and so-called animal temperament, her deceptiveness and potential subversion of the rules of possession and fidelity that insure
the male line.[2]

Natalie Zemon Davis observes that female disorderliness was
grounded in nature rather than nurture, in cold and wet humours
which "meant a changeable, deceptive and tricky temperament"
(p. 125). Physiology accounted for unruly women: shrews, scolds,
transvestites, women who transgressed the rules of womanly decorum, were believed to suffer from hysteria, or a fit of what the Renaissance called the "mother" or the "wandering womb." In the
intervening time between their marriage and its putative consummation after the play's close, Portia has fallen victim to an imaginative fit of the "mother" and become an unruly woman. Her
so-called "hysteria" leads her to act like a man, to bisexuality—she
dresses up like a man and argues the law, imaginatively expressing
her own sexuality by cuckolding her husband with Balthazar. As
Portia says when she returns the ring, "I had it of him: pardon me
Bassanio, / For by this ring the doctor lay with me" (V. i. 258–59).[3]
Instead of the subservient woman of elaborate pledges at III.ii, Portia's speech at V.i.266 ff. is filled with imperatives—"Speak not so
grossly . . . read it . . . Unseal this letter. . . ." Having expressly given
over her house to Bassanio in III.ii, she says in V.i, "I have not yet /
Enter'd my house" (ll. 272–73). She emphasizes her power and secret knowledge by giving Antonio the mysterious letter, but refusing
to reveal how she came by it: "You shall not know by what strange
accident / I chanced on this letter."

It is often said that Act V of *The Merchant of Venice* is unusually
harmonious even for Shakespearean comedy; certainly the world of
usury, hatred, and aggression that characterizes Venice has re-
ceded.[4] But Act V is far from presenting the harmonious view of
love and marriage many have claimed, for even the idyllic opening
dialogue between Jessica and Lorenzo is troubled by allusions to

---

2. Norman Holland presents a number of psychoanalytic accounts of the link between
rings and female sexuality in *Psychoanalysis and Shakespeare* (New York: McGraw-Hill,
1966); for folktale sources, see, for example, the Tudor jest book *Tales and Quick Answers* (1530) cited in Parten (see note 7, p. 257 above).

3. E. A. M. Colman argues in his *The Dramatic Use of Bawdy in Shakespeare* (London:
Longman, 1976) that Shakespeare's bawdy is associated with anarchic and dissident im-
pulses.

4. C. L. Barber claims "No other comedy . . . ends with so full an expression of harmony. .
. . And no other final scene is so completely without irony about the joys it celebrates,"
Shakespeare's Festive Comedy (1957; rpt. Princeton: Princeton Univ. Press, 1972),
p. 187.

unhappy love and broken vows. Lorenzo mockingly calls Jessica a shrew and the play ends on an obscene pun on *ring* and a commonplace joke about female sexuality and cuckoldry, not on the idealized pledges of true love that characterize III.ii.[5] Portia's verbal skills, her quibbles and play with words, her duplicitous representation of herself as an unlessoned girl who vows "to live in prayer and contemplation," even as she rules her household and prepares to argue the law, bring together contradictory attitudes and views toward women and their role and place both in drama and society.[6] Bassanio accepts the oppositions that her play with language enacts: "Sweet doctor, you shall be my bedfellow," he says. But in an aside that scarcely requires a psychoanalytic gloss, Bassanio exclaims "Why I were best to cut my left hand off, / And swear I lost the ring defending it" (V. i. 177–78). Portia's unruliness of language and behavior exposes the male homosocial bond the exchange of women insures, but it also multiplies the terms of sexual trafficking so as to disrupt those structures of exchange that insure hierarchical gender relations and the figural hegemony of the microcosm/macrocosm analogy in Elizabethan marriage. Instead of being "directed, / As from her lord, her governor, her king," Portia resumes her role as lord of Belmont: "Let us go in," she commands. As Davis suggests, in the "little world of the family, with its conspicuous tension between intimacy and power, the larger matters of political and social order could find ready symbolization" (p. 150). The sexual symbolism of transvestism, the transgression of traditional gender roles and the figural transgression of heterosexual relations, the multivalence of linguistic meanings in women's and clowns' speech, all interrogate and reveal contradictions in the Elizabethan sex/gender system in which women were commodities whose exchange both produced and reproduced hierarchical gender relations.

Portia's masterly speech and gift-giving in the play's final scene return us once more to anthropology and to the powerful Big Man of the New Guinea highlands that Mauss describes. To read Portia's transgression as subversive risks the theoretical accusation that her power finally depends on a reversal, on occupying the position of the Big Man, thereby preserving the oppositions that ground gender hierarchy. Even the term for such a gift-giver—Big *Man*—is problematic and suggests the reinscription of binary notions of sexual difference, of male and female, binarisms that inevitably allot to one pole, usually the masculine, a positive value, to the other a

---

5. In *Love's Argument* Novy claims "the threats of possessiveness and promiscuity are both dispelled," but does not explain how this should be so (p. 79).
6. Lisa Jardine analyzes the link between learning in women and sexual "forwardness" in her *SQ* (1987) essay.

negative.[7] From such a perspective, all resistance is always already contained, dissipated, recuperated finally to the *status quo*. But *Derrida's* deconstruction of such inversion, unlike many of its ahistorical and ultimately conservative applications, recognizes that particular strategies, languages, rhetorics, even behaviors, receive meaning only in sequences of differences,[8] and that those sequences of differences are produced within a particular discourse—philosophy or linguistics, for example—or within a particular historical instance. Behaviors and rhetorics signify within particular discourses, histories, and economies. I have therefore argued that the *Merchant* interrogates the Elizabethan sex/gender system and resists the "traffic in women," because in early modern England a woman occupying the position of a Big Man, or a lawyer in a Renaissance Venetian courtroom, or the lord of Belmont, is not the same as a man doing so. For a woman, such behavior is a form of simulation,[9] a confusion that elides the conventional poles of sexual difference by denaturalizing gender-coded behaviors; such simulation perverts authorized systems of gender and power. It is inversion with a difference.

ALAN SINFIELD

How to Read *The Merchant of Venice* without Being Heterosexist†

* * *

I. Antonio vs. Portia

As W. H. Auden suggested in an essay in *The Dyer's Hand* in 1962, the *The Merchant of Venice* makes best sense if we regard Antonio as in love with Bassanio (Auden 1963; see also Midgley 1960). In the opening scene their friends hint broadly at it. Then, as soon as Bassanio arrives, the others know they should leave the two men together—"We leave you now with better company. . . . My Lord Bassanio, since you have found Antonio / We two will leave you" (I. i. 59, 69–70). Only Gratiano is slow to go, being too foolish to realize that he is intruding (I. i. 73–118). As soon as he departs, the

---

7. See Jacques Derrida, *Of Grammatology*, trans. Gayatri C. Spivak (Baltimore: Johns Hopkins Univ. Press, 1977), and *Writing and Difference*, trans. Alan Bass (Chicago: Univ. of Chicago Press, 1978).
8. Derrida, *Of Grammatology*, pp. 19, 33 ff.
9. See Irigaray's discussion of "mimetisme" as self-conscious or reflexive imitation in *Ce sexe qui n'en est pas un*, pp. 134 ff.
† From *Alternative Shakespeares*, Volume 2, ed. Terence Hawkes (London and New York: Routledge, 1996), pp. 123–39. Reprinted by permission of Taylor & Francis.

tone and direction of the dialogue switch from formal banter to intimacy, and the cause of Antonio's sadness emerges:

> Well, tell me now what lady is the same
> To whom you swore a secret pilgrimage—
> That you to-day promis'd to tell me of?
>
> (I. i. 119–21)

Bassanio moves quickly to reassure his friend and to ask his help: "to you Antonio / I owe the most in money and in love" (I. i. 130–31). The mercenary nature of Bassanio's courtship, which troubles mainstream commentators who are looking for a "good" heterosexual relationship, is Antonio's reassurance. It allows him to believe that Bassanio will continue to value their love, and gives him a crucial role as banker of the enterprise.

Whether Antonio's love is what we call sexual is a question which, this essay will show, is hard to frame, let alone answer. But certainly his feelings are intense. When Bassanio leaves for Belmont, as Salerio describes it, he offers to "make some speed / Of his return". "Do not so," Antonio replies:

> And even there (his eye being big with tears),
> Turning his face, he put his hand behind him,
> And with affection wondrous sensible
> He wrung Bassanio's hand, and so they parted.
>
> (II. viii. 37–38, 46–49)

The intensity, it seems, is not altogether equal. As Auden observes in his poem "The More Loving One", the language of love celebrates mutuality but it is unusual for two people's loves to match precisely:

> If equal affection cannot be,
> Let the more loving one be me.
>
> (Auden 1969: 282)

Antonio the merchant, like Antonio in *Twelfth Night* and the Shakespeare of the sonnets, devotes himself to a relatively casual, pampered younger man of a higher social class.

In fact, Antonio in the *Merchant* seems to welcome the chance to sacrifice himself: "pray God Bassanio come / To see me pay his debt, and then I care not" (III. iii. 35–36). *Then* Bassanio would have to devote himself to Antonio:

> You cannot better be employ'd Bassanio,
> Than to live still and write mine epitaph.
>
> (IV. i. 117–18)

As Keith Geary observes, Antonio's desperate bond with Shylock is his way of holding on to Bassanio (Geary 1984: 63–64); when Portia saves Antonio's life, Lawrence W. Hyman remarks, she is preventing what would have been a spectacular case of the "greater love" referred to in the Bible (John 15:13), when a man lays down his life for his friend (Hyman 1970: 112).

That theme of amatory sacrifice contributes to an air of homoerotic excess, especially in the idea of being bound and inviting physical violation. When Bassanio introduces Antonio to Portia as the man "To whom I am so infinitely bound", she responds:

> You should in all sense be much bound to him,
> For (as I hear) he was much bound for you.
>
> (V. i. 135–37)

At the start, Antonio lays open his entire self to Bassanio:

> be assur'd
> My purse, my person, my extremest means
> Lie all unlock'd to your occasions.
>
> (I. i. 137–39)

Transferring this credit—"person" included—to Shylock's bond makes it more physical, more dangerous and more erotic:

> let the forfeit
> Be nominated for an equal pound
> Of your fair flesh, to be cut off and taken
> In what part of your body pleaseth me.
>
> (I. iii. 144–47)

In the court, eventually, it is his breast that Antonio is required to bear to the knife, but in a context where apparent boys may be disguised girls and Portia's suitors have to renounce marriage altogether if they choose the wrong casket, Shylock's penalty sounds like castration. Indeed, Antonio offers himself to the knife as "a tainted wether of the flock"; that is, a castrated ram (IV. i. 114).

The seriousness of the love between Antonio and Bassanio is manifest, above all, in Portia's determination to contest it. Simply, she is at a disadvantage because of her father's casket device, and wants to ensure that her husband really is committed to her. The key critical move, which Hyman and Geary make, is to reject the sentimental notion of Portia as an innocent, virtuous, "Victorian" heroine. Harry Berger regards her "noble" speeches as manipulations: "Against Antonio's failure to get himself crucified, we can place Portia's divine power of mercifixion; she never rains but she pours." Finally, she mercifies Antonio by giving him back his ships (Berger 1981: 161–62; see Hyman 1970; Geary 1984).

Antonio's peril moves Bassanio to declare a preference for him over Portia:

> Antonio, I am married to a wife
> Which is as dear to me as life itself,
> But life itself, my wife, and all the world,
> I would lose all, ay sacrifice them all
> Here to this devil, to deliver you.

Portia, standing by as a young doctor, is not best pleased:

> Your wife would give you little thanks for that
> If she were by to hear you make the offer.
>
> (IV. i. 278–85)

It is to contest Antonio's status as lover that Portia, in her role of young doctor, demands of Bassanio the ring which she had given him in her role of wife. Antonio, unaware that he is falling for a device, takes the opportunity to claim a priority in Bassanio's love:

> My Lord Bassanio, let him have the ring,
> Let his deservings and my love withal
> Be valued 'gainst your wife's commandement.
>
> (IV. ii. 445–47)

The last act of the play is Portia's assertion of her right to Bassanio. Her strategy is purposefully heterosexist: in disallowing Antonio's sacrifice as a plausible reason for parting with the ring, she disallows the entire seriousness of male love. She is as offhand with Antonio as she can be with a guest:

> Sir, you are very welcome to our house:
> It must appear in other ways than words,
> Therefore I scant this breathing courtesy.
>
> (V. i. 139–41)

She will not even admit Antonio's relevance: "I am th'unhappy subject of these quarrels", he observes; "Sir, grieve not you,—you are welcome not withstanding", she abruptly replies (V. i. 238–39). Once more, self-sacrifice seems to be Antonio's best chance of staying in the game, so he binds himself in a different project: *not* to commit his body again to Bassanio in a way that will claim a status that challenges Portia:

> I once did lend my body for his wealth,
> Which but for him that had your husband's ring
> Had quite miscarried. I dare be bound again,
> My soul upon the forfeit, that your lord
> Will never more break faith advisedly.
>
> (V. i. 249–53)

Portia seizes brutally on the reminiscence of the earlier bond: "Then you shall be his surety" (V. i. 254). Antonio's submission is what she has been waiting for. Now she restores Bassanio's status

as husband by revealing that she has the ring after all, and Antonio's viability as merchant—and his ability to return to his trade in
Venice—by giving him letters that she has been withholding.

A gay reader might think: well, never mind; Bassanio wasn't
worth it, and with his wealth restored, Antonio will easily find another impecunious upper-class friend to sacrifice himself to. But,
for most audiences and readers, the air of "happy ending" suggests
that Bassanio's movement towards heterosexual relations is in the
necessary, the right direction (like Shylock's punishment, perhaps).
As Coppélia Kahn reads the play, "In Shakespeare's psychology,
men first seek to mirror themselves in a homoerotic attachment
. . . then to confirm themselves through difference, in a bond with
the opposite sex—the marital bond" (Kahn 1985: 106). And Janet
Adelman, in a substantial analysis of male bonding in Shakespeare's comedies, finds that "We do not move directly from family
bonds to marriage without an intervening period in which our
friendships with same-sex friends help us to establish our identities" (Adelman 1985: 75). To heterosexually identified readers this
might not seem an exceptional thought, but for the gay man it is a
slap in the face of very familiar kind. "You can have these passions,"
it says, "but they are not sufficient, they should be a stage on the
way to something else. So don't push it."

To be sure, Kahn points out that "it takes a strong, shrewd woman
like Portia to combat the continuing appeal of such ties between
men" (1985: 107). And Adelman remarks the tendency towards ca-
suistical "magical restitutions" and the persistence of "tensions that
comedy cannot resolve" (1985: 80). So hetero-patriarchy is not se-
cured without difficulty or loss. None the less, when Adelman writes
"We do not move directly . . . to marriage", the gay man may ask,
"Who are "We"?" And when Kahn says "men first seek to mirror
themselves in a homoerotic attachment", the gay man may wonder
whether he is being positioned as not-man, or just forgotten altogether. If Antonio is excluded from the good life at the end of the
Merchant, so the gay man is excluded from the play's address. The
fault does not lie with Kahn and Adelman (though in the light of recent work in lesbian and gay studies they might want to formulate
their thoughts rather differently). They have picked up well enough
the mood and tendency of the play, as most readers and audiences
would agree. It is the Shakespearean text that is reconfirming the
marginalization of an already marginalized group.

II. Property and Sodomy

The reader may be forgiven for thinking that, for a commentator
who has claimed to be excluded from the *Merchant*, this gay man

has already found quite a lot to say. Perhaps the love that dared not speak its name is becoming the love that won't shut up. In practice, there are (at least) two routes through the *Merchant* for out-groups. One involves pointing out the mechanisms of exclusion in our cultures—how the circulation of Shakespearean texts may reinforce the privilege of some groups and the subordination of others. I have just been trying to do this. Another involves exploring the ideological structures in the playtexts—of class, race, ethnicity, gender and sexuality—that facilitate these exclusions. These structures will not be the same as the ones we experience today, but they may throw light upon our circumstances and stimulate critical awareness of how our life-possibilities are constructed.[1]

In *The Merchant*, the emphasis on the idea of being bound displays quite openly the way ideological structures work. Through an intricate network of enticements, obligations and interdictions—in terms of wealth, family, gender, patronage and law—this culture sorts out who is to control property and other human relations. Portia, Jessica and Launcelot are bound as daughters and sons; Morocco and Arragon as suitors; Antonio and Bassanio as friends; Gratiano as friend or dependant, Nerissa as dependant or servant, and Launcelot as servant; Antonio, Shylock and even the Duke are bound by the law; and the Venetians, Shylock rather effectively remarks, have no intention of freeing their slaves (IV. i. 90–98).

Within limits, these bonds may be negotiable: the Duke may commission a doctor to devise a way round the law, friendships may be redefined, servants may get new masters, women and men may contract marriages. Jessica can even get away from her father, though only because he is very unpopular and Lorenzo has very powerful friends; they "seal love's bonds newmade" (II. vi. 6). Otherwise, trying to move very far out of your place is severely punished, as Shylock finds. It is so obvious that this framework of ideology and coercion is operating to the advantage of the rich over the poor, the established over the impotent, men over women and insiders over outsiders, that directors have been able to slant productions of the *Merchant* against the dominant reading, making Bassanio cynical, Portia manipulative and the Venetians arrogant and racist.

The roles of same-sex passion in this framework should not be taken for granted (I use the terms "same-sex" and "cross-sex" to evade anachronistic modern concepts). For us today, Eve Sedgwick shows this in her book *Between Men*, homosexuality polices the entire boundaries of gender and social organization. Above all, it exerts

---

1. Another way is blatantly reworking the authoritative text so that it is forced to yield, against the grain, explicitly oppositional kinds of understanding; see Sinfield 1992: 16–24, 290–302.

"leverage over the channels of bonding between all pairs of men". Male–male relations, and hence male–female relations, are held in place by fear of homosexuality—by fear of crossing that "invisible, carefully blurred, always-already-crossed line" between being "a man's man" and being "interested in men" (Sedgwick 1985: 88–89; see Dollimore 1992: chs 17–18). We do not know what the limits of our sexual potential are, but we do believe that they are likely to be disturbing and disruptive; that is how our cultures position sexuality. Fear even of thinking homosexually serves to hold it all in place. So one thing footballers must *not* be when they embrace is sexually excited; the other thing they mustn't be is in love. But you can never be quite sure; hence the virulence of homophobia.

If this analysis makes sense in Western societies today, and I believe it does, we should not assume it for other times and places. As Sedgwick observes, ancient Greek cultures were different (1985: 4). In our societies whether you are gay or not has become crucial—the more so since lesbians and gay men have been asserting themselves. An intriguing thought, therefore, is that in early modern England same-sex relations *were not terribly important*. In *As You Like It* and *Twelfth Night*, homoeroticism is part of the fun of the wooing ("Ganymede", the name taken by Rosalind, was standard for a male same-sex love-object); but it wouldn't be fun if such scenarios were freighted with the anxieties that people experience today. In Ben Jonson's play *Poetaster*, Ovid Senior expostulates: "What! Shall I have my son a stager now? An engle for players? A gull, a rook, a shot-clog to make suppers, and be laughed at?" (Jonson 1995: I. ii. 15–17).[2] It is taken for granted that boys are sexual partners (engles) for players; it is only one of the demeaning futures that await young Ovid if he takes to the stage. Moralists who complained about theatre and sexual licence took it for granted that boys are sexually attractive.

"Sodomy" was the term which most nearly approaches what is now in England called "gross indecency"; it was condemned almost universally in legal and religious discourses, and the penalty upon conviction was death. Perhaps because of this extreme situation, very few cases are recorded. Today, staking out a gay cruising space is a sure-fire way for a police force to improve its rate of convictions. But in the Home Counties through the reigns of Elizabeth I and James I—sixty-eight years—only six men are recorded as having been indicted for sodomy. Only one was convicted, and that was for an offence involving a five-year-old boy.[3]

In his book *Homosexual Desire in Shakespeare's England*, Bruce

2. See also Jonson 1995: III. iv. 277–78, V. iii. 580–81. On boys in theatre, see Jardine 1983: ch. 1.
3. See Bray 1982: 38–42, 70–80; Smith 1991: 47–52.

R. Smith shows that while legal and religious edicts against sodomy were plain, paintings and fictive texts sometimes indicate a more positive attitude. This derived mainly from the huge prestige, in artistic and intellectual discourses, of ancient Greek and Roman culture where same-sex passion is taken for granted (Smith 1991: 13–14, 74–76 *et passim*). Smith locates six "cultural scenarios": heroic friendship, men and boys (mainly in pastoral and educational contexts), playful androgyny (mainly in romances and festivals), transvestism (mainly in satirical contexts), master–servant relations and an emergent homosexual subjectivity (in Shakespeare's sonnets). Within those scenarios, it seems, men did not necessarily connect their practices with the monstrous crime of sodomy—partly, perhaps, because that was so unthinkable. As Jonathan Goldberg emphasizes, the goal of analysis is "to see what the category [sodomy] enabled and disenabled, and to negotiate the complex terrains, the mutual implications of prohibition and production" (1992: 20; see Bray 1982: 79). The point is hardly who did what with whom, but the contexts in which anxieties about sodomy might be activated. So whether the friendships of men such as Antonio and Bassanio should be regarded as involving a homoerotic element is not just a matter of what people did in private hundreds of years ago; it is a matter of definition within a sex-gender system that we only partly comprehend.

Stephen Orgel asks: "why were women more upsetting than boys to the English?" That is, given the complaints that boy-actors incite lascivious thoughts in men and women spectators, why were not women performers employed—as they were in Spain and Italy? Orgel's answer is that boys were used because they were less dangerous; they were erotic, but that was less threatening than the eroticism of women. So this culture "did not display a morbid fear of homosexuality. Anxiety about the fidelity of women, on the other hand, does seem to have been strikingly prevalent" (Orgel 1989: 8, 18). Leontes and Polixenes lived guiltlessly together, we are told in *The Winter's Tale*, until they met the women who were to be their wives (I. ii. 69–74). The main faultlines ran through cross-sex relations.

Because women may bear children, relations between women and men affected the regulation of lineage, alliance and property, and hence offered profound potential disruptions to the social order and the male psyche. Same-sex passion was dangerous if, as in the instance of Christopher Marlowe's *Edward II*, it was allowed to interfere with other responsibilities. Otherwise, it was thought compatible with marriage and perhaps preferable to cross-sex infidelity. The preoccupation in writing of this period, is with women disturbing the system—resisting arranged marriages, running off with the wrong man, not bearing (male) children, committing adul-

tery, producing illegitimate offspring, becoming widows and ex-
ercising the power of that position. In comedies things turn out
happily, in tragedies sadly. But, one way or the other, Shakespearean plays, as much as the rest of the culture, are obsessively
concerned with dangers that derive from women.

"We'll play with them the first boy for a thousand ducats", Gratiano exclaims, betting on whether Nerissa or Portia will bear the
first boy-child (III. ii. 213–14). As Orgel remarks, patriarchy does
not oppress only women; a patriarch is not just a man, he is the
head of a family or tribe who rules by paternal right (1989: 10). To
be sure, women are exchanged in the interest of property relations
in Shakespearean plays, as in the society that produced them. But
the lives of young, lower-class and outsider men are determined as
well. In *The Merchant*, as everywhere in the period, we see a traffic
in boys who, because they are less significant, are moved around
the employment–patronage system more fluently than women.
Class exploitation was almost unchallenged; everyone—men as
much as women—had someone to defer to, usually in the household where they had to live. The most likely supposition is that, just
as cross-sex relations took place all the time—Launcelot is accused,
in passing, of getting a woman with child (III. v. 35–36)—same-sex
passion also was widely indulged.[4]

Traffic in boys occurs quite casually in *The Merchant*. Launcelot
is a likely lad. He manages to square it with his conscience to leave
his master, Shylock, but it is unclear where he will go (II. ii. 1–30).
He runs into his father, who indentured Launcelot to Shylock and
is bringing a present for the master to strengthen the bond.
Launcelot persuades him to divert the gift to Bassanio, who is providing "rare new liveries", for the expedition to Belmont (II. ii.
104–105). The father attempts to interest Bassanio in the boy, but
it transpires that Shylock has already traded him: "Shylock thy master spoke with me this day, / And hath preferr'd thee" (II. ii.
138–39). Nor is Launcelot the only young man Bassanio picks up
in this scene: Gratiano presents his own suit and gets a ticket to
Belmont conditional upon good behaviour. And when Jessica assumes the guise of a boy, the appearance is of another privileged
young man, Lorenzo, taking a boy into his service and giving him
new livery: "Descend, for you must be my torch-bearer. . . . Even in
the lovely garnish of a boy" (II. vi. 40, 45). When the young doctor
claims Portia's ring from Bassanio for services rendered, therefore,
a pattern is confirmed.

My point is not that the dreadful truth of the *Merchant* is here
uncovered: it is really about traffic in boys. Rather, that such traffic

---

4. See Jardine 1992; Zimmerman 1992.

is casual, ubiquitous and hardly remarkable. It becomes significant in its resonances for the relationship between Antonio and Bassanio because Portia, subject to her father's will, has reason to feel insecure about the affections of her stranger-husband.

III. *Friendly Relations*

Heroic friendship is one of Smith's six "cultural scenarios" for same-sex relations (1991: 35–41, 67–72, 96–99, 139–43). In Shakespeare, besides the sonnets, it is represented most vividly in the bond between Coriolanus and Aufidius in *Coriolanus*:

> Know thou first,
> I lov'd the maid I married; never man
> Sigh'd truer breath; but that I see thee here,
> Thou noble thing, more dances my rapt heart
> Than when I first my wedded mistress saw
> Bestride my threshold.
>
> (IV. v. 114–19)[5]

Unlike Portia, Aufidius's wife is not there to resent him finding his warrior-comrade more exciting than she.

In his essay "Homosexuality and the Signs of Male Friendship in Elizabethan England", Alan Bray explores the scope of the "friend" (Bray 1990). Even as marriage was involved in alliances of property and influence, male friendship informed, through complex obligations, networks of extended family, companions, clients, suitors and those influential in high places. Claudio in *Measure for Measure* explains why he and Juliet have not made public their marriage vows:

> This we came not to
> Only for propagation of a dower
> Remaining in the coffer of her friends,
> From whom we thought it meet to hide our love
> Till time had made them for us.
>
> (I. ii. 138–42)

On the one hand, it is from friends that one anticipates a dowry; on the other hand, they must be handled sensitively. Compare the combination of love and instrumentality in the relationship between Bassanio and Antonio: the early modern sense of "friend" covered a broad spectrum.

While the entirely respectable concept of the friend was supposed to have nothing to do with the officially abhorred concept of the sodomite, in practice they tended to overlap (see Bray 1990).

---

5. See Sinfield 1994b: 25–37; and Sinfield 1992: 127–42 (this is an extension of the discussion of *Henry V* published first in Drakakis 1985), and 237–38 (on *Tamburlaine*).

Friends shared beds, they embraced and kissed; such intimacies reinforced the network of obligations and their public performance
would often be part of the effect. So the proper signs of friendship
could be the same as those of same-sex passion. In instances where
accusations of sodomy were aroused, very likely it was because of
some hostility towards one or both parties, rather than because
their behaviour was altogether different from that of others who
were not so accused.

The fact that the text of the *Merchant* gives no plain indication
that the love between Antonio and Bassanio is informed by erotic
passion does not mean that such passion was inconceivable, then;
it may well mean that it didn't require particular presentation as a
significant category. What is notable, though, is that Portia has no
hesitation in envisaging a sexual relationship between Bassanio and
the young doctor: "I'll have that doctor for my bedfellow", she declares, recognizing an equivalence (V. i. 33). She develops the idea:

> Let not that doctor e'er come near my house—
> Since he hath got the jewel that I loved,
> And that which you did swear to keep for me.
>
> (V. i. 223–25)

The marriage of Bassanio and Portia is unconsummated and
"jewel" is often genital in Shakespearean writing: the young doctor
has had the sexual attentions which were promised to Portia.
"Ring", of course, has a similar range, as when Gratiano says he
will "fear no other thing / So sore, as keeping safe Nerissa's ring"
(V. i. 306–307; see Partridge 1955: 135, 179). Portia's response to
Bassanio (allegedly) sleeping with the young doctor is that she will
do the same:

> I will become as liberal as you,
> I'll not deny him anything I have,
> No, not my body nor my husband's bed.
>
> (V. i. 226–28)

Notice also that Portia does not express disgust, or even surprise,
that her husband might have shared his bed with a young doctor.
Her point is that Bassanio has given to another something that he
had pledged to her. Nor does she disparage Antonio (as she does
Morocco). Shylock, for the social cohesion of Venice, has to be
killed, beggared, expelled, converted or any combination of those
penalties. Same-sex passion doesn't matter nearly so much; Antonio
has only to be relegated to a subordinate position.

Bray attributes the instability in friendly relations to a decline in
the open-handed "housekeeping" of the great house. Maintaining
retinues such as those Bassanio recruits—young men who look
promising and relatives who have a claim—was becoming anachro-

nistic. So the social and economic form of service and friendship decayed, but it remained as a cultural form, as a way of speaking. The consequent unevenness, Bray suggests, allowed the line between the intimacies of friendship and sodomy to become blurred (1990: 12–13). Don Wayne, in his study of Ben Jonson's poem "To Penshurst" and the country-house genre, relates the decline of the great house to the emergence of a more purposeful aristocracy of "new men" who "constituted an agrarian capitalist class with strong links to the trading community"; and to the emergence, also, of "an ideology in which the nuclear, conjugal family is represented as the institutional foundation of morality and social order". We associate that development with the later consolidation of "bourgeois ideology", but "images and values we tend to identify as middle class had already begun to appear in the transformation of the aristocracy's own self-image" (Wayne 1984: 23–25).

The Merchant of Venice makes excellent sense within such a framework. Portia's lavish estate at Belmont is presented as a fairy-tale place; in Venetian reality Bassanio, an aristocrat who already cultivates friends among the merchant class, has to raise money in the market in order to put up a decent show. At the same time, Portia's centring of the matrimonial couple and concomitant hostility towards male friendship manifests an attitude that was to be located as "bourgeois". This faultline was not to be resolved rapidly; Portia is ahead of her time. Through the second half of the seventeenth century, Alan Bray and Randolph Trumbach show, the aggressively manly, aristocratic rake, though reproved by the churches and emergent middle-class morality and in violation of the law, would feel able to indulge himself with a woman, a young man or both.[6]

If I have begun to map the ideological field in which same-sex passion occurred in early modern England and some of its points of intersection in *The Merchant*, I am not trying to "reduce" Shakespeare to an effect of history and structure. I do not suppose that he thought the same as everyone else—or, indeed, that *anyone* thought the same as everyone else. First, diverse paths may be discerned in the period through the relations between sexual and "platonic", and same-sex and cross-sex passions. These matters were uncertain, unresolved, contested—that is why they made good topics for plays, satires, sermons and so on. Second, playtexts do not have to be clear-cut. As I have argued elsewhere, we should envisage them as working across an ideological terrain, opening out unresolved faultlines, inviting spectators to explore imaginatively the different possibilities. Anyway, readers and audiences do not have to respect closures; they are at liberty to credit and dwell upon the

6. Bray 1982; Trumbach 1987, 1989; Sinfield 1994b: 33–42.

adventurous middle part of a text, as against a tidy conclusion (Sinfield 1992: 47–51, 99–106). As Valerie Traub remarks, whether these early comedies are found to instantiate dissidence or containment is a matter of "crediting *either* the expense of dramatic energy *or* comedic closure" (1992b: 120; see Smith 1992).

Generally, though, there is a pattern: the erotic potential of same-sex love is allowed a certain scope, but has to be set aside. The young men in *Love's Labour's Lost* try to maintain a fraternity but the women draw them away. In *Romeo and Juliet* Mercutio has to die to clear the ground for Romeo and Juliet's grand passion. In *Much Ado About Nothing* Benedick has to agree to kill Claudio at his fiancée's demand. *As You Like It* fantasizes a harmonious male community in the forest and intensifies it in the wooing of Orlando and Ganymede, but finally Rosalind takes everyone but Jacques back into the old system. Yet there are ambiguities as well. In the epilogue to *As You Like It* the Rosalind/Ganymede boy-actor reopens the flirting: "If I were a woman, I would kiss as many of you as had beards that pleased me, complexions that liked me, and breaths that I defied not" (V. iv. 214–17; see Traub 1992b: 128). And Orsino in *Twelfth Night* leaves the stage with Viola still dressed as Cesario because, he says, her female attire has not yet been located. Even Bassanio can fantasize: "Sweet doctor", he says to Portia when she has revealed all, "you shall be my bedfellow,— / When I am absent then lie with my wife" (V. i. 284–85).

And why not? Was it necessary to choose? Although the old, open-handed housekeeping was in decline, the upper-class household was not focused on the marital couple in the manner of today. Portia welcomes diverse people to Belmont; Gratiano and Nerissa for instance, whose mimic-marriage reflects the power of the household. *The Two Gentlemen of Verona* starts with the disruption of friendship by love for a woman, but ends with a magical reunion in which they will all live together: "our day of marriage shall be yours, / One feast, one house, one mutual happiness" (V. iv. 170–71). In a discussion of *Twelfth Night* elsewhere, I have suggested that Sebastian's marriage to a stranger heiress need not significantly affect Antonio's relationship with him (Sinfield 1992: 73). They might all live together in Olivia's house (as Sir Toby does); she may well prefer to spend her time with Maria and Viola (who will surely tire of Orsino) rather than with the naive, swashbuckling husband whom she has mistakenly married. So Antonio need not appear at the end of *Twelfth Night* as the defeated and melancholy outsider that critics have supposed; a director might show him delighted with his boyfriend's lucky break.

This kind of ending might be made to work in the *Merchant*. R. F. Hill suggests it, and Auden reports a 1905 production which had Antonio and Bassanio enter the house together (Hill 1975: 86; Auden 1963: 233). However, Portia plays a harder game than Rosalind and Viola. She doesn't disguise herself, as they do, to evade hetero-patriarchal pressures, but to test and limit her husband. When disguised as a boy she does not, Geary observes, play androgynous games with other characters or the audience (1984: 58). Antonio is invited into the house only on her terms.

Overall in these plays, Traub concludes, the fear "is not of homoeroticism *per se*; homoerotic pleasure is explored and sustained *until* it collapses into fear of erotic exclusivity and its corollary: non-reproductive sexuality"—a theme, of course, of the sonnets (Traub 1992b: 123, 138–41). The role of marriage and child-(son-) bearing in the transmission of property and authority is made to take priority. If (like me) you are inclined to regard this as a failure of nerve, it is interesting that the *Merchant*, itself, offers a comment on boldness and timidity. "Who chooseth me, must give and hazard all he hath"—that is the motto on the lead casket (II. ix. 21). Bassanio picks the right casket and Portia endorses the choice but, as Auden points out, it is Shylock and Antonio who commit themselves entirely and risk everything; and in the world of this play there are penalties for doing that (Auden 1963: 235).

IV. Subcultures and Shakespeare

Traub notes a reading of *Twelfth Night* that assumes Olivia to be punished "comically but unmistakably" for her same-sex passion for Viola. But "to whom is desire between women funny?" Traub asks (1992b: 93). This was my initial topic: must Shakespeare, for outgroups such as Jews, feminists, lesbians, gays and Blacks, be a way of re-experiencing their marginalization? I have been trying to exemplify elements in a critical practice for dissident readers. Mainstream commentators on the *Merchant* (whether they intend to or not) tend to confirm the marginalization of same-sex passion. Lesbians and gay men may use the play (1) to think about alternative economies of sex–gender; (2) to think about problematic aspects of our own subcultures. But (the question is always put): Is it Shakespeare? Well, he is said to speak to all sorts and conditions, so if gay men say "OK, this is how he speaks to us"—that, surely, is our business.

With regard to the first of these uses, the *Merchant* allows us to explore a social arrangement in which the place of same-sex passion was different from that we are used to. Despite and because of the formal legal situation, I have shown, it appears not to have attracted very much attention; it was partly compatible with marriage, and was partly supported by legitimate institutions of friendship, patronage and service. It is not that Shakespeare was a sexual radical, therefore. Rather, the early modern organization of sex and gender boundaries was different from ours, and the ordinary currency of that culture is replete with erotic interactions that strike strange chords today. Shakespeare may speak with distinct force to gay men and lesbians, simply because he didn't think he had to sort out sexuality in modern terms. For approximately the same reasons, these plays may stimulate radical ideas about race, nation, gender and class.

As for using *The Merchant* as a way of addressing problems in gay subculture, the bonds of class, age, gender and race exhibited in the play have distinct resonances for us. The traffic in boys may help us to think about power structures in our class and generational interactions. And while an obvious perspective on the play is resentment at Portia's manipulation of Antonio and Bassanio, we may bear in mind that Portia too is oppressed in hetero-patriarchy, and try to work towards a sex–gender regime in which women and men would not be bound to compete[7] Above all, plainly, Antonio is the character most hostile to Shylock. It is he who has spat on him, spurned him and called him dog, and he means to do it again (I. iii. 121–26). At the trial it is he who imposes the most offensive requirement—that Shylock convert to Christianity (V. i. 382–83). Seymour Kleinberg connects Antonio's racism to his sexuality:

> Antonio hates Shylock not because he is a more fervent Christian than others, but because he recognizes his own alter ego in this despised Jew who, because he is a heretic, can never belong to the state. . . . He hates himself in Shylock: the homosexual self that Antonio has come to identify symbolically as the Jew.
>
> (Kleinberg 1985: 120)[8]

Gay people today are no more immune to racism than other people, and transferring our stigma onto others is one of the modes of self-oppression that tempts any subordinated group. And what if one were Jewish, and/or Black, as well as gay? One text through which these issues circulate in our culture is *The Merchant of Venice*, and it is one place where we may address them.

Works Cited

Adelman, Janet (1985) "Male Bonding in Shakespeare's Comedies", in Peter Erickson and Coppélia Kahn (eds.) *Shakespeare's "Rough Magic"*, Newark: University of Delaware Press.

Auden, W. H. (1963) "Brothers and Others", in *The Dyer's Hand*, London: Faber.

7. See the suggestive remarks in Goldberg 1992: 142, 273–74.
8. Anti-semitism and homophobia are linked by Fiedler 1974: ch. 2, and by Mayer 1982: 278–85.

—— (1969) *Collected Shorter Poems 1927–1957*, London: Faber.
Berger, Harry (1981) "Marriage and Mercifixion in *The Merchant of Venice*: The Casket Scene Revisited", *Shakespeare Quarterly* 32: 155–62.
Bray, Alan (1982) *Homosexuality in Renaissance England*, London: Gay Men's Press.
—— (1990) "Homosexuality and the Signs of Male Friendship in Elizabethan England", *History Workshop* 29: 1–19.
Dollimore, Jonathan (1992) *Sexual Dissidence: Augustine to Wilde, Freud to Foucault*, Oxford: Clarendon Press.
Drakakis, John (ed.) (1985) *Alternative Shakespeares*, London: Routledge.
Fiedler, Leslie (1974) *The Stranger in Shakespeare*, St. Albans: Paladin.
Geary, Keith (1984) "The Nature of Portia's Victory: Turning to Men in *The Merchant of Venice*", *Shakespeare Survey* 37: 55–68.
Goldberg, Jonathan (1992) *Sodometries: Renaissance Texts, Modern Sexualities*, Stanford: Stanford University Press.
Hill, R. F. (1975) "*The Merchant of Venice* and the Pattern of Romantic Comedy", *Shakespeare Survey* 28: 75–87.
Hyman, Lawrence W. (1970) "The Rival Loves in *The Merchant of Venice*", *Shakespeare Quarterly* 21: 109–16.
Jardine, Lisa (1983) *Still Harping on Daughters: Women and Drama in the Age of Shakespeare*, Brighton: Harvester.
—— (1992) "Twins and Travesties: Gender, Dependency and Sexual Availability in *Twelfth Night*", in Susan Zimmerman (ed.) (1992), 27–38.
Jonson, Ben (1995) *Poetaster*, ed. Tom Cain, Manchester: Manchester University Press.
Kahn, Coppélia (1985) "The Cuckoo's Note: Male Friendship and Cuckoldry in *The Merchant of Venice*" in Peter Erickson and Coppélia Kahn (eds.) *Shakespeare's "Rough Magic"*, Newark: University of Delaware Press.
Kleinberg, Seymour (1983) "*The Merchant of Venice*: The Homosexual as Anti-Semite in Nascent Capitalism", in Stuart Kellog (ed.) *Literary Visions of Homosexuality*, New York: Haworth Press.
Mayer, Hans (1982) *Outsiders*, trans. Denis M. Sweet, Cambridge, Mass.: MIT Press.
Midgley, Graham (1960) "*The Merchant of Venice*: A Reconsideration", *Essays in Criticism*, 10: 119–33.
Orgel, Stephen (1989) "Nobody's Perfect: Or Why Did the English Stage Take Boys for Women?", *South Atlantic Quarterly* 88: 7–29.
Partridge, Eric (1955) *Shakespeare's Bawdy*, London: Routledge.
Sedgwick, Eve Kosofsky (1985) *Between Men*, New York: Columbia University Press.
Sinfield, Alan (1992) *Faultlines*, Berkeley: University of California Press; Oxford: Oxford University Press.
—— (1994) *The Wilde Century*, London: Cassell; New York: Columbia University Press.
Smith, Brice R. (1991) *Homosexual Desire in Shakespeare's England: A Cultural Poetics*, Chicago: University of Chicago Press.
—— (1992) "Making a Difference: Male/Male 'Desire' in Tragedy, Comedy and Tragicomedy", in S. Zimmerman (ed.) 1992.
Traub, Valerie (1992) *Desire and Anxiety: Circulations of Sexuality in Shakespearean Drama*, London and New York: Routledge.
Trumbach, Ralph (1987) "Sodomitical Subcultures, Sodomitical Roles, and the Gender Revolution of the Eighteenth Century: The Recent Historiography", in Maccubin, Robert Purks (ed.) *'Tis Nature's Fault*, Cambridge: Cambridge University Press.
—— (1989) "Gender and the Homosexual Role in Modern Western Culture: The 18th and 19th Centuries Compared", in Altman, Dennis; Vance, Carole; Vicinus, Martha; Weeks, Jeffrey (eds.) *Homosexuality, Which Homosexuality?* London: Gay Men's Press.
Wayne, Don E. (1984) *Penshurst: The Semiotics of Place and the Poetics of History*, London: Methuen.
Zimmerman, Susan (ed.) (1992) *Erotic Politics: Desire on the Renaissance Stage*, New York and London: Routledge.

JAMES O'ROURKE

Racism and Homophobia in *The Merchant of Venice*†

* * *

As the work of James Shapiro and Alan Bray has shown, both the presence of Jews and the practice of sodomy were open secrets in Tudor England. What was forbidden by law was routinely over-looked in day to day affairs, unless a Jew or a "sodomite" ran afoul of the law, in which case his sexuality or his Jewishness quickly became a marker of his probable guilt.[1] Another way of describing this phe-nomenon would be to say that in Tudor times both homophobia and anti-Semitism were ordinarily latent presences; it took some special circumstances to make them active forces. The hanging of Lopez in 1594 was one of these circumstances, which involved the exposure of one open secret and the maintenance of another. When Lopez, a convert, protested his innocence on the scaffold and claimed that he "loved the Queen as he loved Jesus Christ," the crowd responded with derisive laughter, and the proof of his guilt was easily adduced: " 'He is a Jew,' they shouted."[2] Even as the Elizabethan mob easily articulated the common understanding of Lopez's true religious alle-giance, they overlooked a second open secret maintained by his prosecutors. Lopez's chief antagonists consisted of the homosocial network of the Earl of Essex's men, and the task of chronicling the Lopez trial for the Essex faction was undertaken by Francis Bacon, whose openly secret homosexuality was well protected by the Essex clique. At the time of the Lopez trial, Essex was attempting to secure Bacon's appointment as Attorney General, at the same time that he was pursuing a vendetta against Lopez over the resistance of William Cecil and of Elizabeth herself. But Bacon's homosexuality, and particularly his association with Antonio Perez, were probably among the reasons for Elizabeth's resistance to his appointment.[3]

---

† From *ELH* 70 (2003): 378–79; 392. Copyright © The Johns Hopkins University Press. Reprinted by permission of The John Hopkins University Press.

1. James Shapiro, *Shakespeare and the Jews* (New York: Columbia Univ. Press, 1986), 72; Alan Bray, *Homosexuality in Renaissance England* (London: Gay Men's Press, 1982), 72–74.
2. William Camden, *The History of the Most Renowned and Victorious Princess Elizabeth*, 4 vols. (London: M. Flesher, 1688), 4:484.
3. The Perez affair and the pursuit of the Attorney General's position are intertwined in vol. 1 of *Memoirs of the Reign of Queen Elizabeth*, ed. and compiled by Thomas Birch from Anthony Bacon's papers and originally published in 1754 (reprint, New York: AMS Press, 1970), 160. This has led to speculation among historians about the connection between the two matters. See Paul Johnson, *Elizabeth I* (New York: Holt, Rhinehart and Winston, 1974), 371; Perez Zagorin, *Francis Bacon* (Princeton: Princeton Univ. Press, 1998), 13; and Lisa Jardine and Alan Stewart, *Hostage to Fortune: The Troubled Life of Francis Bacon* (New York: Hill & Wang, 1999), 161.

Perez, a Spanish émigré who had been investigated by the Inquisition for sodomy in 1592 and who was particularly disliked by Elizabeth, was one of two "Antonios" in the Essex circle at the time of the Lopez prosecution, and Francis Bacon was intimately involved in the circulation of political, financial and personal favors with both of them.[4] The other "Antonio" was Anthony Bacon, Francis's brother, who had been charged with sodomy in France in 1586, and who was by 1594 deeply in debt for money he had borrowed and passed on to Francis.[5] When Francis Bacon lost the Attorney General's position to Coke and was widely supported by many of Essex's enemies for the Solicitorship as a compensatory gesture to Essex, Coke, who was to become a forceful polemicist against "the shamefull sin of sodomy, that is not to be named," continued to argue strongly (and successfully) to Elizabeth against Bacon's advancement. Bacon's description of Lopez in his *True Report of the Detestable Treason Intended by Doctor Lopez*, that he was "of nation a Portugese, and suspected to be in sect secretly a Jew, (though here he conformed himself to the rites of the Christian religion)," shadows Bacon's own maintenance of his openly secret sex life.[6]

The outcomes allotted to Shylock and Antonio at the conclusion of *The Merchant* reflect the fates of Lopez and Bacon in 1594: the Jew's life is destroyed, and the semi-covert homosexual is excluded from the center of the social structure. The downfalls of both characters are produced by the figure of Christian feminine authority, Portia, whose success, as Jonathan Goldberg has argued, "unleashes energies that are racist and homophobic."[7] Both Antonio and Shylock function as scapegoats to the play's comic resolution, and the asymmetrical parallel between them takes its form from the Book of Leviticus, where two goats are chosen, one to be sacrificed, the other to be sent to wander in the wilderness. Portia's question, "Which is the merchant here? and which the Jew?" (4.1.170), recreates the moment in Leviticus when the two goats are poised to discover which is to get the worse news. Through this double scapegoat structure, *The Merchant* outlines the structural similarity of the positions occupied by homosexuals and Jews in Tudor England.

* * *

What happens to Antonio is structurally similar to what happened to Jews, like Lopez, who tried to become Christians by changing their behavior and participating in Christian rituals.

4. Zagorin, 13.
5. Francis Bacon, *The Works of Francis Bacon*, ed. James Spedding et al., 14 vols. (New York: Garrett, 1968), 8:322–23.
6. Bacon, 8:278.
7. Jonathan Goldberg, *Sodometries: Renaissance Texts, Modern Sexualities* (Stanford: Stanford Univ. Press, 1992), 142.

Since Jews fulfilled the necessary scapegoat roles of embodying both the specific guilt associated with money and the more general guilt produced by a religion that taught its members that their salvation depended upon a blood sacrifice, their conversions were never really trusted; they were always suspected of being "really" Jewish. So with Antonio: his relationships with Bassanio and with other men may not be overtly or actively sexual, but the social obsession with sexual purity means that, for his difference, he is stigmatized and compelled to live the role of an internal exile.

* * *

KIM F. HALL

Guess Who's Coming to Dinner? Colonization and Miscegenation in *The Merchant of Venice*†

Samuel Purchas introduces his popular collection of travel narratives, *Purchas His Pilgrimes* (the 1625 sequel to Richard Hakluyt's *Principal Voyages*), by recounting the virtues of trade. He equates the benefits of navigation with Christian charity and leads his reader into the collection proper by envisioning a world converted to Protestantism:

> . . . and the chiefest charitie is that which is most common; nor is there any more common then this of Navigation, where one man is not good to another man, but so many Nations as so many persons hold commerce and intercourse of amity withall; . . . the West with the East, and the remotest parts of the world are joyned in one band of humanitie; and why not also of Christianitie? Sidon and Sion, Jew and Gentile, Christian and Ethnike, as in this typicall storie? that as there is one Lord, one Faith, one Baptisme, one Body, one Spirit, one Inheritance, one God and Father, so there may be thus one Church truly Catholike, One Pastor and one Sheepfold? (1: 56)

Charity may not begin at home, but it certainly ends up there, as the charitable cause of conversion redounds to the economic benefit of the English world. The initial ideal of "commerce and intercourse of amity" among many types of men is replaced by a vision of global unity that denies difference just as Purchas's own language does. (The singular construction ["one Lord, one Faith"] subsumes difference when it replaces the "and" that allows differences

† From *Renaissance Drama* new series 23, "Renaissance Drama in an Age of Colonization," ed. Mary Beth Rose (Evanston: Northwestern University Press, 1992), pp. 87–106. Reprinted by permission of the publisher.

to exist simultaneously ["Jew and Gentile"].) English trade, rather than fostering a mixing of cultures, will eradicate religious differences, as well as cultural and gender differences, under one patriarchal God.

Purchas's glorified version of the end of English colonization similarly serves to efface the multivalent anxieties over cross-cultural interaction that permeate English fictions of international trade. In uniting economics and Christian values, Purchas highlights the fact that colonial trade involves not only economic transactions, but cultural and political exchange as well. The anthropologist Gayle Rubin notes in her influential feminist critique of Lévi-Strauss, "Kinship and marriage are always parts of total social systems, and are always tied into economic and political arrangements" (207). Likewise, the exchange of goods (or even the circulation of money) across cultural borders always contains the possibility of other forms of exchange between different cultures. Associations between marriage, kinship, property, and economics become increasingly anxiety-ridden as traditional social structures (such as marriage) are extended when England develops commercial ties across the globe. Extolling the homogenizing influence of trade suggests that English trade will turn a world of difference into a world of Protestant similitude. However, it leaves unspoken the more threatening possibility—that English identity will be subsumed under foreign difference.

It is this problem of "commerce and intercourse," of commercial interaction inevitably fostering social and sexual contact, that underlies representations of miscegenation in the early modern period.[1] In addition to addressing domestic anxieties about the proper organization of male and female (particularly about the uncontrolled desires of women), the appearance of miscegenation in plays responds to growing concerns over English national identity and culture as England develops political and economic ties with foreign (and "racially" different) nations. This essay will draw on Purchas's dual sense of the all-encompassing nature of trade encounters and colonialism's alleged homogenizing power to suggest the significance of a brief instance of miscegenation in Shakespeare that has been insistently ignored by critics.

---

1. Even though the word *intercourse* did not come to have its current sexual connotation until the eighteenth century, Purchas's use of "commerce and intercourse of amity" resonates powerfully in this way for a modern reader, and I would like to retain this anachronistic sense for the purposes of this paper. Indeed, this paper will read anachronistically throughout. *Miscegenation*, too, is an eighteenth-century term which has particular resonances for the modern American reader. Like "race," the word *miscegenation* is particularly enabled by later scientific discourses; however, the concepts certainly predated the scientific sense. Although there certainly were Renaissance words, such as *mulatto*, for the offspring of certain interracial couples, I prefer to use the term *miscegenation*, just as I play on *intercourse*, to locate an emerging modern dynamic for which there was no adequate language. [The *OED* dates the term "miscegenation" to the nineteenth century (*Editor*).]

Although the most central—and most commented on—problem of difference and trade in *The Merchant of Venice* is between Jew and Christian, more general anxieties about the problem of difference within economic exchange are encapsulated in an instance of miscegenation never staged. In act 3, the audience witnesses a joking interchange between Shylock's servant, Launcelot, and Lorenzo and Jessica about their mixed marriage:

> JES.
> Nay, you need not fear us Lorenzo, Launcelot and I are out,—he tells me flatly that there's no mercy for me in heaven, because I am a Jew's daughter: and he says that you are no good member of the commonwealth, for in converting Jews to Christians, you raise the price of pork.
>
> LOR.
> I shall answer that better to the commonwealth than you can the getting up of the negro's belly: the Moor is with child by you Launcelot!
>
> LAUN.
> It is much that the Moor should be more than reason: but if she be less than an honest woman, she is indeed more than I took her for.
>
> (3.5.28–39)

The Arden edition of *Merchant* helpfully notes that "this passage has not been explained" and suggests, "Perhaps it was introduced simply for the sake of the elaborate pun on Moor/more" (99n35). Their joking conversation no doubt parodically reflects the investment of the commonwealth in sexual practices. Nonetheless, it also begs the question of the difference between Lorenzo's liaison with a Jew and Launcelot's with a Moor. The Renaissance stage abounds with jokes about bastards: if Launcelot's fault was merely the getting of another, there would be no reason to emphasize that this invisible woman is a Moor. In his *Black Face, Maligned Race*, Anthony Barthelemy notes that this exchange reflects ideas of the licentiousness of the black woman typical of the time (124).[2] However, it may be that this pregnant, unheard, unnamed, and unseen (at least by critics) black woman is a silent symbol for the economic and racial politics of *The Merchant of Venice*. She exposes an intricately

2. Eldred Jones sees this moment as the first glimmer of an emerging stereotype of black women (*Othello's Countrymen* 119). He also seems to agree with the Arden editor. He argues that the Launcelot/Moor liaison is an "earthy basic relationship" which completes a structural pattern of romantic relationships in *Merchant*, yet he downplays the relationship's significance: "This cold douche of earthy realism is not unlike the Jacques/Audrey contrast to the Orlando/Rosalind, Silvius/Phebe love types in *As You Like It*. The fact that Launcelot's partner is a Moor only lends emphasis to the contrast" (*Othello's Countrymen* 71).

wrought nexus of anxieties over gender, race, religion, and economics (fueled by the push of imperial/mercantile expansion) which surrounds the various possibilities of miscegenation raised in the play.

II

Before moving into the play itself, I would like to sketch out some of these anxieties over miscegenation by examining one of the play's possible "sub-texts" (Jameson 81). In 1596, despite her earlier support of English piracy in the slave trade, Queen Elizabeth expressed concern over the presence of blacks in the realm. She issued a proclamation to the Lord Mayor of London which states her "understanding that there are of late divers blackmoores brought into this realme, of which kinde of people there are allready here to manie" (qtd. in Fryer 10) and demands that blacks recently brought to the realm be rounded up and returned. This effort was evidently not very successful, as she followed up that proclamation with another order of expulsion:

> . . . whereas the Queen's Majesty, tendering the good and welfare of her own natural subjects greatly distressed in these hard times of dearth, is highly discontented to understand the great numbers of Negars and Blackamoors which (as she is informed) are crept into this realm since the troubles between Her Highness and the King of Spain, who are fostered and relieved here to the great annoyance of her own liege people that want the relief which those people consume; as also for that the most of them are infidels, having no understanding of Christ or his Gospel, hath given especial commandment that the said kind of people should be with all speed avoided and discharged out of this Her Majesty's dominions. . . . And if there shall be any person or persons which are possessed of any such Blackamoors that refuse to deliver them in sort as aforesaid, then we require you to call them before you and to advise and persuade them by all good means to satisfy Her Majesty's pleasure therein; which if they shall eftsoons willfully and obstinately refuse, we pray you then to certify their names unto us, to the end Her Majesty may take such further course therein as it shall seem best in her princely wisdom. (Qtd. in Jones, *Elizabethan Image* 20–21)[3]

While such critical attention as has been paid to this document concentrates on the attempt to discharge Moors from the realm and uses the attempt itself to prove the existence of a viable black

---

3. For a more complete discussion, see Peter Fryer's *Staying Power* (10–12). Fryer provocatively contends that the second order of expulsion was to make up the payment for the return of eighty-nine English prisoners from Spain and Portugal.

presence in England (Newman, "And wash the Ethiop white" 148), the terms of the proclamation demand special attention. The image of large numbers of Moors having "crept into this realm" suggests that they suddenly appeared of their own volition (despite having been "fostered and relieved" here by unnamed residents).[4] The proclamation then lays the fault of this invasion at the foot of Spain, a country already suspect for its past history of interracial alliance.[5] The rest of the document is concerned to prevent contact between these "creeping" invaders and "her own liege" people despite its contradictory contention that Elizabeth's own subjects are the ones "possessed" of blackamoors to the detriment of the state.

Although chronic food shortages occurred throughout Elizabeth's reign and certainly seemed to be a goad to plantation and exploration, her naming of "these hard times of dearth" suggests that both of the expulsions occurred in the context of very immediate state concerns. England from 1594 to 1597 saw dramatic declines in grain harvests (the staple of the lower-class diet), culminating in the famine of 1597. Indeed, much of northern Europe (although, interestingly, not Italy) suffered from famine and starvation from 1595 to 1597. Although the famine in England hit hardest in the northwestern parishes, its effects were felt throughout the realm, as Andrew Appleby notes, "It is abundantly clear, however, that the grain harvest was the heart of the English economy . . . and that its malfunctions were felt, with disastrous results, throughout the kingdom" (137). Private citizens, the Privy Council, and the general public showed concern over the unavailability of bread even in the earliest of those years. These "dear years" carried with them a range of other social dislocations: a reduction in baptismal and

4. The reprintings of this document indicate some confusion. I have used Eldred Jones's transcription of the 1601 draft proclamation in the Cecil papers, which reads "are crept." In contrast, James Walvin's version of this same proclamation (65) reads "are carried," as does the version in Hughes and Larkin (220–21). The facsimile included in Jones (plate 5) appears to me to read "are crept" and I have thus accepted his transcription.

5. English travel writers, not surprisingly, frequently compared their visions of colonial rule with the Spanish model. England saw itself as in part "correcting" the vexed model of colonial rule in Spain. In his *View of the Present State of Ireland*, Spenser outlines one of the sources of this sense of Spain's mixed heritage, as he suggests that Spain's current riches are the inheritance of a long history of invasion, particularly by Africans: "ffor the Spaniarde that now is, is come from as rude and salvage nacions, as theare beinge. As it maye be gathered by Course of ages and view of theire owne historye (thoughe they thearein labour muche to ennoble themselues) scarse anye dropp of the oulde Spannishe blodd lefte in them: . . . And yeat after all these the mores and Barbarians breakinge over out of Africa did finallye possesse all spaine or the moste parte thereof And treade downe vnder theire foule heathenishe fete what euer litle they founde theare yeat standinge the which thoughe afterwardes they weare beaten out by *fferdinando* of *Arraggon* and Elizabeth his wiffe yeat they weare not so clensed but that thorogh the mariages which they had made and mixture with the people of the lande duringe theire longe Continvance theare they had lefte no pure dropp of Spanishe blodd no nor of Romayne nor Scithian So that of all nacions vnder heaven I suppose the Spaniarde is the most mingled moste vncertaine and most bastardlie . . ." (90–91).

marriage rates, a rise in mortality and civil unrest, and, significantly, the unemployment of servant classes. Key government measures were issued in proximity to both expulsions and indicate that the famine generated a degree of class conflict. Elizabeth's order to make starch from bran rather than grain needed for food was issued in the same month as the first order of expulsion. Another proclamation, ending price-fixing and compelling the landed classes to remain in the counties because "her majesty had thus determined for relief of her people to stay all good householders in their countries, there in charitable sort to keep hospitality" (Hughes and Larkin 172), was issued a few months later.

Equally important in the expulsion order is the reference to the religion (or lack of religion) of the Moors, which is based on the supposition that they are a logical group to cut off from state resources because they have "no understanding of Christ or his Gospel." In this time of crisis Christianity becomes the prerequisite for access to limited resources. Certainly, Elizabeth's evocation of the religious difference of the Moor would seem to support the common view that religion, not race, is the defining mark of difference in early modern England.[6] I would argue, however, that even though religion is given as a compelling reason for excluding Moors, emphasizing religious difference only clouds the political reality that the Moors' visibility in the culture made them a viable target for exclusion. In other words, it is their physical difference *in association with cultural differences* (a combination that is the primary basis for the category "race") that provokes their exclusion—not just their religion.

In Elizabeth's proclamation we see what may be a source of the threat posed by Launcelot's Moor. In times of economic stress, visible minorities very often become the scapegoat for national problems. The proclamation shares with *Merchant* an alarm over unregulated consumption. Launcelot's evocation of the scarcity of food through his jesting over the rising price of pork reveals a similar unease over limited resources. Thus, famine, one of the more

6. Kwame Anthony Appiah is the most recent purveyor of this view. In the entry "Race," in *Critical Terms for Literary Study*, he argues, ". . . in Shakespearean England both Jews and Moors were barely an empirical reality. And even though there were small numbers of Jews and black people in England in Shakespeare's day, attitudes to 'the Moor' and 'the Jew' do not seem to have been based on experience of these people. Furthermore, despite the fact that there was an increasing amount of information available about dark-skinned foreigners in this, the first great period of modern Western exploration, actual reports of black or Jewish foreigners did not play an important part in forming these images. Rather, it seems that the stereotypes were based on an essentially theological conception of the status of both Moors and Jews as non-Christians; the former distinguished by their black skin, whose color was associated in Christian iconography with sin and the devil . . ." (277–78). It seems apparent in Elizabeth's document that there was a black presence that had its own reality for Elizabeth and that religion appears as rationale after the fact.

specific rationales for English colonial plantation and expansion, becomes here associated with the black woman. Ultimately both texts draw on and reproduce the same racial stereotype. Just as the image of the black female as consumer of state resources in the twentieth-century United States is statistically inaccurate but politically powerful, so may the black presence have been a threat (albeit small) to white European labor, which is magnified by its very visibility.[7] This sense of privation produces an economic imperative in the play, which insists on the exclusion of racial, religious, and cultural difference. With the finite resources of a Venetian (or Elizabethan) society reserved for the wealthy elite, the offspring of Launcelot and the Moor presents a triple threat that in this world is perceived as a crime against the state. Their alliance is perhaps even more suspect than the ominous possibility of a marriage between Portia and the prince of Morocco, since it would produce a half-black, half-Christian child from the already starving lower classes who threatens to upset the desired balance of consumption. The pun on "Moor/more" further supports this image of the black woman as both consuming and expanding and is particularly striking in a play where the central image is the literal taking of flesh and where Christian males worry throughout about having "less."

* * *

* * * Economic exchanges with an outsider like Shylock open up Venice to sexual and commercial intercourse with strangers; this breach brings with it the threat of economic upheaval and foreign invasion. Social activities such as eating and marriage resonate because of the already permeable borders of the Venetian economy. In defending his insistence on the completion of a legal bond, Shylock comments on the assumed rights of the Venetians to "bond" and to preserve their racial purity in a speech laden with references to problematic communal activities:

> You have among you many a purchas'd slave,
> Which (like your asses, and your dogs and mules)
> You use in abject and in slavish parts,
> Because you bought them,—shall I say to you,
> Let them be free, *marry them to your heirs?*
> Why sweat they under burthens? let their beds
> Be made as soft as yours, and let their palates
> Be season'd with such viands?
>
> (4.1.90–97; emphasis added)

7. Patricia Hill Collins lucidly outlines the connections between the welfare mother and mammy stereotypes, arguing, "Each image transmits clear messages about the proper limits among female sexuality, fertility and Black women's roles in the political economy" (78). See also Angela Davis's description of specific political manipulations of the welfare mother image (23–27).

Rhetorically, Shylock exposes the fears of a chauvinist culture by revealing the Venetians' problematic economic position, suggesting that, in such an open system, the slaves among them may just as well become sons-in-law.[8] The passage may also tie the problem of eating with colonial trade in the reminder ("let their palates / Be season'd with such viands") that the search for spices for aristocratic palates provided much of the momentum for foreign trade. His questions allow for a provocative glance at Queen Elizabeth's dilemma. Producers of labor are also consumers, and the blacks that she wants to exile are a presence precisely because of the increased economic expansion she supported.

As critics have often noted, the language of commerce and trade permeates the Venetian world. This mercantile vocabulary is tied to an erotic vocabulary in much the same way as Titania's description of her Indian votress in *A Midsummer Night's Dream* links the pregnant maid and Indian trade. Like his companion, Bassanio, Antonio begins the play in a melancholy mood; Solanio attributes his sadness not to love, but to the possibility of economic disaster: "Believe me sir, had I such a venture forth, / The better part of my affections would / Be with my hopes abroad" (1.1.15–17). Echoing the eroticized discourse of actual merchant adventure, Solanio's discussion of Antonio's afflictions as "affections" locates the erotic in the economic, particularly as he makes Antonio's fear of losing his ships sound much like the fear of losing a lover:[9]

> should I go to church
> And see the holy edifice of stone
> And not bethink me straight of dangerous rocks,
> Which touching my gentle vessel's side
> Would scatter all her spices on the stream,
> Enrobe the roaring waters with my silks. . . .
>
> (1.1.29–34)

Solanio's displacement is all the more resonant in its religious overtones and its hints at a loss of Christian belief. Foreign adventure proves a dangerous distraction as the stones of the Christian church provoke reminders of the beguiling hazards of trade.

The potential dangers of Antonio's mercantile involvement with foreign Others, read as seductive sexual union, are offset by the rejection of difference in the golden world of Belmont. Bassanio's discussion of his intent to woo Portia suggests an interesting inversion of Antonio's economic adventures. The narrative of his romantic quest is filled with economic metaphors, and his description of Portia makes it obvious that there is an unfavorable balance of trade

---

8. I borrow this multivalent use of "chauvinist" from Susan Griffin (298–305).
9. For more on the gendering of the discourses of travel and trade, see Parker 142.

on the marriage market. Rather than bringing wealth into the country, suitors are coming to Belmont to win away Portia's wealth, as Bassanio notes:

> Nor is the wide world ignorant of her worth,
> For the four winds blow in from every coast
> Renowned suitors, and her sunny locks
> Hang on her temples like a golden fleece,
> Which makes her seat of Belmont Colchos' strond,
> And many Jasons come in quest of her.
>
> (1.1.167–72)

While Antonio participates in the expansion of Venice's economic influence, Bassanio insulates the sexual economy of Venice from foreign "invasion." In language closely approximating Bassanio's, his competitor, the prince of Morocco, "a tawny moor" (and, we presume, a Muslim), frames his own courtship as colonial enterprise and religious pilgrimage when he chooses caskets:

> Why that's the lady, all the world desires her.
> From the four corners of the earth they come
> To kiss this shrine, this mortal breathing saint.
> The Hyrcanian deserts, and the vasty wilds
> Of wide Arabia are as throughfares now
> For princes to come view fair Portia.
> The watery kingdom, whose ambitious head
> Spets in the face of heaven, is no bar
> To stop the foreign spirits, but they come
> As o'er a brook to see fair Portia.
>
> (2.7.38–47)

Morocco reveals the peril of such international competition for wealth (and beauty). The test demanded by Portia's father expands the sex/gender system by opening up the romantic quest to foreign competition, as it were, inviting both the possibility of miscegenation and of another race absconding with the country's money and its native beauty. Morocco explicitly raises this idea and associates it with England:

> They have in England
> A coin that bears the figure of an angel
> Stamp'd in gold, but that's insculp'd upon:
> But here an angel in a golden bed
> Lies all within.
>
> (2.7.55–59)

At the very moment in which he loses the game by making the wrong choice, Morocco raises the specter of a monetary and sexual exchange in England with the image of Portia as an angel in a golden bed. Although the metaphor would seem to deny the comparison ("but that's insculp'd upon: / But here . . ."), Portia is imaged here as the literalized coin of the realm. She, as object of an expanded sex/gender system, can like a coin be circulated among strangers.

The boundaries of Portia's island are hardly impregnable: the surrounding water "is no bar" and no more than a "brook" to outsiders; Portia herself is the open "portal" to Venetian wealth. The sexual and the monetary anxieties of a Venetian state that is open to alien trade are displayed and dispelled in the casket plot, which allows Portia to avoid the threat of contact with others. The prince of Morocco is thus able to attempt to woo but ultimately to lose her. He also loses his right to reproduce his own bloodline, a right not explicitly denied the other suitors (Shell 72). The momentary threat posed by the prince's wooing is dispelled, as is the larger cultural threat posed by the sexuality of the black male. The denial of his fertility should perhaps be looked at in juxtaposition with the fertility of Launcelot's Moor: the prince's sexuality denied, Launcelot then has license to replace him as the Moor's "cultural partner" and to appropriate her body.

The Morocco scene is only the most obvious example of the exclusionary values of Belmont. Portia derides all other suitors for their national shortcomings, reserving her praise for her countryman, Bassanio (a man who at first glance seems to have little to recommend him). Interestingly, the joking about the effects of intermarriage is preceded by the prince of Morocco's attempt to win Portia and Portia's deliverance as he chooses the wrong casket. Portia's response to her narrow escape, "A gentle riddance,—draw the curtains, go,— / Let all of his complexion choose me so" (2.7.78–79), is typical of the generally negative attitudes toward blacks prevalent at the time, but, in true Belmont fashion, in no way reveals the political and economic implications of her aversion.[1]

The economic issues which underlie the romantic world of Belmont rise to the surface in Venice, where there appears to be a real cash-flow problem. Most of the Christian men, it seems, are on the verge of bankruptcy. Bassanio reveals his monetary woes in the

---

1. In his liberally sympathetic discussion of Morocco's rejection, Frank Whigham acknowledges the racism of courtly ideology by noting that "[t]hroughout the scenes with Morocco the element of complexion provides a measure of the exclusive implications of courtesy in Portia's society" (98). However, Whigham then blames the Moroccan prince for his own loss because of "his statement of defiant insecurity regarding his skin color" (98), which is rhetorically out of sync with courtesy theory. His reading remystifies the color problem by blaming it on the prince. Portia never mentions his "imagery of martial exploit and confrontation" (98), only his complexion; so too the tradition of failed suitors indicates to the audience that his unsuitability is not so much a question of rhetorical decorum as racial "propriety." In Morocco's case, "defiant insecurity" may simply be a sensible response to the racism implicit in Portia's courtly ethic.

opening of the play, " 'Tis not unknown to you Antonio / How much
I have disabled mine estate" (1.1.122–23). Despite Antonio's denial, his funds are stretched and the possibility of his financial ruin
is evoked from the very beginning. Tellingly, Antonio has no hope
for a legal remedy from his bargain because strangers in Venice
have certain economic privileges:

> The duke cannot deny the course of law:
> For the commodity that strangers have
> With us in Venice, if it be denied,
> Will much impeach the justice of the state,
> Since that the trade and profit of the city
> Consisteth of all nations.
>
> (3.3.26–31)

In Antonio's case, the very openness of Venetian trade has negative
effects for the city's males. The protection Venetian law should afford its "own natural subjects" is weakened by the economic imperatives of mercantile trade.

In contrast to the males, the women are associated with an abundance of wealth. As we have seen, Portia comes with a large fortune
and Lorenzo "steals" two thousand ducats along with a jewel-laden
Jessica. The comic resolution of the play is not merely the proper
pairing of male and female, but the redistribution of wealth from
women and other strangers to Venice's Christian males. Portia's
wealth goes to Bassanio, Antonio's is magically restored through
her agency, and, most importantly, Shylock's is given over to the
state through a law unearthed by Portia/Balthazar:

> It is enacted in the laws of Venice,
> If it be proved against an alien,
> That by direct, or indirect attempts
> He seek the life of any citizen,
> The party 'gainst the which he doth contrive,
> Shall seize one half his goods, the other half
> Comes to the privy coffer of the state.
>
> (4.1.344–50)

The law that allegedly gave advantage to aliens is counteracted by a
law that repeals that advantage. More than providing an object lesson for Shylock, "hitting him where it hurts," as it were, the punishment makes sure that the uneven balance of wealth in the
economy is righted along racial and gender lines. Antonio's modifi-
cation of the sentence only highlights this impulse, as he insists
that his portion of Shylock's money be passed down "unto the gentleman / That lately stole his daughter" (4.1.380–81). Lorenzo's final expression of gratitude to Portia, "Fair ladies, you drop manna

in the way / Of starved people" (5.1.294–95), typifies the tonality of the play. Portia does indeed drop manna (which she redistributes from the city's aliens) upon the males of Venice: she is the bearer of fortunes for Bassanio, Antonio, and Lorenzo.

Economic alliances in the play are made with expectations of one-way exchange, which is often troped through conversion. Thus Bassanio and Antonio stress Shylock's "kindness" when making the deal in order to give Shylock the illusion of a communal interest and identity rooted in Christian values. Antonio takes his leave, claiming, "The Hebrew will turn Christian, he grows kind" (1.3.174), a phrase which only serves to remind Shylock and the audience that his "kindness" is still contingent. The pun on "kind" used throughout this scene reminds us that the courtesy and "kindness" shown in the play's world is only extended to those who are alike and judged of human "kin" by Christians. Shakespeare also demonstrates how selective such inclusion can be when the duke, in an attempt to make Shylock forgo his bond, invites him into the community, not by imagining a shared humanity, but by creating a cultural hierarchy which stresses Shylock's difference: "From stubborn Turks, and Tartars never train'd / To offices of tender courtesy" (4.1.32–33). Such rhetorical moves only emphasize that the power of exclusion and inclusion rests with what Frank Whigham calls the "elite circle of community strength" and that the outsider is powerless to determine his status within that group (106–07).

The imagery associated with Shylock in the play reveals an ongoing link between perceptions of the racial difference of the black, the religious difference of the Jew, and the possible ramifications of sexual and economic contact with both. We can see clearly how the discourses of Otherness coalesce in the language of the play.[2] In claiming that Chus is one of his countrymen, Shylock gives himself a dual genealogy that associates him with blackness, forbidden sexuality, and the unlawful appropriation of property.[3] Obviously, Shylock's recounting of the Jacob parable has its own cultural overtones and serves to highlight his religious difference.[4] However, his incomplete genealogy is further complicated by the fact that Jacob, the progenitor of the Jews, robbed his brother, Esau, of his

---

2. Shakespeare draws upon a system of associations between the Jew and the black which is as old as Christianity itself. For a brief outline of the association of blackness with the Jew, see Gilman 30–35.

3. For an excellent discussion of the racial and economic ramifications of the Jacob and Esau parable, see Shell.

4. In his *Pseudodoxia Epidemica*, Sir Thomas Browne uses this same parable to explain one theory of the causes of blackness, replacing the biblical injunctions against disobedience with a lesson about the powers of the imagination: "[I]t may be perpended whether it might not fall out the same way that Jacobs cattell became speckled, spotted and ring-straked, that is, by the power and efficacy of Imagination; which produceth effects in the conception correspondent unto the phancy of the Agents in generation" (513).

birthright as eldest brother.[5] Both Jews and blacks become signs for filial disobedience and disinheritance in Renaissance culture. In the two biblical accounts of blackness, Chus (or Cush), the son of Ham, is born black as a sign of the father's sin. A popular explanation of blackness recounted by George Best in his description of the Frobisher voyages shows the problem of disinheritance:

> and [Ham] being persuaded that the first childe borne after the flood (by right and Lawe of nature) should inherite and possesse all the dominions of the earth, hee contrary to his fathers commandement [to abstain from sex] while they were yet in the Arke, used company with his wife, and craftily went about thereby to dis-inherite the off-spring of his other two brethren: for the which wicked and detestable fact as an example for contempt of Almightie God, and disobedience of parents, God would a sonne should be borne whose name was Chus, who not onely it selfe, but all his posteritie after him should bee so blacke and lothsome, that it might remaine a spectacle of disobedience to all the worlde. (Hakluyt, *Principal Navigations* 3: 52)[6]

Like Shylock's genealogy, Best's narrative gives disobedience and disinheritance a crucial role in the formation of difference. In reading Jews and blacks as signs for theft from rightful heirs, such genealogies may have supported the notion for the English reader that these "aliens" usurp the rightful prerogatives of innocent (pre-Christian) victims. (In other words, forcible seizure of their property is excusable because their ownership is suspect.) The Ham story is a bit more problematic because Ham, the originator of the sin, was himself white. Only his offspring, Chus, bears the burden of the original sin, and the blackness thus becomes a reflection of the nether side of a white self. These biblical "sub-texts" help support the play's central action: a circulation of wealth to an aristocratic, male elite that is predicated on the control of difference. Aliens must be either assimilated into the dominant culture (Shylock's and Jessica's conversions) and/or completely disempowered (Shylock's sentence). Their use as explanations for racial difference

5. Lars Engle argues that this story is purposely incomplete: "It is this relation between Jacob and Laban, then, that Shylock is attempting to adduce as an explanation of his own place in the Venetian economy, and, more immediately, as a model for his relation to Antonio" (31).
6. It is in this same narrative that Best includes one of the earliest recorded instances of miscegenation in early modern England, which he uses to refute the climatic theory of the cause of blackness: "I my selfe have seene an Ethiopian as blacke as a cole brought into England, who-taking a faire Englishwoman to wife, begat a sonne in all respects as blacke as the father was, although England was his native countrey, and an English woman his mother: whereby it seemeth this blacknes proceedeth rather of some natural infection of that man, which was so strong, that neither the nature of the Clime, neither the good complexion of the mother concurring, could any thing alter, and therefore wee cannot impute it to the nature of the Clime" (Hakluyt, *Principal Navigations* 3: 50–51).

allows for the organization of property, kinship, and religion within an emerging national—and imperial—identity.

* * *

With their cross-dressing and their active pursuit of female desire, both Portia and Jessica break the constrains of gender; nevertheless, in a text dense with cultural, economic, and gender conflict, glorifying these women as the transgressive disrupters of social order may serve only to obscure the very complex nature of difference for a changing society in which racial categories developed along with changing organizations of gender.[7] To look solely at hierarchies of gender defines the issue too narrowly and valorizes gender as the primary category of difference. Reading Portia as the heroic, subversive female proves particularly problematic when we place her actions in relation to other categories of difference. While her "witty" remarks about her suitors display a verbal acumen and forwardness typical of the unruly woman, her subversiveness is severely limited, for her strongest verbal abilities are only bent toward supporting a status quo which mandates the repulsion of aliens and outsiders. To valorize such cross-dressed figures as liberating Others is to ignore the way their freedom functions to oppress the racial/cultural Others in the play. Portia's originally transgressive act is disarmed and validated by the play's resolution when these "disorderly" women become pliable wives.

Although I have argued that these women serve in some ways as successful comic and economic agents, the play itself does not allow for the same neat elimination of difference offered by Purchas in the opening of this essay. Unlike other Shakespearean comedies, *The Merchant of Venice* ends not with a wedding or the blessing of the bridal bed, but with the exchange of rings and the evocation of adultery. The only immediately fertile couple presented in the play,

7. Among critics of *The Merchant of Venice*, particularly feminists, there is a great deal of debate over the possible feminist implications of Portia's transvestite disguise. Is Portia truly the disorderly, unruly female preached against in tracts against cross-dressing or are such disguises diversions which ultimately serve to restore patriarchal order? Catherine Belsey finds the play less radical than its earlier counterparts: "*The Merchant of Venice* is none the less rather less radical in its treatment of women as subjects . . . [The play] . . . reproduces some of the theoretical hesitation within which it is situated" (195–96). Lisa Jardine locates Portia within a tradition of "confused cultural response[s] to the learned woman" ("Cultural Confusion" 17) and notes that although Portia possesses many threatening advantages over the males in the play, the play still ends with the sexual subordination of women (17). In contrast, Karen Newman finds in Portia a necessary threat to social order: "Portia evokes the ideal of a proper Renaissance lady and then transgresses it; she becomes an unruly woman" ("Portia's Ring" 29). Lars Engle also notes a split between conservative and radical elements in the play; however, he sees Portia as part of the latter precisely because she is the agent of exchange: "On the other hand, more than any other Shakespearean play, *The Merchant of Venice* shows a woman triumphing over men and male systems of exchange: the 'male homosocial desire' of Antonio is almost as thoroughly thwarted in the play as is Shylock's vengefulness" (37). Nonetheless, male homosocial desire (which can be a conservative force) is also a force which threatens the sex/gender system.

Launcelot and the Moor, are excluded from the final scene. Her fe-
cundity exists in threatening contrast to the other Venetians' seeming sterility, particularly as it is created with Launcelot Gobbo, the
"gobbling," prodigal servant whose appetites cannot be controlled.
Like Shylock's absence, their exclusion qualifies the expected resolution of the text and reminds us of the ultimate failure to contain
difference completely even as the play's aliens are silenced. The
Moor, whose presence may be a visible sign for the conflation of
economic and erotic union with the Other in the rhetoric of travel,
provides a pregnant reminder of the problematic underpinnings of
the Venetian economy.

   In her *Literary Fat Ladies*, Patricia Parker charts the appearance
of dilated female bodies in Renaissance texts. While they are
specifically located within the rhetorical technique of dilation,
these "fat ladies" are figures for the delay and deferral that is a central topos of many important Renaissance subtexts such as the
Odyssey, the *Aeneid*, and the Bible (texts that are also key in the
troping of imperial desires). The chief purpose of dilation (amplifi-
cation or the production of *copia*) is mired in an anxiety over uncontrolled excess; hence the texts become as preoccupied with
mastery and control over expansion as with the expansion itself.
Parker argues, "Dilation, then, is always something to be kept
within the horizon of ending, mastery, and control" (14). Certainly
the problem of controlled expansion reverberates within colonial
discourses of the Renaissance as travel writers and editors struggle
to produce texts which allow expansion but always within the con-
fines of conversion and colonial mastery. In some ways, the figure
of the fat lady serves the same purpose as Purchas's introduction:
the promise of profitable conversion within the space allowed by
deferral of the judgment of the Second Coming.

   These fat ladies resonate within a varied field of meanings associated with the judicial, the temporal, the genealogical, and the erotic.
Although Parker does not specifically name Launcelot's Moor in her
catalogue of fat ladies, she too operates within a similar web of
meaning. She appears in the dilated space of the play that postpones
both the resolution of Antonio's dilemma and the consummation of
Bassanio's and Portia's betrothal. Like Parker's first example (Nell
from *The Comedy of Errors*), she is a large presence that is only described. Not permitted to speak, the Moor still encapsulates ideas of
copious fertility and threatening female sexuality.[8] However, unlike
the other Shakespearean fat ladies, Launcelot's Moor cannot be regarded as "a dilative means to a patriarchal end" (19), that is, as a

---

8. Parker draws on Jardine's connection of the figure of the pregnant woman and her
"grossesse" with fertility and threatening sexuality (Jardine, *Still Harping* 131; Parker
18).

momentary disruption of the text or a deferral that contains the promise of an ordered conclusion. Her pregnancy is a reminder of the dangerous result of uncontrolled crossing of borders, of trade that holds the dual (and irreconcilable) promises of the production of new wealth and of an insupportable excess. The end she promises is a mixed child, whose blackness may not be "converted" or absorbed within the endogamous, exclusionary values of Belmont.[9] This dusky dark lady is perhaps more like the women of the *Aeneid*, perpetrators "of delay and even of obstructionism in relation to the master or imperial project of the completion of the text" (Parker 13). She interferes with the "master/imperial" project of *The Merchant of Venice*—the eradication or assimilation of difference. Unlike other fat ladies, her "promised end" signals not resolution, but the potential disruption of Europe's imperial text, because in *Merchant's* Venice—and Elizabeth's England—the possibility of wealth only exists within the dangers of cultural exchange.

Works Cited

Appiah, Kwame Anthony. "Race," *Critical Terms for Literary Study*. Ed. Frank Lentricchia and Thomas McLaughlin. Chicago: U of Chicago P, 1990. 274–87.

Appleby, Andrew B. *Famine in Tudor and Stuart England*. Stanford: Stanford UP, 1978.

Arens, W. *The Man-eating Myth: Anthropology and Anthropophagy*. Oxford: Oxford UP, 1979.

Barthelemy, Anthony Gerard. *Black Face, Maligned Race: The Representation of Blacks in English Drama from Shakespeare to Southerne*. Baton Rouge: Louisiana State UP, 1987.

Belsey, Catherine. *The Subject of Tragedy: Identity and Difference in Renaissance Drama*. London: Methuen, 1985.

Browne, Sir Thomas. *Pseudodoxia Epidemica*. Ed. Robin Robbins. Vol. 1. Oxford: Clarendon, 1981. 2 vols.

Cheyfitz, Eric. *The Poetics of Imperialism: Translation and Colonization from* The Tempest *to* Tarzan. Oxford: Oxford UP, 1991.

Cohen, Walter. *Drama of a Nation: Public Theater in Renaissance England and Spain*. Ithaca: Cornell UP, 1985.

Collins, Patricia Hill. *Black Feminist Thought: Knowledge, Consciousness, and the Politics of Empowerment*. Boston: Unwin Hyman, 1990.

Davis, Angela. *Women, Culture, and Politics*. New York: Random House, 1990.

Engle, Lars. " 'Thrift is Blessing': Exchange and Explanation in *The Merchant of Venice*." *Shakespeare Quarterly* 37 (1986): 20–37.

Fryer, Peter. *Staying Power: The History of Black People in Britain*. Sydney: Pluto, 1984.

Gilman, Sander L. *Difference and Pathology: Stereotypes of Sexuality, Race, and Madness*. New York: Cornell UP, 1985.

Griffin, Susan. "The Sacrificial Lamb." *Racism and Sexism: An Integrated Study*. Ed. Paula S. Rothenberg. New York: St. Martin's, 1988. 296–305.

Hakluyt, Richard. *Discourse of Western Planting*. *The Original Writings & Correspondence of the Two Richard Hakluyts*. Vol. 2. 211–326. Hakluyt Soc. no. 77. London: Cambridge UP for the Hakluyt Soc., 1935. 2 vols.

———, ed. *The Principal Navigations, Voyages, Traffiques, & Discoveries of the English Nation*. Vol. 3. London, 1598–1600. 3 vols.

9. Black Africans become in the Renaissance signs for the impossible, which often comes to include the impossibility of their being subdued to European order. The emblem for the impossible, "washing the Ethiop white," suggests a sense of submission to a European order. Richard Crashaw's poem "On the Baptized Ethiopian" specifically adapts this as a figure for conversion and the Second Coming. For more see Newman, "And wash the Ethiop white," and ch. 2 of my dissertation, "Acknowledging Things of Darkness: Race, Gender and Power in Early Modern England."

Hall, Kim F. "Acknowledging Things of Darkness: Race, Gender and Power in Early Modern England." Diss. U of Pennsylvania, 1990.

Hartwell, Abraham, trans. *A Report of the Kingdome of Congo, a Region of Africa. And of the Countries that border rounde about the same.* 1597. STC 16805.

Hughes, Paul F., and James F. Larkin, eds. *Tudor Royal Proclamations.* Vol. 3. New Haven: Yale UP, 1969.

Hulme, Peter. *Colonial Encounters: Europe and the Native Caribbean, 1492–1797.* London: Methuen, 1986.

Jameson, Fredric. *The Political Unconscious: Narrative as a Socially Symbolic Act.* Ithaca: Cornell UP, 1981.

Jardine, Lisa. "Cultural Confusion and Shakespeare's Learned Heroines: These Are Old Paradoxes." *Shakespeare Quarterly* 38 (1987): 1–18.

———. *Still Harping on Daughters: Women and Drama in the Age of Shakespeare.* New York: Harvester, 1983.

Jones, Eldred D. *The Elizabethan Image of Africa.* Charlottesville: UP of Virginia, 1971.

———. *Othello's Countrymen: The African in English Renaissance Drama.* London: Oxford UP, 1965.

Jonson, Ben. *Every Man out of His Humour. The Complete Plays of Ben Jonson.* Ed. G. A. Wilkes. Vol. 1. 275–411. Oxford: Clarendon, 1981. 4 vols.

Kilgour, Maggie. *From Communion to Cannibalism: An Anatomy of Metaphors of Incorporation.* Princeton: Princeton UP, 1990.

Massinger, Philip. *The Maid of Honour. The Plays and Poems of Philip Massinger.* Ed. Philip Edwards and Colin Gibson. Vol. 1. 117–97. Oxford: Clarendon, 1976. 5 vols.

Newman, Karen. " 'And wash the Ethiop white': Femininity and the Monstrous in *Othello.*" *Shakespeare Reproduced: The Text in History and Ideology.* Ed. Jean E. Howard and Marion F. O'Connor. New York: Methuen, 1987. 143–62.

———. "Portia's Ring: Unruly Women and Structures of Exchange in *The Merchant of Venice.*" *Shakespeare Quarterly* 38 (1987): 18–33.

Parker, Patricia. *Literary Fat Ladies: Rhetoric, Gender, Property.* New York: Methuen, 1987.

Poliakov, Leon. *The History of Anti-Semitism.* Trans. Richard Howard. Vol. 1. New York: Vanguard, 1974–75. 3 vols.

Purchas, Samuel. *Hakluytus Posthumus, or Purchas His Pilgrimes: Contayning a History of the World in Sea Voyages and Lande Travells by Englishmen and others.* London, 1625.

Rubin, Gayle. "The Traffic in Women: Notes on the 'Political Economy' of Sex." *Toward an Anthropology of Women.* Ed. Rayna Reiter. New York: Monthly Review, 1975. 157–210.

Shakespeare, William. *The Merchant of Venice.* Ed. John Russell Brown. The Arden Shakespeare. Cambridge: Harvard UP, 1959.

Shell, Marc. "The Wether and the Ewe: Verbal Usury in *The Merchant of Venice.*" *Kenyon Review* ns 1.4 (Fall 1979): 65–92.

Spenser, Edmund. *A View of the Present State of Ireland.* Ed. Rudolf Gottfried. *The Complete Works of Edmund Spenser: A Variorum Edition.* Ed. Edwin Greenlaw et al. Vol 9. Baltimore: Johns Hopkins P, 1949. 10 vols.

Walvin, James. *The Black Presence: A Documentary History of the Negro in England, 1555–1860.* New York: Schocken, 1971.

Whigham, Frank. "Ideology and Class Conduct in *The Merchant of Venice.*" *Renaissance Drama* ns 10 (1979): 93–115.

R. W. DESAI

"Mislike Me Not for My Complexion":
Whose Mislike? Portia's? Shakespeare's?
Or That of His Age?†

The most significant issue in *The Merchant of Venice* is of course the fate of Shylock. But this concern has assumed the proportions

---

† From *The Merchant of Venice: New Critical Essays,* ed. John W. Mahon and Ellen MacLeod Mahon (New York and London: Routledge, 2002), pp. 305–320. Reprinted by permission of Routledge/Taylor & Francis Books, Inc.

it has during the past fifty years on account of the Holocaust, the culminating horror in the long history of the persecution of the Jewish race in Europe. Shakespeare, ahead of his times, adumbrated in the play a racial conflict that in the twentieth century displayed in full measure what was still embryonic when the play was written at the close of the sixteenth century. History has unlocked the play's secret. Hitherto, understandably, the bulk of criticism has concentrated on this aspect, almost to the exclusion of the strands that the title of my essay indicates.[1]

For, besides Shylock as the Other, there are other Others like the first two suitors who make a bid for the hand of Portia and have, in general, been eclipsed by Shylock. I propose to show that beneath the apparent surface of the happy union of Portia and Bassanio, following the dismissal of the suitors, lies a troubled text that encapsulates what might well be Shakespeare's own unfashionable predilection for "black" that would run counter to the taste of his times. The contradictions that this gives rise to, in what is "express'd, and not express'd" (3.2.183),[2] set off ripples that implicate even a country as remote from Morocco as India, the complexion of whose native women invites a quite unexpected, dual perspective within the play, each one cancelling out the other thereby creating obscurity. Further, I shall argue that paradoxically Portia herself is the Other with reference to the six European suitors whose very absence is a defining presence, and whose ungallant treatment of her, as seen in their having unanimously declined to make a bid for her hand, is endorsed at the play's end in her subjugation and appropriation of her wealth by her own countryman while she, at the same time, becomes the threatening wife.

I

It is all too easy unconsciously to substitute London for Venice, but the specificity of the play's geographical locale in its title should alert us to the importance of its situation, Venice being approximately equidistant from Morocco and Aragon in the southwest, and from England and northern Europe in the northwest. Hitherto recognized in critical opinion on the play as being one of the most prominent trade and financial centers of Renaissance Europe, Venice has not, however, been looked at for its geographical location in southern Europe that Shakespeare invests with sociocultural significance, contextualized by race and color, in *The Merchant of Venice*. Of the eight suitors, six come from northern Europe, in-

---

1. For example, in his recent book-length study of the play, Graham Holderness mentions the Prince of Morocco only in passing (12, 13, 56).
2. Quotations from *The Merchant of Venice* are from the Arden edition, ed. John Russell Brown (London: Methuen, 1967).

clusive of the English suitor Falconbridge whom Portia anatomizes:
though she approves of his looks ("he is a proper man's picture"
1.2.69), a concession that Shakespeare makes to his English audience, no communication between her and the Englishman is possible because "he hath neither Latin, French, nor Italian," while her
knowledge of English, she confesses, is but "a poor pennyworth"
(66ff). Understandably, Shakespeare makes Portia let him off
lightly, but her remark must give us pause: the text self-consciously
and pointedly disowns its own linguistic identity, English, and
asks the audience to imagine its medium to be Italian—a transposi-
tion unique in the canon—to which I will return in the last section
of this essay. Of the six suitors only the Englishman and the
Frenchman have names, though neither of them becomes Portia's
husband—another point that will assume importance in my
argument.

Further, though she dismisses each of her European suitors dis-
dainfully while discussing with Nerissa their national traits, ironically *they* have already rejected her, not regarding either her beauty
or her wealth as sufficient inducements to offset the risk of being
doomed to celibacy should their choice of the right casket miscarry.
When she expresses her revulsion at the prospect of being married
to a "sponge" (the German suitor), Nerissa assures her that all six
of them have backed off:

> You need not fear lady the having any of these lords, they have
> acquainted me with their determinations, which is indeed to
> return to their home, and to trouble you with no more suit, un-
> less you may be won by some other sort than your father's im-
> position, depending on the caskets. (1.2.96–100)

Surprisingly, this inversion of choice, or rather, of no choice, has
not been commented upon, as far as I am aware. Rejected by the
Europeans in humiliating fashion, Portia nevertheless tries to
maintain a brave front before Nerissa by replying,

> I am glad this parcel of wooers are so reasonable, for there is
> not one among them but I dote on his very absence: and I pray
> God grant them a fair departure. (1.2.104ff)

The six northern suitors have refused to submit to the patriarchal
authority exercised by Portia's "dead father" (1. 2. 25), while the
three southern suitors—Morocco, Arragon, and Bassanio—tamely
accept the penalty of castration[3] for making the wrong choice; after
all, this is what the prohibition amounts to:

---

3. For a well documented uncovering of trace elements of castration/circumcision/canni-
   balism in Shylock's design on Antonio's life, see Shapiro (73–91).

> . . . if you choose wrong
> Never to speak to lady afterward
> In way of marriage . . .   (2.1.40–43)

True, Morocco makes a show of preferring a duel for the winning of Portia, but he submits to the terms laid down:

> Mislike me not for my complexion,
> The shadowed livery of the burnish'd sun,
> To whom I am a neighbour, and near bred,
> Bring me the fairest creature northward born,
> Where Phoebus' fire scarce thaws the icicles,
> And let us make incision for your love,
> To prove whose blood is reddest, his or mine.
>
>   (2.1.1–7)

Morocco's identification of Portia with Scandinavia in the extreme north, as his reference to "icicles" suggests, is, of course, erroneous, though understandable, and would have amused the Elizabethan audience. To Morocco anyone belonging to regions beyond the Mediterranean would be "northward born." In *Merchant* geographical distinctions give rise to distinctive phenomenological perceptions, and it seems reasonable to assume that the ears of Shakespeare's audience were more sensitive to such nuances than are those of today's, belonging as we do to a time when even the distinctiveness of various currencies merges into the all-embracing Eurodollar.

Thus at the very outset the play establishes a dichotomy between north and south: the former assertive, preserving selfhood; the latter submissive, yielding to the effacement of self-identity. While Portia's southern suitors idolize her, the northern suitors reject her, thereby undermining her putative supremacy as a universally desirable object of appropriation. Whereas Morocco rapturously exclaims, "From the four corners of the earth they come / To kiss this shrine, this mortal breathing saint" (2.7.39ff), we know that this is an overstatement from an African suitor who, Othello-like, desires a fair-skinned wife, even as in *Titus Andronicus* the Italian male's preference for the Nordic over the Mediterranean may be seen: Saturninus, after proposing to Lavinia, Titus' daughter, summarily rejects her and chooses Tamora, queen of the Goths, despite her being old enough to be his mother, as Tamora herself observes (1.1.331–32). Saturninus frankly spells out his reason for this sudden transfer of his affections: "A goodly lady, trust me, of the hue / That I would choose, were I to choose anew" (262ff). And a few lines later he declares her to be more attractive than "the gallant'st dames of Rome" (371).

The question of complexion was, and still is, a powerful factor in sexual relationships. As recently as 1972, when a referendum on joining the European Union was held in Norway, the Opposition's blunt question to the voters was, "Would you want your daughter to marry a Sicilian?" Portia of course belongs to southern Europe, then as now regarded generally by northern Europe as racially and physically inferior. The French geographer Jean Bodin (1530–1596), whose works were highly influential and very well known during his lifetime, gives a series of sharply contrasting physical and temperamental characteristics of the inhabitants of these two regions from which there can be little doubt that superiority, in his eyes, rests with the northerners. The inhabitants of southern Europe, he informs his readers, are

> of a contrarie humour and disposition to them of the north: these are great and strong, they are little and weake; they of the north, hot and moyst, the others cold and dry; the one hath a big voyce and greene eyes; the other hath a weake voyce and black eyes; the one hath a flaxen haire and a faire skin, the other hath both haire and skin black. (279)

The text of *Merchant* seems to be imbricated with anxieties resulting from Shakespeare's endeavor to give Portia the traits of the northerners in contradiction to her actual southern origin. A strange unease may be detected in Bassanio's reflections as he contemplates the caskets. An Italian himself, he is conscious that the women of his country are in general dark-haired and, therefore, looking at the gold casket he is not unexpectedly reminded of golden-haired wigs that belie the reality lying beneath:

> Look on beauty,
> And you shall see 'tis purchas'd by the weight,
> Which therein works a miracle in nature,
> Making them lightest that wear most of it:
> So are those crisped snaky golden locks
> Which make such wanton gambols with the wind
> Upon supposed fairness, often known
> To be the dowry of a second head,
> The skull that bred them in the sepulcher.   (3.2.88ff)

And enumerating instances from classical literature of the power that golden hair exercises, Robert Burton (1577–1640) concludes his catalog with an ironically whimsical mention of the use of golden-haired wigs by (especially) "Venetian ladies" so as "to catch all comers":

> flaxen hair: golden hair was even in great account, for which Virgil commends Dido, *Nondum sustulerat flavum Proserpinina*

crinem (not yet had Proserpine put up her golden hair), *Et crines nodantur in aurum* (the hair is tied in a golden knot). Apollonius will have Jason's golden hair to be the main cause of Medea's dotage on him. . . . Homer so commends Helen, makes Patroclus and Achilles both yellow-haired, *in aurum coruscante et crispante capillo* (with bright curly golden locks). . . . Leland commends Guithera, King Arthur's wife, for a fair flaxen hair . . . Which belike makes our Venetian ladies at this day to counterfeit yellow hair so much, great women to calamistrate and curl it up. . . . In a word, "the hairs are Cupid's nets, to catch all comers, a bushy wood, in which Cupid builds his nest." (Pt. 3, Sec. 2, Mem. 2, Subs. 2, p. 81)

The Anatomy of Melancholy was not published until 1621, but as Barthelemy notes, it "codifies opinions that were in currency long before its publication" (155n). Bassanio's reflections come close to Burton's, or the other way round. Bassanio deplores "those crisped snaky golden locks" that turn brunettes into blondes "to entrap the wisest" (92–101) and, twenty lines later, on discovering Portia's picture in the lead casket, describes her hair in the portrait as "a golden mesh to entrap the hearts of men / Faster than gnats in cobwebs"—a dubious compliment in the light of his earlier animadversion.[4] A peculiar oppositional current is in evidence here which, I think, must be attributed not so much to Bassanio as to his creator. If this suggestion is rejected, then it seems to me that we are compelled to conclude that Bassanio suspects Portia of wearing a golden-haired wig, both in reality as well as in her portrait. Here we should recall that Julia of *The Two Gentlemen of Verona*, studying the picture of her rival in love, Silvia, wishes she had Silvia's auburn locks—an interesting chiasmus in terms of hair color—so that Proteus might love her instead: "Her hair is auburn, mine is perfect yellow. / If that be all the difference in his love, / I'll get me such a colored periwig" (4.4.194–96), she resolves, while noting, "And yet the painter flattered her a little" (192). And Shakespeare's audience knew of course that after her execution when the decapitated head of Mary, Queen of Scots, was held up by the hair for the viewing of the spectators, it was seen that she had worn a wig for the occasion, while Queen Elizabeth herself, it was discovered after her death, had no less than eighty wigs in her wardrobe. It is not only in Shylock that multiple perspectives emerge, ranging from a broadly farcical character to a martyred Old Testament prophet, but problematics of race, complexion, and culture permeate the entire play.

The message of the lead casket is congratulatory of those who

4. For a startling analysis of hair as "excrement"—Bassanio's term: 1.87—see Wilson (152).

"choose not by the view" (131), yet Bassanio sees the beauty of Portia's hair as a snare. True, he himself is masquerading under false
colors insofar as his "wealth" is all Antonio's, but to suppose that
Shakespeare intended Portia also to be implicated in the practice of
deception by using artificial aids to her beauty would be, perhaps,
too farfetched for dramatic credibility—despite the clear message
of the text. Perhaps, then, a happier alternative would be to turn
from semantics to biographical criticism, namely, Shakespeare's
mind and art, to borrow the phrase from the title of Edward Dowden's book, one of the great milestones in nineteenth-century
Shakespeare criticism. "In such a study as this," Dowden writes in
his introduction, "we endeavour to pass through the creation of the
artist to the mind of the creator: but it by no means prevents our
returning to view the work of art simply as such, apart from the
artist, and as such to receive delight from it" (3).

II

Besides golden-haired wigs and the entrapment of men's hearts in
Portia's hair like gnats in cobwebs, what is it that causes Bassanio's
thoughts, while contemplating the gold casket, to travel to distant
India? One of Antonio's ships, according to Shylock, is bound for
"the Indies" (1.3.16), but this can hardly account for Bassanio's
thought process. Deprecating "ornament" for being deceptive, he
describes it as

> the guiled shore
> To a most dangerous sea: the beauteous scarf
> Veiling an Indian beauty.   (3.2.97–99)

The Arden editor, Brown, rightly points out that the lack of contrast
between "beauteous scarf" and the "Indian beauty" it veils is deficient, but his explanation—"the Elizabethan aversion to dark
skins gives sufficient meaning to the passage. The emphasis is on
'Indian'" (82)—is inadequate: while the first part of his statement
is most probably correct, being, as we shall soon see, substantiated
by Shakespeare himself in his sonnets, the second is unconvincing.
G. B. Harrison offers the same explanation—"dark, which was not
considered beautiful: see sonnet 127" (599). For Arthur Quiller-
Couch and Dover Wilson the passage is "much annotated and possibly corrupt; but if emphasis be laid on the word 'Indian,' and the
Elizabethan horror of dusky skins be borne in mind, does the passage present any real difficulty?" (151). Likewise John Munro: "Indian beauty means a dusky beauty, beautiful in Indian eyes but
not to Western" (I, 465). Other ingenious emendations offered by
various editors as substitutes for "beauty" are "dowdy," "deformity,"

"idol," "gipsy," "favour," "beldam," "bosom," "visage," and even "suttee."

This raises the question of the construction of "India" in Shakespeare. Does the reference denote a specific region, or is it a generic term for all that lies east of Arabia? As I have argued elsewhere, in *A Midsummer Night's Dream* the "lovely boy, stol'n from an Indian king" (2.1.22), whose mother, dying in childbirth, was Titania's companion and sat by her side "in the spiced Indian air" (2.1.123–25), becomes the bone of contention between Oberon and Titania, the boy's very absence from the play being an overruling presence, and the locale suggestive of a specific region on the west coast of India—the modern state of Kerala—famous then (as now) for its export of spices, particularly pepper and cardamom, to all parts of the known world ("England" 4; see also Margo Hendricks). *Dream* was written shortly before *Merchant* and, given the importance attached to the "lovely boy" and his Indian parents, should be sufficient to disabuse our minds of the pejorative meanings attributed to "an Indian beauty" by the numerous editors mentioned earlier. Neither Shakespeare, nor Burton, would have agreed with them. Burton praises "the Indians of old" for practicing selective breeding, the basis of the caste system so greatly admired by Yeats, "the caste system that has saved Indian intellect" (15–16). "An husbandman," Burton observes,

> will sow none but the best and choicest seed upon his land, he will not rear a bull or a horse, except he be right shapen in all parts. . . . In former times some countries have been so chary in this behalf, so stern, that if a child were crooked or deformed in body or mind, they made him away: so did the Indians of old. (Pt. I, Sec. 2, Mem. 1, Subs. 6, p. 215)

Did Shakespeare know of this practice, inducing him to use the adjective "lovely" for the Indian boy? Thomas Bowrey, fifty years after the publication of Burton's work, explored the Coromandel coast of India and pronounced the natives of that region as "for the most part very Streight handsome featured and a well limbed people" (14).

But my aim here is not to offer an explanation for the lack of contrast in lines 97 to 99, but rather to draw attention to the problem as indicative of the trouble the playwright seems to have had in a scene dealing with appearance and reality in the context of skin color, hair color, golden-haired wigs, Indian beauties, and the general Elizabethan attitude to race. In 1596, the year in which *Merchant* was most probably written, the Queen issued a proclamation for the expulsion of "Negars and Blackamoors" from "Her Majesty's dominions" (Jones 20–21; Fryer 10–12), an order consistent with the opening line of sonnet 127, "In the old days black was not counted fair," which posits the general attitude of Europe to the complexion of the Other, but contradicted by Shakespeare's personal attitude: "Thy black is fairest in my judgement's place" (sonnet 131), and, "Then will I swear beauty herself is black, / And all they foul that thy complexion lack" (sonnet 132). Is the celebration of Portia's putative blonde beauty a concession to "the million," as Hamlet might have said, while contradicting Shakespeare's own predilection? Was he going against the grain of his age by expressing his own personal preference for the dark complexion?

For, as we recall, at least two of his most engaging European heroines are not blondes. Beatrice is dark complexioned and therefore unlikely to attract a husband: "Thus goes every one to the world but I," she whimsically laments, "and I am sun-burnt. I may sit in a corner and cry "heigh-ho" for a husband" (2.1.332), and Perdita, daughter of a Russian mother and a Sicilian father, has her mother's features (5.1.224–26) and her father's complexion, which makes Florizel's assertion that "she came from Libya" (5.1.156), though an untruth, plausible.[5] If in these plays the heroines are presented as unabashedly dark-complexioned, in *Merchant*, an earlier play, the heroine's complexion has ambiguous connotations, the subversion of conventional attitudes seeming to surface whenever the question of complexion is addressed.[6] Thus, Portia confides in Nerissa twice: first regarding her apprehension about Morocco's bid for her hand, and then her relief at his discomfiture. For Shakespeare's audience this, presumably, would have been the "correct" reaction to Morocco's presence. Her first statement, "If he have the condition of a saint, and the complexion of a devil, I had rather he should shrive me than wive me" (1.2.123–25); and her second, "A gentle riddance,—draw the curtains, go,— / Let all of his complexion choose me so" (2.7.76–77) are both, however, contradicted by her categorical assurance to Morocco himself:

> Your self (renowned prince) then stood as fair
> As any comer I have look'd on yet
> For my affection.   (2.1.20–22)

We are left with two choices: either to regard Portia as a hypocrite and a dissembler, or to believe that the last quoted utterance

5. As far as I am aware, stage and screen versions of these plays have missed this point. For a detailed examination of this issue, see Desai "What means?" (311–24). Cleopatra, an Egyptian, is of course dark complexioned as she herself says: "that am with Phoebus' amorous pinches black" (1.5.28).
6. Interestingly enough, Shylock's complexion (and Jessica's) in stage and screen productions of the play are shown as "white" which, Biblically speaking, is incorrect. The Jews are the descendants of Shem, Noah's second son, while the Europeans claim descent from Japheth, his eldest son. Metaphorically, and perhaps literally, this distinction is hinted at in Salerio's reference to Shylock's flesh being "jet" (3.1.35). For some excellent insights into these and other related racial issues, see Kaul (1–19).

Tyrone Wilson as Morocco in the Oregon Shakespeare Festival production, 2001. Photograph by David Cooper. Courtesy of the Oregon Shakespeare Festival.

is expressive of Shakespeare's feelings, projected onto Portia, or, to put it differently, that the negative capability Keats attributed to Shakespeare does break down occasionally. My colleague, Professor Urmilla Khanna, tells me of a production of *Merchant* that she saw at Stratford over ten years ago in which, at the first appearance of Morocco, tall, coal-black, strikingly handsome, magnificent in his loosely flowing garments, there was a long pause as he and Portia stared at each other. Portia was surprised and dazzled. Consequent upon this silent exchange, and based on its unspoken implications, I would like to suggest that at the end of 2.7, after Morocco's departure, Nerissa knows that her mistress has fallen hard for him. With Portia's oxymoron, "A gentle riddance,—draw the curtain," Nerissa looks at Portia for a long moment quizzically, without moving. Portia knows that Nerissa knows: "go," Portia orders sharply, her tone a whiplash. And as Nerissa goes, Portia reassures Nerissa, and the audience, and herself (?) that all is well with her sinking back into conventionality: "Let all of his complexion choose me so."

For Morocco, of course, should be depicted onstage as uncompromisingly black, not brown (Figure 10). As is well known, in many nineteenth-century productions of *Othello*, the Moor was shown in the latter coloration despite his describing himself as "black" (3.3.263; 3.3.387; also 1.1.88; 2.3.29). Likewise, the Arden editor of *Merchant*—and he is not the only one—suggests reassuringly for his light-skinned readers that the stage direction for Morocco being "Enter Morocco (a tawny Moor all in white)," his complexion is, "possibly, in contrast to a 'black' Moor," tawny (p. 32). But from Aaron's unambiguous statement in *Titus Andronicus* regarding his son's complexion, it is clear that for Shakespeare "tawny" meant "coal-black." Aaron addresses the boy as "tawny slave," and four lines later sarcastically observes, "But where the bull and calf are both milk-white, / They never do beget a coal-black calf" (5.1.27–32). Strenuous efforts to mitigate Morocco's complexion from black to brown in order to suit European notions of acceptability are misplaced, for Morocco is proud of his complexion: "I would not change this hue," he declares to Portia, "Except to steal your thoughts, my gentle queen" (3.1.11–12), and Aaron asks belligerently, "Is black so base a hue?" (4.2.71).

III

A curious little scene (3.5) at Belmont that has puzzled readers is clearly a reversal of conventional attitudes in the play to the black skin. In an undercutting and dethroning of the white monopoly on sexual attractiveness, Launcelot—the Englishness of whose name is not without significance as I suggest in note 2 below—has made pregnant a "negro" woman who, perhaps, belonged to Morocco's retinue since she is called "the Moor." The scene has been dismissed by editors as problematic,[7] but in a recent, perceptive essay Kim Hall shows "that this pregnant, unheard, unnamed, and unseen black woman is a silent symbol for the economic and racial politics of *The Merchant of Venice*" (94). I would like to divert her argument at this point into a parallel channel and suggest that this woman is once again an expression of Shakespeare's personal challenging of the stereotypical belief that gentlemen prefer blondes. The scene, a vignette, needs to be looked at in its entirely before such an interpretation can claim validity.

7. Brown: "This passage has not been explained; it might be an outcrop of a lost source, or a topical allusion" (99); Harrison: "The scandal is obviously topical but cannot be explained" (603); Quiller-Couch and Wilson: "We are inclined to interpret the reference as a topical one" (158); Munro quotes Furness: "An overlooked fragment of the Old Play which Sh. rewrote" (478).

Replete with sexual innuendo, it begins with Launcelot questioning Jessica's paternity, then Lorenzo suspecting Launcelot of trying to seduce Jessica, followed by his accusing Launcelot of "getting up the negro's belly," and concludes with a dialogue between the two men in which food/dinner becomes a metaphor for sexual appetite: "stomachs" = desire; "cover" = intercourse; "meat" = the flesh trade (Partridge 88, 147, 192). Launcelot rounds off the exchange by saying, "for your coming in to dinner, sir, why let it be as humours and conceits shall govern": in other words, every man to his own taste, as was Launcelot's for the Moor. Thus, the scene is a corrective to Portia's dismissal of Morocco for his "complexion," for, as Professor Hall drily notes, Launcelot and the Moor "are the only immediately fertile couple presented in the play . . . in threatening contrast to the other Venetians' seeming sterility" (108).

Besides this "unheard, unnamed, and unseen black woman," a suitor who has attracted little or no critical attention is the Prince of Arragon. It is all too easy to consider him simply as the second suitor who will, inevitably, choose the silver casket so that we (as well as Portia) might know the secret of the third casket before Bassanio has his turn. But perhaps there is more to him than just this. If Morocco is represented onstage as "tawny" = black, I suggest that Arragon be represented as dark brown, not white. The reason for this is historical. Aragon was under Roman rule till the fifth century, after which it came under the control of the Goths, until the Arabs conquered the kingdom in the early part of the eighth century: Tamora, queen of the Goths, and her liaison with Aaron, the Moor, in *Titus Andronicus*, reflect this confluence. Consequently there was a large exodus of the European-Christian population and an influx of Arabs which went on until around the beginning of the thirteenth century when Aragon, Castile, Navarre, and Portugal were reconquered by the Europeans from the Arabs, and this process continued up to the end of the fifteenth century, when the last Islamic strongholds in Spain were recovered. In 1516, when Charles I of Spain ascended the throne, Aragon became part of a unified Spain while preserving its regional systems of justice, taxation, military service, and currency (Barraclough 124, 143, 150). At the same time, it should not be forgotten that Ottoman power, though losing its grip in the far west, was steadily advancing throughout the Levant, and especially in Syria, Egypt, Tripoli, Algeria, and Tunisia. Accordingly, at the time that Shakespeare was writing *The Merchant of Venice* in the final decade of the sixteenth century, neither the Europeans nor the Arabs could claim ethnic purity, as has been pointed out by Marjorie Raley in her study of *The Tempest* (95–119).

Shakespeare's introduction of the princes of Morocco and Ar-

ragon as suitors indicates a carefully crafted ethnic and racial semiotics without which *Merchant* is an emasculated text. Readers of
this collection of essays on the play are no doubt aware that unlike
the other major themes—the caskets, the money-lending Jew, and
the legal legerdemain—all of which Shakespeare derived from his
sources *Il Pecorone* and the *Gesta Romanorum*—the roles of Morocco and Arragon feature in none of his known sources and are,
therefore, unless some other source comes to light, entirely his own
invention. Modern productions of the play that elide differences in
complexion among the characters, reducing all—except Morocco—
to a common denominator, are as insensitive to the play's message
as were eighteenth-century productions in which these two roles
were often omitted.

Thus, both Morocco and Arragon are the marginalized Other as
far as Portia is concerned, while she, in turn, is, ironically, the
Other to the six northern European suitors who have not esteemed
her worth the hazard, and have departed unscathed. The "wiser
sort" in Shakespeare's audience who knew their history would have
seen in Arragon's complexion his hybrid origin, while noting his
ouster as well as that of Morocco's from the matrimonial arena as
the counterpart of the Jew's ouster from the mercantile arena. If
Shylock is prevented from "thriv"[ing] through "the work of generation" and "breed"[ing] of his ducats by the Venetians (1.3.77–84),
Morocco and Arragon are literally prevented from breeding "in way
of marriage" (2.1.42 and 2.9.13).

Accordingly, a pattern emerges as to the differing complexions of
Portia's suitors, a detail that directors of the play ought to consider:
the six absent northern European suitors, presumably white; Morocco, black; Arragon, swarthy; and Bassanio, tan. To the extent
that Portia is finally matched with the suitor of her choice, and for
other reasons, the closure of the last act may seem satisfying, as ef-
fecting a reconciliation of one set of values with another in terms of
its treatment of law, commerce, friendship, and love, as Danson argues persuasively, but without any consideration of racial difference. As has often been pointed out in contemporary critical
studies of the play, some disturbing questions remain unanswered
(Drakakis 52; Lyon 131–40).

*   *   *

I'd like to conclude by going back to the point I made at the beginning of this essay: that our perspective on the play should be conditioned by what we know concerning the views of Shakespeare's
English audience on race and culture, and that we should not su-
perimpose London upon Venice—something we might do inadver-
tently. Keeping in mind that the English suitor Falconbridge, along
with the other European suitors, has escaped entanglement in the

"crisped snaky golden locks" that the Italian *femme fatale* displays, we might usefully consider at least one—perhaps representative—opinion stated by a northern European on the sexual machinations of—specifically—Italy's females. In *The Schoolmaster* Roger Ascham (1515–68), an Englishman and the Queen's tutor, cautions his countrymen who must "needs send their sons into Italy" that

> [they] shall sometimes fall either into the hands of some cruel Cyclops or into the lap of some wanton and dallying Dame Calypso, and so suffer the danger of many a deadly den. . . . Some siren shall sing him a song, sweet in tune, but sounding in the end to his utter destruction. If Scylla drown him not, Charybdis may fortune to swallow him Some Circes shall make him of a plain Englishman a right Italian. (831)[8]

The tacit, underlying assumption here is, of course, that the English as a race are honest, straightforward, "plain," while the Italians, particularly the women, are devious, dangerous, "wanton." *The Schoolmaster*, published posthumously (1570) and then reprinted in 1571 and again in 1589, was a highly influential work, being one of the earliest educational treatises to be written not in Latin but in English, offering a spirited defense of English as a vehicle for thought and literature. In this context it is possible to see the author's warning against the wiles of Italian women as consistent with his wider aim to establish the English tongue as a worthy substitute for the Latin. At the present time when postcolonial studies have proliferated as a consequence of the great wave of what were former colonies in Asia and Africa becoming free in the wake of India's independence in 1947, it is appropriate that we recognize the parallel between the attitude of these erstwhile colonized peoples to their colonizers, and, correspondingly, the attitude of the Britons to the Roman empire which ruled for nearly 600 years, from 54 B.C. to A.D. 577.[9] Political freedom is seldom accompanied by cultural freedom.

The preoccupation, almost obsessive, even ten centuries later, of Elizabethan dramatists including Shakespeare with Italian (Roman) plots has its parallel in modern India: for example, Satyajit Ray being given a national award only after he had won an Oscar, or some of the most successful contemporary India-born novelists like Salman Rushdie, Arundhati Roy, and Vikram Seth being lionized in the home country only after they had been granted recognition in the west. The opposite, the "hate" side of this love-hate relationship

8. For Freud, it will be recalled, Portia is the Goddess of Death in the guise of the Goddess of Love (67), and for Goddard she falls short of becoming "the leaden casket with the spiritual gold within" (vol. 1, 112).
9. That Shakespeare named Hamlet's "mighty opposite" after the Roman emperor Claudius under whom the actual conquest of Britain took place is surely not by accident.

is to be seen, or, rather, heard, in terms of the shrill denunciation of certain carefully selected items of western culture like beauty pageants, fashion shows, or the observance of St. Valentine's day coming from the self-proclaimed guardians of the old traditions who, however, see nothing contradictory in sending their children to the best English-medium schools, or encouraging them to pursue computer studies with a view to emigrating to the west. I'd like to suggest that *Merchant* encapsulates similar contradictions.

The Englishmen watching *Merchant* may, vicariously, through Falconbridge, the unseen and unheard English suitor, have congratulated themselves for having escaped the clutches of the Italian community which emasculates its men, including Shylock who is stripped of his possessions not only by the Italian state but by his own daughter, an Italian-Jewess. To them, the entrapment of Bassanio, an impecunious Italian, by Portia might have seemed as unenviable and entirely appropriate as was his reciprocal appropriation of her, an heiress, true, but not worth the risk of enforced celibacy. The global vision of Portia's father in which his daughter's "worth" and "sunny locks" attract suitors from all over the world— "For the four winds blow in from every coast / Renowned suitors" (1.1.167–69)—paralleled and reinforced by Venice's international mercantilism covering Tripolis, the Indies, Mexico, and England (1.3.16–18), remains unrealized, for Portia finally gets a husband from nearby Venice: she marries the boy next door. The play seems deliberately to undercut its own large agenda with which it opened. As noted earlier, Shakespeare does not make the English suitor Falconbridge the winner of Portia's hand—something he could easily have done—but faithfully follows his sources whereas, as is well known, in many other plays he made changes with the source material to suit his dramatic purpose.[1] The significance of what he did *not* do in *Merchant* may well be as important as what he did do in his other plays.

To the Elizabethan audience watching the play, the ending would have seemed to stress the divide between play and audience, not just in terms of the unreality of drama or the distinction between fiction and fact ("The best in this kind are but shadows," as Theseus says in *A Midsummer Night's Dream* while watching the enactment of *Pyramus and Thisbe*: 5.1.208–209), but more vitally in *Merchant* than in any other play of Shakespeare's, in terms of an enactment dealing with characters from another country, another culture, another code of values, even another language, in other words, an *Elizabethan* audience watching an *Italian* play. As noted

---

1. The most drastic change of course being the ending of *King Lear*, but also, equally significant, in *The Winter's Tale* where the jealous husband is Sicilian, not Bohemian. For an examination of this change, see Desai "What means?" (312).

at the commencement of this paper, Portia's admission to her poor knowledge of English is a reminder to the Globe audience that the play is really in Italian, the play that they are witnessing on the stage—Shakespeare's play—being merely a translation. This Otherness that the play emphasizes places the action—the reconciliation and restoration at the play's ending—on a detached plane, a spectacle which the audience is intended to admire but not necessarily empathize with.[2] So complete is this divide that even the miracle of Portia possessing secret knowledge of the safe return of three of Antonio's ships becomes acceptable within the play's picture frame:

> Antonio you are welcome,
> And I have better news in store for you
> Than you expect: unseal this letter soon,
> There you shall find three of your argosies
> Are richly come to harbour suddenly.
> You shall not know by what strange accident
> I chanced on this letter.
> *Ant.*   I am dumb!   (5.1.273–279)

All the men in the play are subjugated by Women on Top:[3] Portia and her minions. Antonio is rendered "dumb"; Bassanio and Gratiano are afraid of being made "cuckolds ere we have deserved it" (265); Lorenzo is suspicious of his wife's fidelity on account of Launcelot getting her "in corners" (3.5.26); and Shylock has been completely routed.

If the perspective I have outlined on the play merits plausibility, then though it be true that *Merchant*'s movement from Venice to Belmont is celebratory of matrimony, of identities restored, of synthesis and integration, it is also celebratory of an escape, not only by the six European suitors but the two non-white ones as well, from a possibly disastrous union with an Italian "siren"—to employ Ascham's descriptive term. After all, in the play that Shakespeare wrote just six years later, which also begins in Venice and then moves to Cyprus, miscegenation (narrowly averted in *Merchant*) takes place, and then ends in disaster.[4]

2. In *Merchant* the names of all the characters are Italian—Portia's identity being pointedly associated with her Roman namesake and predecessor (1.2.165–66)—except, remarkably enough, for that of Launcelot Gobbo whose first name is very English, linking him to his predecessor, Malory's Lancelot, also sexually involved with the forbidden woman. In *Hamlet*, written most probably two or three years after *Merchant*, not all of the names are Scandinavian: Claudius, Horatio, Marcellus, Barnardo, Francisco, and Reynaldo are Roman names. That this period was important for Shakespeare is indicated by his making it the historical setting for *Cymbeline*. *Merchant*, we are entitled to speculate, unlike *Hamlet*, was not intended to have an international ambience but to be quintessentially Italian.
3. A phrase taken from Natalie Zemon Davis' chapter "Women on Top."
4. The most powerful modern evocation of Venice as destructive is, of course, Thomas Mann's *Death in Venice*.

Works Cited

Ascham, Roger, *The Schoolmaster* (1570), *The Renaissance in England*. Ed. Hyder E. Rollins and Herschel Baker. Boston: D. C. Heath and Co., 1954.

Barthelemy, Anthony Gerard. *Black Face, Maligned Race: The Representation of Blacks in English Drama from Shakespeare to Southerne*. Baton Rouge and London: Louisiana State University Press, 1987.

Barraclough, Geoffrey, ed. *The Times Atlas of World History*. London: Times Books, 1978.

Belsey, Catherine. "Love in Venice." *Shakespeare Survey* 44 (1991): 41–53.

Bodin, Jean. *The Six Bookes of a Commonweale*. Trans. R. Knolles. London: 1606. Quoted in Margaret T. Hodgen, *Early Anthropology in the Sixteenth and Seventeenth Centuries*. Philadelphia: University of Pennsylvania Press, 1964.

Brown, John Russell, ed. *The Merchant of Venice*. The Arden Shakespeare. London: Methuen, 1967.

Bowrey, Thomas. *A Geographical Account of Countries Round the Bay of Bengal 1669–1679*. Ed. Lt. Col. Sir Richard Carnac Temple. 1905; rpt. Nendeln/Liechtenstein: Hakluyt Society, 1967. Vol. 12, series II.

Burton, Robert. *The Anatomy of Melancholy*. Ed. Holbrook Jackson. New York: Random House, 1977.

Danson, Lawrence. *The Harmonies of "The Merchant of Venice."* New Haven: Yale University Press, 1978.

Davis, Natalie Zemon. *Society and Culture in Early Modern France*. Stanford: Stanford University Press, 1965.

Desai, R. W. "England, the Indian Boy, and the Spice Trade in *A Midsummer Night's Dream*." *The Shakespeare Newsletter*, 48 (1998): 3–4, 26, 39–40, 42.

———. " 'What means Sicilia? He something seems unsettled': Sicily, Russia, and Bohemia in *The Winter's Tale*." *Comparative Drama* 30:3 (Fall 1996): 311–24.

Dowden, Edward. *Shakespeare: A Critical Study of His Mind and Art*. 1875: rpt. London: Routledge and Kegan Paul, 1953.

Drakakis, John. "Historical Difference and Venetian Patriarchy in *The Merchant of Venice*." *The Merchant of Venice*. Ed. Nigel Wood, Theory and Practice Series. Buckingham: Open University Press, 1996. 22–53.

Freud, Sigmund. "The Theme of the Three Caskets." 1913: rpt. *Shakespeare: The Merchant of Venice*. Ed. John Wilders. Houndsville: Macmillan, Casebook Series, 1960. 59–68.

Fryer, Peter. *Staying Power: The History of Black People in Britain*. Atlantic Highlands: Humanities Press, 1984.

Goddard, Harold C. *The Meaning of Shakespeare*. Chicago: The University of Chicago Press, 1951.

Hall, Kim F. "Guess Who's Coming to Dinner? Colonization and Miscegenation in *The Merchant of Venice*." *The Merchant of Venice*. Ed. Martin Coyle. New York: St. Martin's Press, New Casebooks, 1998. 73–91.

Harrison, G. B., ed. *Shakespeare: The Complete Works*. New York: Harcourt, Brace and World, 1968.

Hendricks, Margo. " 'Obscured by dreams': Race, Empire, and Shakespeare's *A Midsummer Night's Dream*." *Shakespeare Quarterly* 47 (1996): 37–60.

Hodgen, Margaret T. *Early Anthropology in the Sixteenth and Seventeenth Centuries*. Philadelphia: University of Pennsylvania Press, 1964.

Holderness, Graham. *William Shakespeare: The Merchant of Venice*. Harmondsworth: Penguin Critical Studies, 1993.

Jones, Eldred D. *The Elizabethan Image of Africa*. Charlottesville: University of Virginia Press, 1970.

Kahn, Coppélia. "The Cuckoo's Note: Male Friendship and Cuckoldry in *The Merchant of Venice*." *Shakespeare's Rough Magic: Renaissance Essays in Honor of C. L. Barber*. Eds. Peter Erickson and Coppélia Kahn. Newark: University of Delaware Press, 1985. 104–12.

Kaul, Mythili. "Background: Black or Tawny? Stage Representations of *Othello* from 1604 to the Present." *Othello: New Essays by Black Writers*. Ed. Mythili Kaul. Washington DC: Howard University Press, 1997. 1–19.

Lyon, John. "Afterword: Prejudice and Interpretation." *The Merchant of Venice*. By John Lyon. Boston: Twayne Publishers, 1988. 131–40.

Mann, Thomas. *Death in Venice*. New York: Viking, 1998.

Munro, John, ed. *Shakespeare: The Complete Works*. New York: Simon and Schuster, 1957. Vol. I.

Newman, Karen. "Portia's Ring: Unruly Women and Structures of Exchange in *The Merchant of Venice*." *The Merchant of Venice*. Ed. Martin Coyle. New York: St. Martin's Press, New Casebooks, 1998. 117–38.

Partridge, Eric. *Shakespeare's Bawdy*. London: Routledge and Kegan Paul, 1968.
Quiller-Couch, Sir Arthur and John Dover Wilson, eds. *The Merchant of Venice*. 1926; rpt.
   Cambridge: Cambridge University Press, 1969.
Raley, Marjorie. "Claribel's Husband." *Race, Ethnicity, and Power in the Renaissance*. Ed.
   Joyce Green MacDonald. Cranbury: Associated University Presses, 1997. 95–119.
Shakespeare, William. *The Merchant of Venice*. Ed. John Russell Brown, London: Methuen,
   Arden edition, 1967.
Shapiro, James. "Shakespeare and the Jews." *The Merchant of Venice*. Ed. Martin Coyle.
   New York: St. Martin's Press, New Casebooks, 1998. 73–91.
Wilson, Scott. "Heterology in *The Merchant of Venice*." *The Merchant of Venice*. Ed. Nigel
   Wood. Buckingham: Open University Press, Theory in Practice Series, 1996. 124–63.
Yeats, W. B. *On the Boiler*. Dublin: The Cuala Press, 1938.

AVRAHAM OZ

The Merchant of Venice in Israel†

* * *

There are not many instances in dramatic history which may better illustrate the unbridgeable gap between "intention" and interpretation than the case of the stage history of *The Merchant of Venice* in Israel. Shakespeare could hardly have anticipated the possibility of his play being performed for a Jewish audience, in Hebrew, in a Jewish state: for him, the probability of such a contingency would barely have exceeded that of an audience of fairies watching *A Midsummer Night's Dream* in fairyland (and, presumably, in fairytongue pentameters). It would seem that in such a context the whole question of the author's intention matters little, if at all. It did matter in Israel, however, as the public controversies surrounding each of the four major productions of the play since the establishment of the professional Hebrew stage in the twentieth century attest.

What lends particular interest to this case of stage history is the continuous dialogue taking place between a developing national consciousness—one which at no point could assume indifference towards Shylock—and a hypothetical original intention attributed to the text. The period concerned was, obviously, crucial for the development of such a national consciousness, and it may be a unique instance in the history of Shakespearean influence where a play readjusted its meaning to take an active part within the framework of a *kairos* totally different from the one in which it originated. For the significance of a Hebrew production of *The Merchant of Venice* clearly transcends the limited realm of the theatre in an age when a totally new national Jewish identity had emerged; in Israel the play is loaded simultaneously with the terror of extermination and the dilemma of might.

† From *Foreign Shakespeare: Contemporary Performance*, ed. Dennis Kennedy (Cambridge: Cambridge University Press, 1993), pp. 60–73. Reprinted by permission of Columbia University Press.

The first Hebrew production of *The Merchant of Venice* was mounted in 1936 at the Habimah Theatre (later to become the National Theatre of Israel). The director, Leopold Jessner (1878–1945), one of the major figures in the rich theatrical life of Berlin during the 1920s, achieved fame as the director of the Staatstheater and the Schiller Theater. A pioneer of German Expressionism, he exerted much influence with his productions of Schiller, Wedekind, and Barlach, as well as Shakespeare's *Richard III* (1920, with Fritz Kortner in the title role), *Othello* (which he directed twice: 1921 and 1932), *Macbeth* (1922) and *Hamlet* (1926, in modern dress).[1] He arrived in Palestine a Jewish refugee, intending to wander on to Los Angeles, after having started his enforced exile in London.

Fifteen years prior to his engagement at the Habimah, Jessner must have attended the colorful and vivacious production of *The Merchant of Venice* by his contemporary and compatriot Max Reinhardt at the Grosses Schauspielhaus, where Werner Krauss's flat-footed, boisterous, almost farcical Shylock retained almost no trace of dignity in the character of the Jew.[2] For Jessner, who always differed from Reinhardt in stressing the conflict of ideas inherent in the plays rather than their spectacular effectiveness, following Reinhardt's example would have been inconceivable, particularly in the Palestine of 1936. As he explained (and he had a good deal of explaining to do), the play was supposed to remain a legend, though one in which the legendary harmony was upset by the special weight of Shylock's role. His was not to be a patient Shylock, accepting his tragic lot quietly; rather he would be a long-struggling Shylock, who eventually falls victim to the treacheries of his adversaries. Not just one Shylock who was beaten in his battle with Christian society: he was to be The Jew.[3]

Much about the spirit of Jessner's production can be gathered from the musical instructions sent with the score by his composer, Karl Rathaus: the overture juxtaposed a decadent Renaissance world (Italian in color), approaching its end, with a long-suffering Jewish one. In the opening scene, set in a lively cafe—the social center of Venetian "golden youth"—a tenor sang a tune associated with the "Hep-Hep," the well-known antisemitic cry of abuse. As was his wont, Jessner made clever use of his famous *Fessnertreppe*,

1. See Herbert Ihering, *Reinhardt, Jessner, Piscator oder Klassikertod* (Berlin: Ernst Rohwolt, 1929); also Ernst Leopold Stahl, *Shakespeare und das deutsche Theater* (Stuttgart: W. Kohlhammer, 1947), 608–14 and *passim*. For a recent appraisal of Jessner's work, see David F. Kuhns, "Expressionism, Monumentalism, Politics: Emblematic Acting in Jessner's *Wilhelm Tell* and *Richard III*," *New Theatre Quarterly* 25 (1991): 35–48.
2. Stahl, *Shakespeare und das deutsche Theater*, 592. See also John Russell Brown's introduction to his New Arden edition of the play (London: Methuen, 1955), xxxvi.
3. Leopold Jessner, "On the Theatre in the Land of Israel and Its Vocation," *Bamah*, 10 (1936): 6 (Hebrew).

a stairway designed to connect various stage levels—an external parallel to the play's immanent structure. A typical employment of this device to stress a point of meaning in a theatrical manner occurred at the trial scene: the Jew, ridiculed by the entire court, his yellow badge attached to the back of his Jewish gaberdine, stood upright on a higher level than the judge, who sat below, speaking his lines in a thundering voice while everybody froze as if suddenly hypnotized.[4]

Predictably, however, the play roused a public controversy. "In spite of Jessner's promises in all his speeches that his production was to stress only those points which will suit the Hebrew stage, most of the gentiles appeared almost as decent human beings," one critic typically complained. "Even Antonio betrayed that touch of somber decency invested in him by the author." Attempting to guide his readers to a better understanding of the spirit of Jessner's production, the same critic added:

> Had our audience been more moderate and attentive, it would have sensed in Shylock something closer to us, to our feelings, and perceived that maybe even today (and perhaps *especially* today) the character of Shylock, as a symbol, is the expression of the Jew's contempt of those who despise him, be it for faults which are in him or such maliciously attributed to him. None of the many details in the play would overshadow the main point, namely that Shylock recognizes his right to detest his enemies, that he realizes his moral advantage over them . . . When Shylock is deserted by his daughter, his last comfort in life, and when he leaves the courtroom, broken and wronged to the core of his being, one gets the feeling that in this very moment his rightfulness pierces the heavens. Yes, they have trodden him under their feet; they have wounded his soul. Helpless, unable to utter a word, to perform even one graceful gesture to fit fairly the tragic moment, his fire of spirit extinct in a moment, he learns that there is no hope and crashes into the abyss opening before him. But the fiery spirit of rage which has left this broken Jew is to haunt the world for ages to come. That is what Shylock symbolizes—the humiliation of Israel, for which there is no pardon in the world for ever and ever![5]

While these were the words of one of Jessner's defenders, others voiced different views. In a mock public trial, organized by the theatre itself and in which Jessner took part as one of the three prosecuted (the author, the theatre, and the director), Shakespeare, though acknowledgment was made to his greatness as a writer, was

4. *Bamah* 11–12 (1937): 31 (Hebrew).
5. Ya'akov Fikhman, "On the Classical Theatre," *Bamah* 11–12 (1937): 8 (Hebrew).

accused of writing "a play in which he invoked an anti-Jewish theme without being informed enough to treat his subject, in a way which produced a false, fictitious, impossible character, interpreted with a strong antisemitic approach, if not on purpose then at least erroneously."[6]

*   *   *

Twenty-three years later, the heroic pathos characterizing Jewish reality in Palestine was considerably modified. The struggle for liberation over, the Israeli community was undergoing a process of stabilization in its eleven-year-old state. And though the Israeli national character was still precarious and highly vulnerable, and the memory of the Jewish Holocaust still fresh, one could now more easily risk a presentation of *The Merchant of Venice* where Shylock was to be exempt from carrying the full weight of Jewish history on his shoulders. This time it was a non-Jewish director, Tyrone Guthrie, who came over to the Habimah (where he had directed a much-acclaimed production of *Oedipus Rex* in 1947) to revive the controversial play. And although the same two actors again alternated the part of Shylock, a significant change of focus was generally expected. Said Meskin:

> When I first played Shylock, I stressed mainly the national, pathetic element. This time I shall endeavor to portray a more human Shylock: he has got a measure of fanaticism—but he has his weaknesses as well. Guthrie has told me that at the beginning of the play Shylock is a thriving merchant, a kind of Rothschild. This has given me much help. I have even obtained a picture of Rothschild.[7]

In Guthrie's modern-dress production, Shylock did indeed physically resemble "a kind of Rothschild." If Jessner's fame as a Shakespearean director rested mainly on his productions of the tragedies, Guthrie felt more at home in Shakespearean comedy, and his production attempted to coax the play as far as possible into that realm. In a busy Venice, he devised a lively and rapid succession of entrances and exits, with Salerio and Solanio portrayed as a pair of American businessmen holding their umbrellas in the rain while passing comments on city affairs, with Gratiano constantly on the move in a dancing step, humming merry jazz tunes—a persistent association of decadent Renaissance Italy with modern American life.

*   *   *

6. *Bamah* 11–12: 24 (Hebrew).
7. In an interview with Michael Ohad, *Dvar Hashavu'a* (Hebrew: February 1959). Guthrie himself opens his introduction to the play in *Shakespeare: Ten Great Plays* (New York, 1962) in the same spirit: "Who is the merchant of Venice? Shylock's part is the most striking and effective, and he is arguably a merchant." Reprinted in Guthrie, *In Various Directions: A View of Theatre* (London: Michael Joseph, 1965).

The next production of *The Merchant of Venice* on the Israeli stage occurred after the most significant experience undergone by national consciousness since the founding of the state in 1948: the 1967 war, which had a dramatic effect on the nation's mentality. The prevailing sense of persecution and self-defensiveness, so far an infinite resource for rationalizing any mistake made in the name of security or any moral conflict resulting from the rights, or "positive discrimination," of Jews in Israel, from now on had to allow for the manifest reality of occupation and might. The euphoric period which followed the war (at least until 1973) was characterized by growing feelings of national pride up to the point of vanity, not unlike those of the Elizabethans in the years immediately following the victory over the Armada. It was now reasonably safe to assume that the self-confident audience would be able to stomach a totally different, non-apologetic approach to the play.

This was the situation when, in 1972, an Israeli-born director addressed himself to the play for the first time in Israel. The "native view" permitted a portrayal of Shylock in the least favorable and most grotesque manner, as if coming directly from the heavily biased drawings of Jews in the Middle Ages. In Yossi Yzraeli's production of the play at the Cameri Theatre of Tel Aviv, everything was far removed from realism: Shylock, in a dark robe and a black bell-shaped hat, stood out among blonde Venetians, all clad in white, against abstract scenery consisting of a white back wall and a white rostrum. Tubal, in black, served only to underline the foreign look of the Jew, while Jessica (not unpredictably) wore a striped dress, with lines of black and white, following her conversion.

One of the major features which marked the production was its persistent departure from the individuality of character. I have dwelt elsewhere on one example of this practice, the experimental doubling of Morocco and Arragon, both played by the actor playing Bassanio, and thus lending a reinforced unity to the choice of the three caskets.[8] If this device might still have been accommodated within the boundaries of realistic characterization (e.g., Bassanio eliminating alternatives in disguise), making all the Christians in Venice look alike transcended the boundaries of individuality to the point of rendering them, in some respects, as a collective entity. Typical of this approach was the treatment of Antonio in the trial scene: the stage was totally bare but for a black stool on which Antonio sat with a huge black cross fastened to his back. Thus made a type of Christ, Antonio himself did not become an object of empathy; the pathos and compassion evoked by the scene were

---

8. See Avraham Oz, "The Doubling of Parts in Shakespearean Comedy: Some Questions of Theory and Practice," in *Shakespearean Comedy*, ed. Maurice Charney (New York: New York Literary Forum, 1980), 175–82.

directed to the figure of Christ beyond him rather than to Antonio in person.

The action was further circumscribed by a surrounding framework: the show opened with a Passion-like procession, with mummers in masks, and Shylock, his Jewish nose grotesquely prolonged, bending under the weight of the cross. Another symbolic procession followed the trial scene. But the most dominant element of this enveloping framework was the constant presence of a puppet theatre peering over the white back wall, reflecting, reverberating, and multiplying the action underneath by means of puppets in the likeness of the actual characters on stage. The puppet-show was used as a visual commentary on the action, sometimes comically imitating it, sometimes making visual interscenic connections, and occasionally even providing alternative action. The most outstanding example of the latter practice occurred when, as the background to Lorenzo's exhortation on music (act 5, scene I), the puppet-play enacted a symbolic ritual in which Shylock was baptized by the Christians.

The production, though in many respects lively and entertaining, was considered an artistic (and box-office) failure, its symbolism much too obvious and far from convincing.[9] Predictably, much of the critical controversy focused on the portrayal of Shylock. Even though, in the final analysis, Yzraeli's interpretation was meant to render Shylock as the victim of a sterile Christian society, his intentions were thwarted, for much of the audience, by the Jew's repellent appearance and mannerisms. Unlike Jessner and Guthrie, who chose for the part typically heroic actors, Yzraeli gave the role to a notable comedian, Avner Hyskiahu, whose style of delivery generally consists of a nervous staccato. Under the director's instructions, Hyskiahu played Shylock as "a shrewd old Jew, his posture, his gait, his manner of speaking reflecting a life spent making shrewd, furtive money deals, a man accustomed to abuse. He delivers his key speech ("Hath not a Jew eyes?") snarling at the two *goyim* [gentiles], practically spitting in their faces. He is a worm turned, but still a worm."[1] The controversy over the production once again served to expose the age-old prejudices concerning the play:

> It is but natural that we Jews are practically allergic to a typical antisemitic interpretation, which blurs Shylock's cry of pain and protest, stirring the heart of any human being, be it a Jew, a Christian, or other. In this the play was deprived of its

9. Originally, Yzraeli planned to set the play within a large cathedral, somewhere in Europe, where the townsfolk were mounting a Passion play with the local Jew forced to play the villain of the piece. This was abandoned during rehearsals, giving rise to a somewhat patched-up framework which eventually circumscribed the actual production.

1. M. Kohanski, *The Jerusalem Post*, 24 Mar. 1972.

tragic power and poetic flavour which are, in spite of the various amusing moments abounding in *The Merchant of Venice*,
the very core of the play.[2]

This, however, was a fairly moderate reaction. Not surprisingly, the
production in general, and the portrayal of Shylock in particular,
were most fiercely attacked by the more radically nationalistic
press.

Avner Hyskiahu repeated Shylock in yet a different production,
in 1980, again at the Cameri Theatre, directed this time by a non-
Jewish director from the Royal Shakespeare Company, Barry Kyle.
In many ways Kyle's production was not distinguishable from any
likely production of the play at his home theatre in Stratford. Set in
no specific locality or period (Portia was dressed as a typical Renaissance lady while Launcelot Gobbo appeared on stage riding an
ancient motorcyle), Christopher Morley's impressive scenery subtly
captured the symbolism of the three caskets: a golden back wall
(made of shutters typical of Tel Aviv verandas) and golden bridges,
surrounding waters of silver hue, and a lead-colored central plat-
form.

In his program note (entitled "Two Outcasts of Society: Shylock
and Antonio") Kyle stressed the allegorical significance of the play,
as his interpretation attempted to communicate it:

> The money world, though bound by contracts and stamped by
> passion, must depend on friendship.

Kyle marked value as binding together the two stories of the plot:
the value of friendship, of marriage pledge, and of money. Time has
turned Shylock into a racist stereotype; yet in the play Shylock is
condemned not because of his Jewishness but because he lets
money rule him. This condemnation has nothing to do with anti-
semitism, says Kyle, since it also applies to the Prince of Morocco
and Arragon, as well as to the young Christians of Venice, including
Bassanio. Shylock, whose world is stamped by gold and silver, ig-
nores the quality of mercy. Once wronged, Kyle said in his initial
talk to the actors, Shylock easily falls prey to revenge in succumbing to the logic and mentality of terrorism. Triggering one of the
most charged terms in the life of the Middle East, Kyle allowed the
tokens of local topicality to penetrate his conception of the play.

Such an attitude towards "a fellow countryman," however,
proved an obstacle even for actors who took part in the production
itself. At a certain point during rehearsals, Kyle was persuaded by
some of the actors (though not before a thorough argument with
many of the others) that in order for the message of concord and

2. Hayim Gamzu, *Ha'aretz* (Hebrew), 20 Mar. 1972.

love to be accepted by the target audience, Antonio's first stipulation regarding Shylock's conversion had better be dropped. Thus, while in 1972 the ritual symbolizing Shylock's baptism was virtually enacted on stage, no mention of his possible conversion was made to the audience of 1980, polarized between cultural assimilation with the west and a fervent, often fundamentalist search for traditional roots. It was the radically nationalistic part of the audience who failed to notice Kyle's conception of Shylock as "succumbing to the logic and mentality of terrorism." Social, economic, and political circumstances in Israel in the 1980s, a second decade of occupying another people's homeland, have had their effect of the national consciousness. Looking back on the long history of Jewish suffering up to the Holocaust, many in Israel have made it a flag "not to be made a soft and dull eyed fool, to shake the head, relent and sigh, and yield to [gentile] intercessors" (3.3.14–16). For those, Shylock's cry of defiance, "My deeds upon my head" (4.1.202) was justified in context, since "Jewish" and "the logic and mentality of terrorism" had become mutually exclusive concepts. This strange mixture of resenting Shakespeare's alleged antisemitism and identifying with Shylock's motives lent special significance to a topical image of a terrorist act, which, in the political context of the Middle East, is hardly confined to any one-sided allegorical interpretation.

Even though Kyle's production failed to make its political point, it was a crucial step towards setting the play in the contemporary Israeli context. Kyle's attitude towards Shylock surely would have antagonized the old historicist school, for the term "terrorism" could enter neither the discourse nor the supposed "master narrative" of the Renaissance. But there is another, more basic difficulty. From the stance of normative social order, terrorism must signify crime. Terrorism may not necessarily be politically motivated; but Shylock convinces neither the Venetian court nor the majority of Shakespeare's critics in his motiveless malignity. What is he, then? A political dissenter? And if so, what would be the moral position of a political terrorist in the Renaissance? Within the discourse of crime, the term "political terrorism," meaning the use of violence to press individuals or society to meet political demands, may betray a peculiar sense of moral (if not legal) legitimation. As Uri Eisenzweig argues, the physical reality of terrorism "appears to be dramatically unquestionable," whereas its actual legal content is missing from most judicial systems.[3] While terrorism must emanate from a logical procedure which stands outside the normative order, it draws for its validity on a different, meta-normative order, which

3. See Uri Eisenzweig, "Terrorism in Life and in Real Literature," *Diacritics* (Fall 1988): 32.

recognizes the dominant ideology as only one of several orders competing in the sociopolitical consciousness. Such an extra-official validity has no place in any legitimate code of values, and thus it may exist exclusively in the realm of text. The performative nature of the terrorist text thus becomes indispensable in this process. It is the word of Shylock's bond which becomes the symbolic, hence the essential, meaning of the terrorist act he performs. The consummation of the act of terrorism is not the actual deed (such as the cutting of the pound of flesh), nor is its author's real identity (as a Jew, a moneylender, or a Pantaloon) of necessary significance at the crucial moment. This may explain the discrepancy between Shylock's prominence in the play and his relatively brief presence on the scene, as well as his much-debated absence from the play after the trial scene.

And yet the legal content of terrorism, missing from most judicial systems, does reside in Shakespeare's Venetian book of laws. Any play composed during the reign of Elizabeth could not ignore the constant danger of contrivance by strangers, which may explain the peculiarly anti-alien nature of Shakespeare's Venetian legislation that otherwise pretends to be liberal and egalitarian. There is no sense in which such a private assault contrived by one individual against another should be distinguished ethnically or nationally, unless that distinction between alien and citizen implies an act of political subversion, or, in other words, political terrorism.

Shylock does not belong with those precursors of modern terrorism, such as Brutus, who use violence against tyranny. Yet if Shylock does not take hostages illegally, his act of appropriating the law itself is not entirely devoid of ideological grounds. Hardly an Iago-like "motive-hunter," Shylock provides some solid reasons for his stubborn insistence on his bond, none of which has to do with ideology; and yet some tokens of ideological motivation are still betrayed in his behavior. To cite but one example, whether or not we are to believe Jessica's evidence concerning her father's initial intentions to harm Antonio, her reference to Tubal and Chus as Shylock's "countrymen" (3.2.284) is telling. We do not know which is their common "country" of origin, but this expression, together with Shylock's repeated references to his "nation" and "tribe," casts an ideological shade on his attitude throughout the play.

Beside the particular case of his Jewishness, Shylock represents a more generally subversive element within the dominant Christian, capitalist order in Venice. Together with Othello he belongs in the company of "aliens," whose danger to the ideological integrity of the Venetian ruling class is so menacing that special legislation had to be issued to curb their rights and activities within the liberal state. Shylock is no self-styled machiavel like Marlowe's Barabas, who defies the law entirely. Thus his complaint cannot find any institutional outlet until his specific function within the trade-capitalist process which moves Venetian economy is directly addressed. Significantly enough, this opportunity occurs when emotion is mixed with business: the financial implications of court-ing Portia belong to the subversive parts of "pure" love in the same way that Shylock the alien is a necessary constituent of the Vene-tian economic system. Once Shylock is allowed to interfere with the financial operations of Venice's prince of merchants, the sub-versive process of rebellion is set in motion.

Throughout the play Shylock is consistently urged to adopt a "gentle" attitude ("We all expect a gentle answer, Jew"). This is but another way of demanding that he embrace a "gentile" ideology, a demand which is finally imposed on him legally with the verdict of the trial, which suddenly turns out to be his own. Shylock's percep-tion of the law of Venice is indeed "alien," since the use he makes of the Venetian constitution rests on the word of the law but con-tradicts its spirit. It is, in fact, the very essence of Shylock's terror-ism: he consciously subverts the soul of Venetian order, namely its book of laws, and turns it upon itself. The only counter-measure Venice could take against Shylock's act of legal terrorism is to sub-vert the spirit of language on which the law rests in order to re-establish the normal procedures of justice and social order by which Venice's mainstream ideology abides. And it is significant that this is brought about by an "alien" of a different order, a woman disguised as a man, a country feudal who comes from afar, in order and in time.

Unlike his modern counterparts, Shylock never dreams of insti-tuting a new order, where the ruling authorities will emanate from below, equally representing all the town's residents. His imaginary example of abolishing slavery (4.1.90–98) remains a parable, with-out anybody knowing his own opinion on the matter. We do not even know for sure whether he would have pursued his murderous act to the very end, had not Portia's "tarry" stopped him at the last moment. Nor is it crucial for us, or even for Shakespeare, to know, since, as we have noted before, the terrorist act performed by Shy-lock is consummated on the textual or symbolic level. As Grant Wardlaw is not alone in arguing, "terrorism is primarily theatre."[4] The gist of this notion is nothing but an extension of the textual identity of the terrorist act, as it is often expressed by a note or a telephone call which brings it to public attention, into the perfor-mative ritual of the theatrical gesture. Shylock need not act further, since, as the play as a whole shows us, his function in the plot is

---

4. Grant Wardlaw, *Political Terrorism* (Cambridge: Cambridge University Press, 1982), 38.

nothing but that of a catalyst. It is, in other words, the reaction of normative society to an extraterritorial act that the play is about.

Without resorting to the critical fallacies of traditional historicism, *The Merchant of Venice* may still be made to show us the ways in which, by temporarily taking hostage the Venetian law, and while the entire audience of the theatre of terrorism hold their breath, Shylock manages to bring forth the very target of political terrorism, exposing the moral fragility of the dominant ideology. His act succeeds in undermining the notion of reality as integrated and rational, as appropriated by the dominant ideology. In his *Geschichtsphilosophische Thesen* Walter Benjamin tells us that only from the stance of the victors is history viewed as a unitary process. In this respect Shylock is a loser. But as a political terrorist he celebrates the losers' victory in naming the name of the game. In this he disappears as a Jew, or a Pantaloon, or even as an "alien" in the general sense. As the author and perpetrator of the "terrorist" text of his bond he coerces the legal system to produce a counter-terrorist text of a similar nature, whereby it exposes itself, at least for one cathartic moment, to its own ideological limitations.

It is hard to predict to what extent the future stage history of *The Merchant of Venice* in Israel will reflect sociopolitical developments in the way it has been doing in the past century, or what course it may take. I believe that the intricate view of Shylock as representing the ideological complexities of terrorism, initially propounded in Barry Kyle's production, may shed new light on the age-old apologetic approach to the play, adopted in its stage and critical history by Jews and non-Jews alike. The easy transformation of Shylock from one form of minority affiliation to another renders the ideological content of the play more general. In a very peculiar way it is expressed in Rafi Bokai's film *Avanti Popolo* (Israel, 1986), which depicts the escape of two Egyptian soldiers through the Israeli lines in Sinai in the attempt to reach the Egyptian border. When captured by a group of Israeli soldiers one of the two Egyptians starts to recite Shylock's "hath not a Jew eyes" speech. An Israeli soldier comments: "He has changed the parts!" Has he, indeed? Portia, clad as a young male judge, opens the process of justice in the Venetian court, asking: "Which is the merchant here? and which the Jew?" (4.1.170). It is the very question that any judicious reading of the play must attempt to leave open.

REWRITINGS AND APPROPRIATIONS

JOHN CUNNINGHAM

[Prologue for a Revival of *The Merchant of Venice* at the Time of the Parliamentary Bill for Naturalizing the Jews]†

'Twixt the sons of the stage without pensions or places[1]
And the vagabond Jews[2] are some similar cases.
Since time out of mind, or[3] they're wronged much by slander,
Both lawless alike have been sentenced to wander.
Then faith, 'tis full time we[4] appeal to the nation
To be joined in this bill for na-tu-ra-li-za-ti-on.
Lard,[5] that word's so uncouth! 'Tis so irksome to speak it!
But 'tis Hebrew, I believe, and that's taste, as I take it.

Well, now to the point: I'm sent here with commission
To present this fair circle[6] our humble petition.
But conscious what hopes we should have of succeeding
Without (as they phrase it) sufficiently bleeding;
And convinced we've no funds, nor old gold we can rake up,
Like our good brothers, Abraham, Isaac, and Jacob;
We must frankly confess we have nought to present ye
But Shakespeare's old sterling—pray let it content ye.

Old Shylock the Jew, whom we mean to restore ye.
Was naturalized oft by your fathers before ye.
Then take him tonight to your kindest compassion;
For to countenance Jews is the pink[7] of the fashion.

---

† From *Poems, Chiefly Pastoral* (1766), pp. 165–66. The poem's full title in the source is "A Prologue Spoke by Mrs. G——, in an Itinerant Company, on Reviving *The Merchant of Venice* at the Time of the Bill Passing for Naturalizing the Jews." The date of this parliamentary legislation was 1753. The bill aroused such strong antisemitic sentiment in Britain that it was repealed in 1760. All notes are the Editor's.
1. Itinerant actors without a permanent stage venue.
2. Wandering because they had no homeland.
3. Unless.
4. The actors.
5. Lord.
6. The audience.
7. Height.

IAIN CRICHTON SMITH

Shylock†

Shylock, on you in the house of grey ledgers,
interest, red ink, offices, the moon shines down
a balloon of circuses, without gravity.

The students in long cloaks sing among nightingales.
Rings are exchanged, the constancy of hands,
Italy is a night of a million stars.

There is no justice for the knotted heart.
Law becomes feminine, engagements of night streams,
night is when lovers kiss among wise owls.

Your author is unjust to you, Shylock.
On your Jewish bible of iron there flicker green leaves.
Laughter rebounds from your locked and beaten chest.

Imagination is against you, and your daughter
enters the coach at midnight. Let you stand
in your convict clothes striped with a pitiless prose,
watching her ride into an exile of Gentiles,
into the exile of youth. The moon shines down.
What shall you say of its coin fruitfully changing?

ALAN SILLITOE

Shylock the Writer‡

Humanity is good to bait fish with,
Salt fish that dries in the throat
And needs vodka to turn it down.

Such human quality pressed
A jackboot onto his vocation.
A mob was set on him whose rage
Needed no stoking.

A writer has eyes, hands, a heart
A pen that sometimes scratches

† From *Collected Poems* (Manchester: Carcanet Press, 1992), pp. 354–55. Reprinted by permission of Carcanet Press Limited.
‡ From *Collected Poems* (New York: HarperCollins, 1993), p. 229. Reprinted by permission of HarperCollins Publishers Ltd.

Like a rose-thorn at a gardener's vein.
He borrows words

And lends them out at interest,
Turns from each season and
With no humility or ignorance
Tells a story to keep the world quiet.

KARL SHAPIRO

Shylock†

Ho, no, no, no, no, my meaning in saying he is a good man is to
have you understand me, that he is sufficient.
—THE MERCHANT OF VENICE

Home from the court he locked the door and sat
In the evil darkness, suddenly composed.
The knife shone dimly on the table and his eyes
Like candles in an empty room
Shone hard at nothing. Yet he appeared to smile.

Then he took up his talith[1] and his hat
And prayed mechanically and absently closed
His fingers on the knife. If he could realize
His actual defeat or personal doom
He must die or change or show that he was vile.

Nevertheless he would remain and live,
Submit to baptism, pay his fines,
Appear in the Rialto as early as tomorrow,
Not innocently but well aware
That his revenge is an accomplished fact.

And poverty itself would help to give
Humility to his old designs.
His fallen reputation would help borrow
A credit of new hate; for nothing will repair
This open breach of nature, cruel and wracked.

His daughter lies with swine, and the old rat
Tubal will be obsequious
To buy off his disgrace and bargain on his shame.
Despair can teach him nothing at all:
Gold he hates more than he hates Jesus' crown.

† From *Collected Poems 1940–1978* (New York: Random House, 1978), p. 79. Copyright © 1978 Estate of Karl Shapiro by arrangement with Wieser & Elwell, Inc., New York.
1. Prayer shawl [*Editor*].

The logic of Balthasar[2] will fall flat
On heaven's hearing. Incurious
As to the future, totally clear of blame,
He takes his ledgers out of the wall
And lights them with a taper and sits down.

LEONARD NATHAN

Shylock in New York†

I met Shylock in my sleep
last night under the occult sign
of the three balls.[1] "Grandfather,"
I cried, "man of many shadows,
is that you? If it is, I think
you have something for me, something
precious to be handed down
with love through generations,
wander where they will."

He merely shrugged, then smiling
a bitter archaic smile, reached
into a dark recess or pocket
of his gabardine and offered
me a stone redder than ruby,
harder than diamond. "Grief," he said.
"To suck if not to swallow,
and pass on. Enjoy."

2. Hans Urs von Balthasar was an ecumenical Catholic theologian whose thought was influential on Vatican 2 and Pope John the 23rd. Balthasar's "logic" held, among other
things, that love unites people who are different even as it establishes their difference
[Editor].
† From *Michigan Quarterly Review* 41.4 (2002): 568. Reprinted by permission of the author.
1. Traditional sign of a pawnbroker's shop [Editor].

FIONA PITT-KETHLEY

Shylock†

> I am a Jew. Hath not a Jew eyes? hath not a Jew hands, organs, di-
> mensions, senses, affections, passions? . . . If you prick us, do we
> not bleed? if you tickle us do we not laugh? if you poison us do we
> not die?

I like Shylock. When playing him at eleven
I learned to sympathise with him and see his point of view.
(My version was more Sweeney Todd[1] than Jew.
I pulled my hair round, tied up as a beard,
wore a loose preaching-gown and velvet cap
and brandished mother's bread knife in the Court.)

He had more guts and more integrity
than all the Gentile bastards in that play.
(The noble Portia I do not admire—
for all her estimable logic in the dock,
all she attained was union with a wimp
who obviously preferred his man-friend's charms,
yet needed marriage to a girl with cash.)

Some words of Shylock's still remain with me,
24 years away from playing his part—
the speech in which he states the outcast's case
and pleads the same humanity for Jews.

The man I loved—a bastard-Gentile-type—
saw me as far less human than Mankind,
less human than the women in his life,
especially his wife (although she screws around
and treats him like a dog). I'm just
"a character", he's said as much—far "too
eccentric" for his love. (Do I not bleed?)

Though not a Jew, I am a Jew to him.

Feelings? I haven't got the things to hurt.
If I had "Jewish gaberdine" he'd spit
on it for sure—well, metaphorically.

---

† From *London Review of Books* 12.2 (25 Jan. 1990): 8. Reprinted by permission of the
London Review of Books (www.lob.co.uk).
1. Legendary London barber who killed his customers with a razor, then had his lover serve
up their remains in meat pies [*Editor*].

And yet this Gentile craves what I have got—
no, unlike Shylock, I've no cash to lend—
he'd like my sympathy for all *she*'s done.
(It doesn't occur the tales might cause me pain.)
And, curiously, he *also* wants my love—
though he's no thought of ever paying back.

Revenge is sweet—almost as sweet as sex.
No smart-arse Portia'll spring to his defence.
"The quality of mercy is not strained . . ."
Mercy? I've not seen much of it around,
"strained" or unstrained. I'll get my pound of flesh.
I've learned my lesson from poor Shylock's case—
I'll settle for the bastard's blood as well.

OTHER REWRITINGS AND APPROPRIATIONS

Dramatic and Musical Adaptations

This list and the ones that follow are selective. Only works in English are included. "See Gross" refers the reader to John Gross, *Shylock: A Legend and Its Legacy* (New York: Simon & Schuster, 1992), originally published in Britain as *Shylock: Four Hundred Years in the Life of a Legend* (London: Chatto & Windus, 1992).

Armstrong, Gareth. *Shylock*. London: The Players' Account, 1999. [Playscript for one actor, performed by Gareth Armstrong. Conjures up a whole cast of real and imaginary characters to explore issues of race and religion. See <www.britishcouncil.org/.../arts-drama-directory-small-scale/arts-drama-directory-gareth-armstrong.htm>.]

Britten, Benjamin. "Fancie: Tell me where is fancy bred." In *Ceremonie of Carols*, Naxos Audio CD, 1995. [A setting of the song from 3.2 for unison chorus & piano. Also available in sheet music. See <http://laurasmidi.com>.]

Brougham, John. *Much Ado about a Merchant of Venice*. New York: S. French, 1868. [Burlesque with topical satire of Wall Street. It had numerous performances in 1869 and remained popular into the 1890s. See Gross, p. 220.]

Carter, Elliott. "Tell Me Where Is Fancy Bred." In *Twentieth-Century Voices in America*, Vox Audio CD, 1995. [A setting of the song from 3.2 for alto voice and guitar. Commissioned by Orson Welles for use in a 1938 Mercury Theater production of the play. Also available in sheet music. See <www.sheetmusicplus.com/pages.html>.]

Dixon, Ed. *Shylock*. [Musical. Dixon received a Drama Desk nomination for his performance in this work in 1987.]

Einhorn, Edward. *A Shylock*, play performed in New York, 1996. [Postmodern look at Shakespeare's play and antisemitism. Excerpts are available online at <www.untitledtheatre.com/Shyscript.htm>.]

Ervine, St. John. *The Lady of Belmont*. London: Allen and Unwin, 1923. [Playscript. Produced in London, 1927. Ten years later the marriages are falling apart. Bassanio has spent most of Portia's money and wants to have an affair with Jessica. Shylock is mellower and more prosperous than ever. See Gross, pp. 228–29.]

Farquhar, Robert. *Portia Pulls a Pinch Play: A Shakespearean Burlesque.* Franklin, Ohio: Farquhar Play Bureau, 1930. [Playscript. According to WorldCat, there are only two library copies extant.]

Granville, George, Lord Lansdowne. *The Jew of Venice, 1701.* Rpt. London: Cornmarket, 1969. [Popularized satirical version of the play that held the London stage for forty years from its first performance in 1701. See Gross, pp. 108–10.]

Greenwell, Peter, and Gordon Snell. *The Three Caskets.* [Musical described as a "one-act operetta." First performed in London, 1956.]

Gurney, A. R. *Overtime: A Modern Sequel to The Merchant of Venice.* New York: Dramatists' Play Service, 1996. [Playscript. Premiered in San Diego, 1995. Starts with the wedding feast of Portia and Bassanio and goes on to consider issues of antisemitism and homophobia.]

Haynes, Roger, and Paul Bentley. *Fire Angel.* [Rock opera that premiered in London, 1977. Restages *The Merchant of Venice* in the New York Mafia underworld.]

Irving, Henry. "On Playing Shylock." In *Irving's Impressions of America,* ed. Joseph Hatton. Boston: Osgood, 1884, pp. 224–33. [Irving was a celebrated Shylock who performed the role regularly during the 1880s and beyond. Available online at <www.classicaltheatre.com/id61.htm>.]

Leich, Roland. "Portia and Her Suitors: Four Verses from William Shakespeare's *The Merchant of Venice.*" Vienna, Virginia: Vienna Woods Music, 1996. [Musical score. Setting for high voice and piano of "Tell me where is fancy bred," "All that glisters is not gold," "The fire seven times tried this," and "You that choose not by the view."

"Leiron-Young, Mark. *Shylock: A Play.* Vancouver: Anvil Press, 1996. [Playscript. After a production of *The Merchant of Venice* has been cancelled, the Jewish actor who performed Shylock finds himself condemned by his own community.]

Marowitz, Charles. *Variation on the Merchant of Venice.* [1977 play. Takes place in Palestine in 1946. Shylock, Tubal, and Jessica are working for the Jewish underground. See Gross, pp. 334–35.]

Poulenc, Francis. "Fancy." In *Hey, Ho, the Wind and the Rain: Songs from Shakespeare's Plays.* Audio CD, Tadpole, 2003. [Setting of the song from 3.2 performed by boy soprano Lorin Wey and instrumentalists.]

Scott, Munroe. *Shylock's Treasure (A Reconciliation) A Comedy in Three Acts.* (Toronto: Playwrights Canada, 1982). [Playscript. First produced Ontario, 1978. Twenty years after *The Merchant of Venice,* the major characters get back together, restage the trial, convict Antonio, and achieve reconciliation.]

Stewart, Patrick. *Shylock: Shakespeare's Alien.* [One-man show designed to explore the sympathetic side of Shylock. Performed by Stewart in Leeds, England, 2001.]

Sullivan, Sir Arthur. Incidental Music to *The Merchant of Venice.* 1871; *Incidental Music.* Audio CD, Marco Polo, 1994. Sullivan is best known for his "Gilbert and Sullivan" operettas. Audio samples available at <www. amazon.com> and <www.arthursullivan.net/incidental/venice/serenade. mid >.]

Talfourd, Francis. *Shylock, or The Merchant of Venice Preserved.* New York: S. French, n.d. (1850s). [Popular stage burlesque first produced in London in 1853 and described in its longer title as "the stray leaves of a Jerusalem hearty-joke." See Gross, p. 220.]

Thomson, Virgil Garnett. "Tell Me Where Is Fancy Bred." *Shakespeare*

Songs for High Voice and Piano. New York: Southern Music Publishing, 1961. [Musical score. Setting of the song from 3.2.]

Vaughan Williams, Ralph. *Serenade to Music*. London: Oxford University Press, 1961. [Musical score. Setting of the lines on music from 5.1.60 and ff. for soloists, chorus and orchestra. Available in numerous Audio CD performances.]

Welles, Orson, dir. *The Merchant of Venice*. United States: Pearl, 1999. [Audio CD of the Mercury Theater Production, 1938–39, with incidental music by Elliott Carter. See also *The Merchant of Venice: The Mercury Shakespeare* (New York: Harper, 1939).]

Wesker, Arnold. *The Merchant*. 1980; rev. ed. London: Methuen, 1983. [Playscript. Also called *Shylock*. Produced in New York, 1977. Zero Mostel was to take the title role but died during rehearsals. Shylock and Antonio are close friends horrified by the consequences of their "nonsense bond." See Gross, p. 335.]

Wilson, David Henry. *Shylock's Revenge*. Taunton, Somerset: Hope Corner, 1986. [Play first performed in Hamburg, 1989. Shylock gets back his possessions and becomes a Jew again. Elements of burlesque, but also serious treatment of antisemitism, racism, and the power of money. See Gross, pp. 335–36.]

Novels, Short Stories, and Poems

• indicates a work included in this Norton Critical Edition.

Auchincloss, Louis. "Black Shylock." In *Second Chance: Tales of Two Generations*. Boston: Houghton Mifflin, 1970, pp. 3–18. [Short story. The eighth-grade class at a posh Manhattan school performs the play featuring Shylock in blackface, with unexpected results.]

Barham, Rev. Richard Harris (writing under the pseudonym Thomas Ingoldsby). "The Merchant of Venice: A Legend of Italy." In *The Ingoldsby Legends*, second series. London: Richard Bentley, 1842. [A comical verse retelling of the story of the play. Available online. See <www.exclassics. com/ingold/ing30.htm>. See also Gross, pp. 221–22.]

Bates, Margret Holmes. *Shylock's Daughter: A Novel*. Chicago: Charles H. Kerr, 1894. [Loosely based on *The Merchant of Venice* but updated to nineteenth-century America. A usurious senator sets his daughter to seduce a young political opponent in the hope of suppressing the young man's programs for rural reform.]

•Crichton Smith, Iain. "Shylock." In *Collected Poems*. Manchester: Carcanet Press, 1992), pp. 354–55.

•Cunningham, John. "Theatrical Prologue for a Revival of *The Merchant of Venice* when the Bill Had Passed for Naturalizing the Jews." In *Poems, Chiefly Pastoral*. Newcastle: T. Slack, 1771, pp. 165–66.

Edgeworth, Maria. *Harrington*. Ed. Susan Manly. Peterborough, Ontario: Broadview Press, 2004. [Novel originally published in 1817. Harrington, a recovering antisemite, encounters the historical figure Charles Macklin, a celebrated eighteenth-century actor of Shylock, and attends a highly charged production of *The Merchant of Venice* in which Macklin stars.]

Hawke, Simon. *The Merchant of Vengeance*. New York: Forge, 2003. [Mystery. Young Will Shakespeare is determined to outdo Marlowe's *Jew of Malta* and ends up precipitating events that parallel the plot of his as yet unwritten *Merchant of Venice*.]

Isler, Alan. "The Monster." In *The Bacon Fancier*. New York: Viking, 1997, pp. 3–41. [Short story. Shylock's predicament from the point of view of the seventeenth-century Venetian ghetto.]

Jong, Erica. *Shylock's Daughter: A Novel of Love in Venice*. 1986; rpt. New York: Harper Collins, 1995: [Formerly titled *Serenissima*. An actress doing a film based on *The Merchant of Venice* finds herself back in the sixteenth century and in love with Will Shakespeare.]

Kellerman, Faye. *The Quality of Mercy*. New York: W. Morrow, 1989. [Mystery. The secretly Jewish daughter of Dr. Rodrigo Lopez meets William Shakespeare and they combine forces to seek justice for their respective causes.]

Lamb, Charles, and Mary Lamb. "The Merchant of Venice." In *Tales From Shakespeare*. London: Thomas Hodgkins, 1807. [Retelling for children. Available in modern editions and online at <www.eldritchpress.org/cml/tfsmofvenice.html>.]

Levy, Newman. "The Merchant of Venice." In *Theatre Guyed*. New York: Alfred A. Knopf, 1933, pp. 3–6. [Burlesque poem with the moral "When you take a bride / Choose one with legal training."]

Lewisohn, Ludwig. *The Last Days of Shylock*. New York and London: Harper, 1931. [Novel. After the trial, Shylock bitterly reflects on Jewish persecution, then travels eastward, eventually reconciling with Jessica, who has been deserted by Lorenzo.]

•Nathan, Leonard. "Shylock in New York." *Michigan Quarterly Review* (2002): 568.

•Pitt-Kethley, Fiona. "Shylock." *London Review of Books* 12.2 (25 January, 1990): 8.

Pressler, Mirjam. *Shylock's Daughter*. Trans. Brian Murdoch. New York: Fogelman Books, 2001. [The story from Jessica's point of view for children].

Rasley, Alicia. *Poetic Justice*. New York: Kensington, 1994. [Romance novel loosely based on the play. Jessica must marry with her uncle's approval in order to win his inheritance. She is courted by a much poorer man who passes a test to win her.]

•Shapiro, Karl Jay. "Shylock." In *Collected Poems 1940–78*. New York: Random House, 1978, p. 79.

•Sillitoe, Alan. "Shylock the Writer." In *Collected Poems*. New York: Harper Collins, 1993, p. 229.

Witwer, H. C. "The Merchant of Venice." In *The Classics in Slang*. New York: Grosset and Dunlap, 1927, pp. 73–86. [Comic prose adaptation in 1920s slang.]

Wolfe, Humbert. "Shylock Reasons with Mr. Chesterton." In *Shylock Reasons with Mr. Chesterton and Other Poems*. Oxford: Basil Blackwell, 1920. [Poem. Dramatic monologue exploring issues of antisemitism through Shylock's expostulations with G. K. Chesterton, who made widely publicized anti-Jewish remarks during his long career as a writer.]

Radio, Television, and Film

Badiyi, Reza, dir. "Out of Mind, Out of Sight." Season 1, episode 11 of *Buffy, The Vampire Slayer*. May 19, 1997. [TV show episode loosely based on *The Merchant of Venice*. A student ostracized by others seeks revenge and the play is quoted in a classroom scene.]

Burton, Hal, dir. *The Merchant of Venice*. 1955. [Version for television with Rachel Gurney as Portia and Michael Hordern as Shylock.]

Gold, Jack, dir. *The Merchant of Venice*. BBC-TV, 1980. [VHS, made for TV as part of the BBC-Time-Life Shakespeare series. Available in DVD from Ambrose Video.]

Horrox, Alan. *The Merchant of Venice*. London and Warwick: Tetra Films for Channel 4 Schools, 1996. [Film version made for TV. Available in the UK from Trumedia. See <www.imdb.com/title/tt0138606/>.]

King, Burton, dir. *None So Blind*. 1923. [Silent film. Also known as *Shylock of Wall Street*. Loosely based on *The Merchant of Venice*. A complicated tale of love and finance in which a Jewish pawnbroker loses his daughter to a gentile and uses revenge money to become a moneylender on Wall Street, only to find his granddaughter eventually enmeshed in a similar romance.]

Lasry, Pierre, dir. *Shylock*. Montreal: National Film Board of Canada; Princeton, New Jersey: Films for the Humanities and Sciences, 1999. [Documentary film. Looks at the history of Shylock in performance against a backdrop of the history of antisemitism. Video clips available at <www2.uoguelph.ca/dfischli/multimedia/video/nfb.cfm> .]

Miller, Jonathan, and John Sichel, dirs. *Merchant of Venice*. Artisan Entertainment, 1999. [VHS. Sichel's version, made for TV, of Miller's 1970 National Theatre production of the play, with Laurence Olivier as Shylock and Joan Plowright as Portia.]

Nunn, Trevor, dir. *The Merchant of Venice*. Chatsworth, California: Image Entertainment, 2004. [DVD. Henry Goodman as Shylock. Uses theatrical sets, but shot as a film.]

Radford, Michael. *The Merchant of Venice*. Arclight, 2004. [Film version starring Al Pacino as Shylock, Jeremy Irons as Antonio, and Joseph Fiennes as Bassanio.]

Rubinstein, Harold. *Shylock's End*. In *Shylock's End and Other Plays*. London: Gollancz, 1971. [Radio play.]

Selwyn, Don, dir. *Maori Merchant of Venice*. New Zealand, 2002. [Film version of the play in Maori with English subtitles. See <www.maorimerchantofvenice.com>.]

Welles, Orson, dir. "The Merchant of Venice" (in five parts). Episode of *The Cavalcade of Literature*. [Radio show, aired August 16, 23, and 30, and September 6 and 13, 1941.]

———, dir. *Merchant of Venice*. United States, 1969. [Film version made for TV with Orson Welles as Shylock. Two of the three reels were stolen and have never been recovered. See <www.sensesofcinema.com/con tents/directors/03/welles.h tml>.]

West, Walter, dir. *The Merchant of Venice*. UK, 1916. [Silent film version.]

Selected Bibliography

• indicates a work included or excerpted in this Norton Critical Edition.

GENERAL INTRODUCTIONS TO SHAKESPEARE

The Bedford Companion to Shakespeare: An Introduction with Documents, ed. Russ Mc-Donald. Boston: Bedford Books, 1996.
The Cambridge Companion to Shakespeare, ed. Margreta de Grazia and Stanley Wells. Cambridge: Cambridge University Press, 2001.
The Oxford Companion to Shakespeare, ed. Michael Dobson and Stanley Wells. Oxford: Oxford University Press, 2001.

BIBLIOGRAPHIES AND COLLECTIONS OF ESSAYS ON *THE MERCHANT OF VENICE*

•Bloom, Harold, ed. *Major Literary Characters: Shylock*. New York and Philadelphia: Chelsea House, 1991.
Coleman, Edward, ed. *The Jew in English Drama: An Annotated Bibliography*. 1943; rpt. New York: New York Public Library, 1970.
Huffman, Clifford Chalmers, ed. *Love's Labor's Lost, A Midsummer Night's Dream, and The Merchant of Venice: An Annotated Bibliography of Shakespeare Studies, 1888–1994*. Binghamton: Medieval and Renaissance Texts and Studies, 1995.
•Mahon, John W. and Ellen MacLeod Mahon, eds. *The Merchant of Venice: New Critical Essays*. New York and London: Routledge, 2002.
Wheeler, Thomas. *The Merchant of Venice: An Annotated Bibliography*. New York: Garland, 1985.
Wheeler, Thomas, ed. *The Merchant of Venice: Critical Essays*. New York: Garland, 1991.
Wilders, John, ed. *Shakespeare, The Merchant of Venice: A Casebook*. London: Macmillan, 1969.
Wood, Nigel, ed. *Theory in Practice: The Merchant of Venice*. Buckingham and Philadelphia: Open University Press, 1996.

OTHER CRITICAL AND HISTORICAL STUDIES

Adelman, Janet. "Her Father's Blood: Race, Conversion, and Nation in *The Merchant of Venice.*" *Representations* 81 (Winter, 2003): 4–30.
Babcock, Barbara, ed. *The Reversible World: Symbolic Inversion in Art and Society*. Ithaca: Cornell University Press, 1977.
Belsey, Catherine. "Love in Venice." *Shakespeare Survey* 44, ed. Stanley Wells. Cambridge: Cambridge University Press, 1992, pp. 41–53.
Berger, Harry, Jr. "Marriage and Mercifixion in *The Merchant of Venice*: The Casket Scene Revisited." *Shakespeare Quarterly* 32.2 (1981): 155–62.
Boose, Lynda E. "The Comic Contract and Portia's Golden Ring." *Shakespeare Studies XX*, ed. J. Leeds Barroll. New York: Burt Franklin, 1998, pp. 241–54.
Brewer, John, and Roy Porter, eds. *Consumption and the World of Goods*. London: Routledge, 1993.
Bruster, Douglas. *Drama and the Market in the Age of Shakespeare*. Cambridge: Cambridge University Press, 1992.
Bullough, Geoffrey. *Narrative and Dramatic Sources of Shakespeare*. Vol. 1. New York: Columbia University Press; London: Routledge and Kegan Paul, 1966, "*The Merchant of Venice,*" pp. 442–514.

345

Bulman, James C. *The Merchant of Venice: Shakespeare in Performance*. Manchester: Manchester University Press; New York: St. Martin's Press, 1991.

Callaghan, Dympna. *Shakespeare without Women: Representing Gender and Race on the Renaissance Stage*. London: Routledge, 2000.

Chaudhuri, Sushi. *Merchants, Companies, and Trade: Europe and Asia in the Early Modern Era*. Cambridge: Cambridge University Press, 1999.

Chojnacki, Stanley. *Women and Men in Renaissance Venice: Twelve Essays on Patrician Society*. Baltimore: Johns Hopkins University Press, 2000.

•Cohen, Derek. "Shylock and the Idea of the Jew." In *Major Literary Characters: Shylock*, ed. Harold Bloom. New York and Philadelphia: Chelsea House, 1991, pp. 305–316.

Cohen, Stephen A. " 'The Quality of Mercy': Law, Equity, and Ideology in *The Merchant of Venice*." *Mosaic* 27.4 (1994): 35–54.

•Cohen, Walter. "*The Merchant of Venice* and the possibilities of Historical Criticism." *ELH* 49 (1982): 765–89.

Cox, Catherine S. "Neither Gentile Nor Jew: Performative Subjectivity in *The Merchant of Venice*." *Exemplaria* 12.2 (2000): 359–83.

•Danson, Lawrence. *The Harmonies of* The Merchant of Venice. New Haven and London: Yale University Press, 1978.

•Desai, R. W. " 'Mislike Me Not for My Complexion': Whose Mislike? Portia's? Shakespeare's? Or That of His Age?" In *The Merchant of Venice: New Critical Essays*, ed. John W. Mahon and Ellen MacLeod Mahon. New York and London: Routledge, 2002, pp. 305–23.

Drakakis, John. " '*Jew*. Shylock is my name': Speech Prefixes in *The Merchant of Venice* as Symptoms of the Early Modern." In *Shakespeare and Modernity: Early Modern to Millennium*, ed. Hugh Grady. London and New York: Routledge, 2002, pp. 105–21.

Edelman, Charles, ed. *Shakespeare in Production: The Merchant of Venice*. Cambridge: Cambridge University Press, 2002.

•Edelman, Charles. "Which is the Jew that Shakespeare Knew?" Shylock on the Elizabethan Stage." *Shakespeare Survey* 52, ed. Stanley Wells. Cambridge: Cambridge University Press, 1999, pp. 99–106.

Engle, Lars. " 'Thrift is Blessing': Exchange and Explanation in *The Merchant of Venice*." *Shakespeare Quarterly* 37.1 (1986): 20–37.

———. *Shakespearean Pragmatism: Market of His Time*. Chicago: University of Chicago Press, 1993.

Floyd-Wilson, Mary. *English Ethnicity and Race in Early Modern Drama*. Cambridge: Cambridge University Press, 2003.

Freeman, Jane. " 'Fair Terms and a Villain's Mind': Rhetorical Patterns in *The Merchant of Venice*." *Rhetorica* 20.2 (2002): 149–72.

Freinkel, Lisa. "*The Merchant of Venice*: 'Modern' Anti-Semitism and the Veil of Allegory." In *Shakespeare and Modernity: Early Modern to Millennium*, ed. Hugh Grady. London and New York: Routledge, 2002, pp. 122–41.

•Freud, Sigmund. "The Theme of the Three Caskets." *The Standard Edition of the Complete Psychological Works* 12, Trans. James Strachey. London: Hogarth Press, 1958.

Gross, John. *Shylock: A Legend and Its Legacy*. New York: Simon and Schuster, 1992.

Habib, Imtiaz. *Shakespeare and Race: Post-colonial Praxis in the Early Modern Period*. Lanham, New York, and Oxford: University Press of America, 2000.

Halio, Jay, ed. *The Merchant of Venice*. Oxford: Oxford University Press, 1998.

•Hall, Kim F. "Guess Who's Coming to Dinner? Colonization and Miscegenation in *The Merchant of Venice*." *Renaissance Drama* new series 23, ed. Mary Beth Rose. Evanston: 1992: Northwestern University Press and the Newberry Library Center for Renaissance Studies, 1992, pp. 87–111.

———. *Things of Darkness: Economies of Race and Gender in Early Modern England*. Ithaca: Cornell University Press, 1995.

Holderness, Graham. *William Shakespeare: The Merchant of Venice*. New York: Penguin Books, 1993.

Holland, Peter D. "*The Merchant of Venice* and the Value of Money." *Cahiers Élisabéthains* [*Elizabethan Notebooks*]: *Late Medieval and Renaissance English Studies* 60 (October 2001): 13–30.

Holmer, Joan Ozark. *The Merchant of Venice: Choice, Hazard, and Consequence*. New York: St. Martin's Press, 1995.

•Knight, G. Wilson. *The Shakespearian Tempest*. London: H. Milford, Oxford University Press, 1932.

Knudson, Roslyn. *Playing Companies and Commerce in Shakespeare's Time*. New York: Cambridge University Press, 2001.

Lampert, Lisa. *Gender and Jewish Difference from Paul to Shakespeare*. Philadelphia: University of Pennsylvania Press, 2004.

•Lelyveld, Toby. *Shylock on the Stage*. Cleveland: The Press of Western Reserve University, 1960.

•Lerner, Laurence. "Wilhelm S. and Shylock." *Shakespeare Survey* 48, ed. Stanley Wells. Cambridge: Cambridge University Press, 1995, pp. 61–68.

Leventen, Carol. "Patrimony and Patriarchy in *The Merchant of Venice*." In *The Matter of Difference: Materialist Feminist Criticism of Shakespeare*, ed. Valerie Wayne. Ithaca, New York: Cornell University Press, 1991, pp. 59–79.

•Lewalski, Barbara K. "Biblical Allusion and Allegory in *The Merchant of Venice*." *Shakespeare Quarterly* 13.3 (1962): 327–43.

Luxon, Thomas H. "A Second Daniel: The Jew and the 'True Jew' in *The Merchant of Venice*." *Early Modern Literary Studies* [online journal] 4.3 (1999): 1–37. http://purl.oclc.org/emls/04–3/luxoshak.html>.

Lyon, John. *Twayne's New Critical Introductions to Shakespeare: The Merchant of Venice*. Boston: Twayne, 1988.

Mahood, M. M., ed. *The Merchant of Venice*. 1987; rpt. Cambridge: Cambridge University Press, 2003.

Marchitello, Howard. "Disembodied Letters and *The Merchant of Venice*: Writing, Editing, History." *ELH* 62 (1995): 237–65.

McPherson, David C. *Shakespeare, Jonson, and the Myth of Venice*. Newark: University of Delaware Press; London: Associated University Presses, 1990.

Metzger, Mary Janell. " 'Now by My Hood, a Gentle and No Jew': Jessica, *The Merchant of Venice*, and the Discourse of Early Modern English Identity." *PMLA* 113.1 (1998): 52–63.

Muldrew, Craig. *The Economy of Obligation: The Culture of Credit and Social Relations in Early Modern England*. New York: St. Martin's Press, 1998.

•Newman, Karen. "Portia's Ring: Unruly Women and Structures of Exchange in *The Merchant of Venice*." *Shakespeare Quarterly* 38.1 (1987): 19–33.

•Orgel, Stephen. *Imagining Shakespeare: A History of Texts and Visions*. Houndmills, Basingstoke: Palgrave, 2003, "Imagining Shylock," pp. 144–62.

•O'Rourke, James. "Racism and Homophobia in *The Merchant of Venice*." *ELH* 70 (2003): 375–97.

•Oz, Avraham. "Transformations of Authenticity: *The Merchant of Venice* in Israel." In *Foreign Shakespeare: Contemporary Performance*. Cambridge: Cambridge University Press, 1993, pp. 56–75.

———. *The Yoke of Love: Prophetic Riddles in The Merchant of Venice*. Newark: University of Delaware Press; London: Associated University Presses, 1995.

Patterson, Steve. "The Bankruptcy of Homoerotic Amity in Shakespeare's *Merchant of Venice*." *Shakespeare Quarterly* 50.1 (1999): 9–32.

Rackin, Phyllis. "The Impact of Global Trade in *The Merchant of Venice*." *Shakespeare Jahrbuch* [Shakespeare Yearbook], vol. 138, ed. Ina Schabert. Germany: Verlag und Druckkontor Kamp GMBH Bochum, 2002, pp. 73–88.

Rozmovits, Linda. *Shakespeare and the Politics of Culture in Late Victorian England*. Baltimore: Johns Hopkins University Press, 1998.

•Shapiro, James. *Shakespeare and the Jews*. New York: Columbia University Press, 1996.

•Sinfield, Alan. "How to Read *The Merchant of Venice* without being Heterosexist." In *Alternative Shakespeares, vol. 2*, ed. Terence Hawkes. London and New York: Routledge, 1996, pp. 122–39.

Spiller, Elizabeth A. "From Imagination to Miscegenation: Race and Romance in Shakespeare's *The Merchant of Venice*." *Renaissance Drama* new series 29, ed. Jeffrey Masten and Wendy Wall. Evanston: Northwestern University Press, 2000, pp. 137–64.

Wrightson, Keith. "Estates, degrees, and sorts: Changing perceptions of society in Tudor and Stuart England." In *Language, History, and Class*, ed. Penelope Corfield. Oxford: Basil Blackwell, 1991, pp. 30–52.

Yaffe, Martin D. *Shylock and the Jewish Question*. Baltimore: Johns Hopkins University Press, 1997.